KEY ENVIRONMENTS

General Editor: J. E. Treherne

GALAPAGOS

The International Union for Conservation of Nature and Natural Resources (IUCN), founded in 1948, is the leading independent international organization concerned with conservation. It is a network of governments, non-governmental organizations, scientists and other specialists dedicated to the conservation and sustainable use of living resources.

The unique role of IUCN is based on its 502 member organizations in 114 countries. The membership includes 57 States, 121 government agencies and virtually all major national and international non-governmental conservation organizations.

Some 2000 experts support the work of IUCN's six Commissions: ecology; education; environmental planning; environmental policy, law and administration; national parks and protected areas; and the survival of species.

The IUCN Secretariat conducts or facilitates IUCN's major functions: monitoring the status of ecosystems and species around the world; developing plans (such as the World Conservation Strategy) for dealing with conservation problems, supporting action arising from these plans by governments or other appropriate organizations, and finding ways and means to implement them. The Secretariat co-ordinates the development, selection and management of the World Wildlife Fund's international conservation projects. IUCN provides the Secretariat for the Ramsar Convention (Convention on Wetlands of International Importance especially as Waterfowl Habitat). It services the CITES convention on trade in endangered species and the World Heritage Site programme of UNESCO.

IUCN, through its network of specialists, is collaborating in the Key Environments Series by providing information, advice on the selection of critical environments, and experts to discuss the relevant issues.

Frontispiece. Satellite (Landsat C) image of western Galápagos Islands. Note the molten lava flowing down the northeast flank of Sierra Negra in the lower central part of the image. The eruption (see Chapter 2, Fig. 6) was in its seventh day, on 19 November 1979, and a white vapour cloud parallels the flow while lower haze covers the slopes to the west. Summit calderas are clear on the major volcanoes but clouds characteristically banked against the southeast flanks of several higher volcanoes are spilling into and obscuring the Sierra Negra caldera. More detailed air photographs of Tagus Cove, Volcán Ecuador, and Fernandina Caldera appear in Chapter 2.

KEY ENVIRONMENTS

GALAPAGOS

Edited by

R. PERRY

Foreword by

HRH THE DUKE OF EDINBURGH

Published in collaboration with the

INTERNATIONAL UNION FOR CONSERVATION OF
NATURE AND NATURAL RESOURCES

by

PERGAMON PRESS

OXFORD · NEW YORK · TORONTO · SYDNEY · PARIS · FRANKFURT

U.K.	Pergamon Press Ltd., Headington Hill Hall, Oxford OX3 0BW, England
U.S.A.	Pergamon Press Inc., Maxwell House, Fairview Park, Elmsford, New York 10523, U.S.A.
CANADA	Pergamon Press Canada Ltd., Suite 104, 150 Consumers Road, Willowdale, Ontario M2J 1P9, Canada
AUSTRALIA	Pergamon Press (Aust.) Pty. Ltd., P.O. Box 544, Potts Point, N.S.W. 2011, Australia
FRANCE	Pergamon Press SARL, 24 rue des Ecoles, 75240 Paris, Cedex 05, France
FEDERAL REPUBLIC OF GERMANY	Pergamon Press GmbH, Hammerweg 6, D-6242 Kronberg-Taunus, Federal Republic of Germany

First edition 1984

Library of Congress Cataloging in Publication Data

Galápagos.
(Key environments) (Contribution no. 355 of the
Charles Darwin Foundation for the Galápagos Isles)
Includes index.
1. Natural history—Galápagos Islands. I. Perry,
Roger. II. Series. III. Series: Contribution . . . of
the Charles Darwin Foundation for the Galápagos Isles;
no. 355.
QH123.C45 no. 355 [QH198.G3]   574.9866'5s   83-13143
[508.9866'5]

British Library Cataloguing in Publication Data

Galápagos.—(Key environments)
1. Natural history—Galápagos Islands
I. Perry, R. II. Series
508.866'5   QH198.G3

ISBN 0-08-027996-1 hardcover

This volume forms Contribution No. 355, of the
Charles Darwin Foundation for the Galápagos Isles.

Printed in Great Britain by A. Wheaton & Co. Ltd., Exeter

U.K.	Pergamon Press Ltd., Headington Hill Hall, Oxford OX3 0BW, England
U.S.A.	Pergamon Press Inc., Maxwell House, Fairview Park, Elmsford, New York 10523, U.S.A.
CANADA	Pergamon Press Canada Ltd., Suite 104, 150 Consumers Road, Willowdale, Ontario M2J 1P9, Canada
AUSTRALIA	Pergamon Press (Aust.) Pty. Ltd., P.O. Box 544, Potts Point, N.S.W. 2011, Australia
FRANCE	Pergamon Press SARL, 24 rue des Ecoles, 75240 Paris, Cedex 05, France
FEDERAL REPUBLIC OF GERMANY	Pergamon Press GmbH, Hammerweg 6, D-6242 Kronberg-Taunus, Federal Republic of Germany

First edition 1984

Library of Congress Cataloging in Publication Data

Galápagos.
(Key environments) (Contribution no. 355 of the
Charles Darwin Foundation for the Galápagos Isles)
Includes index.
1. Natural history—Galápagos Islands. I. Perry,
Roger. II. Series. III. Series: Contribution . . . of
the Charles Darwin Foundation for the Galápagos Isles;
no. 355.
QH123.C45 no. 355 [QH198.G3] 574.9866'5s 83-13143
[508.9866'5]

British Library Cataloguing in Publication Data

Galápagos.—(Key environments)
1. Natural history—Galápagos Islands
I. Perry, R. II. Series
508.866'5 QH198.G3

ISBN 0-08-027996-1 hardcover

This volume forms Contribution No. 355, of the
Charles Darwin Foundation for the Galápagos Isles.

Printed in Great Britain by A. Wheaton & Co. Ltd., Exeter

KEY ENVIRONMENTS

GALAPAGOS

Edited by

R. PERRY

Foreword by

HRH THE DUKE OF EDINBURGH

Published in collaboration with the

INTERNATIONAL UNION FOR CONSERVATION OF
NATURE AND NATURAL RESOURCES

by

PERGAMON PRESS

OXFORD · NEW YORK · TORONTO · SYDNEY · PARIS · FRANKFURT

The general problems of conservation are understood
by most people who take an intelligent interest in the state
of the natural environment. But if adequate measures are to
be taken, there is an urgent need for the problems to be
spelled out in accurate detail.

This series of volumes on "Key Environments" concentrates
attention on those areas of the world of nature that are under
the most severe threat of disturbance and destruction. The
authors expose the stark reality of the situation without
rhetoric or prejudice.

The value of this project is that it provides specialists,
as well as those who have an interest in the conservation of
nature as a whole, with the essential facts without which it is
quite impossible to develop any practical and effective
conservation action.

1984

Preface

The increasing rates of exploitation and pollution are producing unprecedented environmental changes in all parts of the world. In many cases it is not possible to predict the ultimate consequences of such changes, while in some, environmental destruction has already resulted in ecological disasters.

A major obstacle, which hinders the formulation of rational strategies of conservation and management, is the difficulty in obtaining reliable information. At the present time the results of scientific research in many threatened environments are scattered in various specialist journals, in the reports of expeditions and scientific commissions and in a variety of conference proceedings. It is, thus, frequently difficult even for professional biologists to locate important information. There is consequently an urgent need for scientifically accurate, concise and well-illustrated accounts of major environments which are now, or soon will be, under threat. It is this need which these volumes attempt to meet.

The series is produced in collaboration with the International Union for Conservation of Nature and Natural Resources (IUCN). It aims to identify environments of international ecological importance, to summarize the present knowledge of the flora and fauna, to relate this to recent environmental changes and to suggest, where possible, effective management and conservation strategies for the future. The selected environments will be re-examined in subsequent editions to indicate the extent and characteristics of significant changes.

The volume editors and authors are all acknowledged experts who have contributed significantly to the knowledge of their particular environments.

The volumes are aimed at a wide readership, including: academic biologists, environmentalists, conservationists, professional ecologists, some geographers, as well as graduate students and informed lay people.

John Treherne

Contents

1 The Islands and their History   1
  R. Perry

2 Geology of Galápagos Islands   15
  T. Simkin

3 Oceanographic Setting of the Galápagos Islands   43
  G.T. Houvenaghel

4 The Galápagos Climate: Present and Past   55
  P.A. Colinvaux

5 Lichens and Bryophytes   71
  W.A. Weber and S.R. Gradstein

6 Endemism and Evolution in Terrestrial Plants   85
  D.M. Porter

7 Native Climax Forests   101
  U. Eliasson

8 Changes and Threats to the Vegetation   115
  O. Hamann

9 The Inshore Fish Fauna of the Galápagos Islands   133
  J.E. McCosker and R.H. Rosenblatt

10 The Giant Tortoises: A Natural History Disturbed by Man   145
  Tj. de Vries

11 The Large Iguanas of the Galápagos Islands   157
  I. Eibl-Eibesfeldt

12 The Endemic Land Birds   175
  P.R. Grant

13 The Seabirds   191
  M.P. Harris

14 The Galápagos Seals   207
   Part 1. Natural History of the Galápagos Sea Lion
        I. Eibl-Eibesfeldt
   Part 2. Natural History of the Galápagos Fur Seal   215
        F. Trillmich

15   Native Land Mammals   225
      D. A. Clark

16   Introduced Fauna   233
      H. N. Hoeck

17   Marine Environment and Protection   247
      G. M. Wellington

18   The Path of Conservation   265
      Part 1.   J. Black M.
      Part 2.   G. T. Corley Smith   269

19   Contributions to Science from the Galápagos   277
      R. I. Bowman

      Index   313

CHAPTER 1

The Islands and their History

ROGER PERRY

Formerly at the Charles Darwin Research Station

Contents

1.1.	The Islands	1
1.2.	Arrival of Plants and Animals	4
1.3.	Early Visitors	7
1.4.	Settlement	10
1.5.	The Age of Darwin	12
	References	14

1.1. The Islands

In March 1535, a ship carrying the Spanish bishop, Fray Tomás de Berlanga, on a voyage from Panama to Peru was becalmed off the coast of South America. Although by no means an unusual event in itself, this heralded what was to become one of the strangest and perhaps most unexpected voyages of discovery. Swept to the west by a strong off-shore current, the vessel was carried deep into the still largely unexplored eastern Pacific. Drifting for over a week, the bishop and his companions came at length to a group of barren volcanic islands. After further delays, landing parties scrambled ashore, their most desperate need now being for water to replenish supplies that were running dangerously low on board.

An official account of the expedition, including the hardships of their return journey to the mainland, was duly sent by Fray Tomás in a letter to Charles V, Holy Roman Emperor. In this the bishop recorded the position of the islands and described the tortured scenes that they had encountered on land. These have the appearance, he wrote, 'as though sometime God had showered stones'; the soil is 'like dross, worthless, because it has not the power of raising a little grass, but only . . . thistles like prickly pears'. Amid the many problems that beset him, Fray Tomás yet found time to observe and comment on the tameness of the birds ('so silly they do not know how to flee'), the great numbers of seals and iguanas, and tortoises (*galápagos*) so large 'that each could carry a man on top'. Of water, only with the greatest difficulty did they procure enough to fill a few casks and so continue their voyage.

Reading those lines written four and a half centuries ago, one catches a timeless glimpse of the islands that are the subject of this volume. No one would deny the Galápagos an aspect of elemental harshness. No one can stand

1

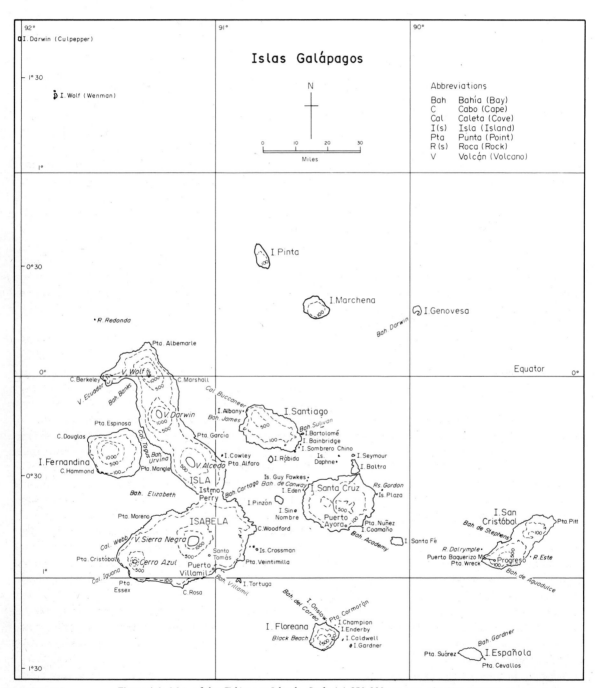

Figure 1.1. Map of the Galápagos Islands. Scale 1:1,250,000; contours in metres.

unmoved by the desolate wastes of lava, relieved here and there by gaunt clumps of cactus. These have brought many enduring descriptions of the islands: some visitors have found there 'heaps of cinders . . . magnified into mountains', others their vision of the 'cultivated parts of hell'. Whatever the images they have seldom been compromising. Even in Tomás de Berlanga's great age of discovery one senses that there was a remote and perplexing strangeness about the Galápagos; little though could it have been realized that a remarkable natural paradise had been found, one that was to become the preoccupation of scientific thought in generations to come.

These islands belong today to Ecuador, the country with the nearest continental landmass to the east. They straddle the equator, 800 to 1,000 km from the mainland, and span a distance of nearly 300 km between north and south. Thus, they form a scattered archipelago (Fig. 1.1), spread over 45,600 sq km of ocean, comprising 13 principal islands, with a further 65 or so named islets, rocks and reefs. The total land area is some 7,800 sq km.

The largest of these islands is Isabela, with just over half the total land surface of the archipelago. It stretches in a 130 km arc of five volcanoes and the remains of a sixth, once separate islands which are now joined by the coalescence of lava on their flanks. The rounded outlines of these peaks, deceptively bland in appearance (Chapter 19, Fig. 8), rise to heights of between 1,100 and 1,700 m, making this backbone of Isabela the most salient feature on the Galápagos skyline. Visible but well separated from Isabela are three further islands each with an area exceeding 500 sq km: Fernandina, Santiago and Santa Cruz. Beyond Santa Cruz, in the extreme east, lies a fifth major island, San Cristóbal, with the present day administrative centre and port of Baquerizo Moreno. The best known of the smaller islands, in descending order of size, are: Floreana, Marchena, Española, Pinta, Baltra, Santa Fé, Pinzón and Genovesa.

A visitor surveying this broad horizon of distant and enigmatic peaks inevitably comes to wonder which island holds the greatest interest and the greatest attraction for biologists. The question, however, is a difficult if not impossible one to answer, for each tends to have its own character, extending in many cases to distinctive races or species of plants and animals. Island differentiation occurs among many groups of terrestrial organisms, and it is the archipelago as a whole, with its complex of islands and their peculiar inhabitants, that has elevated the Galápagos to their unique place in science.

But the visitor comes initially not to look perhaps for differentiation but for some more unifying theme to link these unusual islands. Firstly, they will be found to have an overriding sense of youthfulness. The islands are volcanic and represent the exposed parts of a group of huge basaltic volcanoes that have risen from the bed of the sea. Everywhere are betrayed signs of the islands' cataclysmic origins. Lava streaks their sides, descending as frozen rivers, often as black as coal, that have spread and hardened into the stark and varied landscapes. Cones of cinder and scoria stud the lowlands, reminding one in places of the symmetry and close formation of groups of pottery kilns. Even where the ground has yielded to plant life, one has to move warily among tumbled blocks and ridges of lava. In geological terms, the islands are recent. Dating studies place the age of the islands in the order of 3 to 5 million years (page 17), with the visible land surfaces generally very much younger. Volcanic activity continues, with the most frequent eruptions now occurring on the western islands of Fernandina and Isabela.

This sustained volcanism provides an element of instability to the environment with all this means in terms of ecological opportunity. It also adds asperity to harsh conditions already imposed by the climate. Unlike most equatorial regions, the Galápagos Islands are not particularly hot and humid; they lie instead in a dry zone of the Pacific, where temperatures are kept abnormally low by cool upwellings in the sea. This results in peak daytime temperatures during the warmer months, January to May, barely averaging 29°C—several degrees lower than might be expected at similar latitudes on the mainland coast. In August this average upper limit in the islands falls to 19°C.

Because of these conditions, the smaller islands and the coastal lowlands of the larger are desert-like in character. Subjected to prevailing southeasterly winds, they suffer what may be termed a 'trade wind drought'. Periods of rain are brief, and water quickly drains away through the porous volcanic soils. Cacti and xerophytic scrub are the main components of the vegetation, with scattered trees, such as *Bursera*, losing their leaves during the dry season. Only after persistent rains in the early part of the year do these low-lying areas wear a mantle of green.

Inland, different climatic conditions prevail. A sharp contrast will be noticed by anyone making a journey into the interior of one of the larger islands, such as Santa Cruz, Santiago or Isabela. The upper slopes of these islands are high enough and extensive enough to displace upwards significant moisture-bearing air masses, and these benefit the land with increased precipitation. So while the lowlands perhaps are experiencing drought, the upper parts of the islands may be receiving moisture in the form of mist precipitation or drizzle, locally known as *garúa*. At elevations between 200 and 500 m there begin the dense and often lugubrious forests, rich in epiphytes, which bear a striking though superficial resemblance to the cloud-forests of the Andes. It is these moist highlands, with their lingering cloud cover and greater depths of soil, that have been favoured for agricultural development over the years, and so have suffered appreciable change. Higher still, above this humid belt, forests characteristically give way to open landscapes of fernbrake and sedge, which crown the summits of the major volcanoes.

Between these two extremes—the dry lowlands and the lush highlands—there is a graduated series of floral and faunal change. Six, and in places seven, vegetation zones may be recognized on Santa Cruz, in a horizontal distance of barely 15 km (Table 1.1). On a clear day one may look inland from the shore and identify these bands of vegetation, the uppermost delineated perhaps by higher-riding blankets of cloud. The variation of life that results from this altitudinal zonation is a theme that is constantly to recur in this book.

Table 1.1. Vegetation Zones on the Southern Slope of Santa Cruz (after various authors)

		Zone	Altitude guide
1	Littoral Zone	Mangroves and associated strand species	0–10 m
2	Arid Zone	Dry-season woodland ('Cactus Forest')	10–50 m[1]
3	Transition Zone	Semi-deciduous woodland	50–200 m
4	Scalesia Zone	Closed evergreen forest	200–450 m[2]
5 (a)	Brown Zone[3]	Mossy open evergreen forest[4]	450–650 m
(b)	Miconia Zone	Mossy evergreen scrub[4]	
6	Fern-Sedge Zone	Non-wooded evergreen or summit pampa	650–850 m

[1] Increasing in some areas to 100 m
[2] Areas with *Scalesia* extend exceptionally to 750 m
[3] An extension of, and integrated by some authors with, Scalesia Zone
[4] Now greatly reduced by farming
Floristic compositions of these zones are described on pages 73–79 and 102, and climatic factors inducing these zones on page 58.

Associated plant and animal communities are affected not only by soil conditions, exposure and prominence of the islands but by a highly-irregular weather pattern. Virtually rainless years are not unknown, and periodic drought is a recurrent feature. Once in a while the dominant oceanic conditions in the islands fail. They fail in the sense that the cool upwellings are suppressed by warmer water flowing from the west, resulting for a time in truly tropical conditions of temperature and humidity. These may bring sharp and heavy rains, but it is a period generally accompanied by prolonged calms at sea, when the islands, enveloped in transparent stillness, have to many their aura of greatest charm.

1.2. Arrival of Plants and Animals

How life came originally to these young and remote shores and, once there, adapted to the rigours of an alien existence is a subject that has absorbed scientific thought ever since Charles Darwin's famous visit in 1835. All the evidence now affirms that the islands have never been in closer contact with the mainland, either by means of a land-bridge (such has been postulated in the past), or by hypothetical islands providing stepping-stones that once aided in the dispersal of species from the mainland. So one turns to other agencies to bring this about—an exercise in deduction and speculation.

It is worth stressing at the outset the close affinities that exist between plants and animals of the islands and those of South America. The land birds have their closest allies there; so too do the reptiles, including the iguanid lizards and giant tortoises. Inshore fishes have been derived essentially from the continental eastern Pacific area (Walker, 1966), and all groups of terrestrial invertebrates that have been studied show a similar pattern of fragmentation from a wider neotropical fauna.

For plants rather more specific facts have emerged. An overwhelming percentage of the islands' non-endemic vascular flora also occurs on the mainland of South America, with only a few species (1%) being of Mexican and Central American origin (Porter, 1976). Of the endemics virtually all have their closest known relatives in South America. Mosses, on the other hand, show an exceptional and close correlation with Central America, a circumstance that has been adduced as resulting from the warm-sea trade winds operating in their favour (page 82).

Most scientists today accept the various agencies of long-distance dispersal as being responsible for bringing life to the Galápagos Islands. These include: (1) wind and air currents; (2) oceanic drift, either by swimming, floating or carried on natural rafts of vegetation; and (3) dispersal by means of birds. In the main, these would have buoyed chance colonists passively to the islands; only in the cases of a few birds and insects would behavioural traits coupled with flight powers probably have led to dispersion—though these again carried the inevitable uncertainty of arrival at a colonizing destination.

Transportation by air currents would have brought spores of such plants as ferns and their allies and orchids. Dr. Porter refers in Chapter 6 to the relative effectiveness of wind dispersal in these groups and, as would be expected, to a correspondingly low incidence of endemism they have to the islands. Lichens also have the ability to survive transportation over long distances, carried as dust-like particles in the air, and here again one comes across individual species that have a generally wide range of distribution.

Floating rafts of vegetation have long been visualized as vehicles for stranded organisms. Detached islets of plant debris are a common sight on the mainland rivers of Ecuador, many of these eventually reaching the sea on the coast of Guayas. On occasions, these natural rafts have been observed many miles from the mainland and drifting steadily in the direction of the Galápagos. Ultimately, a few perhaps are to contribute their cargo of palms and other continental trees to the debris that has been found at times stranded on the beaches of the islands. Such rafting probably also accounts for the arrival of small reptiles, oryzomine rodents and terrestrial invertebrates. It is unlikely however that many plants would have survived this hazardous means of crossing, apart from mangroves and other species adapted to extreme saline conditions.

By contrast, fruits, seeds and vegetative disseminules that can be carried by birds escape the exigencies of an amphibious landing. The importance of birds as agents bringing new plant colonists to the islands has recently emerged with increased clarity (Porter, 1976). During the northern winter, migrant birds bolster the resident avifauna of the Galápagos Islands, with such species as whimbrel and blue-winged teal regularly visiting humid areas inland. Adventitious plant material could be carried either attached to the feet, legs or plumage of these migrants, or internally in the digestive tract. From an analysis of dispersal mechanisms in plant genera represented in the islands, it has been deduced that perhaps 60% of all *natural* introductions of vascular species have been brought about by birds. An interesting point arising from this, however, is that the main migration routes of birds as they appear today is with Central America—rather than with South America from where the majority of plants originate; so changing climatic conditions are implied. Needless to say, it is from the unravelling of such apparent dissension that new facts are continually emerging about the islands and the origin of their life.

The new factor today is man. Almost everywhere he has become the main agency bringing new species to islands. This applies to plants as well as to groups such as the terrestrial invertebrates, which still present however a largely enigmatic picture. Some far-reaching migratory species, such as the danaid butterflies, *Danaus plexippus* and *D. gilippus*, occur regularly in the islands, suggesting that distances from the mainland are attainable from time to time by some groups. At the other extreme, notably sedentary species like land snails, ants and beetles all show a high degree of endemicity to the islands. All this is to be expected. What often hampers more specific analyses is a meagre state of our knowledge of the range of species on the mainland—information that is needed before assigning derivations to those of the islands. It is the terrestrial invertebrates that present one of the widest and most fertile fields for future distribution studies.

The way in which the tortoises arrived at the islands has given rise to much inspired conjecture. Their genus, *Geochelone*, is represented on the South American mainland by several small-to medium-sized species, and it is generally assumed that the progenitors of present Galápagos animals were correspondingly small in size. It is also believed that these tortoises were carried floating passively to the islands. There is no doubt that such a journey would have been fraught with untold hazards, but the odds against a successful outcome appear not quite so remote when they are viewed against a time scale involving hundreds of thousands of years. It is also conceivable, or perhaps likely, that only a gravid female arrived to establish the founding colony. Subsequently, lava flows could have been a factor occasionally trapping individuals and so forcing survivors to take to the sea, from whence they colonized new parts of the archipelago.

During four centuries man has collected and transported giant tortoises in the archipelago. The intention has usually not been for these animals later to escape, but some may well have been transferred to smaller islands (such as Rábida) for temporary storage, or cast overboard when circumstances for some reason required decks to be cleared for action. Such incidents could have accounted for the origin of stray and enigmatic animals found on Rábida and Fernandina (Chapter 10). Man may also have been responsible for another anomalous groups of 'saddle-backed' tortoises which appeared a few years ago in the northwest of

Figure 1.2. The highlands of Santa Cruz: in the absence of mammalian competitors, tortoises became the dominant grazing herbivores on the Galápagos Islands. (Photograph by Alan Root).

Santa Cruz (Snow, 1964). But, despite a multitude of disturbances over the years, remarkably few such inconsistencies exist, and this remains a cardinal feature of the scientific interest in these islands.

Two endemic vertebrates, the Galápagos fur seal and Galápagos penguin, belong to genera that are associated pre-eminently with the cool south temperate or subantarctic seas. That these species should thrive today alongside tropical coral fish and frigate birds is one of the bizarre and fascinating attractions of the Galápagos. Their ancestors presumably found their way north by following the cool waters of the Humboldt Current.

Finally, it is always interesting to record new, and in some sense documented, arrivals at the islands, for these point to the dynamic processes involved in colonization. Over the past two decades the cattle egret (*Bubulcus ibis*) has settled in the Galápagos, following an expansion of its range through South America coupled with the availability of a vacant niche. The same may be true of the paint-billed crake (*Neocrex Erythrops*), a notoriously secretive species, yet one first recorded on the islands in 1953 and since found breeding on Santa Cruz and Floreana (Harris, 1974).

The Galápagos Islands are not without their notable absentees. Aquatic animals are poorly represented—as one might suspect from the paucity of suitable habitats on the islands. But freshwater of a permanent nature does exist, as at the lake of El Junco on San Cristóbal (Fig. 5, Chapter 4). Amphibians, mayflies and caddis-flies—all of which occur abundantly on the mainland—presumably never overcame the barrier of the sea to reach the archipelago. Large terrestrial mammals similarly failed to make the crossing, thus leaving the way free for the tortoises to develop and become the large grazing herbivores on land, a position they enjoyed until the comparatively recent advent of man with domestic livestock.

1.3. Early Visitors

After their discovery the Galápagos Islands fell, in Spanish eyes, within the sphere of influence of the Catholic Kings, but remained what they were: an alien and unpromising land on the edge of the New World. So they were destined to continue for the greater part of the next three centuries, never being occupied or settled by the Spaniards.

It was 11 years before the next recorded visit, when Diego de Rivadeneira, a fugitive from the civil war between rival factions of the Spanish conquerors of Peru, was carried by the prevailing currents to the islands. Like his predecessor, he arrived short of food and water and only regained the continent after a long and difficult voyage. In 1570, the Galápagos Islands appeared on the map of the Flemish cartographer, Abraham Ortelius, under the name 'Insulae de los Galopegos', thus formally identifying the islands with their giant tortoises. But by this time another and more mystical name was coming into use: the Enchanted (or Bewitched) Isles. This arose for a prosaic enough reason, that of the problem of navigating among the islands, for the unaccountable calms and currents still continued to puzzle and tax the ingenuity of mariners.

The vagaries of the oceanic currents lay behind one of the strangest of all stories concerning the Galápagos. This is worth recounting even in the narrative of this book, for it has far from been erased from the history of the islands. One of the redoubtable figures of pre-Conquest Peru was the Inca, Tupac Yupanqui, an ambitious monarch who was reputed to have led a voyage of exploration into the Pacific before the end of the 15th century. Details of this were handed down orally by the early Peruvians (who had no written language) and recorded by the Spaniards. Tupac Inca's voyage, it was said, involved a great many men, who embarked on a fleet of balsa rafts and sailed with him into the western sea. They were away for almost a year and when they returned brought back gold, a black slave and the skin and jawbone of an animal that was said to be a horse. More significantly, they reported the finding of two islands, which they called Hahuachumbi (Outer Island) and Ninachumbi (Island of Fire).

One thing that is clear is that none of these trophies could have been derived from uninhabited volcanic islands such as the Galápagos. Nevertheless, the Spanish chronicler, Pedro Sarmiento de Gamboa, who compiled an official history of the Incas (1572), did identify Tupac Yupanqui's discovery with the archipelago, an assumption that has long cast its shadow over authenticated knowledge of the islands.

Where the Inca went on his great voyage is of course a very interesting question. There is little doubt that the Galápagos archipelago was within the range of early Peruvian craft, which had sails and could be steered by a system of moveable centre-boards. And it must appear at least probable that occasional vessels were carried to the islands in the same way as those of the bishop and Rivadeneira. The route of a balsa adrift in the eastern Pacific might well be to the Galápagos and from there back in a great arc in the direction of Central America (as was demonstrated by the *Balsa Pacífica*, which passed through the islands in 1965). But whether the Inca made so circuitous a journey, and collected his trophies at subsequent landfalls, is a question that can now never be answered. Gold it might finally be remembered was a fatal lodestone in the early days of the Conquest and one all too likely to erode the foundations of truth; could there have been exercised that indelible trait of a canny Andean people to tell the Spanish adventurers what they most wanted to hear?

The story of possible pre-Columbian visits to the Galápagos does not in fact end there. In 1953, an expedition of the Norwegian ethnologist, Thor Heyerdahl (page 303), found pottery sherds at coastal sites on the islands of Santiago, Santa Cruz and Floreana. These remains were referred to types of early earthenware vessels known from northern Peru and the area near Guayaquil (Heyerdahl and Skjölsvold, 1956). The problem in relating these finds to early mainland sources is that each of the Galápagos sites concerned (and a further one since discovered in the highlands of Santiago) has yielded remains from the buccaneering or whaling periods. So the possibility cannot be discounted that the earthenware fragments derived instead from water-carrying vessels taken ashore during post-Conquest times. Other artefacts described by Heyerdahl (1978), namely a terracotta flute, chalk-stone spinning whorl and flint and obsidian scrapers, are less easy to explain, though similar care has to be exercised in eliminating later sources. And there the matter rests; the most the islands may have been was a seasonal fishing outpost during prehistoric times.

In the event, the early history of the islands was scarcely less colourful. The lure of the rich treasure fleets of the Spaniards constantly drew adventurers to the Pacific and it was in the Galápagos that English buccaneers found a base for their activities. From the islands they launched raids on the long open coast between Panama and Callao, returning to refit and victual their ships and to divide spoil. Their association with the islands extended from the late 17th century to the middle of the 18th century, with the names of Edward Cooke, Ambrose Cowley, William Dampier, Edward Davis and Lionel Wafer among the better-known of these men who became a thorn in the sides of successive Spanish viceroys.

The attractions of the islands lay in their safe and secluded anchorages, where there was little fear of reprisals from the Spaniards, in the fresh food available (in Dampier's view 'no pullet eats more pleasantly' than a Galápagos tortoise) and, once they had been located, in several tolerably reliable sources of freshwater. A reader interested in tracing this period of Galápagos history will find several published narratives of the buccaneers, with Dampier's (1697), in particular, providing a fascinating early seafarer's glimpse of the islands.

After the buccaneers, the Spaniards took a renewed though temporary interest in the islands through the voyages of Alejandro Malaspina and Alonso de Torres. Subsequently, they became a base for Pacific whaling fleets, a period that was to have its own far-reaching repercussions on the wildlife of the islands. This began with the voyage of Captain James Colnett, R.N., who undertook to explore new whaling grounds on behalf of merchants of the City of London. He twice visited the Galápagos, in 1793 and 1794, when he saw how conveniently the islands were placed for refitting and victualling ships. The tortoises were an obvious attraction—as they had been to the buccaneers—for they were a convenient source of fresh meat in the days before the advent of canning and refrigeration and when ships were away from home ports for 2 or 3 years at a stretch. In a short time British ships were coming increasingly to the islands, soon to be followed by those of the New England whaling fleets. With the hundreds of vessels these combined fleets entailed, the drain on the populations of tortoises began to tell, despite the many tens or even hundreds of thousands of these reptiles that had at one time roamed the islands. First one race and then another was brought perilously close

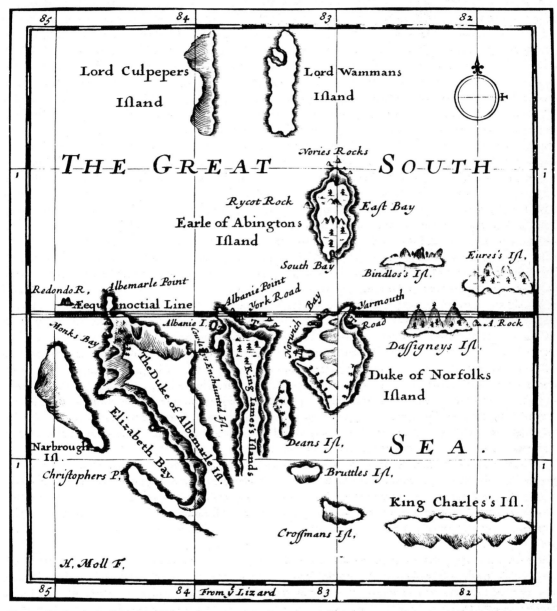

Figure 1.3. Cowley's chart of the Galápagos Islands. Comparison with the modern chart (Figure 1.1) shows discrepancies in scale (particularly of some smaller islands) and a southerly displacement of King James's Island (Santiago) and Eures's Island (probably Genovesa). The anchorage in the west of the Duke of Norfolk's Island (Santa Cruz) corresponds to Bahía Conway, which gives the position for Dean's Island (Pinzón).

English names with their official Ecuadorian equivalents (in both cases subsequent better-known names appear in parenthesis) are as follows: Narbrough Island: Fernandina; Duke of Albemarle Island: Isabela; King James's Island: San Salvador (Santiago); Dean's Island (Duncan): Pinzón; Duke of Norfolk's Island (Indefatigable): Santa Cruz; Brattles Island: Tortuga; Crossman's Island: Crossman (Los Hermanos); King Charles's Island: Santa María (Floreana); Dassigney's Island (Chatham): San Cristóbal; Eures's Island (Tower): Genovesa; Bindlos's Island: Marchena; Earl of Abington's Island: Pinta; Lord Wamman's Island (Wenman): Wolf; Lord Culpeper's Island: Darwin. Further synonyms appear in Slevin (1959) (Figure source: Cowley, Captain W.A., *Collection of Original Voyages*, 1699).

to extinction. The pogrom continued with the arrival of fur traders who came to deplete the stocks of seals. It was a sombre period as we would judge it today, resulting in the ruthless over-exploitation of these species. In the 1830s, when Ecuador assumed sovereignty of the islands, the first settlers arrived and set about their own sustained hunting of the islands' wildlife.

In turning to the names of the islands one comes to a subject that is at once complex and confusing. The earliest names are those recorded by Ambrose Cowley in his chart of 1684 (Fig. 1.3). These honoured kings of the Stuart line and British high officials, not a few of whom had shown what some would regard as a lamentable degree of leniency towards the buccaneers. Colnett made a more comprehensive map, using these English names but evidently running into difficulties with some of the islands which over the years had received a succession of names. He christened several that had remained unidentified and, for good measure, substituted a few names of his own. In 1832, the islands became known officially as the *Archipiélago del Ecuador* (Archipelago of the Equator = Ecuador) and Spanish names were adopted. Among the earlier of these were San Carlos (for Charles, now Floreana) and Olmedo (for Santiago, formerly James). Sixty years later, this collective name was changed to *Archipiélago de Colón* (Archipelago of Columbus), in celebration of the fourth centenary of the discovery of America. At the same time different epithets came into being for the individual islands, these now recalling the ships of Christopher Columbus and the people who had helped finance his expeditions. These remain the official Ecuadorian names today, although, unhelpfully, they are not in every case the ones in general usage among Spanish-speaking people of the islands. Thus, over the centuries, some islands have received a compendium of titles, with one at least (Santa Cruz) acquiring eight. It is perhaps one of the minor ironies of cartographic history that so few of these names bear much relevance to the people and events associated with the islands. The one bright and constant thread is the name *Galápagos*, which continues to be accepted and used, both in Ecuador and the outside world.

1.4. Settlement

The islands had no aboriginal people and the first human impact of importance on the environment was brought about by the exploitation of tortoises and by the introduction of domestic livestock. The formal ceremony of annexation to Ecuador was conducted on Floreana by Colonel Ignacio Hernandez on 12 February 1832. Later that year the first settlers arrived, many of them political detainees who had escaped a sentence of death for one of deportation. Floreana was chosen for the venture as it was already used as a port-of-call by whalers (where they had their famous barrel post office at Bahía del Correo) and the island had some known potential for cultivation. Earlier in the century, a recalcitrant though enterprising castaway, Patrick Watkins, had lived for several years on the island growing pumpkins and other produce which he exchanged for liquor on board visiting ships.

Under the guidance of José Villamil, a general of the Ecuadorian independence movement, the young settlement grew and prospered for a few years. Forest was cleared in the high saddle forming the centre of Floreana, where maize, sugar cane, sweet potatoes, bananas, melons and citrus fruits were grown. Animals were introduced, among them cattle, horses, pigs and donkeys. It is not difficult to envisage a certain buoyancy in the early days of the settlement, but any optimism must gradually have given way to the realization that the island was small and one subject moreover to the debilitating effects of drought. Privation was one thing, but hopes turned to disillusionment when it was found that the government in Quito intended using the new colony as a penal settlement. During the troubled years that followed the island suffered the vicissitudes of abandonment and recolonization, with outbreaks of violence and lawlessness. After a final period of desertion the island was reoccupied in 1929. Even these latest years have hardly passed unclouded, for Floreana has been the scene of some of the most bizarre and publicized events in the archipelago's recent history (Strauch, 1936, Wittmer, 1961). Today, a visitor finds a cluster of wooden houses on the coast near the open roadstead at Black Beach. From there a narrow rocky trail heads inland, taking one amid dry thorn scrub to half-a-dozen scattered smallholdings in the hills. This part of the island, with its louring peaks and overgrown plantations, seems to hint darkly at Floreana's strained and melancholy past.

Settlement followed a similar pattern elsewhere. After various desultory attempts, San Cristóbal was colonized in 1869. Manuel Cobos, a member of a prominent Guayaquil family, started a venture to harvest a lichen, known as orchil (*Roccella babingtonii*), which was used in the dye industry. Very largely through his own tyrannical efforts, Cobos was also able to develop the high volcanic terrain into one of the leading sugar plantations of Ecuador. The sugar together with coffee and hides were exported for a time to the mainland. The enterprise eventually entered a decline, in part one surmises through the impoverishment of the thin volcanic soils, and then, in 1904, Cobos suffered death at the hands of his workers. Despite these setbacks the settlement continued and eventually became the administrative capital of the archipelago, centred today on the port of Baquerizo Moreno.

Interest in southern Isabela had followed in 1895 when a group of vagrants were gathered from the streets of Guayaquil and sent as a colonizing expedition. Eighty persons arrived to found the tiny port of Villamil and a village inland on the humid slopes of the volcano of Sierra Negra (Santo Tomás). By the beginning of this century, two hundred colonists were established on the island, making a living by raising cattle and exporting sulphur, seal skins and tortoise oil. Their heyday, if such it was, came to an end when the government chose this island as a new site for a penal colony.

Santa Cruz, the fourth island to be inhabited, was settled in the 1920s. It is an unusual story in that its pioneers were members of a Norwegian colonizing expedition. The inspiration for this venture appears to have been derived from the book by William Beebe, *Galápagos: World's End* (1924), which, though by no means inaccurately, painted a picture of the islands which highlighted their romantic side to the layman enduring the long winters of northern Europe. This triggered what would be known today as an exercise in real estate. Although its instigators rapidly faded from the scene they were instrumental in sending out groups of families who were quite ill-prepared for the ordeal of starting a new life under the harsh and arid conditions of the Galápagos. Some died and many more returned to their native Norway, but the few that remained somehow managed to scrape together a living and were joined in time by settlers from the mainland. Together they developed the smallholdings, or *chacras*, that today occupy much of the humid zone inland. Meanwhile, the coastal village of Puerto Ayora (at Academy Bay), with its painted houses and exotic flowering shrubs, has grown to become the largest and in many ways most colourful settlement in the archipelago. It is connected by road across the highlands to the air terminal at Baltra, thus enabling Santa Cruz to outstrip San Cristóbal and become the centre of a small but flourishing tourist industry.

Today, there are between five and six thousand inhabitants of the islands. The great majority of these are Ecuadorians, but people who have direct links with a dozen other countries are represented and give communities a sometimes surprisingly cosmopolitan flavour. English is spoken as a second common language. These population centres are confined to sectors of the four inhabited islands (San Cristóbal, Santa Cruz, Isabela and Floreana), with a small air force detachment at Baltra. The rest of the archipelago forms territory of a national park. Life for the islanders is regulated to a certain extent by the rules of living in an area of outstanding scientific interest, but there are compensations. The islands have provincial status, and many families have been able to move away from the traditional pursuits of fishing and subsistence farming to reap some of the direct benefits of tourism.

Altogether, settlement affects about 12% of the land surface of the archipelago. Whilst this may not appear large, it does involve the greater part of the fertile humid zone environment with its tracts of immemorial 'tortoise country'. Elsewhere, the land generally has proved too arid and too barren for any form of agricultural pursuit or livestock husbandry. In many ways one must be thankful that this has been so, for without the protective armour imposed by the volcanic terrain the story of the Galápagos would have been a very different one, and it is doubtful if such a book as this, taking the undiminished environment for its theme, would have been written.

But the consolation extends beyond this. Anyone visiting the islands finds a certain enchantment amid the

Figure 1.4. Pinnacle Rock, Bartolomé Island, with the highlands of Santiago beyond. An aerial photograph of this scene appears as Fig. 2, Chapter 2.

broad vistas of the lowlands that have been so little influenced by the hand of man. This is an important feature in the promotion of the tourism that has now become a part of the Galápagos scene. The legacies of earlier, uncontrolled settlement are there, but disguised, reflected in the depleted state of the tortoise populations and in the reduced ranges of iguanas and some birds. Equally unobtrusive at first is the influence of alien plants and animals, which have had a subtle though no less crucial impact on the environment. These today represent the main threats to the islands' indigenous wildlife.

1.5. The Age of Darwin

The circumstances that brought a former student of theology to the position of naturalist on board H.M.S. *Beagle* and so set in train a sequence of ideas that culminated in the theory of organic evolution need no retelling here. For the Galápagos, it meant a visit that has come to eclipse all other historical events in the islands.

H.M.S. *Beagle* spent just 5 weeks in Galápagos waters. Yet what emerged from the visit was Charles Darwin's remarkably perceptive account of the islands. That perception encompassed their isolation, the geological youthfulness of the land, and the character of plants and animals that had found their way there from the mainland of South America. Darwin's interest had been fired by what he had already seen of life on the mainland, where species had many similarities with those of the islands, yet differed in marked ways. Somehow, in a not so very distant past, chance migrants must have traversed 1,000 km of sea to colonize those austere shores; and once there descendants of these had changed or become modified, each to its own particular ends. In that 'little world within itself . . .', wrote Darwin (1890), 'we seem to be brought near to that great fact—that mystery of mysteries—the first appearance of new beings on this earth'.

The impressions gained by Darwin in the Galápagos Islands matured in his mind over many years. What his observations of the unique life there had enabled him to do was to consider the idea of the non-fixity of species. When he eventually set forth his explanation he established both the process of evolution and the mechanism of natural selection as the force operating to create new species. The epochal paper outlining Darwin's ideas, together with Alfred Russel Wallace's advancing the same thesis, was presented to the scientific world at a meeting of the Linnean Society of London on 1 July 1858. The following year *The Origin of Species* burst upon a complacent Victorian England. The resulting controversy raged well into this century and incidentally brought recognition to the Galápagos as a remarkable natural laboratory of evolution.

The succeeding years one must now view against the times. Scientific endeavour arose in large part from collecting expeditions designed for the enrichment of museums and the description of new species. The main emphasis of growing interest in the Galápagos was in collecting, which resulted in the compilation of inventories of the islands' fauna and flora and in the study of systematics based on these collections. Among the scientific visitors who followed Darwin in the last century were the Swedish botanist Nils Andersson, the colourful and controversial Louis Agassiz, Theodor Wolf, who came at the instigation of the Ecuadorian Government, and George Baur, a geomorphologist who wrote about the islands and their origins. In 1897, the expedition of Frank Webster and Charles Harris made collections for Lord Rothschild who was assembling series of the world's giant tortoises in his museum at Tring. Succeeding this was the even more extensive expedition of Edmund Heller and Robert Snodgrass from Stanford University.

Before turning away from the early expeditions—a fuller account of which may be found in Slevin (1959)—mention should be made of the long association of the California Academy of Sciences with the Galápagos Islands. In 1905, Rollo Beck headed a year-long expedition on the schooner *Academy*, which made the most thorough studies of the vertebrates and vascular plants that had so far been undertaken. Most remarkable among these collections was an almost complete range of the giant tortoises known to inhabit the islands. Allan Hancock's voyages of *Velero III* in the 1930s continued this tradition and association with California, which culminated in the Galápagos International Scientific Project of 1964 (Bowman, 1966).

This spate of scientific interest did not leave the host country unmoved. In 1934, the Ecuadorian Government promulgated the first laws protecting wildlife in the archipelago and, 25 years later, under mounting pressure, declared the islands a national park. This finally set aside all unoccupied land for the protection of native plants and animals. In the same year, 1959, an international organization, the Charles Darwin Foundation for the Galápagos Isles, came into being to advise Ecuadorian authorities on the needs of the park and to coordinate scientific research. To further both these aims a permanent biological research station was set up at Academy Bay on Santa Cruz, the most central island of the group. Ten years later, the advent of organized tourism and the inauguration of a Galápagos National Park Service heralded a period of new and comparative stability in the islands.

Today, it is not easy to appreciate just how critical were the post-war years and the protracted representations and mounting pressures that led to the establishment of a permanent scientific presence on the islands (Eibl-Eibesfeldt, 1959, Bowman, 1960). That there came about a successful change in philosophy may be attributed to a few far-sighted individuals who guided the inception of the Charles Darwin Research Station (*Estación Científica Charles Darwin*). Ultimately, at the heart of this change was the unique quality of the islands and the potential they offered for development as a centre for research and education.

In the Galápagos Islands there are some of the world's most striking examples of adaptive radiation. These include the geospizine finches, mockingbirds, tortoises, iguanas and, among plants, the groups of *Scalesia* and *Opuntia*, all of which receive due mention in this book. What is notable is that the patterns of interisland variation in the Galápagos have remained remarkably intact—a situation, unhappily, that has not been accorded to other oceanic island groups which had a comparable wealth of evolutionary diversity. Despite the many disturbances and despite earlier fears, the Galápagos has suffered few species losses.

New sciences and new disciplines constantly bring fresh insights into the conditions moulding the Galápagos Islands and their environment. Over the past quarter century behavioural studies have gained a special emphasis, facilitated by the extraordinary tameness of many endemic vertebrates. To the ecologist, there is an infinitely extending field of research. Today, it is the turn of the entomologist, marine biologist, lichenologist and volcanologist to shed new light on the origins of life on the islands. In a very real sense, each scientist coming to the Galápagos works in the shadow of others. It is the composite picture, the mosaic that they have built, that is the substance of this volume, a portrait of a group of islands unfettered by time, where the processes of adaptive change may be discerned with a clarity denied to other parts of the world.

References

Beebe, W. (1924) *Galápagos: World's End*. Putnam's Sons, New York.

Bowman, R.I. (1960) *A Biological Reconnaissance of the Galápagos Islands during 1957*. UNESCO, Paris.

Bowman, R.I. (1966) *The Galápagos: Proceedings of the Symposia of the Galápagos International Scientific Project*. University of California Press, California.

Dampier, W. (1697) *A New Voyage Round the World*. London.

Darwin, C. (1890) *Naturalist's Voyage Round the World*. John Murray, London.

Eibl-Eibesfeldt, I. (1959) Survey on the Galápagos Islands. *Unesco Mission Reports*, **8**, 1–31.

Harris, M.P. (1974) *A Field Guide to the Birds of Galápagos*. Collins, London.

Heyerdahl, T. (1978) *Early Man and the Ocean*. Allen and Unwin, London.

Heyerdahl, T. and Skjölsvold, A. (1956) Archaeological evidence of pre-Spanish visits to the Galápagos Islands. *Mem. Soc. Amer. Arch.*, 12.

Porter, D.M. (1976) Geography and dispersal of Galápagos Islands vascular plants. *Nature, Lond.* **264**, 745–746.

Sarmiento de Gamboa, P. (1572) *History of the Incas*. Hakluyt Soc., **XXII**, Cambridge 1907.

Slevin, J.R. (1959) The Galápagos Islands: A History of Their Exploration. *Occ. Papers Cal. Acad. Sci.*, **XXV**, 1–150.

Snow, D. (1964) The Giant Tortoises of the Galápagos Islands. *Oryx VII*, 277–290.

Strauch, D. (1935) *Satan Came to Eden*. Jarrolds, London.

Walker, B.W. (1966) The Origin and Affinities of the Galápagos Shorefishes in *The Galápagos*. Edited by R.I. Bowman. Pages 172–174. University of California Press, California.

Wittmer, M. (1961) *Floreana*. Michael Joseph Ltd., London.

CHAPTER 2

Geology of Galápagos Islands

TOM SIMKIN

National Museum of Natural History, Smithsonian Institution, Washington, D.C

Contents

2.1. Introduction   16
2.2. Setting   16
2.3. Age   17
2.4. Historic Volcanism   18
2.5. Eruptive Styles and Products   19
    2.5.1. Lava fountaining and vent formation   19
    2.5.2. Lava flows and tubes   19
    2.5.3. Explosive volcanism and fragmental deposits   21
    2.5.4. Fumaroles and gas   24
    2.5.5. Rock compositional variation   24
2.6. Volcano Development   26
    2.6.1. Volcano spacing   26
    2.6.2. Rift systems   27
    2.6.3. Calderas and pit craters   28
    2.6.4. Volcano growth and form   32
2.7. Faulting   34
    2.7.1. Uplift   34
    2.7.2. Seismicity   36
2.8. Erosion and Other Surface Processes   36
    2.8.1. Weathering and alteration   37
    2.8.2. Water movement above sea level   37
    2.8.3. Marine erosion   38
    2.8.4. Sedimentation and beaches   38
2.9. Conclusions   38
    Acknowledgements   39
    References   39

2.1. Introduction

The Galápagos Islands—Herman Melville's 'five-and-twenty heaps of cinders'—owe their existence above sea-level to their youthful volcanic nature. They are there because they are volcanically young. Furthermore, the dry equatorial climate slows the weathering of rock into soil and withholds the moisture that would soon cloak such volcanic features in vegetation if they were found in wetter climates. The result is a stark landscape quite alien to the experience of most visitors. Most visitors, though, quickly recognize variety in this landscape, and sense that its history is inextricably tied to that of the wild and wondrous organisms living on its surface. This chapter attempts to summarize what is known of the archipelago's physical history, and to review the active processes that have shaped (and continue to shape) these special islands.

2.2. Setting

Plate tectonics—the concept that revolutionized the earth sciences in the 1960s—tells us that most of the world's volcanism takes place at plate boundaries: either along the deep oceanic rift system, where plates are spreading apart with the creation of new oceanic crust, or where plates are colliding with thinner crust being subducted under thicker at island arcs or continental margins. But the Galápagos Islands are not explained by either setting. They lie over 1000 km west of the magnificent continental margin volcanoes of the Ecuadorian Andes, and equally far east of the point where the Pacific's major rift, the East Pacific rise, turns northward to form the Gulf of California. At this major bend in the East Pacific Rise another rift system—the Galápagos Spreading Center—heads eastwards from this 'triple junction' to pass north of the Galápagos Islands (Fig. 2.1). Southward spreading from this center is slow (3 cm/yr) relative to the fast (>7 cm/yr) eastward spreading from the East Pacific Rise, resulting in a net crustal movement toward the east-southeast in the Galápagos Islands region. Although the Galápagos Spreading Center has provided the dramatic 1977 discovery of bizarre hydrothermal vent communities 2.5 km below the surface and subsequent observations on the oceanic rift system (Corliss *et al.*, 1979, Ballard *et al.*, 1982), the site of this detailed work is over 400 km east of the Galápagos archipelago and shares only its name with the islands. To understand the origin of the islands we must go beyond the fundamental plate tectonics elements of spreading centers and subduction zones.

An early corollary of the new hypothesis of Earth's behavior has been the idea of 'hotspots', rooted deep in the mantle, supplying lava to and through overlying crustal plates as they move slowly along. The Hawaiian Islands have been the type example of this process, with ages growing progressively older to the northwest (in the direction of plate movement) from the currently active hotspot at the southeast end of the chain, but the Galápagos were listed as another example in Wilson's (1963) initial statement of the idea. The concentration of recent volcanism in the western islands defines the hotspot, and plate movement to the east-southeast explains the older islands and submarine ridge in that direction as former products of the hotspot. By the time of Morgan's (1971) extension of the concept, the presence of the Galápagos Spreading Center was known and he suggested that ancient products of the Galápagos hotspot had, through past millions of years, been deposited to the north as well as the south. Plate motion on that side of the spreading center is to the northeast, explaining the submarine Cocos Ridge as another 'plume' of volcanic material being carried away from the Galápagos hotspot. Thus the hotspot idea explains not only the main features of island ages, but also the broader physiographic features of the region. The shallow submarine platform of the Galápagos archipelago has steep slopes to the west and south, but gentle slopes to the northeast and east where it is essentially the intersection of the Cocos and Carnegie Ridges. This is exactly the physiographic pattern to be expected from a fixed mantle hotspot that has, over the last 25 million years, supplied volcanic products to two overlying plates, one moving to the northeast and the other to the east-southeast (Hey, 1977). The Galápagos spreading

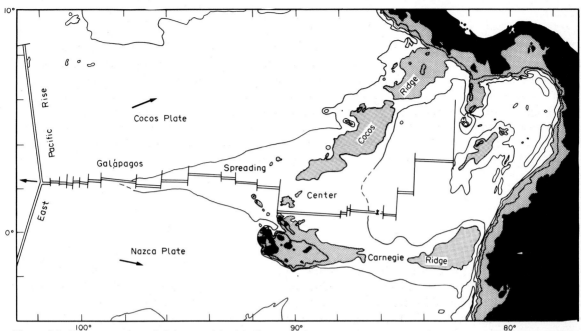

Figure 2.1. Tectonic setting of Galápagos Islands. Plate boundaries from Hey (1977) and bathymetry from Chase (1968). Bathymetric contour intervals at 500 fathoms (914 m) and area above 1000 fathoms (1829 m) shown by stipple pattern. Site of deep-sea hydrothermal vent explorations on the Galápagos Spreading Center (Corliss *et al.*, 1979) marked by **asterisk**. Absolute plate motion vectors (arrows) also from Hey (1977).

center that separates these two plates has received many detailed studies (see for example, Johnson *et al.*, 1966, and Schilling *et al.*, 1982), with particular attention to the striking petrochemical variation along its axis, and all have tended to strengthen the basic idea that a deep mantle hotspot exists under the western Galápagos Islands. The regional gravity data of Case and others (1973) and the isotope data of White and Hofmann (1978) are also compatible with a Galápagos hotspot.

2.3. Age

The question that biologists constantly ask geologists in Galápagos is 'how old are the islands?' 'how long has evolution had to work here?' Marine geophysical techniques, particularly the dating of seafloor magnetic anomalies, indicate that the oceanic crust on which the islands are built can be no older than 10 million years. However, the hotspot concept described above clearly implies that the islands are much younger than their underlying crust. Attempts to date the island rocks themselves have encountered several difficulties: (1) young lava flows tend to cover older ones, (2) erosion in most parts of these arid islands is too slow to cut through to the older interior, (3) potassium, the parent element whose radioactive decay to argon is most commonly measured in age determinations, is present in only very small quantities in most Galápagos rocks, and (4) the dry, rubbly lava flows that make up so much of the Galápagos have daunted much diligent searching for the islands' oldest rocks (Herman Melville wrote of the islands 'The interior of most of them is tangled and difficult of passage beyond description; the air is sultry and stifling; an intolerable thirst is provoked, for which no running stream offers its kind relief'). Nevertheless, much progress has been made, with the most recent radiometric work (Bailey, 1976) yielding confident ages around 3.3 million years for Española. Although Española lavas had been interpreted by McBirney and Williams (1969) as uplifted submarine flows, Hall and others (1980) have since found evidence that they are subaerial, confirming that true islands existed in Galápagos at least 3.3 m.y. ago.

Allan Cox (1983) has tabulated radiometric and magnetic age determinations from the Galápagos. No rocks older than 0.7 m.y. have been found on the historically volcanic islands of Fernandina, Isabela, Santiago, and Pinta, nor on the northern islands of Genovesa, Marchena, or Culpepper. A 0.72 m.y. age has been measured from Wenman, and the central islands of Santa Cruz, Baltra, Rábida, Pinzón, and Floreana have rocks in the 0.7–1.5 m.y. age range. Ages of 2.6–2.8 m.y. have been measured on Santa Fé rocks and an uncertain 4.2 m.y. (±1.8 m.y.) age from Plazas, off the northeast coast of Santa Cruz. The 3.3 m.y. age for Española has been discussed above, and Cox estimates that the old volcano of southwest San Cristóbal is older than 2.4 m.y. (Colinvaux, 1968, has reported a 4 m.y. date for this volcano, but the dated rock was not collected in place and may represent pre-island growth). Cox concludes (as did Hey, 1977) that the earliest Galápagos Islands probably emerged 3 to 5 million years ago, and there is no geologic evidence that the islands have ever been connected, even by a chain of islands, with the mainland. These ages would seem to conflict with some fossil evidence from the islands—particularly the late Miocene (5–10 m.y.) ages reported by Durham (1965) for the invertebrate fossils found on northeast Santa Cruz—however, Lipps and Hickman (1982) have recently concluded that most Galápagos fossils are represented by living species and that most island fossil deposits are not older than 2 million years. Evolution has had only a few million years in which to work in the Galápagos, and these islands—in contrast to other still-active ocean archipelagos like the Azores, Canary, and Samoa Islands—are remarkably young.

The remainder of this chapter will discuss the main geologic features of Galápagos with emphasis on the processes that have formed them. Because the islands are so young, and their formative processes so vigorously continuing, the origin of most features is obvious without great leaps of imagination.

2.4. Historic Volcanism

The oldest documented eruption was in 1797 from Volcán Wolf,* although earlier visitors observed volcanism from unspecified parts of the archipelago. The historic volcanism of Galápagos has been catalogued by Richards (1962) and both updated and condensed by Simkin and others (1981). Fifty-three eruptions are known, from 8 volcanoes, and another 6 volcanoes carry evidence of probable eruptions within the last few thousand years or less. Most eruptions have produced basaltic lava flows, commonly from linear fissures, rather than the violently exploding ash and pumice characteristic of the more gas-rich, siliceous volcanoes at colliding plate margins.

By any measure, the Galápagos are amongst the most active oceanic volcano groups in the world. During the last 15 years, when reportage of Galápagos volcanism has been reasonably complete, only Hawaii has been active in more years (10, to 7 each for Galápagos and Réunion, in the Indian Ocean; Iceland was active in 6 and no other deep ocean island group was active in more than 3). Simkin and Siebert (in press) have suggested measures of volcanic 'vigor' that allow crude comparisons of different volcanic groups. These show Galápagos to be among the dozen most vigorous groups in the world; roughly comparable to Japan, and more active than regions such as the Philippines, Mexico, and the West Indies. It is certain, however, that the historic record for Galápagos is incomplete, probably even in recent years. The 1979 eruption of Cerro Azul, from a vent low on its east flank, was well recognized in Galápagos (Moore, 1980B), but it was not until 2 years later that Moore, upon climbing to the summit, saw lava within the caldera that she did not remember from pre-1979 visits. Inspection of photographs taken by other summit visitors in 1979 narrows the date of the summit flow to within a few months of the flank eruption, and they may well have been

---

* An arguably older eruption on Santiago is dated, but was not witnessed. The prominent lava flow in James Bay contains fragments of marmalade pots stashed by buccaneers in 1684 (Heyerdahl, 1963). The flow was mentioned by Darwin, thus bracketing its age between 1684 and 1835: one of the rare uses of marmalade pots in volcano-chronology.

synchronous. Even more recently, an unnoticed eruption produced small lava flows visible on the 26 March, 1982, air photographs of Fernandina (Fig. 2.9) that were not present when we walked past that area 15 months earlier (4 December 1980). Normally the earliest hours of Galápagos eruptions are the most spectacular and activity is often virtually ended in a day or two—clouds or topography may obscure that activity or there may simply be no human observers near enough to see the show.

2.5. Eruptive Styles and Products

People who drink bubbly liquids know that removing the bottle cap reduces pressure on the liquid, allowing gas to escape from solution. They also know that shaking the bottle, or holding it at the wrong angle, can disastrously affect the way in which the liquid leaves the bottle. Molten magma is also a bubbly liquid, and its gas content is an important factor affecting the way it exits its container. The degassing and consequent expansion of molten liquid as it nears the surface is a driving force behind most eruptions, and the varied eruptive products on Galápagos can be better appreciated if the (now-departed) gas phase is considered. In part because of the changes caused by degassing during eruption, geologists use the word 'magma' to refer to the gas-containing liquid before it reaches the surface, and 'lava' for the relatively gas-poor liquid that then flows on to the surface.

The other, much more obvious, factor to consider is that molten Galápagos lava, at temperatures above 1,000°C, cools to the solid state at a wide variety of rates, depending on the temperature of the surrounding material and the volume of the liquid. Small fragments thrown high into the air above an erupting vent may chill instantly as the spun glass fibers of 'Pele's hair'; larger clots of liquid splattered on to nearby cold rock may cool in seconds as a thin, hard, skin; and meters-thick lava flows may retain a molten liquid interior capable of movement and redistribution for months after the end of the eruption.

2.5.1. Lava fountaining and vent formation

Driven by expanding gases, lava commonly fountains above its vents and may reach spectacular heights. In the August, 1982, eruption of Volcán Wolf, for example, fountains were reported from caldera floor vents to the rim, a vertical distance of over 600 meters and rivalling the famous 1959 fountains from Kilauea Iki, in Hawaii. However, degassed lava may also well quietly out of other vents—even nearby vents in the same eruption—without pyrotechnic display. Varied fountaining behavior, and even the varied wind dynamics at the time of eruption, lead to equally varied spatter cones built around different vents. A cone wall may be destroyed by the later opening of a nearby vent, or carried down slope by flowing lava. An eruption is a changing, dynamic process: not only is the material arriving at the surface changing as the eruption progresses, but the surface itself is also changing as solidifying lava alters the landscape around the vents. Few Galápagos visitors will be lucky enough to see lava fountaining, but its products are well displayed at recent vents around Sullivan Bay (Santiago) and southeastern Genovesa. On a much smaller scale, vent shapes can be inspected with ease on the Sullivan Bay lava flow, where the advancing thin edge has flowed over and trapped water concentrations that then exploded, drilling vertically through the thin flow to produce a small 'rootless' vent, or hornito, perhaps less than a meter in diameter, on the surface of the flow.

2.5.2. Lava flows and tubes

Most of us have seen pictures of lava flowing colorfully down hill, but on Galápagos we can explore the now-cooled surfaces of such flows and recognize many details of their mobile history. Thin crusts have been wrinkled into parabolic arcs by the flow of underlying lava, thicker crustal plates have been rafted together before freezing into rock, and still-fluid lava has oozed from cracks in nearly-solid flows to form bulbous protrusions on fracture surfaces that are obviously late in the flow's history. Such features are beautifully displayed at places like Sullivan Bay (Fig. 2.2) and Punta Espinosa (Fig. 6.6)—they testify to the great fluidity of these flows. The retained gases contributing to that fluidity are evidenced by the countless small gas bubbles, or vesicles, 'frozen' in the rock and visible on any fractured surface.

The infinitely less attractive counterpart to these smooth-surfaced, fluid, *pahoehoe* flows ('pa-hoy-hoy'), are the spiny, cindery surfaces of the dreaded *aa* ('ah-ah') flows. These are not experienced by most tour visitors to Galápagos for the simple reason that nobody walks on them by choice, but they are common in the islands and a typical example can be seen at the end of the marked trail at Punta Espinosa. They are turgid, viscous flows, relative to the more fluid pahoehoe, and cliff sections through such flows reveal a downward gradation from the clinkery, fragmental surface into a massive interior. The flow base is again fragmental because flows move like great caterpillar tractor treads, with rubble from the top tumbling down the advancing flow front to be overridden at the base. Just as there are many gradations in lava viscosities and flow regimes, there are many gradations in lava flow surfaces and types, but the aa/pahoehoe classification is adequate for most Galápagos lava flows.

Any lava flow moving down slope seeks the easiest hydraulic path and, as the flow grows larger in its initial channel, often overspills its own sides. Cooling of countless, thin overspills builds hard natural levees that serve to contain the flow in its own channel. Well-developed channels decorate the west-facing scarp of Isla Bartolomé, and oblique sun angles can make visible from great distances the larger channels that lace the steep slopes of the bigger volcanoes.

Lava tubes, or tunnels, have attracted much interest in Galápagos where several have been mapped by

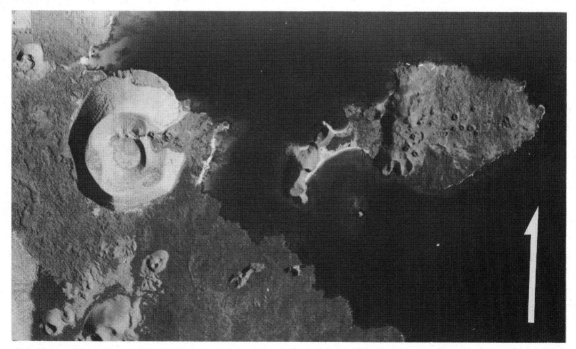

Figure 2.2. Sullivan Bay, eastern Santiago, and Isla Bartolomé. Vertical air photograph (by US Air Force) taken in 1946. Pinnacle Rock is to left of white beach on northwest side of island and the common landing dock is near the northernmost tip in the center of the island. The prominent tuff cone of Cerro Inn (left center of photograph) was formed by explosive eruptions. Around the start of this century, highly fluid lava flows covered about 50 km² south of Cerro Inn, burying parts of other cones and leaving the remarkably ropy flow surfaces of Sullivan Bay. Activity later resumed at Cerro Inn, adding spatter and scoria to the breached east side of the cone. (Arrow corresponds to distance of 1 km).

Balazs (1975), Montoriol-Pous (1978), and others (Fig. 19.13). Commonly 5 m in diameter and hundreds of meters long, these natural caves have provided refuge for former Galápagos animals and protection for their remains. They have thus been fertile collecting sites for vertebrate paleontologists (Steadman, 1981, 1982). The formation of lava tubes has been observed on Hawaii (Peterson and Swanson, 1974) both by the crusting over of lava streams near vents (such as the flow channels described above) and by the coalescence of pahoehoe toes at sluggish flow fronts on gentler, more distant, slopes. 'As a pahoehoe toe budded from the flow front, a skin chilled around it. The skin inflated like a balloon as more lava oozed into it. Eventually the skin broke open owing to excess fluid pressure, and lava emerged as a new toe that rapidly became encased in its own skin. Repetitions of this budding process gradually lengthened the flow and developed a small tube, whose overlying crust thickened to form a rigid shell.' (Peterson and Swanson, 1974, p. 215). As the tubes developed, they eroded downward from shallow depths to at least 13 m deep, cutting into underlying older flows. When the flow of lava ended at the vent some or all of the lava drained out to leave a long, empty tube system. Because they transport large volumes of lava long distances with very little heat loss, lava tubes are recognized as important elements in the growth of large, broad, basaltic shield volcanoes.

2.5.3. Explosive volcanism and fragmental deposits

Nearly all historic Galápagos eruptions have produced lava flows, with only a small proportion of fragmental deposits, and inspection of the great caldera wall sections of lavas in Galápagos finds only thin and infrequent fragmental deposits. These proportions are reversed, however, in the historic eruptions of the world, over 73% of which have been explosive and only 24% of which have produced lava flows (Simkin *et al.*, 1981). The reason for this is that most of the world's known volcanoes are at converging plate boundaries, and are made of more siliceous, more viscous, gas-rich magma than the basaltic materials of Galápagos. Gas does not escape easily from viscous, silica-rich magma, and the result near continental margins is more explosive eruptions and volcanoes that are dominated by their fragmental deposits.

Fragmental deposits do exist in Galápagos, though, and are well known to anyone who has visited places like Tagus Cove, Bartolomé, or James Bay. These light-colored, regularly-layered deposits form what appear from the sea to be truncated cones as high as 395 m and up to 3.5 km across at the base (Fig. 2.3). Darwin regarded them as 'the most striking feature in the geology of this Archipelago' (1844, p. 112) and was the first to recognize that such features formed by the explosive interaction of hot, basaltic lava and cold water. Lava high in the feeding conduit is fragmented by the thermal shock of sudden, cold-water quenching, and the instantaneous volume expansion of water flashing to steam hurls the fragments upward, often along with larger fragments of older rock torn from the walls of the vent. The lava need not even be molten and fresh: the right mix of cold water and heated older rocks can produce explosive eruptions without the direct participation of any fresh, molten material. In any case, these fragments are thrown high in the air, with larger fragments falling back near the vent, some smaller ones landing further away, and none falling directly back into the vent (because of the continuing vertical blasts there). The inevitable result of this process is a circular cone shaped like an inverted **W** in cross-section (Fig. 2.4). Such cones are common around Galápagos coastlines, and are also found in summit calderas (Fernandina, Cerro Azul, and Marchena) where lakewater, rather than seawater, has been responsible for the explosive reaction. The collective term for fragmental materials of all sizes is 'tephra', and the consolidated, hardened, finer-grained deposits are called 'tuff'.

The above discussion has emphasized the simple fall of fragments thrown high above the vent in the building of these cones. Another process prominent in many Galápagos explosive eruptions is that known as base surge. Base surges were first recognized as ring-shaped density currents expanding laterally away from the base of mushroom clouds at thermonuclear test blasts. In explosive eruptions, they carry fragmental debris horizontally: eroding underlying deposits in some places, depositing dune-like cross-bedding in others, and plastering wet ash layers on any immovable vertical surface that is in the way. Evidence of base

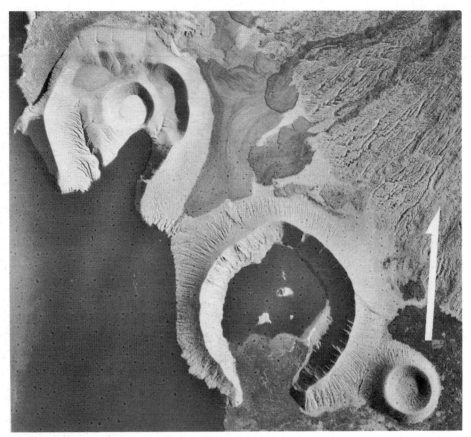

Figure 2.3. Tagus and Beagle cones, west central Isabela. Vertical air photograph (by US Air Force) taken in 1946. Explosive interaction of hot lava and cold seawater has built several cones of fragmental material. Renewed activity at Tagus has built an inner, nested cone that is filled (like the larger cone to the south) with a saline lake near sea level. Later lava flows from Volcán Darwin, to the north east, have ponded behind these cones and entered the breached south end of Beagle Cone (see panorama in Chapter 4, Fig. 3). The outside diameter of Beagle (3 km) places it amongst the largest cones in Galápagos. (North arrow corresponds to distance of 2 km).

surge is clear in the deposits of Fernandina's 1968 explosive eruption, and can be seen in older deposits such as the bedded ash cliffs around the south shore of James Bay. Other modifying influences on the above description of cone formation include winds and the later addition of lava.

Darwin noticed that most southeast rims of these cones are low, and he explained this as erosion by trade-wind waves and swells. The prevailing southeasterly winds must also modify the depositional process described above (*during* formation of the cones) by building the leeward rim at the expense of the windward. A resurgence of less explosive eruptions may also modify the 'inverted **W**' shape by adding a smaller cone within a larger (as at Tagus Cove, Fig. 2.3). One of the most interesting modifications of the 'inverted **W**', however, comes from the addition of unfragmented, liquid lava. In some eruptions, such as the famous 1963–7 eruption of Surtsey, off the south coast of Iceland, the explosions eventually build a fragmental cone large enough to shield the ascending magma from contact with cold seawater. Molten lava then reaches the surface without exploding and may proceed to fill the inner cone and perhaps even coat the outer surface like chocolate on a giant ice cream cone. This process is important in island growth because fragmental deposits are very soft, relative to lava flows, and will not long survive vigorous erosion by pounding surf unless protected by hard lava. Examples of various stages of this process can be seen in Galápagos: lava filled cones

Figure 2.4. Natural cross-section through cone at Buccaneer Cove, Santiago. Only half of the cone is shown, with the central vent near the right margin of the photograph. View (looking southwest) shows both inward- and outward-dipping layers formed by fluctuating conditions at the time of eruption.

(or remaining parts thereof) are at Daphne Minor, Buccaneer Cove (Fig. 2.4), and Bartolomé just southwest of Pinnacle Rock; the lava that once filled the conduit at Buccaneer Cove is now stripped bare as a solitary, dark vertical column; and the island of Champion, north of Floreana, is nearly completely coated by lavas with only a few bays cut through into the softer fragmental deposits beneath.

Three other features of interest in explosive volcanism are accretionary lapilli, bomb sags, and distant airfall deposits. Accretionary lapilli are concentrically layered spheres, many as large as peas, that are concentrated in some layers of cones such as Tagus Cove's. They form either when small grains fall through the eruptive cloud's turbulent mix of water vapor and fine ash, picking up muddy coatings like tiny snowballs, or when the raindrops associated with some eruptive clouds act as nucleii collecting fine ash on their way down through the cloud. Bomb sags are formed when large blocks, hurled upwards during an eruption, land on moist, not-yet-fully-consolidated layers of earlier fragmental material. The resulting down-warping of these layers, often with the large block still in place, can be seen from boat rides along cliff sections displaying the internal layering of large cones like Tagus or Cabo Cowan. While the tuff cones discussed above are built by the nearby deposits of explosive eruptions, some ash is carried far from the vent and may build a significant airfall deposit if the eruption is large. The 1968 Fernandina eruption left up to 17 m of fragmental deposits on the caldera floor, 5 m on the western rim, 15 cm at the coast (11 km to the west), and lightly dusted a merchant vessel 350 km to the west. No adequate stratigraphy of far-traveled ash deposits has been attempted in Galápagos, but there have clearly been massive explosions in the islands that dwarf the 1968 Fernandina eruption. Much of the outer flank of Alcedo is mantled with thick, trachytic pumice (McBirney and Williams, 1969), and the outer slopes of Marchena—where not covered by younger flows—are made up of thick basaltic tephra deposits.

Although most of this discussion has centered on tuff cones, the features built of finely fragmented basalt where hot magma and cold water meet in explosive proportions, it must be obvious that many gradations exist between them and the spatter cones, or cinder cones, built by lava fountaining as described in section 2.51. Linear fissure eruptions, crossing an Oregon lakeshore several million years ago, built tuff cones in what was then a shallow lake but cinder cones on the drier side of that former shoreline (Heiken, 1971). In Galápagos, steep-sided cinder cones are common on the dry, outer slopes above sea-level, but cindery, scoriaceous layers may also be found in near-shore tuff-cones, resulting from fluctuations in water access to the vent (or its subsurface conduit) during the course of the eruption.

2.5.4. Fumaroles and gas

Volcanism does not end with the end of an eruption. Thick lava flows (thicknesses of 50 m have been measured on Galápagos) may retain a liquid interior for a year or more, and continue to lose heat for decades. But huge magma chambers, filled with molten liquid and thermally blanketed by the overlying volcanic edifice, cool for many millions of years after their last eruption. The fumaroles and hot springs of many volcanic regions are surface reminders of these hot materials below.

Rainfall percolates downward through porous rocks, but if it encounters hot rock it is heated, becomes less dense, and rises back to the surface as steam. This may or may not contain volcanic gases, but the heat source is commonly still-cooling magma, and late gases from that magma commonly mix with the vapor on its way to the surface. These surface concentrations are called 'fumaroles', or 'solfataras' if sulfur precipitation is pronounced. They are located on major vertical fractures, like caldera boundary faults, that provide an easy passage to the surface and are often found near recent eruptive fissures, where still-cooling magma is very close to the surface.

In the submarine environment—with an abundance of the water that is usually in short supply above sea-level in Galápagos—these hydrothermal systems work very efficiently, and submersible explorations of submarine volcanoes have recently found hydrothermal deposits, including metallic sulfides, concentrated on caldera walls and recent vents (Lonsdale et al., 1982). Galápagos fumaroles are most vigorous in climatically wet periods, when water supply is high, and are best seen in the early mornings, when the relative coolness of the air results in more condensation above the warm emanations. In Antarctica, such condensation results in the construction of huge ice towers over fumarolic vents.

In Galápagos, fumaroles are known from all the historically active volcanoes, plus Volcán Ecuador (northwest Isabela), Marchena, Santa Cruz, and Santa Fé. They provide many warm, moist habitats for ferns, mosses, and other moisture-loving organisms. Nordlie and Colony (1973) have described the fumarole that displayed geyser-like water fountaining through the 1960s on the caldera wall of Volcán Alcedo. The gas flowed at a velocity around 6 m/sec and was dominantly water vapor with large proportions of CO_2 and various sulfurous components. The associated pools, of mixed value to the large Alcedo wildlife population, carry a high boron content, abundant opal deposits, and temperatures to 96°C in one. The same authors have studied the most active fumarolic area in Galápagos, in Sierra Negra caldera, where a high vapor plume can often be seen from distant parts of the archipelago. Here gas vent temperatures reach 235°C, delicate sulfur crystals are formed at lower temperatures, and melting of sublimated deposits has produced liquid sulfur flows up to 225 m long.

2.5.5. Rock compositional variation

Whether lava flowed quietly or was fragmented explosively, its composition is of considerable interest to geologists. Variations in the products of a volcano provide clues to processes within that volcano and to the development of the archipelago as a whole. Some variations are obvious to the naked eye, such as the relative abundance of crystals that were already growing in the magma at the time it reached the surface. Large plagioclase feldspar crystals, for example, make up 10–15% of a typical Fernandina rock, and are clearly seen as white, lath-shaped crystals several mm in length. They were carried to the surface in suspension during eruption, but there the transporting liquid basalt cooled swiftly, with no time for growth of large crystals, and now forms a dark, fine-grained matrix around the feldspars. In the northern islands, large feldspar crystals make up a remarkable 60–80% of some individual flows, but these flows are interspersed with flows that carried no crystals at all. In their admirably detailed study of Pinzón volcano, Baitis and Lindstrom (1980) found repeated cycles of volcanic ash, overlain by several aa flows carrying no large crystals, which in turn were overlain by a thick series of crystal-rich flows before the next cycle began with more ash. They suggest that these sequences result from differentiation of a shallow magma chamber, with crystals growing and settling toward the bottom while gas pressure increased toward the top. After many—perhaps thousands—of years, gas pressure exceeded the confining pressure of the overlying rocks and explosive eruptions brought silica-rich, differentiated pumice and ash to the surface. These were then followed by completely liquid flows and, eventually, the crystal-rich liquid from deep in the zoned magma chamber. Addition of more basaltic liquid from depth would then have initiated another of the 7 cycles mapped by Baitis on the 260 m sea-cliff section of southwest Pinzón.

Similar, although not as pronounced, concentrations of olivine crystals are found in the picritic lavas of Volcán Ecuador, Cerro Azul, and elsewhere. Even larger particles, however, are carried to the surface with some Galápagos lavas. The slow cooling of magma in deep chambers forms coarsely-crystalline rocks of large, interlocking mineral grains, including some rocks formed by the gravity settling of early-formed, heavy crystals on the magma chamber floor. These may later be broken and fragments transported to the surface in alkaline basalt flows. Floreana lavas display many such deep-seated rock fragments, or xenoliths, and these valuable samples of the crust beneath Galápagos have been described by McBirney and Williams (1969) and Bow (1979).

Most Galápagos rocks, though, look very much the same, and most obvious color variations—from black, to brown, to red—are more the result of variation in oxidation than any fundamental variation in composition. Careful work with microscopes and chemical analyses is needed to recognize these more significant variations. The status of such detailed work (Simkin et al., 1972) is not sufficiently advanced in most parts of the archipelago to allow satisfying generalizations, but some observations are clear. For example, the lavas of Fernandina are monotonously unchanging in composition, with specimens from the steep caldera walls and many locations on the flanks falling within a narrow range of tholeiitic basalt composition. This constancy contrasts dramatically with the wide range of compositions on the much smaller volcano of Pinzón. Nordlie and others (1982) find compositional variations that fit his 1973 suggestion that the western volcanoes can be placed in the following developmental sequence: Cerro Azul (youngest), Wolf, Fernandina, Darwin, Alcedo, Sierra Negra (oldest). They point out that chemical distinctions between the youngest and oldest volcanoes in this sequence—adjacent to each other and both recently active—shows that there is little connection between magma chambers at depth.

While the large western volcanoes are built of tholeiitic basalt, those of the central part of the archipelago (including San Cristóbal) are mainly basalts of alkalic parentage. This pattern is reversed by smaller volcanoes, with alkali basalts on Volcán Ecuador, in the west, and tholeiitic rocks making up the central islands of Pinzón and Rábida. A broader complication is the finding (Baitis and Swanson, 1976, Bow, 1979) of low-K_2O tholeiitic basalts, comparable to those of the oceanic spreading centers, on the dominantly alkaline islands of Santiago and Santa Cruz. These young flows are related to the east-trending normal faults and aligned vents recognized by Swanson and others (1974) on Santiago and 6 other islands to the southeast. These features are believed to be related, in turn, to the east-trending Galápagos Spreading Center just to the north of the archipelago (Fig. 2.1). While it is easy to say that the islands are dominantly basaltic, with striking variation on some islands, there is much diversity, and more detailed petrologic data are needed.

The ultimate origin of Galápagos rocks is the earth's mantle, many tens of kilometers below the surface. Recent attempts to understand the nature of this mantle include the petrologic work of Bow (1979), the isotope work of White (1979), and the trace element analyses of Shimizu and others (1981).

2.6. Volcano Development

Having discussed the building materials of volcanoes—the small-scale features seen close at hand by Galápagos travelers—attention should be turned to the larger features that they build. This section will discuss the spacing of Galápagos volcanoes, their two dominant features of linear rift zones and broadly circular calderas, and the various volcano shapes that result.

2.6.1. Volcano spacing

Darwin (1844) noticed that many Galápagos volcanoes were aligned along parallel northwesterly axes and that roughly perpendicular lines could also be drawn to connect volcanic centers in a grid pattern. The intersection of major vertical fracture systems in the earth's crust creates a vertical line of weakness well suited to the ascent of magma. Darwin's map allowed a very regular grid pattern to be constructed linking Galápagos volcanoes, but more accurate charting of the islands has forced subsequent investigators either to draw less regular grids or to shift the positions of awkwardly placed volcanoes. Both alternatives have been followed. Shand (1937) likened Galápagos crust to a slab of chocolate—easy to break by bending, until the size of the remaining fragments approaches the thickness of the slab—in suggesting that the regular spacing of the grid might reflect the thickness of the local crust. Vogt (1974) has used the most recent bathymetric data to update this approach, finding an average inter-volcano spacing of 42 km: a not unreasonable plate thickness for Galápagos and comparable to other volcanic archipelagos (such as the Azores) in similar tectonic settings.

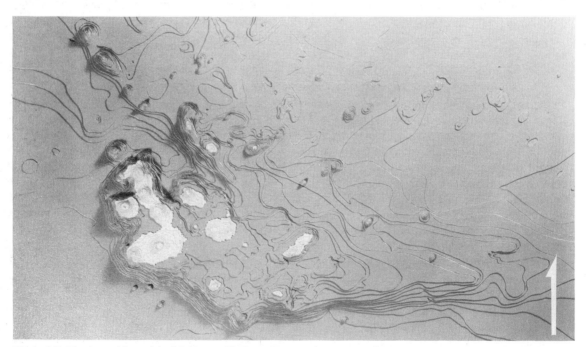

Figure 2.5. Physiographic model of Galápagos Platform. Topographic contours from American Geographical Society map of Galápagos and bathymetry from Chase (1968). Vertical exaggeration of model is 2:1 and scale can be estimated by 3½ km abyssal depths to the west of the platform and 1½ km elevations of the higher western volcanoes. Model by Lana Everett Turner and the author.
(North arrow corresponds to a distance of 100 km).

He also concludes that the islands are under a north-south least principal stress, with partial melts from the Galápagos hotspot flowing mainly northward to fill the gap created by the spreading center there. The spacing of Galápagos volcanoes is intriguing to anyone who likes to draw lines on maps, but a look at the bathymetric setting of these volcanoes (Fig. 2.5) quickly draws attention to the striking submarine features of the archipelago. The seamounts and linear northwesterly scarps of Galápagos have received virtually no investigation by marine geologists/geophysicists and such work is essential to a true understanding of the islands.

2.6.2. Rift systems

Most Galápagos eruptions are from a line of vents, indicating a subsurface planar fracture (providing easy passage for magma seeking the surface), rather than from a single, central vent. Fissure eruptions in many parts of the world begin with a 'curtain of fire', or low continuous fountaining from a fracture perhaps kilometers in length. Commonly, though, a part or parts of this fracture soon become favored pathways for the ascending magma, and flow at one or more portions soon increases as activity declines (and eventually dies) along the rest of the fissure. On a broader scale—in time as well as space—this pattern probably explains the distribution of Galápagos volcanoes along the regional, 'Darwinian' fractures described above. The northern island of Pinta, for example, is crossed by northwesterly lines of vents paralleling the elongation of the island and the submarine ridge on which it stands. Its 777 m summit is the highpoint along this ridge because it is the center of the most voluminous outpouring of lava. The high ridge along the equator, joining Wolf and Volcán Ecuador to the west, is clearly a constructional feature, built by aligned vents along a regional rift system. Several other volcanoes on Isabela are linked by lines of vents, showing that deepseated rift systems—as well as the simple overlapping of nearby volcanoes—are involved in the development of the largest of Galápagos Islands (Fig. 2.5).

Broadly regional rifting has already been mentioned in connection with the east-west fractures recognized by Swanson and others (1974) on Santiago and other islands to the southeast. Many of these have fed relatively young lava flows from aligned vents, and they seem related to the east-west spreading center north of the archipelago. The 1958 eruption of Fernandina issued from fissures that crossed the south end of the caldera rim in an east-west direction neither radial nor circumferential to the volcano center.

Most fissure eruptions, however, are aligned either radially or circumferentially. Gravitational stresses on isolated, simple shield volcanoes result in radial fissure eruptions in fan-like arrangement down the outer flanks. The north flanks of both Cerro Azul and Wolf show good examples of such flows. However, regional rift systems also produce fissures that are geometrically radial to the volcano, and it may be a matter of interpretation whether a radial fissure results from local distention or a more regional pattern. With so many regional patterns having been proposed for Galápagos, it is often difficult to be confident that a particular radial feature is unequivocally the product of local distention.

Circumferential fissures are also common in Galápagos. 'No other calderas in the world display such spectacular circumferential fissures' (Williams and McBirney, 1979, p. 205). The 1979 eruption of Sierra Negra was from such a fissure, 2.6 km long (Fig. 2.6), and most of the older flows seen on Fernandina, the eastern flanks of Wolf, and others are also from such fissures. As many as 4 concentric rows of vents are found around some caldera rims, although their length and number vary and no single fissure can be traced around a full circle. There is no significant vertical offset of the rocks on either side of the fissures. They are, in other words, fractures rather than faults, but the circumferential fault systems forming the calderas also produce many fissure eruptions. This description of circumferential features leads directly to discussion of the calderas themselves.

Figure 2.6. Eruption of Sierra Negra, 14 November, 1979. Second evening of eruption from circumferential vents near skyline known locally as Volcán Chico. Elizabeth Bay in foreground. Photograph from south rim of Alcedo by Lynn Fowler. See frontispiece for another view of this eruption.

2.6.3. Calderas and pit craters

Calderas are roughly circular collapse depressions found near the summits of many volcanoes, and those of the Galápagos are sufficiently distinctive to serve as type examples of calderas with well-developed circumferential fissures (Williams and McBirney, 1979). They form above magma chambers—the large regions perhaps 2–5 km down where magma often accumulates as a staging area on its way to the surface—and they are the direct result of the instability of those chambers. As magma accumulates, hydraulic pressure attempts to 'raise the roof' of the chamber, producing fractures in the overlying roof. If the chamber roof is broadly circular, the fractures will be broadly cylindrical. Subsequent removal of magma from the chamber—by eruption, withdrawal, or lateral intrusion of the volcano's flank—removes critical support for the overlying cylinder of roof rock and it drops into the newly vacated magma chamber (Fig. 2.7). The result is a broadly circular depression, or caldera, at the surface of the volcano. This process may be repeated many times, with as many variations as there are changes in the developing chamber(s), and eruptions may repeatedly flood the floor of the surface caldera.

Sierra Negra is the largest Galápagos caldera in area, measuring 7 by 10 km across. It is somewhat larger in area than the famous calderas of Crater Lake, Oregon, and Krakatau, but is dwarfed by many others (including, in the ocean island setting, that of Kauai, Hawaii). The deepest caldera in Galápagos is on Fernandina, where the floor now reaches 1120 m below the summit rim (and only 350 m above sealevel), while the shallowest is that of Marchena, a caldera ranking between Darwin and Alcedo in area but now filled to overflowing by recent eruptions. Calderas with diameters in the 1–2 km range are found on Pinzón, Santiago, and Genovesa, but the larger western volcanoes all have calderas in the 4–10 km range. Most Galápagos travelers do not make the hard day's trudge necessary to see these larger calderas, but many anchor in Darwin Bay, the slightly off-center caldera of Genovesa, or sail across the Equator looking at the magnificent 'giant's armchair' of Volcán Ecuador—the small volcano of northwest Isabela that has had its western half down-faulted to reveal a natural cross-section complete with caldera floor perched halfway down from the summit rim (Fig. 2.8).

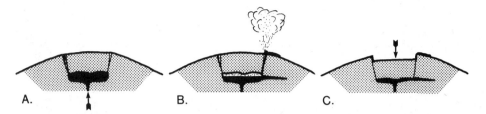

Figure 2.7. Schematic cross-sections of simplified caldera collapse sequence. (A) Additions to near-surface magma chamber hydraulically create ring fractures above chamber margin, (B) removal of magma by eruption (up) or intrusion (to side) removes support under overlying block, and (C) block collapses, along ring fractures, into vacated chamber creating circular depression at surface.

Although calderas are well known in most volcanic parts of the world, their formation occurs only rarely in terms of human lifetimes. In June of 1968, however, Fernandina caldera was dramatically enlarged when its floor dropped 350 m in the largest collapse known since the 1912 events at Katmai, Alaska. Only small parts of the 1968 events were witnessed, but modern remote sensing devices and subsequent investigations have helped piece together the story of this unusual collapse (Simkin and Howard, 1970).

Before the collapse began, a small eruption was seen on Fernandina's southeast flank. This was followed, 3 weeks later, by a major explosive eruption from the east side of the caldera floor, an area where fumarolic activity had increased greatly in the preceding year. The eruptive cloud, more than 15 km high, was seen throughout the archipelago, and its deposits were described in section 2.5.3. The largest explosion was recorded by microbarographs throughout the hemisphere and caused the residents of Puerto Baquerizo Moreno, 220 km to the east, to think that the nearby Naval Base had blown up. One day later, a major Galápagos earthquake swarm began to be recorded around the world. Filson and others (1973) interpret these earthquakes as the shocks produced by the caldera block, roughly 2 km in diameter, dropping 350 m in approximately 75 increments (each averaging nearly 5 m) over a 9-day period. A group from the Darwin Station, led by Roger Perry, climbed to the rim at the peak of this swarm, but the caldera was completely obscured by dust from the constant rock avalanches down the interior walls. They had, in fact, some difficulty standing, on this day when over 200 separate earthquakes were recorded by the Darwin Station seismograph (150 km to the east), but the group made good speed back down the mountain. Three weeks after the collapse began the caldera was still frequently filled with dust, but only a few earthquakes were felt each day. Views of the caldera floor showed that it had subsided intact, but with the greatest drop at the southeast end where a large lake had formed (Fig. 2.9). The lake level continued to rise during the following months, but at a decreasing rate, as groundwater percolated down to the lowered base level. Rockfalls down the oversteepened slopes continued for years, but also at decreasing frequency, and most slopes had stabilized by 1977.

Life returned quickly to the caldera, but many organisms have had their troubles around that unquiet lake. Four eruptions have taken place within the caldera since 1968 and all have heated the lake vigorously by the addition of large volumes of hot lava. A new genus of nematode, identified in water collected before the first of these eruptions, was not present in water collected afterward. The first people to reach the lake after the 1978 eruption, 7 weeks after it began, recorded water temperatures of 46°C (115°F). When we arrived a month later we found many dead ducks by the shoreline (but the lake water had cooled to a comfortable 32°C or 90°F). Colonization of the barren 1968 ash deposits has been dramatic—completely barren ash near the margin of the caldera rim deposit in 1970 was covered with barely penetrable, 2–3 m-high shrub forest by

Figure 2.8. Volcán Ecuador, northwest Isabela, from air and sea. Vertical air photograph (by US Air Force) taken in 1959 shows eastern half of volcano, the western half having been downfaulted below sealevel. The smooth primary outer slopes have been eroded on the north and south, the arcuate caldera rim is clear in the center of the picture, and later volcanism has produced lava flows and a prominent tuff cone at the western shore. The sea view from the west, looking into the natural cross section, shows the summit rim, 808 m above sealevel, and remnant caldera bench halfway below it. The equator crosses this volcano at the extreme west tip, Cape Berkeley, to the left of both photographs.
(North arrow in upper photograph corresponds to a distance of 2 km).

1978. In the only systematic study of the biota's response to the dramatic geophysical events of 1968, Lynn Hendrix (1981) has been monitoring the vegetation changes along a measured transect at the rim since 1971.

Pit craters, such as those by the roadside near the summit of Santa Cruz, also result from collapse in much the same way that calderas form (or that sinkholes form in limestone terrain). Pit craters are distinguished from explosion craters by the near total lack of explosive deposits around their rims. Their formation has been witnessed on Hawaii (Macdonald and Eaton, 1964) where magma was withdrawn from a narrow fissure in 1955. This left a cavity that was then enlarged, by melting and stoping of overlying rocks, until a small explosion broke a hole through to the surface with the escape of concentrated gasses. The hole, initially 6 m in

Figure 2.9. Fernandina caldera before and after the 1968 collapse. Vertical air photographs taken in 1946 (above, by US Air Force) and 1982 (below, by Instituto Geográfico Militar, Quito). Prehistoric collapse(s) created the elliptical caldera rim before more recent collapse isolated the prominent benches at either end of the caldera leaving the lake-filled floor shown in the 1946 photograph (see also Chapter 11, Fig. 7). The 1968 collapse utilized an even smaller diameter boundary fault and tilted the floor down 350 m to the southeast. The prominent tuff cone in the center of the caldera rode the subsiding block down 280 m, but is now partially submerged. Subsequent eruptions near the edge of the southeast bench in 1972, 1973, and 1977 have poured lava into the new lake, forming lava deltas, and the prominent 1978 flows from the northwest bench covered much of the newly collapsed floor on their way to the lake. The small black lava flows on the south rim in the 1982 photograph were erupted sometime in the 15 months preceding the photograph. They issued from a 900 m circumferential fissure and flowed both south (where they ponded against an older row of circumferential vents) and north (where they reached a high flat bench). Circumferential vents are well shown on the 1946 photo, and one turns radial to the northwest, but those near the west rim have been largely masked, in the lower photograph, by the thick tephra deposits of 1968.

diameter, soon widened by collapse of overhanging walls to leave a circular, vertical-walled pit like those found on Galápagos. The narrowest of the prominent pit craters on the 'back', or east flank, of Volcán Ecuador is 125 m deep (Fig. 2.8), and a small crater near the southwest rim of Fernandina caldera was greatly enlarged during the 1968 eruption (stones dropped into it now fall for 8 long seconds before hitting the bottom, corresponding to a depth of 260 m). In other parts of the world pit craters exceed 1 km in diameter, overlapping in size with small calderas, but calderas form over central magma chambers whereas pit craters most commonly develop over rift zones. The 'Chain of Craters Road' on Kilauea, Hawaii, passes 12 major pit craters along the prominent East Rift Zone of that volcano.

2.6.4. Volcano growth and form

Having discussed various elements of Galápagos volcanism raises the question of how they fit together to form the distinctive volcanoes that make up the islands. McBirney and Williams (1969) have likened the shape of Galápagos volcanoes to 'overturned soup plates' in order to emphasize the steep slopes (between flattish summits and gently-dipping outer flanks) that distinguish them from the 'overturned saucer' shapes of the better-known Hawaiian volcanoes. These Galápagos slopes measure 15–35° to the horizontal (see profile in Chapter 6, Fig. 6), in contrast to the 2–12° slopes of Hawaiian volcanoes. The development of radial rift zones has dominated the growth of Hawaiian volcanoes (Fiske and Jackson, 1972); has influenced the growth and location of some Galápagos volcanoes (particularly Pinta); and has played an important role in building their gently-dipping outer subaerial flanks (Nordlie, 1973). Nevertheless, radial rift zones are not as well developed on Galápagos as they are on Hawaii—possibly, as Nakamura (in press) suggests, because Galápagos lacks the thick oceanic sediment layer that has influenced the earliest stages of volcano development on Hawaii—and they cannot account for the steep subaerial flanks that are the most distinctive morphologic feature of Galápagos volcanoes. For this it seems reasonable to look at two other distinctive Galápagos features: the well-developed calderas and the striking circumferential vent systems.

Calderas are natural accompaniments of near-surface magma chambers, and near-surface magma chambers are undoubtedly present through most of the growth history of oceanic volcanoes. Calderas are therefore not confined to a narrow time stage in a volcano's history, nor do they develop in a simple series of sequential steps. A comparison of Cerro Azul and Fernandina calderas illustrates the complexities of caldera development. The embayed walls of Cerro Azul suggest several small calderas—perhaps collapses into cupolas above a main chamber—partially engulfed by a later and larger collapse. However, this 'evolutionary' trend from smaller to larger caldera diameters is reversed on Fernandina, where the three major collapses evident have had successively smaller dimensions (Fig. 2.9). The filling of calderas by lava lakes obscures such earlier stages of caldera development and makes caldera histories seem less complex than they really are.

Volcanism may bury a summit caldera completely, as on Hawaii's Mauna Kea (Porter, 1972), but burial does not necessarily mean the end of caldera development. Marchena's caldera is nearly buried, for example, but by vigorous, petrologically youthful basalt flows hardly suggestive of a volcano's last gasp. There is evidence to suggest shallow calderas buried at the summits of Santa Cruz, Floreana, and San Cristóbal. Small volcanoes—such as Pinzón, Volcán Ecuador, and Genovesa—have small calderas and even Rábida has a 'caldera-like depression' (Swanson et al., 1974) measuring less than a kilometer across. Furthermore, a new generation of detailed bathymetric mapping is finding calderas to be a common feature of small, young volcanoes on the deep sea floor (e.g. Lonsdale and Spiess, 1979). There is every reason to believe that calderas are present through most of the evolutionary history of Galápagos volcanoes.

Circumferential vents, like calderas, are a consequence (albeit special) of near-surface magma chambers, and may likewise be present through much of a volcano's history. Most of us have been conditioned to think of volcanoes as being fed from a point source, producing a conical shape like Fuji's, or a linear source, producing a ridge-like shape such as Hekla's. However, the circumferential vents of Galápagos show us clearly that volcanoes may also be fed from a broadly cylindrical source, and the inevitable product of such a source is a Galápagos-like shape. The reason for such a source is clear from consideration of Fiske and Jackson's (1972) elegant model for rift zone growth on Hawaii. They showed, both by theory and by experimental models, that gravitational stresses in a topographic ridge tended to orient subsurface intrusions of magma parallel to the axis of that ridge, extending and building it through time. As soon as the first caldera collapse takes place on a volcano's summit, a broadly circular ridge is created, and a broadly cylindrical fracture system has probably developed as well (Section 2.63, Fig. 2.7). Magma subsequently moving out of the chamber below would be expected, by the Fiske and Jackson model, to seek out fractures beneath the crest of the newly-formed circular ridge, building it further through circumferential vent eruptions.

Once the growth of a circular ridge is begun, gravitational stresses contribute to its continued development, and several processes should contribute to formation of the steep outer flanks and flattish summit benches so well displayed in Galápagos. The vents themselves concentrate lava on the growing ridge in the form of spatter, or scoria cones, some reaching heights of 20–30 m and others combining to form a virtual wall of scoria. Flows from upslope may pond behind such walls, and lava from Fernandina's 1958 eruption at one point flowed circumferentially between older concentric vent lines for 900 m without finding an exit to continue radially down hill. Some lava flows *into* the caldera—from summit vents as well as caldera boundary faults—rather than outward, and Fernandina's newest eruption (Fig. 2.9) illustrates this as well as ponding behind circumferential scoria cones. All circumferential eruptions leave magma in the feeding fissures, as dikes, helping to distend the ridge and steepen outer slopes. Another important contributor to steep Galápagos slopes is the fact that some flows, either because of small volume or high viscosity, simply do not travel very far from their feeding vent. Such flows must build the ridge at the expense of the lower flanks, and a study of surface flow lengths on Fernandina (Simkin, 1972) shows that there are many such flows.

Several factors, then, combine to suggest that circumferential vents should build a volcano with flattish summit flows, steep outer flanks, and an intermittently active central caldera. Circumferential vents are clearly present and active in Galápagos, and the expected morphology is also present. An obvious question, though, is why this combination is not more common on basaltic volcanoes. Circumferential vents are known from other volcanoes (e.g. Niuafo'ou, Suswa, Kilauea) and may well be more common than reported, but they are obviously not widespread. One reason may be that western Galápagos volcanoes have developed nearly concurrently, each relatively independent of nearby neighbors. It is the presence of older and larger neighboring volcanoes, with their dominating stress fields, that have influenced the development of radial rift zones on young Hawaiian volcanoes. A contributing reason may be that Fernandina flows appear to be more viscous than those on Hawaii–perhaps because of their typical load of 10–15% crystals—and their ratio of aa to pahoehoe is lamentably higher. Since lava tubes are developed almost exclusively in pahoehoe flows (Peterson and Swanson, 1974), this means that transport of molten lava to lower slopes by this highly efficient process is less common on Fernandina than on Hawaii.

Multi-beam sonar techniques are now finding that many sea-floor volcanoes have steep flanks, a flattish summit bench, and a central caldera. Recent manned exploration of two of these (Lonsdale *et al.*, 1982) found sub-horizontal flows on the narrow summit benches and evidence of circumferential feeder vents. Estimates of the number of active sea-floor volcanoes run over 1,500 in the Pacific Ocean alone (Batiza, 1982), and a high proportion of those surveyed in detail show 'Galápagos-like' morphology. Perhaps the gently-dipping shield volcanoes of Hawaii may soon be thought of as the exceptions amongst oceanic central volcanoes.

2.7. Faulting

Another major process affecting Galápagos is faulting—the movement of large blocks of the earth's crust with respect to one another. Two specific types of faulting have been discussed above, the regional fracture pattern under 2.61 and caldera collapse under 2.63, but other types of faulting have also modified the Galápagos landscape.

All Galápagos travelers landing at the Baltra airstrip (Fig. 2.10) quickly see evidence of recent faulting: either driving north down the steep fault scarp to meet a boat at Caleta Aeolian or taking the ferry across the downdropped block separating Baltra from Isla Santa Cruz to the south. Between the flat-lying lava flows that make up the island of Baltra are thin layers of limestone bearing shallow-water marine fossils (Hertlein, 1972). These lava flows, then, were once below sea level, and the east-trending faults so well shown on Figure 2.10 record differential levels of uplift. Much of northeastern Santa Cruz has also been uplifted, and the small, offshore islands of Plazas show tilting as well as uplift, like two parallel trap-doors lifted along east-trending faults that tilt their surfaces gently to the north. Similar east-trending faults have created Bahía Academy on the south coast of Santa Cruz. The bay and village of Puerto Ayora are in a down-dropped block bounded on one side by the north-facing cliff forming the inner harbor and on the other by the south-facing cliff, or barranco, behind the tortoise pens at the Darwin Station. These faults may extend over 20 km to the east (Laruelle, 1967) where the uplifted submarine lavas of Santa Fé have been broken into subparallel, east-trending fault blocks. McBirney and Williams (1969) remarked that some of these faults formed within the last few thousand years; Tjitte de Vries reported fumaroles from them in 1971; and Bruce Nolf has found post-faulting, subaerial volcanism on the island.

Although faulting has been an important process throughout Galápagos history, all of it has apparently been 'normal faulting': one crustal block moving up or down, with respect to its neighbor, along a near-vertical fracture or fault plane. As should be expected from the extensional tectonic setting, no evidence is known for either the thrust faulting (one block over or under another) of convergent plate boundaries or the tear faulting (blocks shifted horizontally without vertical movement) of offsets along spreading plate boundaries.

2.7.1. Uplift

The vertical faulting described above has uplifted large areas of the central Galápagos, and Swanson and others (1974) regard this as a broad, tectonic uplift related to the Galápagos Spreading Center to the north. The east-trending fault system in the islands supports this interpretation, but localized uplifts are also known in the islands, and more detailed geologic mapping is needed for full understanding of the regional uplift pattern. On southern Isabela, inland from the coastal village of Villamil, are 1 km^2 of uplifted fossiliferous limestones, sandy beaches hundreds of meters from the coast, and a variety of shallow lagoons. Two historic examples of even more local uplift provide good illustrations of the dynamic nature of the Galápagos.

In 1954, a Disney film crew was sailing along the west coast of Isabela when they noticed a remarkably white stretch of shoreline at Urvina Bay. Closer investigation showed that the white color was shallow-water coral and calcareous algae now stranded as much as 4 m above sea level. Also stranded were lobsters, marine turtles, and even a few fish, indicating that the uplift had been both swift and recent (Couffer, 1956). The uplift of this bay, and nearly 6 km of adjacent shoreline, has been interpreted as a response to near-surface magma movement because an eruption from Volcán Alcedo, 15 km to the east, was reported later that year (Richards, 1957). However, K.A. Howard's careful comparison of Alcedo's 1946 and 1960 air photographs finds no new lavas anywhere on the upper flanks, as reported for the 1954 eruption, and a more likely location for that eruption is Sierra Negra, over 40 km south of Urvina Bay.

More recently, uplift at Punta Espinosa, on Fernandina, has resulted in a tourist landing dock that now

Figure 2.10. Isla Baltra, northeast Santa Cruz, and east-trending fault blocks. Vertical air photograph (by US Air Force) taken in 1959 shows remnants of World War II military base and prominent fault scarp just north of the currently-used (eastern) airstrip. Parallel faults have isolated Baltra from Santa Cruz, to the south, and Seymour, to the north. (North arrow corresponds to a distance of 2 km).

stands fully out of the water at lower stages of the tide. Contrary to the situation at Urvina Bay, however, Punta Espinosa was raised in several steps. In mid–September 1974, marine invertebrate studies by Jerry Wellington indicated approximately 30 cm of recent uplift at Espinosa. This was 6 weeks after a local earthquake, and more earthquakes—resulting in further uplift—were recorded during the following year. In February, 1976, Wellington estimated the total uplift at 80–90 cm and there has been no apparent movement since then. Although the total uplift was not large, some mangrove trees have died, along with many stranded barnacles, and M.P. Harris noticed that flightless cormorants moved their nests forward as the shoreline receded. Such biologic changes must have taken place with countless uplifts in the past.

Evidence of large-scale submergence is not obvious in Galápagos, but as Darwin pointed out (1839, p. 560) "the movement itself tends to conceal all evidence of it". Subsidence is to be expected as plate motion carries older volcanoes away from hotspots and spreading centers (Menard, 1969) and this is another reason to urge modern marine geological investigations of the archipelago. On the islands themselves, however, the abundant evidence of Galápagos uplift testifies to the dynamic, ongoing growth of these islands.

2.7.2. Seismicity

Discussion of rock fracturing and the uplift of large crustal blocks demands discussion of the shock waves recorded from these events. Acharya (1965) has summarized the seismic, or earthquake history of Galápagos prior to 1962, and in the next years a network of seismographs was installed around the world (including one at the Darwin Station) that resulted in a major increase in both the number of earthquakes located and the accuracy of those locations. In 1968, however, this worldwide seismographic network received an unusual test in the form of the Fernandina caldera collapse (section 2.6.3). Here the true earthquake epicenters were clearly known—the dropping caldera block—but the hypocenters located routinely from distant seismograms plotted from Roca Redonda to Cerro Azul (Filson et al., 1973). These location errors (as much as 134 km) preclude any detailed knowledge of Galápagos seismicity, but some useful generalizations can be made.

The largest earthquake known in the islands was magnitude 6.5 (m_b) in 1954. Although the frequency of earthquakes normally increases exponentially as magnitude decreases, Galápagos events smaller than magnitude 4.0 are generally too small to be located by the worldwide network and those smaller than 4.4 are rarely recorded. In the 18 years since the worldwide net was established, 22 earthquakes or earthquake swarms have been located in the islands, and only 4 years have been apparently quiet. The magnitude range during that period has been 3.8–5.7 (m_b) and the median value 4.7. Most locations are in the western islands, but some are to the east and a few are off the Galápagos platform to the west and south. A separate seismic zone lies to the north of Pinta on the transform, or wrench fault that offsets the Galápagos Spreading Center (Fig. 2.1). This active zone has produced 17 earthquakes, or earthquake swarms, in the last 18 years, including earthquakes that have preceded 4 separate Galápagos eruptions by only a few weeks. The magnitude range in this zone has been 4.1–5.6 (m_b) and the median value 4.8.

Although several of the islands' 9 eruptions in that 18-year period have apparently been triggered by local earthquakes, others have been seismically quiet. The islands have also experienced several earthquake swarms that have had no associated surface volcanism. However, earthquake swarms on carefully monitored volcanoes, such as those of Hawaii and Iceland, have been shown to mark the subsurface movement of magma. Large swarms have been located in the vicinity of Volcán Wolf (early 1973) and Fernandina (spring of 1971).

2.8. Erosion and Other Surface Processes

Volcanism and faulting alter the Galápagos landscape in dramatic, often spectacular, events of short duration. Other processes make equally major alterations in the Galápagos landscape by small, unspectacular, but relentless changes, over long periods of time. In the mild, dry climate and relatively calm seas of Galápagos, these processes are not as effective as they are in other environments, but they are nonetheless important and will be discussed briefly below.

2.8.1. Weathering and alteration

Lava flow surfaces decompose through time by a variety of mechanical and chemical processes, eventually forming soil. Differential expansion and contraction with temperature change helps to disintegrate rock, and surface temperature measurements on Fernandina's 1968 ash range from 4° to 49°C (39–120°F). Plants break up rock with rootlets and their own organic decomposition products. Fumarolic vents actively leach and alter basaltic rock as documented by Colony and Nordlie (1973) on Sierra Negra. But effective weathering in most areas require moisture (combining with elements from the atmosphere, the biosphere, and the rocks themselves) to produce acids capable of sustained disintegration of rock. Such moisture is present in some parts of the islands, with an annual rainfall of 2.6 m having been measured in the highlands of Santa Cruz, but in most areas it is not. Consequently, weathering is slow in the drier parts of the islands. Darwin referred to the 'general indecomposable character of the lava' (1844, p. 114), and Cox (1971) describes a San Cristóbal lava flow that appeared to be no more than a few decades old, but is probably (on the basis of its paleomagnetism) considerably more than several centuries old. Baitis and Lindstrom (1980, p. 372) call attention to 'the lack of extensive soil development or erosion in the past several hundred thousand years following the final activity on Pinzón'.

Unfortunately little work has been done on the soils of Galápagos since the tragic death of Jacques Laruelle, in 1967. His own work, from 1963 onwards, is summarized in his book (1967), and Eswaran and others (1973), and Morrás (1977) have added to that work on Santa Cruz. Clearly, though, the soils of Galápagos depend heavily on the distribution of moisture—that essential ingredient in the disintegration of lava—and the distribution of fragmental deposits from explosive eruptions (see 2.5.3). Fragmental deposits may mantle a whole volcano, like Alcedo (see frontispiece), providing an easy footing for vegetation that could not be created on a hard lava surface by thousands of years of normal weathering.

2.8.2. Water movement above sea level

Most lava flows are severely broken up during the cooling process. They are therefore notoriously porous: rainfall swiftly disappears into cracks, and permanent running streams are not found on Galápagos. However, volcanic ash deposits—particularly the fine ash that is the last to fall—can compact to form a very impervious surface, and heavy rains are not unknown even at lower elevations in Galápagos (the Darwin Station recorded 15 cm of rainfall in one 24 hour period in 1976). Rain on a fresh ash surface, then, quickly runs off down hill, rapidly eroding the soft, fragmental deposit in the process. Radial valleys with intervening ribs are formed by such erosion on the flanks of Galápagos tuff cones, and the process is dramatically shown on the deposits of Fernandina's 1968 eruption. Two years after the eruption, erosion had already cut 6 m deep, V-shaped gulleys into the soft, fragmental materials on the caldera floor, and after 4 more years the underlying lava flows were exposed, flooring a 6 m wide ephemeral stream bed, bounded by 7 m high vertical walls of tephra.

Groundwater movement below the surface is also an important process in Galápagos. Groundwater dissolves parts of the material through which it passes and later may precipitate these dissolved salts when encountering changed conditions. Waters percolating through the 1968 fragmental deposits of Fernandina, for example, have precipitated the sodium sulfate thenardite as a white coating on the steep walls cut by the above-mentioned erosion. Higher temperature movement of water and vapor through tuff cones harden these initially soft layers, in the palagonitization process, making them better able to withstand the forces of erosion. Redistribution of elements from the freshly fragmented glass actually weakens the former glass but strengthens the total rock (palagonite tuff) by depositing these elements, particularly silica, as a strong cement binding the fragments together. Because the movement of water and vapor through tuff cones is likely to be irregular, the resulting cementation may also be irregular. Certainly the resistance to erosion of Galápagos tuff cones is often irregular, with segments like the much-photographed Pinnacle Rock of Bartolomé standing isolated from the remainder of its cone (Chapter 1, Fig. 4). More work needs to be done on the palagonite tuffs of Galápagos, where they were first recognized by Darwin, and on the subsurface movement of groundwater so important to residents of the archipelago.

2.8.3. Marine erosion

The most dramatic continuing force on Galápagos is the pounding surf, and evidence of its power is to be found in islands such as Wenman, Culpepper, Española, and Roca Redonda that are mere erosional remnants of their former structures. The sea surface is rarely mirror-like in Galápagos, and travelers hoping to land on seemingly quiet shores often find, on closer inspection, crashing waves that relentlessly modify the coasts. The ability of coastal materials to withstand such pounding varies widely, as discussed above under both the 'coating' of tuff cones (2.5.3) and their cementation (2.8.2). However, little is known of the rates at which marine erosion works in Galápagos. Darwin described the large palagonite cone of Tortuga (Brattle) Island as 'in a ruined condition, consisting of little more than half a circle open to the south' (1844, p. 109). Nearly 150 years later, the island remains 'little more than half a circle', reminding us that well-cemented tuff cones are not destroyed overnight, but comparison of Darwin's comments on Bahía de Aguadulce (Freshwater Bay) with today's Buccaneer Cove, on Santiago, shows more substantial changes over the years.

2.8.4. Sedimentation and beaches

The other side of the erosion coin is sedimentation: material removed from one place being later deposited in another. The 1968 fragmental deposits eroded from the floor of Fernandina caldera have been redeposited (along with periodic additions of lava) on the floor of the caldera lake, and material eroded from Galápagos coastlines is redeposited (along with marine organisms and detritus) offshore. Johnson and others (1976) report sea-floor sediment thicknesses of about 500 m over much of the shallow Galápagos Platform, but note some areas scoured clear of sediment by strong bottom currents.

Some material eroded from Galápagos coastlines, however, is simply shifted by long-shore currents and redeposited nearby as beach sands. Beautiful, long beaches are found on many of the islands, particularly near the fragmental deposits of explosive eruptions. The composition of these beach sands varies, from place to place, depending on the available materials nearby. Altered volcanic glass is a common constituent, and some sands are rich in coral and shell fragments. The white sands of Marchena are rich in feldspar, from the large feldspar crystals common in lavas from that island (2.5.5), and there is a much-visited green olivine sand beach at Punta Cormorant, on Floreana. Olivine-rich xenoliths from the crust below Floreana are common in the lavas of that island, and were explosively fragmented, along with the liquid lava that carried them to the surface in the eruption building the prominent cone at Punta Cormorant. The development of a large beach, though, is a long and complicated process. Galápagos beaches are not easily renewable resources, and it is a matter of concern that sand has recently been stripped from several beaches on Santa Cruz for use in building construction on that island.

2.9. Conclusions

The processes that shape geologically vigorous volcanic islands are those that shape our planet, but they are particularly vivid on Galápagos. There are no examples, it must be admitted, of glacial sculpturing, and the huge changes wrought by man elsewhere have been fortunately slight in Galápagos. The only major geologic processes *not* displayed in Galápagos, are the deep burial, metamorphism, overthrusting, and compressive folding of the world's subduction zones. These will come, though, in about 20 million years when (if current plate motions continue) the present islands will be buried under South America.

Acknowledgements

Students of Galápagos, both resident and migratory, are as remarkable, in many respects, as the more celebrated wildlife of the islands. I am fortunate in having met many fine teachers, helpers and friends through Galápagos and space does not permit mention of all those to whom I owe a substantial debt. Among those who have generously supplied information about Galápagos eruptions, though, I especially thank Tui De Roy Moore, Dagmar Werner, a succession of Darwin Station staff members, and ham radio operators Bud Devine and Forrest Nelson. Many friends have helped make field work more enjoyable as well as educational and I particularly thank Bruce and Penny Nolf, Pete Hall, Tui Moore, and Bob Smith. The manuscript has benefited from thoughtful reviews by Dick Fiske, Bill Melson, and Bruce Nolf. Mary McGuigan has conjured many manuscript drafts in and out of the word processor with skill and admirable good humor. Lastly, I thank my wife, Sharon, not only for help on Galápagos volcanoes but also for answering more 'is this paragraph clear to a non-geologist?' questions than any non-geologist should be called upon to answer.

References

The essential review of Galápagos geology is the memoir by McBirney and Williams (1969). A chronologic list of geological treatments of the whole archipelago, excluding those listed by McBirney and Williams, is: Wolf (1892), Lewis (1956), Sauer (1965), Williams (1966), McBirney and Aoki (1966), Laruelle (1967), Case and others (1973), Durham and McBirney (1975), Hall (1977), Moore (1980), and Cox (1983). Since the 1969 memoir, geological treatments of the western islands include: Simkin and Howard (1970), Simkin (1972), Nordlie and Colony (1973), Colony and Nordlie (1973), Delaney and others (1973), and Nordlie (1973). Discussions of the central islands include: Hertlein (1972), Swanson and others (1974), Baitis and Swanson (1976), Bow (1979), and Baitis and Lindstrom (1980). Other post-1969 discussions of individual islands include those of Cox (1971) on San Cristóbal, and Beate (1979) on Genovesa. The list below also omits many references when later related work by the same author is cited.

The interested reader is referred to the authoritative volcanological textbooks by Macdonald (1972) and Williams and McBirney (1979). The excellent photographic compilation by Carr and Greeley (1980) illustrates and discusses many Hawaiian examples of volcanic features common in Galápagos.

Acharya, H.K. (1965) Seismicity of the Galápagos Islands and vicinity. *Bull. Seis. Soc. Am.*, **55**, 609–617.

Bailey, K. (1976) Potassium-Argon ages from the Galápagos Islands. *Science*, **192**, 465–466.

Baitis, H.W. and Lindstrom, M.M. (1980) Geology, petrography, and petrology of Pinzón Island, Galápagos Archipelago. *Contributions to Mineralogy & Petrology*, **72**, 367–386.

Baitis, H.W. and Swanson, F.J. (1976) Ocean rise-like basalts, within the Galápagos Archipelago. *Nature*, **259**, 195–197.

Balazs, D. (1975) Lava tubes on the Galápagos Islands. *Nat. Speleological Soc. Bull.*, **37**, 1–4.

Ballard, R.D., van Andel, T.A. and Holcomb, R.T. (1982) The Galápagos Rift at 86°W: 5, variations in volcanism, structure, and hydrothermal activity along a 30-kilometer segment of the rift valley. *Jour. Geophys. Res.*, **87**, 1149–1162.

Batiza, R. (1982) Abundances, distribution and sizes of volcanoes in the Pacific Ocean, and implications for the origin of non-hotspot volcanoes. *Earth & Planetary Sci. Letters*, **60**, 195–206.

Beate, B. (1979) Geología y petrografía de la Isla Genovesa, Galápagos. *Tesis de Grado, Escuela Politécnica. Quito.* 81 pp.

Bow, C.S. (1979) The geology and petrogenesis of the lavas of Floreana and Santa Cruz Islands, Galápagos Archipelago. *Ph.D. Thesis, Univ. Oregon*, 308 pp.

Carr, M.H. and Greeley, R. (1980) *Volcanic features of Hawaii*. Washington, NASA Scientific & Technical Information Branch, SP-403. 211 pp.

Case, J.E., Ryland, S.L., Simkin, T. and Howard, K.A. (1973) Gravitational evidence for a low-density mass beneath the Galápagos Islands. *Science*, **181**, 1040–1042 (see also **184**, 808–809).

Chase, T.E. (1968) *Sea floor topography of the Central Eastern Pacific Ocean*. U.S. Dept. Interior, Fish and Wildlife Service, Bureau of Commercial Fisheries, Circular 291.

Colinvaux, P.A. (1968) Reconnaissance and chemistry of the lakes and bogs of the Galápagos Islands. *Nature*, **219**, 590–594.

Colony, W.E. and Nordlie, B.E. (1973) Liquid sulfur at volcán Azufre, [Sierra Negra], Galápagos Islands. *Economic Geology*, **68**, 371–380.

Corliss, J.B., Dymond, J., Gordon, L.I. Edmond, J.M. and others (1979) Submarine thermal springs on the Galápagos Rift. *Science*, **203**, 1073–1083.

Couffer, J.C. (1956) The disappearance of Urvina Bay. *Natural History*, **65**, 378–383.

Cox, A. (1971) Paleomagnetism of San Cristóbal Island, Galápagos. *Earth & Planet. Sci. Letters*, **11**, 152–160.

Cox, A. (1983) Ages of the Galápagos Islands. In: *Patterns of Evolution in Galápagos Organisms*. Edited by R.I. Bowman, M. Berson and A.E. Leviton, Am. Assoc. Adv. Sci., Pacific Div., San Francisco (in press).

Darwin, C. (1844) *Geological observations on volcanic islands*. Smith, Elder & Co., London, 175 pp.

Delaney, J.R., Colony, W.E., Gerlach, T.M. and Nordlie, B.E. (1973) Geology of the Volcán Chico area on Sierra Negra Volcano, Galápagos Islands. *Geol. Soc. America Bull.*, **84**, 2455–2470.

Durham, J.W. (1965) Geology of the Galápagos. *Pacific Discovery*, **18**, 3–6.

Durham, J.W. and McBirney, A.R. (1975) Galápagos Islands. In: *Encyclopedia of World Regional Geology*. Edited by R.W. Fairbridge. Dowden, Hutchinson, & Ross, Stroudsburg, Pa., 285–290.

Eswaran, H., Stoops, G. and De Paepe, P. (1973) A contribution to the study of soil formation on Isla Santa Cruz, Galápagos. *Pedologie*, **23**, 100–122.

Filson, J., Simkin, T. and Leu, L.K. (1973) Seismicity of a caldera collapse: Galápagos Islands 1968. *Jour. Geophys. Research*, **78**, 8591–8622.

Fiske, R.S. and Jackson, E.D. (1972) Orientation and growth of Hawaiian volcanic rifts: the effect of regional structure and gravitational stresses. *Proc. Roy. Soc. London, A*, **329**, 299–326.

Hall, M.L. (1977) *El volcanismo en el Ecuador*. Quito, Biblioteca Ecuador, 120 pp. (17–37 Galápagos).

Hall, M.L., Ramon, P., and Yepes, H. (1980) The subaerial origin of Española (Hood) island and the age of terrestrial life in the Galápagos. *Noticias de Galápagos*, **31**, p. 21.

Heiken, G.H. (1971) Tuff rings: examples from the Fort Rock-Christmas Lake Valley Basin, south-central Oregon. *Jour. Geophys. Research*, **76**, 5615–5626.

Hendrix, L. (1981) Post-eruption succession on Isla Fernandina, Galápagos. *Madrono*, **28**(4), 242–254.

Hertlein, L.G. (1972) Pliocene fossils from Baltra (South Seymour) Island, Galápagos Islands. *Proc. Calif. Acad. Sciences Fourth Series*, **XXXIX**, no. 3, 25–46.

Hey, R. (1977) Tectonic evolution of the Cocos-Nazca spreading center. *Geol. Soc. America Bull.*, **88**, 1404–1420.

Heyerdahl, T. (1963) Archaeology in the Galápagos Islands. *Occ. Papers Calif. Acad. Sci.*, no. 44, 45–51.

Johnson, G.L., Vogt, P.R., Hey, R., Campsie, J. and Lowrie, A. (1976) Morphology and structure of the Galápagos Rise. *Mar. Geol.*, **21**, 81–120.

Laruelle, J. (1967) *Galápagos*. Natuurwet Tijdschr, 236 pp.

Lewis, G.E. (1956) Galápagos Islands (Archipiélago de Colón) Province. *Geol. Soc. Am. Memoir*, **65**, 289–291. (*Handbook of South American Geology*, Edited by W.F. Jenks).

Lipps, J.H. and Hickman, C.S. (1982) Paleontology and geologic history of the Galápagos Islands. *Geol. Soc. America, Abstracts for Annual Meeting*, 548.

Lonsdale, P., Batiza, R. and Simkin, T. (1982) Metallogenesis at seamounts on the East Pacific Rise. *Mar. Tech. Soc. Journal*, **16**(3), 54–61.

Lonsdale, P. and Spiess, F.N. (1979) A pair of young cratered volcanoes on the East Pacific Rise. *Jour. Geology*, **87**, 157–173.

Macdonald, G.A. (1972) *Volcanoes*. Englewood Cliffs. Prentice-Hall, 510 pp.

Macdonald, G.A. and Eaton, J.P. (1964) Hawaiian volcanoes during 1955. *U.S. Geol. Surv. Bull.*, **1171**, 170 pp.

McBirney, A.R. and Aoki, K. (1966) Petrology of the Galápagos Islands. In: *The Galápagos*. Edited by R.I. Bowman, Univ. Calif. Press, Berkeley, 71–77.

McBirney, A.R. and Williams, H. (1969) Geology and petrology of the Galápagos Islands. *Geol. Soc. Amer. Memoir*, **118**, 197 pp.

Melville, H. (1856) The Encantadas. In: *Piazza Tales*. Dix & Edwards, New York 66 pp.

Menard, H.W. (1969) Growth of drifting volcanoes. *Jour. Geophys. Res.*, **74**, 4827–4837.

Montoriol-Pous, J. and de Mier, J. (1977) Contribución al conocimiento vulcano-espeleológico de la.Isla de Santa Cruz (Galápagos, Ecuador). *Speleon*, **23**, 75–91.

Moore, T. De Roy (1980A) *Galápagos – islands lost in time*. Viking, N.Y. 71 pp text & 293 color photos.

Moore, T. De Roy (1980B) The awakening volcano. *Pacific Discovery*, **33**(4), 25–31.

Morgan, W.J. (1971) Convection plumes in the lower mantle. *Nature*, **230**, 42–43.

Morgan, W.J. (1978) Rodriguez, Darwin, Amsterdam . . . A second type of hotspot island. *Jour. Geophys. Res.*, **83**, 5355–5360.

Nakamura, K. (in press) Why do long rift zones develop better in Hawaiian volcanoes? – a possible role of thick oceanic sediments. *Proc. 1980 IAVCEI symp. on oceanic volcanism, Azores Univ.*

Nordlie, B.E. (1973) Morphology and structure of the western Galápagos volcanoes and a model for their origin. *Geol. Soc. America Bull.*, **84**, 2931–2956.

Nordlie, B.E. and Colony, W.E. (1973) Fumarole with periodic water fountaining, Volcán Alcedo, Galápagos Islands. *Geol. Soc. America Bull.*, **84**, 1709–1720.

Nordlie, B.E., Thieben, S.E. and Delaney, J.R. (1982) Chemical composition of the basalts of Cerro Azul, Volcán Wolf, and Sierra Negra, Western Galápagos Islands. *IAVCEI-IAGC Scientific Assembly, Reykjavik, Iceland, Abst.*, 41.

Peterson, D.W. and Swanson, D.A. (1974) Observed formation of lava tubes. *Studies in Speleology*, **2**, 209–222.

Porter, S.C. (1972) Buried caldera of Mauna Kea volcano, Hawaii. *Science*, **175**, 1458–1460.

Richards, A.F. (1957) Volcanism in Eastern Pacific Ocean Basin: 1945–1955. *Cong. Geol. Internatl.*, 20 sess, 19–31.

Richards, A.F. (1962) Archipiélago de Colón, Isla San Felix and Islas Juan Fernández. *Catalog of Active Volcanoes of the World 14*, IAVCEI Rome, 50 pp.

Sauer, W. (1965) *Geología del Ecuador*. Quito, Talleres Graficos del Ministerio de Educación, 383 pp. (344–360 on Galápagos).

Schilling, J.-G., Kingsley, R.H. and Devine, J.D. (1982) Galápagos hot spot spreading center system. 1. Spatial petrological and geochemical variations (83°W–101°W). *Jour. Geophys. Res.*, **87**, 5593–5610.

Shand, S.J. (1937) *Earth Lore*. Thos. Murby & Co., London, 2nd Ed.

Shimizu, H., Masuda, A. and Masui, N. (1981) Rare-earth element geochemistry of volcanic and related rocks from the Galápagos Islands. *Geochem. Jour.*, **15**, 81–93.

Simkin, T. (1972) Origin of some flat-topped volcanoes and guyots. *Geol. Soc. America Memoir*, **132**, 183–193.

Simkin, T. and Howard, K.A. (1970) Caldera collapse in the Galápagos Islands, 1968. *Science*, **169**, 429–437.

Simkin, T., Reeder, W.G. and MacFarland, C. (Eds.) (1974) *Galápagos Science: 1972 status and needs*. Published by Smithsonian for Charles Darwin Foundation, Wash., D.C., 87 pp.

Simkin, T. and Siebert, L. (in press) Explosive eruptions in space and time: a look at the Holocene record. In: *Explosive Volcanism*. Edited by F.R. Boyd, Washington, National Academy of Sciences.

Simkin, T., Siebert, L., McClelland, L., Bridge, D., Newhall, C., and Latter, J.H. (1981) *Volcanoes of the World*. Stroudsburg, Pa., Hutchinson Ross, 240 pp.

Steadman, D.W. (1981) Vertebrate fossils in lava tubes in the Galápagos Islands. *Proc. 8th Internatl. Cong. of Speleology*, 549–550.

Steadman, D.W. (1982) The origin of Darwin's Finches (Fringillidae, Passeriformes). *Trans. San Diego Soc. of Natural History*, **19**(19), 279–96.

Steadman, D.W. and Ray, C.E. (1982) The relationships of Megaoryzomys curioi, an extinct Cricetine rodent (Muroidea:Muridae) from the Galápagos Islands Ecuador. *Smithsonian Contrib. Paleobiology*, **51**, 23 pp.

Swanson, F.J., Baitis, H.W., Lexa, J. and Dymond, J. (1974) Geology of Santiago, Rábida, and Pinzón Islands, Galápagos. *Geol. Soc. America Bull.*, **85**, 1803–1810.

Vogt, P.R. (1974) Volcano spacing, fractures, and thickness of the lithosphere. *Earth & Planetary Sci. Letters*, **21**, 235–252.

White, W.M. (1979) Pb isotope geochemistry of the Galápagos Islands. *Carnegie Inst. Wash. Yearbook*, **78**, 331–335.

White, W.M. and Hofmann, A.W. (1978) Geochemistry of the Galápagos Islands: implications for mantle dynamics and evolution. *Carnegie Inst. Wash. Yearbook*, **77**, 596–606.

Williams, H. (1966) Geology of the Galápagos Islands. In: *The Galápagos*. Ed. R.I. Bowman. Univ. Calif. Press, Berkeley, 65–70.

Williams, H. and McBirney, A.R. (1979) *Volcanology*. San Francisco, Freeman, Cooper, 397 pp.

Wilson, J.T. (1963) Hypothesis of earth's behaviour. *Nature*, **198**, 925–929.

Wolf, T. (1892) *Geográfica y geología del Ecuador*. Casa de la Cultura Ecuatoriana, Quito (1975 republished), 798 pp. (517–542 on Galápagos).

CHAPTER 3

Oceanographic Setting
of the Galápagos Islands

GUY T. HOUVENAGHEL

Université Libre de Bruxelles, Belgium

Contents

3.1. Introduction   44
3.2. Regional Oceanography Around the Galápagos   44
     3.2.1 Water circulation in the eastern equatorial Pacific   44
         3.2.1.1. The South Equatorial Current (SEC)   45
         3.2.1.2. The Equatorial Countercurrent (ECC)   45
         3.2.1.3. The Equatorial Undercurrent (EUC)   45
         3.2.1.4. Equatorial upwelling   46
     3.2.2. The water masses   46
         3.2.2.1. Tropical surface waters   46
         3.2.2.2. Subtropical surface waters   46
         3.2.2.3. Equatorial surface waters   47
         3.2.2.4. Subtropical subsurface waters   47
         3.2.2.5. Antarctic Intermediate Water   47
         3.2.2.6. Pacific Deep Water   47
         3.2.2.7. *El Niño* phenomenon   47
3.3. Oceanography of the Galápagos Archipelago   48
     3.3.1. Analysis of some parameters   48
         3.3.1.1. Surface temperature   48
         3.3.1.2. Thermal structure   49
         3.3.1.3. Salinity   50
         3.3.1.4. Nutrients   50
         3.3.1.5. Oxygen   50
         3.3.1.6. Primary production   51
         3.3.1.7. Plankton biomass   51
     3.3.2. Upwelling and circulation patterns in the archipelago 51
         3.3.2.1. Undercurrent and topography-induced
             upwellings   51
         3.3.2.2. The seasonal pattern   52
3.4. Conclusions   53
     References   53

3.1. Introduction

The Galápagos Islands are located in a part of the eastern Pacific where the distribution of water masses and oceanic circulation are intricate. The size and geomorphology of the archipelago convey enormous importance to the ocean in determining the environment of the islands.

The archipelago is formed from the emerging tops of huge submarine volcanoes with rather steep slopes and rising from a $40,000\,km^2$ wide platform at a depth of $1,300\,m$. It is thus made of scattered insular units, isolated from each other by deep waters (Houvenaghel, 1977). As a result, the littoral waters, which cover about $6,000\,km^2$, are divided into numerous bodies surrounded by the ocean.

The oceanographic properties in the surface waters are under the influence of the meteorology (wind speed and direction) as shown by Bjerkness (1966), Wyrtki (1966, 1975), Donguy and Henin (1980); they also regulate the local climate (Houvenaghel, 1974b).

The major fact in the oceanography of the Galápagos Islands is the presence of cold waters at the surface. Many informants dealing with this explain that the cold water is brought into the Galápagos region by the Peru Current, also called the Humboldt Current. Moreover, since this current comes from the south along the South American mainland, references to antarctic influences reaching the Galápagos are often given. This erroneous assumption is based upon the confusion which is made between the concept of an oceanic current and the transport of a water mass. The lack of sufficient data until recent years about oceanography in the Galápagos has also been responsible for perpetuating this idea of an antarctic influence.

The present contribution summarizes the major facts of the oceanography around and within the archipelago, one of the most extraordinary oceanic environments in the world.

3.2. Regional Oceanography Around the Galápagos

3.2.1. Water circulation in the eastern equatorial Pacific

Much of the surface circulation in the equatorial region of the oceans is dominated by the westerly flow of water set up primarily by the trade winds. In the Pacific, these westward surface currents are the North Equatorial Current (NEC) located between 10 and 20°N and the South Equatorial Current (SEC) between 5°N and 10°S. Since the meteorological equator (Intertropical Convergence Zone) lies north of the geographical equator, tradewinds and SEC are crossing it. Both NEC and SEC are separated by a narrow current, the Equatorial Countercurrent (ECC) flowing east in a belt, corresponding to the Intertropical convergence Zone where winds are light and variable (doldrums).

Along the American mainland, in both hemispheres, waters are driven towards the equator, forming the California Current in the north, and the Peru Current in the south. At low latitudes these currents turn to the west feeding the equatorial currents, NEC and·SEC.

From data gathered by oceanographic expeditions between 1928 and 1964, Wyrtki (1966) calculated a circulation model showing that the balance between the westward outflows and the advections feeding them could not be reached without taking into account a subsuperficial eastward current, the Equatorial Undercurrent (EUC) discovered by Cromwell—and often referred to as the Cromwell Current. According to this model, waters carried by the EUC to the east, and as far as the continent, contribute to the SEC, to the upwellings off northern Peru and to a lesser extent to the NEC. More than half the water driven by the SEC south of the equator could be of EUC origin.

In the equatorial corner of the Eastern Pacific, from Cabo Corientes (Mexico) down to Ecuador, the circulation is further complicated by advections and local features like upwellings and surface heating.

This rough description of the circulation in the Eastern Equatorial Pacific shows that the Galápagos Islands may be influenced by many current systems, especially since the whole circulation described above fluctuates in strength and position from season to season and from year to year. Such fluctuations associated with regional meteorology have been discussed by Donguy and Henin (1980). The main elements involved in this circulation are briefly described hereafter.

3.2.1.1. The South Equatorial Current (SEC)

The SEC drives superficial waters over the entire region around the Galápagos. At its northern boundary, at 4° to 5°N, the speed is maximum (about 50 cm/sec) but not stable during the year. To the south, the speed reduces but the current remains stable and noticeable down to 10°S. In the vicinity of the equator its thickness (i.e. depth range) is reduced (20 to 50 m) because of the presence of the EUC. Further south, the current is deeper, and reaches a 'thickness' of 200 m. The flowrate of the SEC is very high (60.10^{12} cm^3/sec) as a result of its multiple feeding from the Peru Current, ECC, EUC and upwellings. The SEC is strong from July to January and weak from February till June.

3.2.1.2. The Equatorial Countercurrent (ECC)

The eastgoing ECC is narrow, only 300 to 700 km wide according to the seasons, located between 8° to 12°N and 4° to 6°N. East of 110°W, its flow is slightly deviated to the south. When reaching close to the mainland, the flow rate (10.10^{10} m^3/sec) decreases and part of the water turns north, joining the NEC, while the other, going south, joins the SEC and the Peru Subsuperficial Current. The ECC may influence the north of the Galápagos archipelago. From May to August this current is strong, while it is weak or absent during the rest of the year.

3.2.1.3. The Equatorial Undercurrent (EUC)

Located just at the equator, the EUC is a rather stable subsuperficial current which extends from 160°E in the western Pacific eastward to the vicinity of the Galápagos. An hydrologic feature associated with this is the characteristic attenuation of the thermocline and its rise towards the surface at the equator. The EUC is fed by waters of subtropical origin moving equator-ward just under the surface layer (or Ekman layer) and which, when reaching the equator, are escaping from the Coriolis forces and so taken up by the EUC.

This current is rather narrow (300 km wide) with a 'thickness' of 200 to 250 m. The upper boundary, deeper in the central Pacific, reduces progressively to the east, reaching 50 m or less in the vicinity of the Galápagos. Old charts indicate eastward flows in surface waters at the equator, a feature, according to Jones (1969), linked to the weakening of the tradewinds and which could be due to the rise of the EUC close to the surface.

Knauss (1966) shows that during the cold season, the EUC decreases before reaching 96°W and passes through the north of the Galápagos, with only a small branch to the south of the islands. During a warm season Christensen (1971) found that the axis of the EUC lay 80 km south of the equator and at a depth of 75 m. Another strong branch also passes to the north of the Galápagos and proceeds further east with slight deviation. The EUC, or its branches, are noticed close to the mainland (Stevenson and Taft, 1971, Houvenaghel, 1976).

In the central Pacific, the flow of the EUC (40.10^{12} cm^3/sec Montgomery and Stroup 1962) and its speed 100 to 150 cm/sec Knauss, 1966) are high. In the eastern Pacific, the dissipation of the EUC by mixing, upwelling and friction much reduces these figures. Knauss (1966) measured flow rates of 8.10^{12} cm^3/sec at 93°W west of the Galápagos, and 4.10^{12} cm^3/sec at 87°W to the east of them. Christensen (1971) noticed a flow of 3.10^{12} cm^3/sec in the branch passing to the north of the islands only. According to Wyrtki (1966) and Bennett (1963) about half the potential energy of the EUC is dissipated by friction.

According to our observations in the archipelago and analyses of hydrologic data (Houvenaghel, 1973, 1974, 1978), the slowing down of the EUC when approaching the Galápagos, and its deviations induced by the islands' topography, appear to be the most important feature of the oceanography of the Galápagos.

3.2.1.4. Equatorial upwelling

During their journey to the east, the waters of the upper part of the EUC are driven to the surface by equatorial upwelling. This is noticed on surface temperature charts by the sharp belt of cold surface waters at the equator.

This equatorial upwelling is the result (because of the earth's rotation) of strong steady winds (southeast tradewinds) crossing the equator. The mechanism is as follows. When wind blows on the water, the upper layers of the water move to the right of the wind in the northern hemisphere, and to the left in the southern hemisphere. As a consequence, easterly tradewinds crossing the equator induce a divergent movement in the surface waters, which tend to spread away at the equator and create there some kind of hydrological valley. This is filled, by compensation, from waters surfacing from below. These subsuperficial waters, involved in the upwelling belong to the EUC. At the surface, these cool waters move away to the west, driven by the SEC.

3.2.2. The water masses

Owing to the water circulation and its fluctuations around the Galápagos, the islands are washed by water masses of different origins and characterized by different thermohaline, chemical and biological properties.

3.2.2.1. Tropical surface waters

The tropical surface waters are low in salinity, from 33.8‰ down to less than 30‰, and with temperatures above 25°C. They are superficial, forming a thin layer, 20 to 50 m thick, bordered to the south by the ECC. These warm, light waters remain to the north of an oceanic equatorial front which, starting at about 4°S along the coast of South America, crosses the equator east of the Galápagos and runs then to the west between 1° and 3°N. This boundary, very sharp near the coast, but fading offshore, separates the tropical surface waters in the north from colder, saltier subtropical and equatorial surface waters in the south. This front corresponds to a region where the thermocline reaches the surface.

From May to November, the temperature gradient across the front reaches 5 to 6°C, while the salinity difference amounts to 1‰. From January to March, there are no obvious temperature differences, but salinities are still contrasting. When the Niño phenomenon develops, the front disappears permitting the extension of tropical surface water southward along the coast of South America.

3.2.2.2. Subtropical surface waters

The subtropical surface waters, characterized by their high salinity (35‰) and broad range of temperatures (15° to 28°C), drift out of the central part of the subtropical anticyclonic gyre of the South Pacific, where evaporation exceeds precipitation. To the east, these waters extend towards the South American mainland but without reaching it because of the presence of coastal upwellings. To the north, the boundary is not conspicuous since the subtropical waters mix progressively with equatorial surface waters.

3.2.2.3. Equatorial surface waters

Equatorial surface waters are intermediate between subtropical surface waters in the south and tropical surface waters in the north. Temperatures fluctuate but remain higher than 20°C. Salinities of 34 to 35‰ result from mixing and advections of the different waters feeding the SEC.

3.2.2.4. Subtropical subsurface waters

The presence of a layer of water with its salinity maximum at the depth of the permanent thermocline characterizes the vertical structure of the hydrology of the eastern equatorial Pacific. These waters with high salinity, called subtropical subsurface waters, are derived from subtropical surface waters formed in wintertime at the surface in the gyre. Becoming denser (rising salinity, lowering temperature), these waters sink to moderate depths, remain at equilibrium and flow towards the mainland and the equator. During this journey they come under the influence of the lower parts of the SEC, which lead them progressively to the west. On approaching the equator, these high salinity waters are included and mixed with the EUC, which drives them to the east.

3.2.2.5. Antarctic Intermediate Water

Below the Subtropical Subsurface Waters, salinity decreases in the water column to a minimum at about 700 to 900 m depth. This represents the northernmost influence of the Antarctic Intermediate Water which contributes to upwellings off middle and southern Peru (south of 15°S).

3.2.2.6. Pacific Deep Water

Underneath the layer of Antarctic Intermediate Water, at greater depth, water with uniform properties (1.5°C and 34.7‰), called Deep Water, or Common Water, fills the rest of the ocean.

3.2.2.7. El Niño phenomenon

El Niño is a phenomenon during which an unusual warming of the surface waters occurs in the entire eastern equatorial Pacific. This is well known along the coasts of Ecuador and Peru where waters are normally cool because of local coastal upwellings. El Niño is sporadic but persistent, with important biological and economic consequences like the disappearance of the anchovy with the subsequent death of piscivorous seabird producers of guano along the Peruvian coast. It starts usually between November and March. Typical El Niño years were 1953, 1957–58, 1965, 1972, 1975, 1976–77.

This apparent regional perturbation belongs to a large scale oceanwide air-sea oscillation. Different mechanisms explaining El Niño have been proposed. For Bjerknes (1966), when tradewinds are weak, the upwellings are weaker; warm waters from north of the equator may then move freely to the south. This phenomenon could be predicted by observing the differences in atmospheric pressure between central and eastern Pacific (Quinn, 1974). For Wyrtki and his co-workers (1975, 1977), *El Niño* is preceded by a period during which the tradewinds are rather strong and lead to the accumulation of huge volumes of warm water in the western Pacific. This is demonstrated by the rise of the sea level in the west (10 cm) and a lowering of 5 cm in the east. When these winds weaken, waters accumulated in the west are not retained by wind pressure and so tend to return to the east. As a consequence, in the eastern tropical Pacific, the sea level rises and the thermocline sinks spectacularly. The massive advection of light surface warm water overcomes the local cooling—already reduced by the weakening or even stopping of upwellings along the South American coast. At the equator, for the same reasons, the local depression due to the divergence disappears, as well as the equatorial upwelling associated with it. The eastgoing ECC discharges high amounts of warm water, with low salinities due to rainfalls, which are able to flow to the south since there remain no upwellings, thermal front or antagonistic winds to counteract their extension.

The intensity and duration of *El Niño* depends primarily on the amounts of warm water accumulated in the west during the preceding year.

3.3. Oceanography of the Galápagos Archipelago

Progress in the knowledge of the oceanography of the Galápagos results from the analysis of data gathered at stations in the vicinity of the archipelago during oceanographic expeditions. At present this information is scarce and limited. Wooster and Hedgpeth (1966) reviewed information available at that time. Goering and Dugdale (1966), Barber and Norton (1968) and Wiebe *et al.* (1968) focussed their interest on the submerged crater that forms an isolated basin in Bahía Darwin (Genovesa Island). Siebert (1971) briefly described a hydrologic profile in Bahía James (Santiago Island), and Pak and Zaneveld (1973) analysed the EUC to the east of the Galápagos. The compilation of all oceanographic station data and bathythermographic profiles in archives at the data bank of the National Oceanic and Atmospheric Administration (NOAA, Washington, USA) enables us to analyse hydrologic features broadly affecting the archipelago. During a Belgian expedition to the Galápagos Islands in 1967–68, based at the Charles Darwin Research Station, we made hydrologic, chemical and biologic observations. This, together with data gathered at the same time by the Stanford Oceanographic Expedition 17 and 19 Cruises, which worked at some 14 stations in the Galápagos area, gave us the opportunity to study oceanographic conditions in the archipelago and more specifically its seasonal fluctuations (Houvenaghel, 1973, 1974, 1978).

3.3.1. Analysis of some parameters

3.3.1.1. Surface temperature

The annual cycle of temperature in the islands is documented by series of daily measurements in the surface waters at Puerto Baquerizo Moreno (San Cristóbal Island), from 1958 (IGY) till 1963 (Abbot, 1966), and by the Charles Darwin Research Station at Bahía Academia (Santa Cruz Island) since 1965 (Houvenaghel, 1973, 1974, 1978). The Galápagos year is divided into distinct hot and cool periods. Warming starts in October–November, develops in December and reaches maximum in February–April but may last until June. Lower temperatures are encountered during the rest of the year, especially in August–September. Although they concern different series of years, both sets of data exhibit significant differences of temperature regime between two localities distant by only 80 km from each other. In Bahía Academia, the monthly means range from 21.5°C in August to 25.2°C in April; the absolute daily minimum is observed in July (17.8°C). In San Cristóbal, the monthly means are from 18.5°C in September to 24.8°C in March, with an absolute daily minimum of 15.0°C in November. The cold period in San Cristóbal is also longer than in Santa Cruz, indicating geographical differences in surface temperature distribution. Information about the surface temperature over the rest of the archipelago is scarce (Stewart 1911, Abbott 1966). We have worked out about 1,250 surface temperature data measured ourselves or gathered from the Charles Darwin Research Station and NOAA data bank (Houvenaghel 1974). The computation of these data for areas measuring 1° by 1° confirm that the thermal regime is different according to the region of the archipelago. To the north, surface waters remain warm all the year round and may in summer approach 30°C. To the west, surface waters are always colder than elsewhere; while in the south the cold character decreases eastwards. This computation also indicates local surface coolings at Cabo Berkeley (Isabela), Punta Espinosa (Fernandina) and on the west coast of San Cristóbal. Some less important cold spots are the east coast of Santa Cruz, to the south and northeast of Isabela, Bahía James (Santiago), Floreana and Española; all these are related to local upwellings.

The monthly analyses of surface temperature at the scale of the archipelago demonstrates the evolution in time and space of antagonistic cold and warm influences. Warm waters from the north are prevented from extending towards the south by local upwellings, which maintain a large cold spot to the west of Isabela. From April onwards (March during colder years) this cold area expands. A tongue of cold water passing to the north of Isabela appears first. Soon after, in April–May, the cold area expands eastward to the south of Isabela. In June–July (during the colder years) this area reaches the equator east of the islands. The return of the warm waters in September, reducing progressively the cold water area. The migrations of warm equatorial surface water from the north to the south is faster east of the archipelago. When they return to northern positions, the warm waters first leave the western and eastern approaches of the archipelago. In the central part waters are usually less cool and local heating is common. Such local heating take place in bays where water circulation is reduced. Bahía Elizabeth (Isabela) is a good example.

3.3.1.2. Thermal structure

The basic feature of the thermal structure in the Galápagos is the presence of a permanent thermocline that is closer to the surface at the equator than it is to the north or south (Cromwell, 1958, Wyrtki, 1965).

The analysis of the thermal structure in the Galápagos is based—beside hydrologic station data—upon some 450 bathythermographic profiles in archives at the NOAA.

To the north and the northeast of the archipelago, an upper mixed layer (about 25 m deep and with increasing depth to the north) is limited in depth by the thermocline in which gradients of 0.3°C/m are found. To the west and south of the archipelago such a highly stratified thermal structure disappears during the cold season, or may even be lacking throughout the year. Here the thermocline is always weak, with gradients from 0.05°C/m to 0.18°C/m and frequently reaching the surface, thus revealing an upwelling pattern. When locating the position where the thermocline intersects the surface we may deduce that this occurs above, or in the vicinity of, the southern slopes of the underwater relief of the archipelago. This relation between topography and upwelling is also shown by hydrological transects across the archipelago. In the transition region between the well stratified waters in the north and northeast and the upwelling regions in the south and west, the thermocline is irregular and thick with relatively weak gradients. This characterizes the waters in the central part of the archipelago.

Within the thick thermocline found in these waters a staircase structure is often found, and a distinct secondary superficial thermocline may also be present. This staircase structure indicates the presence of complicated circulation with antagonistic components, which are the superficial waters flowing to the west and the subsuperficial waters flowing to the east. The secondary superficial thermocline noticed in these waters is a consequence of local heating and is linked with an increase in stability of the superficial layer. This occurs in the central part of the archipelago, in bays or downstream of an upwelling area. Such a secondary thermocline may be related to the seasonal shallow thermocline described by Wyrtki (1965) for Peruvian waters; however, in the Galápagos this feature is not restricted to the warm season but may be found throughout the year.

3.3.1.3. Salinity

Salinity helps to describe the extensions of the upwelling waters and their subsequent mixing and heating when flowing downstream. The upwelled waters are characterized by high salinity and contrast with tropical surface waters from the north and northeast. This extension of the cool saline waters at the surface starts in April and reaches its maximal area (of 35‰) in May–June. Later on, the 34‰ isoline appears first to the north and the east of the islands, then spreads over the archipelago in such a way that it may cross the 1°N latitude as early as September. During the warm season, the tropical surface waters never reach further south than the north of Isabela in the western part of the archipelago, or the southern coast of Santa Cruz in the central area. This helps to explain small scale geographical differences in surface waters, such as those noticed between Bahía Academia and San Cristóbal.

Profiles and transects describing the vertical distribution of salinity across the archipelago show maximum salinity waters as those typically belonging to the EUC. The salinity maximum observed in 1968 within the islands are characterized by properties (thermosteric anomaly among them) which correspond to those measured the same year in the EUC core to the west of the Galápagos (93°W) by the Piquero and Eastropac Cruises (Taft and Jones 1973). These transects demonstrate that the maximum salinity waters are involved in feeding the upwellings already identified by their thermal properties. This indicates that local upwellings around and within the Galápagos are related to the EUC activities.

3.3.1.4. Nutrients

Analyses of nutrient distributions and their seasonal evolutions in 1968, in relation to thermohaline properties, indicate that, in the core of maximum salinity corresponding to EUC water, phosphates, silicates and nitrates are high with maximum values of 2.0, 20.0 and 26.5 μg at/l respectively. For nitrates, values are rather low; 0.35 μg at/l or less. In surface coastal waters of the central part of the archipelago (around Bahía Academia) nitrates, silicates and phosphates reach low values corresponding to consumption patterns. For phosphates, about half of the data show an enrichment up to 2.9μg at/l in these coastal waters. The same happens to nitrites, where the majority of samples are enriched in comparison to their values in the maximum salinity core approaching the islands. The vertical distribution of nutrients in the water column confirm the properties described above, especially those for the nitrites, which are characterized by maximal values just above the pycnocline at the bottom of the upper layer. For the phosphates, enrichment processes take place in shallow waters. This nutrient distribution, well documented in 1968, clearly indicates that the waters on the southern coast of Santa Cruz are not undercurrent waters reaching this central region. They are instead recently upwelled waters which, owing to solar heating, become lighter, and in which primary production as well as some regeneration occur. This is also demonstrated by transects across the archipelago which show that above the pycnocline, in the upper layer and downstream from upwelling areas, nutrient concentrations are lower than those in the maximum salinity core of the undercurrent. Besides consumption patterns, phosphate enrichments are also noticeable above shallow bottoms.

The eutrophication of the Galápagos area, which sustains rich biological activities, is the result of the input at the surface of nutrient rich waters belonging to the undercurrent.

3.3.1.5. Oxygen

The presence of waters that are recently upwelled and belonging to the EUC is also attested by the distribution of dissolved oxygen. In about 130 surface samples, taken throughout the archipelago, values range from 2.25 ml/l to 6.20 ml/l, corresponding to 43 to 119% saturation. 77% of the samples were undersaturated. In coastal and inshore waters at Bahía Academia, dissolved oxygen values were at, or just above, saturation, indicating that the waters in this region had been drifting in the upper layers long enough to allow biologic productions to increase the oxygen content. This emphasizes the conclusions already drawn from the analysis of nutrient levels in these waters.

3.3.1.6. Primary production

During our measurements at fixed stations in Bahía Academia, no distinct seasonal cycle of primary production could be deduced. The only general rule is that peaks of production occur when the water quality has changed. In the warm season this corresponds to the horizontal advection of tropical surface waters. During the cold season peaks show up when the presence of cold nutrient-rich waters is noticed.

From the relations between primary production and nutrients, it may also be concluded that primary production is higher in those waters where phytoplankton has been developing over some days.

3.3.1.7. Plankton biomass

A pattern of distribution of surface plankton biomass resulted from the analysis of 250 samples scattered throughout the archipelago. No seasonal cycle or trend was discernible as for primary production. The samples from typical upwelling areas, such as those to the west and south of Isabela, were low, with biovolumes of $5\,ml/100\,m^3$ or less. In coastal and inshore waters, and especially next to upwelling zones, the biovolumes are much more important. Values as high as $82\,ml/100\,m^3$ have been found to the north of Isabela.

As a general rule, the highest plankton biomass is found in waters of high salinity and high temperature. This means that biologic production is enhanced by upwellings, but that high plankton development only takes place in these upwelled waters after they have been drifting for some time in the upper layer. The explanation for such a delayed start to biologic production in nutrient-rich upwelling waters has been given by Barber and Ryther (1969), who demonstrated that in the EUC waters a better phytoplankton development was obtained when organic chelators were added to the medium. Such organic matter, absent in the EUC waters, are produced by biological activity in surface waters.

3.3.2. Upwelling and circulation patterns in the archipelago

3.3.2.1. Undercurrent and topography-induced upwellings

The EUC is the major phenomenon in the oceanography of the Galápagos. This current brings to the islands quantities of cold fertile waters that counteract the advection of warm tropical surface waters. The EUC flow patterns through the archipelago as deduced from our analyses are summarized in Figure 3.1. Shaded areas indicate the strongest and most regular upwelling zones. Both features, flow pathways and upwellings, are linked directly to the submarine topography of the archipelago which introduces obstacles along the eastgoing path of the undercurrent. This has the effect of deflecting waters to the north, to the south, or to both sides of the archipelago, and in the piling up and rising of waters upstream from the obstacles, resulting in upwelling to the surface.

The circulation pattern, the distribution of watermasses in the surface layer and the subsequent mixing are complicated by the presence of the west drift, the SEC, which carries the superficial layer along. All the physical, chemical and biologic parameters describing the surface properties suggest that the waters driven by this surface current are upwelled waters that are more or less mixed and progressively heated while flowing downstream to the west.

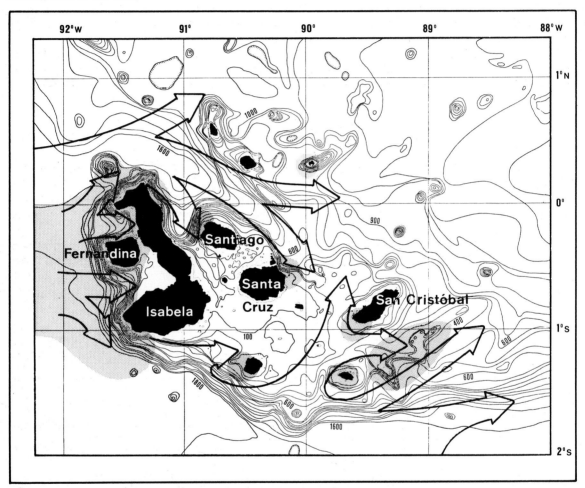

Figure 3.1. Bathymetric chart of the archipelago showing the main flows of the east-going Equatorial Undercurrent (schematized by arrows) and the location of the most prominent upwellings (shaded areas), (sounding in fathoms), from Houvenaghel 1978.

3.3.2.2. The seasonal pattern

Oceanographic conditions in the Galápagos fluctuate seasonally. In the summer, when the Intertropical Convergence Zone migrates to the southern hemisphere, the dominant feature in the surface circulation is the presence of a southeast flow of warm tropical surface waters (with temperatures of 27°C and above and salinities of 33‰ or less) coming from the north. At that time of the year, a local patch of colder waters is still present to the west of Isabela. From the salinity distribution, we may deduce that the warm tropical surface waters do not normally reach the southern edge of the archipelago.

Later in the year, from March–April onwards, the upwelling zone originating west of the islands extends (mainly) to the south and east, bringing more and more cold saline and fertile waters into surface layers.

From June to August, but especially in August, the eastgoing waters driven by the undercurrent counteract with the westgoing surface waters drifting with the South Equatorial Current. This leads to a circulation pattern suggesting the presence at the level of the archipelago of a broad cyclonic movement in which surface temperatures may rise due to local heating.

During the final part of the year, the eastgoing flow passing to the north of the archipelago increases and isotherms move locally towards the north.

At the turn of the year, in December–January, a sudden decline in the extension of the cold waters occurs when the summer season brings tropical surface waters back to the south.

The annual cycle of the surface circulation pattern coincides with meteorologic seasons in the region, especially the annual southern shift of the Intertropical Convergence Zone. However, upwellings in Galápagos waters are present throughout the year.

3.4. Conclusions

Physical, chemical and biologic parameters demonstrate the presence of upwelled waters in the Galápagos area and depict their distribution within and around the archipelago. All the oceanographic properties in the Galápagos are determined or influenced directly or indirectly by waters flowing with the undercurrent. The terrestrial environment is also dependent upon these marine influences, which are responsible for severe climatological and ecological conditions.

The sharp isolation of the Galápagos Islands provided by the local upwellings and the selecting conditions they impose upon life are the leading factors promoting species isolation and endemism in this remarkable archipelago.

References

Abbott, D.P. (1966) Factors influencing the zoogeographic affinities of Galápagos inshore marine fauna in *The Galápagos*. Edited by R. Bowman. Pages 108–122. Univ. Calif. Press, Berkeley and Los Angeles

Barber, R.T. and Norton, J. (1968) Hydrography of Bahía Darwin, Isla Genovesa. *Cruise Report S.O.E.*, **17**, 78–84. (Unpublished document).

Barber, R.T. and Ryther, J.H. (1968) Organic chelators: factors affecting primary production in the Cromwell Current upwelling. *J. Exp. Marine Biol. Ecol.*, **3**, 191–199.

Bennett, E.B. (1963) An oceanographic atlas of the Eastern Tropical Pacific Ocean, based on data from Eastropac Expeditions in October–December 1955. *Bull. Int. Am. Trop. Tuna Comm.*, **8**(2), 33–135.

Bjerknes, J. (1966) A possible response of the atmospheric Hadley circulation to equatorial anomalies of ocean temperature. *Tellus*, **18**, 820–829.

Christensen, N. (1971) Observation of the Cromwell Current near the Galápagos Islands. *Deep Sea Res.*, **18**, 27–33.

Cromwell, T. (1958) Thermocline topography, horizontal currents and 'ridging' in the eastern tropical Pacific. *Bull. Int. Am. Trop. Tuna Comm.*, **3**, 135–144.

Donguy, J.R. and Henin, C. (1980) Surface conditions in the eastern equatorial Pacific related to the intertropical convergence zone of the winds. *Deep Sea Res.*, **27**, 9A, 693–714.

Goering, J.J. and Dugdale, R.C. (1966) Denitrification rates in an island bay in the equatorial Pacific Ocean. *Science*, **154**, 505–506.

Houvenaghel, G.T. (1973) Contribution à l'étude de l'écologie marine des Iles Galapagos. *Mém. Acad. r. Sci. d'outre mer Cl. Sci. Natl. Méd.(N.S.)*, **14**, 1–102.

Houvenaghel, G.T. (1974a) Etude océanographique de l'Archipel des Galapagos et mise en évidence du rôle des conditions hydrologiques dans la dermination du peuplement des Iles. Thesis. Université Libre de Bruxelles.

Houvenaghel, G.T. (1974b) Equatorial Undercurrent and climate in the Galápagos Islands. *Nature*, **250**, 565–566.

Houvenaghel, G.T. (1976) Evolution annuelle de la température de l'eau de mer en surface dans la Baie de Pánama et au large des côtes ecuadoriennes. *Ciel et Terre Bull. Soc. Belge d'Astronomie de Météorologie et de Physique du Globe*, **92**, 4, 201–224.

Houvenaghel, G.T. (1977) Description de la géomorphologie marine de l'archipel des Galapagos. *Cah. du Pacifique*, **20**, 223–239.

Houvenaghel, G.T. (1978) Oceanographic conditions in the Galápagos Archipelago and their relationships with life on the islands in *Upwelling Ecosystems*, Edited by R. Boje and M. Tomczak. Pages 181–200. Springer-Verlag, Berlin Heidelberg

Houvenaghel, G.T. and Houvenaghel, N. (1974) Aspects écologiques de la zonation intertidale sur les côtes rocheuses des Iles Galapagos. *Marine Biol.*, **26**, 135–152.

Jones, J.H. (1969) Surfacing of the Pacific Equatorial Undercurrent, direct observation. *Science*, **163**, 1449–1450.

Knauss, J.A. (1966) Further measurements and observations of the Cromwell Current. *J. Mar. Res.*, **24**, 205–240.

Love, C.M. (1972) *Eastropac Atlas*. U.S. Department of Commerce, Washington.

Montgomery, R.B. and Stroup, E.D. (1962) Equatorial Waters and Currents at 150° west, in July–August 1952. Baltimore, John Hopkins Press.

Pak, H. and Zaneveld, J.R. (1973) The Cromwell Current on the east side of the Galápagos Islands. *J. Geophys. Res.*, **78**, 7845–7859.

Quinn, W.H. (1974) Monitoring and predicting El Niño invasions. *J. Appl. Meteor.*, **13**,(7) 825–832.

Siebert, J. (1971) Some oceanographic observations in the Galápagos Islands. *Am. Zool.*, **11**, 405–408.

Stevenson, M.R. and Taft, B.A. (1971) New evidence of the Equatorial Undercurrent east of the Galápagos Islands. *J. Mar. Res.*, **29**, 2, 103–115.

Stewart, A. (1911) A botanical survey of the Galápagos Islands. *Proc. Calif. Acad. Sci. Ser.*, **4**,(1), 7–288.

Taft, B.A. and Jones, J.H. (1973). Measurements of the Equatorial Undercurrent in the Eastern Pacific in *Progress in Oceanography*. Edited by B.A. Warren. Pages 47–110. Pergamon Press, Oxford.

Wiebe, P., Cox, J. and Malone, T. (1968) A hydrographic survey of Darwin Bay *Cruise Report S.O.E.*, **19**, 44–56 (Unpublished document).

Wooster, W.S. and Hedgpeth, J.W. (1966) The oceanographic setting of the Galápagos in *The Galápagos*. Edited by R. Bowman. Pages 100–107. Univ. Calif. Press, Berkeley and Los Angeles.

Wyrtki, K. (1965) The thermal structure of the eastern Pacific Ocean. *Deutsche Hydrogr. Z. Ergänzungsheft*, 1–84.

Wyrtki, K. (1966) Oceanography in the Eastern Equatorial Pacific Ocean in *Oceanography and Marine Biology*. Edited by H. Barnes. Pages 33–68. Allen and Unwin, London.

Wyrtki, K. (1975) 'El Niño': The dynamic response of the equatorial Pacific Ocean to atmospheric forcing. *J. Phys. Oceanogr.*, **5**,(4) 572.

Wyrtki, K. (1977) Sea level during the 1972 El Niño. *J. Phys. Oceanogr.*, **7**,(6), 779.

CHAPTER 4

The Galápagos Climate: Present and Past

PAUL A. COLINVAUX

The Ohio State University, Department of Zoology, Columbus, Ohio, USA

Contents

4.1. Introduction   55
4.2. *El Niño* and the Coming of the ITCZ   58
4.3. Impact of the Immediate Sea   61
4.4. Sedimentary Clues to the Galápagos Ice Age   63
4.5. Possible Ice-Age Climates of the Galápagos   66
4.6. Implications of Ice-Age Climate for Life on the Galápagos   68
References   69

4.1. Introduction

The Galápagos are true desert islands, although on the equator. Tropical islands are usually wet. If they were a few degrees of latitude further north, the Galápagos too would be wet. They would also be wet if South America was a different shape. Furthermore, global pressure systems from far away press upon the Galápagos climate to keep the islands in the desert state we know.

The detailed forces that drive the Galápagos climate are complex, and the great geographer, Glenn Trewartha (1961), described the region as having one of the 'Earth's problem climates'. Yet some of the main forces at work are clear enough. The primary cause of Galápagos drought is the wind and the way the wind drives the sea. The islands lie close to where winds and current systems meet, and their peculiar climate depends on the subtleties of that meeting. If winds or currents were pushed differently, as perhaps they might have been in an ice age, then the Galápagos would have a different climate.

Well to the north of the Galápagos, out in the open, landless Pacific, is the climatic equator where the wind systems meet. This is the doldrums, the heat girdle of the earth, a region for which climatologists have an uglier name in jargon: ITCZ, or Intertropical Convergence Zone. This is a very wet place, where towering cliffs of white cumulus climb high, and deluge the sea beneath with water they cannot hold in the cold of the upper air.

The doldrums are the start of the heat engine that drives the winds and currents of air and sea. The equatorial sun heats the air, expanding it, causing it to rise. Up, too, goes water vapor, hurled from the sea surface by the kinetic motions of warm molecules. In the cumulus cloud of the upper air, the condensing water gives back its heat, warming a packet of air already high above the sea, causing it to rise still more.

This process can be magnified over very warm shallow seas, where the hot air is soggy with moisture. The air, heated both below and above, begins to storm upward, faster and faster, until a hurricane is born. But over the open Pacific north of the Galápagos, the sea is not that warm, nor the air that moist.

Yet the rising air of the doldrums does suck in copious masses of air from both north and south to feed the climbing columns. The heat engine has been switched on. Air must come in low over the sea from high latitudes to take its turn at being heated over the doldrums; and air must flow back overhead to fill the void. This basic circulation is permanent, as long as the earth is heated along its girdle of doldrums by the sun.

The winds rushing to take their place in the climbing masses at the ITCZ are the trade winds. The Galápagos Islands are in the path of the southern contingent, near the end of their journey. The trade winds must blow for ever; as every sailor knows they do so blow. But the trade winds do not come directly from the south or the north, but from the southeast or northeast, due to a very simple process partly hidden from understanding by a foreign-sounding name, Coriolis force.

Think of the southern trade wind as it flows northwards across the ocean towards the Galápagos and its eventual extinction by the climb over the doldrums. This wind is actually moving sideways with the spin of the earth as well as forwards from the suck of the heat engine. When the trades start on their journey far to the south, the sideways motion is comparatively slow because the spherical earth is narrow there and its surface velocity modest. But as the trades travel on towards the equator they cross a surface that moves faster and faster. And it takes time for the wind to be accelerated to the new spinning speed, west to east. So the trades lag behind the spin of the earth, which shows up as an apparent deflection to the east.

A more formal way of stating what happens is that angular momentum is conserved. The process is perhaps more easily imagined if we think of air going in the opposite direction, south from the equator. Such air would start with a large sideways, west to east velocity. As it moves out it reaches parts of the earth moving more slowly so that conserving its angular momentum would make the wind turn in the direction of the earth's rotation to the left. Air going south has to lose angular momentum. But trade wind air going north has to gain angular momentum, being deflected into the earth's spin, to the east. This also is to the left.

We may say that air slides out from under the southern trade winds so that they are deflected to the left, becoming the southeast trades. It is this process of slippage of a fluid moving over a rotating surface to which we have given the grand-sounding name of Coriolis force. In the southern hemisphere the slippage (deflection) is to the left; in the northern hemisphere it is to the right. So all trade winds are partly east winds. And all returning winds coming overhead from the equator northwards or southwards are bent until they become westerlies.

So the trade winds blow on the Galápagos from the southeast. And this is the prime fact that makes the shape of South America important, because southeast of the Galápagos there is nothing but sea. The South American coastline tapers away to the east itself, giving the trades a clear run from their start far to the south. And this is important because the trades have all those miles to blow the sea along with them.

The southeast trades drag along with them the Humboldt Current, sometimes called the Peru Current. Parallel with the slanting coastline of South America this mighty current is forced to flow. But it is a fluid moving over rotating land, just like the trade winds themselves. The land slips from under it and the Humboldt Current is deflected ever more to the left.

The Humboldt Current turns due west well before the trades have completed their journey to the doldrums; Coriolis force sees to that. In fact the Humboldt, or rather its successors, go on turning to the left far out in the Pacific until the current has swept clear round the ocean, completing a titanic gyre. Most of the time this westward (left) turning of the Humboldt means that it does not reach the Galápagos at all but sweeps past well to the south. Yet the water movements caused by its passing are decisive for the Galápagos climate (Palmer and Pyle, 1966).

The vital consequence of the turning of the Humboldt Current is that surface water is forced away from the land. Throughout the journey past northern Chile and along the coast of Peru the current is driven on, partly parallel to the coast yet always with a turning movement out to sea. This means that water must flow in behind the advancing waters of the current. And this water can come only from below. It is an upwelling.

Water comes out of the depths, hauled up along the continental edge beside Peru and spread over the sea surface behind the water that is driven onward by the trades. This upwelled water comes from the dark depths where no life has drained it of nutrients and so it is fertile, giving rise to the legendary fisheries of Peru and the hunting grounds of the guano birds. But, more important for the Galápagos, the water also is cold.

All the way from Peru to the Galápagos, the trade winds are cooled by upwelled water from below, and kept cool. It is a cool dense mass of air that streams towards the Galápagos over the cold sea. But this air is a thin surface sheet only, no more than a thousand or two feet thick. It is topped by an inversion: warm air over cold. This is the inevitable consequence when there is a long fetch of smoothly moving air gliding over a cold sea. The cold bottom air fails to rise and becomes like a stable river, a separate fluid crossing the ocean just above the sea surface. But overhead there is subsiding air, which comes down as part of the returning circulation driven by the heat engine. Subsiding air must compress as each packet falls to low elevations of high pressure. And to compress air is to yield heat. This provides warm air to set over the cool winds of the eastern Pacific.

When you fly to the Galápagos from mainland Ecuador you can see this inversion underneath you marked by endless ranks of thin stratus clouds. These thin clouds lie just under the inversion, which is as far as slowly rising air in the surface winds can get. Small water droplets are squeezed out of this air by the limited expansion of its limited climb, but the droplets cannot be very large.

While you fly over the sea, these clouds that mark the inversion are far below you, since the inversion is only a few thousand feet from the sea. But as your aircraft descends towards its landing on the Galápagos you can see the thin cloud in profile, stretched out as a flat sheet to the horizon and beyond.

This pattern is quite unlike that of the trade winds most sailors know. Usually the trades flow over water that is ever warmer as the journey to the equator progresses. The bottom air collects both heat and water vapor from the ocean and rises in packets to great heights. Then you see lovely trade-wind skies like those near Jamaica: mounting cumulus clouds 20,000 ft high; some turning into brief showers of heavy rain.

Figure 4.1. Stratus cloud layer on the flank of Fernandina. The clouds mark the inversion with a top at about 3000 ft. The rim of the volcano is nearly 5000 ft. Stripes on the mountain are lava flows, there being almost no vegetation in this view. Photograph taken from Punta Espinosa.

But the cold Peruvian sea sends trade winds to the Galápagos only as thin streams under their inversion. When they hit a low island very little happens; perhaps a little more condensing of fine droplets from the disturbance so that a light stratus cloud is formed near sea level. This we call the *garúa*, the clammy mists familiar to those who go to the Galápagos in July.

Larger islands reach to the inversion so that a belt of stratus cloud sits like a band, high on the windward side of the island (Fig. 4.1). Plants in this belt are soaking wet from fog drip and the ground is kept moist by frequent light showers. The classic view of Isla Santa Cruz from the south off Academy Bay is shaped by this belt of stratus cloud. Underneath is the brown desert, then an abrupt transition to cloud and greenery, finally a summit relatively free of cloud poking through. On the higher islands like Fernandina the emergence of the dry top of the mountain above the clouds is clearer still (Fig. 4.1). The lee sides of all the islands gets very little water under this regimen, often little more than fog blown over from the windward side (Fig. 4.2, center).

Such is the climate and its causes for most of the year in the modern Galápagos. The resulting weather stamps on the larger islands their characteristic pattern of vegetation: cactus scrub or *Bursera graveolens* woodland on the lee sides and on a coastal strip all round the island; a gradient up into evergreen forest at cloud height; *Miconia* and treeferns in the wettest cloud layer; and the bare treeless uplands. Yet there are times when it really rains on the Galápagos, even in the deserts. Obviously something can destroy the normality of the Galápagos climate, though not for long.

4.2. *El Niño* and the Coming of the ITCZ

Rain comes to the Galápagos when the sea warms. This is one way of putting it, and it is certainly true. There are now a number of records correlating rainfall on the larger islands with sea temperature. Yet the warming is not much, just a degree or two. It has no local importance that the sea warms a little but it is a sign that something dramatic has happened to the weather.

What seems to happen is that weather usually found near the doldrums has moved south to reach the Galápagos. There has been a displacement of the climatic equator through several degrees of latitude and the Galápagos is removed from its prevailing odd climate and given the weather usually found closer to the intertropical convergence. The warm water is a part of this general motion, a sign that the weather has changed rather than a cause of the change. This system of weather comes south to the Galápagos every year between December and March, though how long it stays and how strongly it is impressed vary greatly.

The prudent scientist writing a general essay has to be very cautious about explaining the cause of this moving of the ITCZ. He does not quite dare to say that we know not why it happens, because that would not be strictly true. Contributing causes are known. But a completely satisfactory explanation may still be some way off.

The normal position of the climatic equator is north of the geographic equator, not synchronous with it as you might expect. Certainly the ultimate arbiter of this fact is the distribution of land and sea over the whole earth, with most of the land being in the northern hemisphere. This sets inequalities in the force of winds and currents, and the ITCZ ends up north of the real equator. Perhaps it is pushed there by the southern winds driving on over their large fetch of ocean unimpeded by land.

Movements of the ITCZ are correlated with pressure changes on the grandest scale, particularly with the 'southern oscillation'. This is the name given to a pattern of observed fact, essentially that high pressure over New Guinea and the northern Australian region is correlated with low pressure over the eastern Pacific where the Galápagos lies (Lamb, 1972). We observe that masses of air at opposite ends of the Pacific must be coupled and we talk of an oscillation in the atmosphere as if masses of air were connected like the ends of a teeter-totter. The coupling must be very complex, apparently still beyond the reach of an hypothesis of prime causes. But the annual march of the ITCZ down towards the Galápagos is directed by whatever directs the southern oscillation itself, since these events are in synchrony.

It is possible to say in a very general way how much rain the Galápagos get in each December to March period from a knowledge of pressure changes over New Guinea alone (Quinn, 1971). This, of course, does not tell us directly what drives the advance and retreat of the ITCZ on to the Galápagos, but it does show that

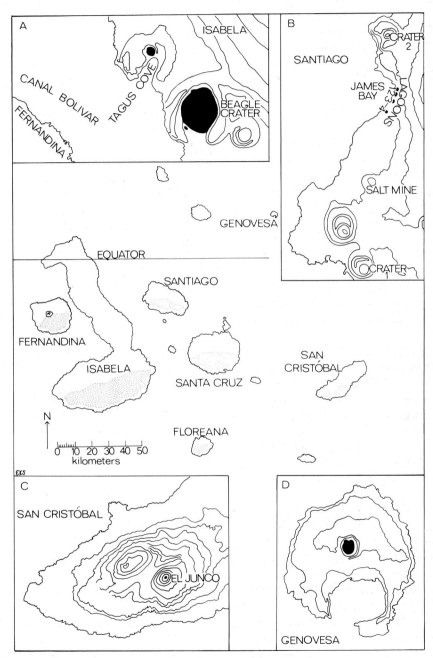

Figure 4.2. Lakes of the Galápagos Islands. Only the crater lake on Genovesa and the maar lake, El Junco, on San Cristóbal hold ancient sediments. The contours round El Junco were drawn by hand one day in 1966 when the clouds lifted. Shaded areas on the sketch map (center) are the moister parts of the islands.

global forces are behind these events. A global trend brings both warm water to the islands once a year and the rain of the doldrums. It is no local happening that fixes the peculiar Galápagos weather.

When Galápagos islanders notice the water warming and the clouds gathering in January, they do not say 'here comes the ITCZ' or 'the doldrums' but rather '*El Niño* is coming!' Yet there might be an argument about whether it is really going to be '*El Niño*' or whether they are about to have 'an *El Niño* year'. For the annual southern march of ITCZ is the basis for the *El Niño* legends, though there are various meanings given to that evocative term (see also Chapter 3.2.2.7).

The prime legend belongs to Ecuador. When the ITCZ comes down to the geographic equator or below, the whole weather system of the southeast trades and the Humboldt Current falters. Winds blow less certainly along Peru, the current pours less vigorously, and there are less upwellings pressing to fill the void along the coast. A direct response is the running of a new narrow coastal current *southwards* down the coast of Ecuador. This is a current of warmer water, fed from equatorial masses of warmed surface water. The effect on the southern coast of Ecuador is both dramatic and welcome, because it brings rain. Sea breezes, warm and wet, come to the desert shore, are thrown up by the desert heat, and drop rain. The people see this blessing at Christmas, the time of the Christ child, and call it in gratitude '*El Niño*'. 'The child comes!'

Scholarly accuracy requires that we realize that '*El Niño*' is the name of a current that comes every December to the coast of Ecuador. But Anglosaxon oceanographers and climate people have forgotten the rules of scholarly primogeniture. They take *El Niño* to mean all the phenomena of air and sea associated with the march of ITCZ (Lamb, 1972). I remember first holding forth on this meaning of *El Niño* to an Ecuadorian colleague as we discussed the Galápagos climate only to be told, '*El Niño* is a current'. I stood corrected.

The *El Niño* Current certainly does not reach the Galápagos Islands, it even goes the wrong way. But the whole syndrome associated with the coming of the ITCZ does, and it comes every year. To call this whole syndrome '*El Niño*' is now respectable, even in Ecuadorian Spanish. So there are two basic meanings to the annual coming of *El Niño*: the coastal current and the whole weather pattern.

But the meaning heard by a wider public is still another:—not an annual event at all but an intermittent Act of God, possibly coming every 7 years. To the press, and to some oceanographers, *El Niño* means an extreme expression of the whole climatic syndrome that happens only intermittently. Warm water floods far to the south, the whole upwelling system collapses along the Peruvian coast, fisheries fail, and heavy rain scours the Peruvian desert. This is spectacular, but then anything carried to extreme inclines to spectacle.

One of these extreme '*El Niño* years' means a very rainy season on the Galápagos, and one that is unusually prolonged. But the difference is only one of kind. Rains of a sort come within a month or two of the usual time every year and *El Niño* on the Galápagos is an annual event, just as is the Ecuadorian current, called *El Niño* because it comes as a blessing at Christmas.

A prime consequence for Galápagos life is that there are strong seasons, even though the islands lie on the equator. But the seasons are irregular. There are no obvious environmental cues to tell life of the Galápagos desert when the rain is coming; not day-length, not regularity, not time-elapsed since the last rain. So the life of the desert must be adapted to living in an unpredictable environment.

One of the most striking of these adaptations is the opportunistic deciduousness of the *Bursera graveolens* trees. To most Galápagos visitors these are gaunt, leafless objects, remarkably evenly spaced and looking like a northern apple orchard in a dry winter. But let it rain and they will grow bright green, compound leaves vary rapidly so that the brown slopes are verdant within days. And when the ground dries up the *Bursera* trees will drop their leaves, just as do the trees of old or New England in the Fall. Only there is no Autumn on the Galápagos, just a 'fall' of leaves when it suits the trees best. *El Niño* makes the hillsides green, whenever he cares to come.

4.3. Impact of the Immediate Sea

It is easy to exaggerate the coldness of the Galápagos ocean. The water is cool by equatorial standards, yet far from cold. Most of the year typical surface water is 20°C, perhaps with a range from 19–21°C, which is significantly warmer than the 15–18°C of the coastal upwellings off Peru. Indeed, most of the Galápagos most of the time are not supplied with upwelled water.

Neither are the Galápagos supplied with 'the cold waters of the Humboldt Current' as so many articles about the islands say. This current is immensely important to the Galápagos, as we have seen, because its tendency to veer from the coast of Peru generates the cold upwellings that cool the trade winds. Notice, incidentally, that the crucial cold water of this process is hauled from the depths by the passage of the Humboldt—not brought from Antarctica by a form of long-distance transport. The temperature of the current itself is of lesser importance than the upwelling it causes. But, although the Humboldt fashions indirectly the Galápagos air, it scarcely delivers any water to the islands, though it points in the right direction.

The actual movement of Galápagos surface water is complicated, since the islands sit at the junction of global current systems (see preceding chapter) as well as of global wind systems. There can be much local confusion. But the important thing to life on the islands is that the surrounding water is not usually upwelled. It is not as cold as upwelled water and, far more important, it is not fertile.

The desert Galápagos Islands sit in somewhat desert Pacific sea. The desert properties of this local ocean certainly are not as extreme as in the blue waters of the central Pacific, which are one of the world's most infertile places, comparable only to the greater deserts on land. Fertility is raised over this barren standard because there are shallows round the Galápagos, local coastal effects, and the temporary upwellings of the western approaches, of which more in a moment. But, in the main, Galápagos waters are not very productive (Maxwell, 1972).

A clue to the unproductivity of the sea is before the eyes of every visitor in the blueness of the oceans. Blue ocean is always desert ocean. The blue color comes because light goes deep into the sea, eventually to be reflected back with all but its high-energy blue wavelengths absorbed in the water (Colinvaux, 1978). But this is possible only if there are few plants to trap the blue. A cold fertile upwelling is green, and the Peru fisheries must look like the North Sea or Long Island Sound in summer.

So the blue, cool but not cold, water which bathes most of the Galápagos most of the year, is only moderately productive. The oceanic birds which use the Galápagos as a base must often hunt far for their food. One of the nicest illustrations of this is the view from Genovesa where streams of red-footed boobies fly in endless lines, over the horizon and far away, as they journey to fishing grounds we scarcely know.

When the rains come between January and April, the water warms, perhaps to 25°C and productivity is probably at its lowest. How important this is to the lives of the shores, I doubt if we know. The significance may be minimal because coastal ecosystems depend for their nutrients on the continual flux of water against land. Even water with low nutrient concentrations can support productive ecosystems then, because fixed life can sieze on nutrients as they flow by, even when the concentration is low. This is the reason that highly productive coral reefs can thrive in the desert waters of the open Pacific.

So the Galápagos have a mix of surface waters, not the cold of upwellings but with some input from cooler streams. The mean temperature is too low for coral reefs to form, yet not low enough to denote the presence of fertile water from deep below. But this generality has important, if intermittent, exceptions. Temporary upwellings do happen to the west, and these are vital to some of the more spectacular Galápagos animals, to penguins, flightless cormorants, and the crowded shores of Fernandina and Isabela.

Perhaps the best known of all Galápagos spectacles is the crowded shore of Punta Espinosa on Fernandina. It is there that male marine iguanas sun themselves, two thousand at a time. This is, too, the best place to see penguins and flightless cormorants, and pelicans of Punta Espinosa breed only when the temperature of the water offshore falls sharply, perhaps as low as 17°C. When this happens, it is always a localized western event affecting sea areas round Fernandina and adjacent Isabela only. There is no regularity to the happening. There may be 6 months, perhaps 12 or more, of the usual cool water, then within days the water is cold and has turned green with algal life.

We have had researchers camped out on the shore of Fernandina waiting for this to happen (Boersma, 1974). The birds tell you if you fail to watch your thermometers, for there is a flurry of feeding as boobies, pelicans, gulls and the rest converge from far away to feed in swarms on the small fish which the fertile waters hold. Male penguins start to bray like donkeys in upwelling time as they 'lightly turn to thoughts of love'. Pelicans lay eggs, cormorants pair off; the bustle of reproduction is switched on for all the birds. This can happen in any calendar month. There is no regularity to it. The response is to an unpredictable upwelling.

The best explanation of what is happening is that a current known as the Cromwell Stream has washed against the islands from the west. This is an undercurrent, frequently called the Equatorial Undercurrent (EUC), although some of us find the phrase 'Cromwell Stream' comes more easily to the lips (Lamb, 1972). It runs from West to East, meandering along the equator across the Pacific. It appears to return water piled up at the western side of the ocean.

Sea level is actually about 70 cm higher at the New Guinea side than at the South American side. This is because surface currents on both sides of the equator flow from east to west, each driven by trade winds coming from the east. As a result water is piled up down stream and there must be a flow back. Some portion of this flow back appears as the Cromwell Stream. It pours deep under the surface currents whose flow it counteracts.

There are no walls or banks to channel the Cromwell Stream and its path must meander on its long journey, often pushed one way or another, perhaps after long lags, by the pressures round the migrating ITCZ. It is thus perfectly rational that the stream should miss the Galápagos for much of a year, but yet hose against the islands from time to time. It might then haul up local upwellings against the island shores, bringing fertile water and small fish for the birds of Punta Espinosa (Maxwell, 1972).

Probably this account is too simple for what really goes on behind the western upwellings, though it fits what we see well enough. But, however complex the causes, the pattern is of local, irregular, unpredictable upwellings along that coast. They also often do not last long. And this is a pattern crucial to the environment of the remarkable fauna of Punta Espinosa.

Galápagos penguins are the best-studied of the Punta Espinosa fauna (Boersma, 1977; see also Chapter 13.1.4). They breed nowhere else than these western shores where the upwellings come, and they breed only during the short passage of an upwelling, no matter when this might be. You can see adult penguins swimming in all parts of the archipelago, but if you would see them breed you must go to the west coast and wait for an upwelling. If you are unlucky, you might have to wait 6 months or a year.

The penguins can support an adult from the limited fishing to be had in the poorly productive blue water round the islands, and they wander about the sea lanes at their fishing. But to breed they must have plentiful food within comfortable swimming distance of a nest. Only a coastal upwelling gives them this. But the Galápagos environment is without cues to tell the penguins when an upwelling is coming. They are like the *Bursera* trees waiting, without advanced information, for rain. They must be ready to respond when the thing actually happens.

Both at sea and on the desert land, therefore, there is much about the Galápagos climate which is unpredictable. First thoughts of the islands are always that they are desert islands; brown land floating on blue sea. Yet there are good times, both on land and sea, and these come every year. The moulding fact for much of Galápagos life is that these good times are impossible to predict.

4.4. Sedimentary Clues to the Galápagos Ice Age

I have searched the Galápagos archipelago for sediments that should hold records of ice-age time (Colinvaux, 1968). Ancient lakes or bogs are what we need to reconstruct climates of the past. I found both, though only a single lake, El Junco on Isla San Cristóbal, is old enough to hold a record of the ice age.

There are raised peat bogs on the Galápagos, particularly in the highlands of Santa Cruz, above the *Miconia* belt near the feature called Media Luna. These are raised, domed, *Sphagnum* bogs, closely similar to their counterparts in Northern Europe or Minnesota. Two very nice ones occupy old explosion craters. One is 5 m thick and I have a single radiocarbon determination from the bottom of it of about 5000 B.P. (years before present).

That the Santa Cruz bogs should grow rapidly at about one meter a millennium seems reasonable considering the present climate. The bogs lie under the stratus cloud, always moist, and so hidden by fog that I have found it necessary to walk on compass bearings in order to find them. This is classic bog-forming climate, and the presence of the bogs show that this climate has persisted for at least the last 5000 years. Yet it is curious that no bogs are older than this. In north temperate regions bogs have been growing for 10,000 years since the climate change that marked the final last gasp of the ice age. Perhaps the youth of Galápagos bogs says no more than that suitable craters or other hollows are only 5000 years old. There is, however, perhaps a suggestion that a climate favorable to bogs did not exist more than 5000 years ago. This would be a conclusion so interesting that it had best be set aside to await supporting data.

I made a round of the Galápagos lakes, probing the bottom of each for sediments (Fig. 4.2). The crater lake at Tagus Cove on Isabela has a bottom of salt and lava. It is very young. Large Beagle Crater (Fig. 4.3; see also Fig. 2.3, Chapter 2) not so far away, and where Darwin tried to drink but found the water 'salt as brine' is also young, with only 15 cm of sandy sediment in the middle. The crater lakes on Santiago, and the Bainbridge crater lake are little better. And of all the salt crater lakes only Arcturus, the lake in the middle of Genovesa, holds sediment (Fig. 4.4). Under 30 m of water there is beautifully banded mud, nearly 5 m thick. But this mud spans only the last 4 to 6000 years and is not old enough to help with the ice-age climate (Goodman, 1972).

There is only one permanent fresh water lake on the whole Galápagos archipelago: El Junco. There are various ponds, typically 10 to 20 m across on Santa Cruz and other islands. Probably they all dry up at times and none has an ancient record in its mud. But El Junco holds a record of more than 40,000 years, making it a candidate to be one of the oldest small lakes in the world. It is tempting to say, 'Trust the desert Galápagos to have something spectacular in fresh-water lakes'.

Figure 4.3. Panorama of Beagle Crater Lake from the Northwest. The basin is a huge tuff ring, now largely filled, with lava flows (foreground) having entered the breached low rim to the south.

Figure 4.4. Arcturus Lake on Genovesa. The lake occupies the crater in the center of Isla Genovesa (Fig. 4.2). The water is nearly twice as salty as sea water and 30 m deep. In the bottom is 5 m of mud spanning 4–6000 years. Trees lining the shore in places are mangroves (*Rhizophora mangle*).

'El Junco' is really the name of a hill, one of the peaks round the rim of the weathered volcano that forms the southwestern half of San Cristóbal. The hill overlooks a broad flat depression which is all that remains of the old caldera. In really wet years this flat expanse floods to a depth of a few inches, giving rise to old travellers' tales of a large lake at the summit of San Cristóbal. It was these travellers' tales that took me to the island in 1966. The inhabitants of Puerto Baquerizo Moreno (Wreck Bay) and the village of Progreso soon put me right about the existence of a big lake: but there was a little lake, a 'laguna' on top of El Junco. The lake is small, just 273 m across at its widest point, but the water is 6 m deep and under that is mud. We mapped El Junco, and called its lake by the name of the hill for want of a better name (Fig. 4.2).

The basin of El Junco lake is an explosion crater, technically known as a 'maar'. Explosion craters like this often are blasted on the rims of volcanos. They are quite different from the main crater or 'caldera' which is the collapsed magma chamber of the volcano. They are like shell holes with gently sloping sides and low rims of rubble. El Junco occupies an example of an explosion crater good enough for a text book (Fig. 4.5).

A particular beauty of a crater on top of a hill is that the basin is 'closed'. El Junco has no inlet and no outlet, perhaps being best thought of as like a saucer of water perched on a mound. The only run-off to reach the lake is from the narrow crater rim itself. There are no springs to feed it; no streams to drain it. This means that the water level of the lake must be sensitive to any change in precipitation or evaporation.

If the weather on top of El Junco hill was ever much wetter than now, the crater should fill until water poured over the crater rim. This has happened from time to time since there is a small ditch cut through the rim at the lowest point (Fig. 4.5). Water level has been close to the ditch in recent years so that probably all that is needed for an overflow is heavier than usual rains of the kind that must come when the ITCZ moves further south than usual. But the overflow can never have been very sustained because the ditch is narrow and obviously has never held a considerable stream.

Figure 4.5. Panorama of El Junco Lake from the Crater Rim (1966). Towards the left one of our drilling rafts and a separate rubber boat give a sense of scale. To the left of the raft can be seen the notch cut when the lake overflowed.

If the weather was ever much drier, water in El Junco crater should dry completely. Indeed, any permanent lake in such a place is unexpected, and a permanent lake dependent entirely on direct precipitation, without any feeding stream from a distant catchment, is positively startling. The sediments do show that the lake has dried in the past, but not for the last 10,000 years.

There are nearly 16 m of sediment in El Junco, but most of it was collected in dry times (Colinvaux, 1972). Fig. 4.6 shows the pattern. About 3 m of organic gyttja, typical brown lake mud, overlies a large mass of red clay. An array of radiocarbon dates shows that the organic mud spans the last 10,000 years, and the red clay must have been put down before that. 10,000 B.P. is the age now generally accepted for the end of the last ice age in the north, so the sediment profile of El Junco looks like a response to global changes in climate associated with an ice age.

The organic mud is nicely banded and laminated, and without any significant mineral layers. This makes it certain that the mud was all dropped under water so that there has been a lake in the crater for all of the last 10,000 years. But there are some regions of blacker mud, particularly between 2 and 3 m in the sediment cores that look like mud found today in the shallows, close to the reed beds that ring the lake. No such black mud lies today under the 6 m of water of the open lake. This suggests that there was a long period, from about 6000 to 3000 B.P. when the lake was much shallower than now, although it certainly persisted.

But the underlying red clay can only mean that the crater was without water before 10,000 B.P. We examined the red clays by X-ray diffraction and by thin section to identify their minerals and structure (Colinvaux, 1972). They are amorphous clay with concretions of gibbsite and haematite, a mineral composition that makes it certain that they did not form under water. But the thin sections do show flow lines that suggest movement by water. These two kinds of evidence show clearly how the clays got there: they were weathered under air round the crater rim and washed down to the crater floor by showers that might be very rare. It is a desert that knows rain only very rarely of which the red clay speaks.

The red clay has no organic matter in it at all, no fossils for reconstructing the past and no carbon to be used for radio-carbon dating. From looking at the clay itself all one could say was that it was deposited in a dry time of unknown duration. But this vague statement could be greatly strengthened when we found earlier organic deposits buried deep within the clay (Fig. 4.6).

This deeply buried organic matter is lake gyttja like that of the last 10,000 years, though more compressed. It is nicely laminated, clearly undisturbed. It marks a time when the crater held a lake quite like the present. And it was deposited at a time so remote as to be beyond the reach of radiocarbon dating: the actual determination said more than 48,000 B.P.

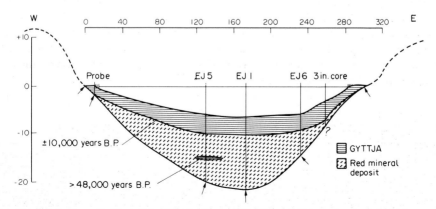

Figure 4.6. Cross Section of the El Junco Basin. EJ5, EJ1, and EJ6 are the sites of the three borings that penetrate to the rock basin. Arrows are points at which the basin is believed to have been identified. Vertical exaggeration is 3:1. All measurements are in meters.

The El Junco sediments show, therefore, that twice El Junco has held a lake and twice it has been without water. Each of these episodes seems to have been prolonged. They can have been caused only by the existence of different climatic regimens.

There is more than a suggestion of ice-age events in the timing and scale of these changes. For all of postglacial time, the last 10,000 years, El Junco held a lake. Throughout the time of the last glacial maximum about 20,000 B.P. the crater held no water. It looks as if a lake in El Junco is a nonglacial or interglacial event, and that a dry basin is an ice-age condition. This suggests that the older lake mud records the time of the last major nonglacial time, which is certainly consistent with the radiocarbon stipulation that it is old. The bottom red clay then is an earlier glaciation still.

Dating the El Junco deposits, therefore, suggests that there has been major climatic change on the Galápagos in synchrony with the coming and going of glaciers far away in the north. In general terms the Galápagos were drier in ice-age times than in inter-glacials like the present. The next stage is to try to understand what this general picture actually meant for the weather of the Galápagos in the past.

4.5. Possible Ice-Age Climates of the Galápagos

Perhaps the first thing to be said is that El Junco sediments yield the only direct evidence of Galápagos climates of the ice age that we possess. Perhaps they will prove to be the only record from the islands themselves that we will ever possess. Conserve, therefore, El Junco. Let no one drain it or dig out its mud for we will certainly want to look at it again.

There will be records from both the deep sea and from the South American mainland that will help with understanding past Galápagos climates, and some of us are working on these possibilities. There are already data from deep sea cores in the central Pacific, but none decisive for reading the Galápagos past. For the moment we must reconstruct that past from the El Junco record alone, knowing full well the dangers of but a single source.

Yet, there is one additional clue in the El Junco mud which encourages our extrapolation from the one lake to the whole archipelago. This is the record of spores of water ferns of the genus *Azolla*. Modern El Junco has *Azolla* growing round the edges in the shallows. The plants look like duck-weed, a little pinkish in color and with frilly edges to the leaves. El Junco mud is richly supplied with the dead ghosts of their spores, particularly of the structures called massulae which can be identified to species. So diagnostic are these massulae that the best way to identify a population of *Azolla* to species is with massula structure. We find massulae of *Azolla filiculoides* Lam. in every sample of the surface mud spanning the last 10,000 years, and this is the only *Azolla* species in the postglacial mud.

There are, of course, no *Azolla* massulae in the red clay of the great drought, but there are some in the mud of that ancient lake which we suspect of being of interglacial age. These massulae, however, are of another species, *Azolla microphylla* Kaulf (Schofield and Colinvaux, 1969). *A. microphylla* is unknown from the modern Galápagos where all collections are of *A. filiculoides*.

Once an ancient lake in El Junco held a population of *A. microphylla*, but the lake dried up and the population was extinguished. A long time later, probably more than 30,000 years later, El Junco again held a lake and it was recolonized by *Azolla*, but of another species. If during those 30,000 years there were ponds on the Galápagos where *Azolla* could live we would expect *A. microphylla* to have persisted and so be handy for the recolonization of El Junco. But when the modern lake filled a different *Azolla*, *A. filiculoides*, had to be brought from the mainland more than a 1000 km away. Presumably *A. microphylla* was extinct on the Galápagos by then.

The *Azolla* story, therefore, strongly suggests that the drought which dried El Junco dried all the lesser ponds of the archipelago as well, giving confidence that El Junco was responding to climatic change affecting the whole Galápagos region.

The problem, then, is to define a Galápagos climate that will deny standing water to the El Junco crater. A first step must be to understand something of the water budget of the modern lake. And alas we have no measurements. I did once try for funds to establish instruments on El Junco to measure the water budget throughout the year, but failed to find the money. Meanwhile we can make reasonable statements about what the main items in that water budget must be.

Water inputs are of two kinds; fog drip and drizzle from the stratus clouds throughout the year and the annual, and very variable, rains. The only output of importance appears to be evaporation, though there may be some trivial seepage through the rim. If the lake surface was continually exposed to the equatorial sun, it seems reasonable to suppose that the lake should quickly dry. This is what happens to all other basins on the islands that fill in the March rains. We must suppose that El Junco lake is spared this fate because almost permanent clouds protect it from the sun.

I once spent a week camped on the rim of El Junco, and there was only one day in which the clouds lifted enough to let me see the surrounding land well enough to make a sketch map (Fig. 4.2). There really is a lid of clouds protecting the lake from being dried by evaporation. The sediment record suggests that that lid has been intact these last 10,000 years, a most prolonged monotony of fog.

Without measurements it is hard to assess the input to the lake by condensation of cloud and the light drizzle that falls from it. It does not, however, seem likely that this can do much more than offset evaporation, and there must be a suspicion that the real rains of the January to April period are needed to fill the lake.

The best model budget for the modern lake, then, shows water being contributed annually with the rains brought when the ITCZ comes south and that this water is prevented from drying up during the rest of the year by the stratus cloud cover. This gives us two ways in which a change of climate could dry the lake: the annual rains could fail or the stratus cloud cover could be removed: or, of course, both.

It is tempting to imagine the stratus cloud removed in ice-age time as a result of the world-wide change of sea level (the so-called eustatic fall in sea level). Sea level was roughly 100 m lower than now during glaciations, entirely to provide the great mass of water locked up in the world ice sheets. I like to say that an ice age is a time when they take 100 m out of the world oceans, make a giant ice cube from it, and store the ice cube on the land. The sea is shallower, and places remote from the ice like the Galápagos Islands gain in altitude a matter of 300 ft. The effect on El Junco was to raise the lake surface 100 m higher into the clouds. This is not, however, enough to thrust the lake into the clear air above the cloud layer. It would take a relative raise of several 100 m to do this.

If we want to remove the clouds then we must look to climatic change that stripped the stratus from the Galápagos entirely, and not just play with the relative height of El Junco. But the stratus is associated with the whole peculiar climatic pattern that makes the Galápagos a desert in the first place. Since El Junco sediments say that the islands were even more desert in ice-age time, it seems necessary to leave the desert mechanism intact, requiring that some stratus cloud was always there.

We can call upon other circumstantial evidence for the permanence of stratus cover, right through the ice age and beyond, in the existence of endemic Galápagos plants that require moist clouds. Most notable of these is the Galápagos tree-fern, *Cyathea weatherbiana*. Not only is it reasonable that this plant must have been in the Galápagos for longer than the last 10,000 years but the El Junco sediments give direct evidence that this was so because we find *Cyathea* spores in the ancient buried organic matter deposited more than 48,000 years ago. This endemic plant must have survived the ice age on the Galápagos and it requires a moist, foggy environment. This, then, is direct evidence that the stratus clouds persisted, at least at some intensity.

Another approach to the problem is to ask what sediments should be present in El Junco if the stratus cloud system was removed but the ITCZ rains were allowed to recur every year at roughly their present intensity. The pattern then should be that the crater would hold a lake for part of each year; every April there should be water in the basin, but this should then progressively dry. Next January the lake would fill once more. Every year a lake would persist for part of the year, often for more than 4 months, before drying out. But if this happened, there would be clear traces in the sediments, almost certainly taking the form of banded deposits, possibly even denying the red clay any chance to form at all. The El Junco mud denies that there was an ephemeral lake in the crater in ice-age time: it says there was no lake at all.

The El Junco record thus brings us to the position where we know two things about the ice-age climate with some certainty. Firstly the characteristic Galápagos desert climate which now prevails for most of the year prevailed in ice-age time too. The ice-age islands knew the *garúa* just as now, and the larger volcanoes poked their summits into a sheet of stratus cloud.

The second property of the ice-age climate was that there was not enough precipitation to fill basins with water, in spite of the cloud drizzle. It seems almost inescapable from this that there were few of the heavier rains of the January to April period in the ice age.

I have argued (Colinvaux, 1972) that the most parsimonious way of arranging the necessary climate on the Galápagos is to deny the ITCZ its annual pilgrimage south so that the rainy season never came to the Galápagos in those days. This, however, is hard to allow from what we know of the pressure systems correlated with the annual march of ITCZ.

Obviously the position of the convergence at any time results as a tension between conflicting forces, some pushing north, some pushing south. Among these forces are the steepness of the pressure gradients on either side. There are modern data to show that the passage of the ITCZ in any one year depends, for instance, on the steepness of pressure gradients in the northern hemisphere.

Newall (1973) has argued that pressure gradients in the northern hemisphere during an ice age should have been so steep that the ITCZ cannot have remained north of the Galápagos as I suggested. A direct effect of the ice sheets themselves would be to squeeze the weather systems of the north into a narrower band of latitude. Circulation driven from the heat engine of the doldrums (the Hadley cell circulation) should have been more intense and there would be a powerful push to drive the climatic equator to the south. There were no offsetting pressures from the southern hemisphere, because there were no extra ice sheets there. The result should be that the ITCZ in ice-age times would have been south of its present position. It could not have remained in its more northerly setting year-round as I proposed.

These two points of view must be resolved without placing the convergence over the Galápagos at any time of the year, for this would have brought rain to the Galápagos on a scale excluded by the El Junco sediments. Perhaps the convergence was less important in the ice-age atmosphere, becoming much less defined as it is in other parts of the modern world (Lamb, 1972). We shall know the truth of this proposition in time from records in mainland South America and from the deep sea, and we are looking for them.

One thing seems certain: the dry ice-age climate of the Galápagos cannot be arranged by appealing to minor changes in winds or temperature of the oceans. Certainly these were present, and colder sea, more intense upwelling along the Peruvian coast, a stronger inversion, and even more stable trade winds would deepen the prevailing desert conditions on the Galápagos as some have argued (Houvenaghel, 1973; Simpson, 1974). But the El Junco data suggest that something more was required, probably a displacement or dissolution of the Intertropical Convergence Zone.

4.6. Implications of Ice-Age Climate for Life on the Galápagos

For the best known animals and plants of the Galápagos, the ones tourists see on the desert coasts, the weather of the ice age would have been much like present weather most of the time: sun and *garúa* chasing each other through the day. But the plants would have had to go without the January to April rains. Perhaps there were fewer *Bursera graveolens* groves then, and more stands of cactus. For the plants able to cope with even less rain than they get now, the islands would actually have allowed larger populations—because the space covered by desert was bigger. The new land drained by the falling sea would be desert land. In the ice age, therefore, cactus-dominated deserts may have spread over a larger real estate than their modern counterparts.

The fauna of the coast probably lived at least as well as now, possibly better. All would depend on the amount of upwelling, and this might be hard to predict. We know that there was more upwelling far away along the Peru coasts and elsewhere, from the record of phosphate deposits on the guano islands (Hutchinson, 1950), but this does not tell us the nutrient supplies to Galápagos waters. As we pointed out earlier, it is essential to free one's mind from the idea that the Galápagos ocean is part of the Humboldt current, or that it should take its fertility from Peru. What we really need to know to assess the sea food of the old Galápagos is the history of the western upwellings that feed the penguins and flightless cormorants now. Unfortunately we do not yet have a clear model of present causes, let alone the pattern of the past.

There were places in the ice-age highlands where fog-drip let moisture-loving plants persist in hollows. But is likely that there was less forest in the wetter uplands than now. What there was managed without a rainy season. And the highlands of the highest mountains in an ice age may have been very dry indeed; red deserts colored like the clay of El Junco rather than the tundra-like landscape we see today.

But these changes were ones with which most of the present Galápagos plants and animals could cope. If any used the rainy season as an environmental cue, perhaps for reproduction, they might have fared ill. Actual dependence on the annual rains for resources also would have been fatal, but very few Galápagos plants or animals probably are so dependent. The exceptions are the true moisture loving plants like the water fern *Azolla* for which the coming of the ice age spelt local extinction.

References

Boersma, P.D. (1974) The Galápagos Penguin: A Study of Adaptations for Life in an Unpredictable Environment. Ph.D. Thesis, The Ohio State University.

Boersma, P.D. (1977) An Ecological and Behavioral Study of the Galápagos Penguin. *The Living Bird*, **15**, 43–93. Cornell Laboratory of Ornithology.

Colinvaux, P.A. (1968) Reconnaissance and Chemistry of the Lakes and Bogs of the Galápagos Islands. *Nature*, **219**, 590–594.

Colinvaux, P.A. (1972) Climate and the Galápagos Islands. *Nature*, **240**, 17–20.

Colinvaux, P.A. (1978) *Why Big Fierce Animals Are Rare*. Princeton University Press, Princeton, N. J.

Goodman, D. (1972) Tower Island Bird Colony. Ph.D. Thesis, The Ohio State University.

Houvenaghel, G.T. (1974) Equatorial Undercurrent and Climate in the Galápagos Islands. *Nature*, **250**, 565–566.

Hutchinson, G.E. (1950) Survey of Existing Knowledge of Biogeochemistry. 3. The Biogeochemistry of Vertebrate Excretion. *Bull. Amer. Mus. Natur. Hist.*, **96**, 554 p. + plates 1–16.

Lamb, H.H. (1972) *Climate: Present, Past and Future*. Methuen and Co. Ltd. London.

Maxwell, D.C. (1974) Marine Primary Productivity of the Galápagos Archipelago. Ph.D. Thesis, The Ohio State University.

Newell, R.E. (1973) Climate and the Galápagos Islands. *Nature*, **245**, 91–92.

Palmer, C.E. and R. L. Pyle (1966) The Climatological Setting of the Galápagos. In: *The Galápagos*. R.I. Bowman, Ed. 93–99.

Quinn, W.H. (1971) Late Quaternary Meteorological and Oceanographic Developments in the Equatorial Pacific. *Nature*, **229**, 330–331.

Schofield, E.K. and P.A. Colinvaux (1969) Fossil *Azolla* from the Galápagos Islands. *Bull. Torrey Bot. Club*, **96**, 623–628.

Simpson, B.B. (1975) Glacial Climates in the Eastern Tropical South Pacific. *Nature*, **253**, 34–36.

CHAPTER 5

Lichens and Bryophytes

W.A. WEBER★ AND S.R. GRADSTEIN†

★University of Colorado Museum, University of Colorado, Boulder, Colorado, USA; †Botanical Museum and Herbarium, University of Utrecht, Utrecht, Netherlands

Contents

5.1. Introduction 71
5.2. Lichens 72
5.3. Bryophytes 76
5.4. Epilogue 83
References 84

5.1. Introduction

Compared to other biogeographers, a botanist is at a distinct disadvantage when he tries to speak to laymen about his subject. Animal geographers have easily visualized groups—lions, giraffes, elephants, tapirs, tortoises, penguins and albatrosses—that most people have known about since they started reading children's books. These animals also tend to have, within their clans, similar ways of life. Plants, however, with the exceptions of such groups as oaks, willows and elms, are not readily visualized by most people, and natural selection does not work on them so conspicuously at the genus level but at the lowest taxonomic level—the species or below. In other words, with a few notable exceptions, one cannot get a grasp of a genus of plants by general aspect and way of life. A genus of flowering plants may in extreme instances have an aquatic species, a woody species, a shrubby and an herbaceous one. One cannot hope to approach the subject of plant geography without a very intimate knowledge of a lot of families, genera and species. Even the Galápagos genus *Scalesia* violates our traditional sense of the genus by including trees and shrubs, and leaves with dissected as well as simple leaves (Chapter 6, Fig. 3).

Among cryptogamic plants (mosses, lichens, ferns, fungi and algae) the situation is complicated further by the fact that the differences important in taxonomy are usually microscopic. While one can learn to recognize some of the well-marked species in these groups by having them shown to him, to gain a real knowledge of these groups is a long, painful, frustrating and unending process. Even most botanists who develop a serious and successful acquaintance with the flowering plants never dabble with the crytogams.

Because of space limitations, we are unable to give the reader an elementary introduction to the two major groups of cryptogams dealt with here: bryophytes—including mosses, leafy liverworts and thallose liverworts, and lichens—symbiotic combinations of ascomycetous or basidiomycetous fungi with various genera of green and blue-green algae. There are good primers available elsewhere. We will assume that the reader has a general knowledge. Some arguments, however, which do not require much professional knowledge will be developed that are relevant to the general problem of transport, colonization, reproduction and evolution—questions that are seldom addressed in elementary texts. In the following discussion, the lichen and moss material is presented by Weber, and the liverwort material by Gradstein.

5.2. Lichens

Before 1964 (the date of the Galápagos International Scientific Project, GISP), bryophytes and lichens on the Galápagos were known intimately only to the birds, who use them for nest-building, and to Ecuadorian prisoners, who presumably were employed to collect one species of lichen—*Roccella babingtonii*—for the orchil dye factories on the mainland. Botanists generally concentrated on flowering plants, and casually collected only the odd lichen or moss that was conspicuous. When I was invited to join the GISP expedition I vainly searched through Beebe and other authors looking for descriptions of the cryptogamic vegetation or for evidence of these plants in their photographs. Only a suggestion of lichens appeared in a color spread in *Life Magazine* showing a land iguana stretched out on a leaning trunk of mangrove!

Nevertheless, some botanists did realize that lichens constituted a significant part of the Galápagos flora. Svenson (1935) was so impressed with the lichen flora that he singled out the lichens as being in great need of study on the islands, pointing out that the 'orchilla moss' once used in dyes, 'represented the only vegetable product of the Islands that was of any commercial value'. Farlow wrote (1902): 'Judged by the collections of previous expeditions as well as those of Messrs. Snodgrass and Heller, the lichen flora must be striking in appearance and abundant. Naturally the collections include principally the larger and more showy species of foliose and fruticulose habit, which are in most cases identical with species found along the Pacific Coast of America from California to Chile.' Svenson (1935), describing Genovesa Island, wrote: 'The trees . . . have swollen and twisted branches cluttered with white coralliform lichens.' Howell (1942) on Santa Cruz Island, wrote: 'On steep wet slopes . . . a peculiar fluffy lichen (*Dictyonema*) produces queer mounds of grayish-white.' And Stewart (1912) related: 'When one lands for the first time on almost any of the islands, one is immediately struck with the great abundance of lichens. This is true not only of the larger and higher islands, which reach sufficient elevation to receive a considerable amount of moisture from the fogbanks which strike their sides . . . but it is true also . . . of the lower islands . . . where desert or semi-desert conditions prevail.'

Nevertheless, the Galápagos was not officially visited by a professional lichenologist until 1964, and all that was known about the lichens was based on examination of herbarium specimens collected by non-lichenologists. My shipboard symposium contribution (Weber, 1966) on the state of the art was very simple and brief.

When we landed at Academy Bay, I had no idea what to expect; I supposed that I probably would have to range far and wide to find suitable localities. My first assignment on shore was to watch the baggage against thievery—a silly precaution—and when I was relieved I decided to take a short walk back into the cactus forest. I was absolutely stunned! Every rock and tree, even many cactus pads were completely covered with white, yellow, red, brown and gray lichens. How anyone could have avoided getting them exposed on film is still a mystery to me. I remember sitting down on a lava boulder and bursting into tears. How, in 6 weeks, could I ever 'get on top' of this amazing array of lichen species? My enthusiasm must have been obvious, because Bob Usinger later wrote (1972), in his autobiography, '[Dr. Weber] came in from his first day of field work like a small boy from a candy shop.'

A few days later on my first walk up to the highlands of Santa Cruz, I was just as overwhelmed by the luxuriance and variety of mosses and liverworts that hung in great curtains over the fences, covered the cultivated citrus with masses of soaking vegetation, and formed great velvet coverings over the upper branches of the native trees. Even the packed wet soil of trails becomes carpeted, in wet season, by the flat green ribbons of thallose liverworts.

Sailing around the islands, one can hardly lose sight of the lichen-covered lava rocks gaudily splashed, as if painted, with white and yellow crustose lichens. In fact, I have not seen such an abundance of conspicuous lichens anywhere else except on the coast of Chile and southern California. The seacoast is the first point that a visitor sees, so this should be a good place to begin our introduction to Galápagos lichens and bryophytes.

The growth forms of lichens—fruticose (shrub-like), foliose (leaf-life) and crustose (crust-like) are only broad categories bridged by intermediate types, and they do not always coincide with the limits of the genus. To get a quick introduction to the variety of lichens the best place might be South Plaza Island, a place visited by everyone. The boulders found along the crest just above the landing are representative of coastal outcrops all over the archipelago, and of the species' geographical affinities. The white crust dominating the rocks is mostly *Arthothelium galapagosensis* (endemic), most closely related to a Chilean species. The yellow crust is *Lecanora pseudopinguis* (endemic), related to a Southern Californian type. Orange crusts belong to *Caloplaca isidiosa*, known from the coast of Brazil and Chile. A brown-tan species with black fruits is *Buellia galapagona* (endemic) related to species in Chile.

Among the fruticose lichens, the most distinctive is a chalky-white one with gnarled wormlike branches. This is *Roccella galapagoensis* (endemic), related to the Chilean *R. portentosa*. This *Roccella* does not produce the chemical compound producing the royal purple dye, but another species abundant on the shrubs of the thickets at the top of the island is the classic orchilla lichen, *Roccella babingtonii*, found from California to Chile. A number of green cylindric or flattened fruticose lichens cover the rocks and bushes. These are *Ramalina*. One usually does not think of lichen populations as being dynamic, but they have their 'highs' and their 'crashes'. In 1964 I collected as many as 9 species of *Ramalina* in great abundance on the shrubs along the path between the Darwin Station and Puerta Ayora. On three subsequent visits I never found more than a very few plants. Evidently these species are relatively short-lived, and disintegrate quickly when over-mature, new colonies being established only as a result of some special combination of climatic conditions, probably involving the establishment of standing water in the cracks of the bark.

This short excursion demonstrates two fundamental questions about Galápagos lichens. The lichens of the shore rocks are, to a great extent, endemic to Galápagos, and are closely related to counterparts on the Chilean, or on the southern Californian coast. What climatic characteristics are common to these areas? How did the lichens arrive here, and how long have they been isolated? That all of these areas are foggy coasts is obvious, and the entire family of Roccellaceae is evidently restricted to such places. Lichens reproduce by various methods of propagation by accidentally or deliberately fragmenting, the alga and the fungus being carried together by some agency. The agency is not likely water, nor very likely wind currents, but in my opinion probably the feathers of birds. Propagula most likely are picked up through contact with the rock, and deposited by preening, moult, or death. We know virtually nothing about speciation or evolution in lichens (this involves coevolution of the symbionts), but the taxonomic picture suggests that it is an exceedingly slow process, since we see little present-day evidence of lichens evolving except at a chemical level. Is our current estimate of the age of the Galápagos realistic in terms of the time needed for lichen speciation? I think not, but here geologic and botanical evidence, as in the case of continental drift and plate tectonics, may eventually be reconciled.

Crustose lichens are extremely abundant and diversified on the trunks of trees throughout the dry zones. The stems of mangroves above high tide level display mosaics of different colors of which probably the most striking are the brilliant deep orange-red crusts of *Pyrenula cerina* and the more clear yellow *Anthracothecium ochraceoflavum*. The ghostly white trunks of the *palo santo* trees, *Bursera graveolens*, owe a great deal of their pallor to extensive colonies of white or grey crustose lichens. While the dense shrubbery of the littoral zone probably gets enough moisture to support the fruticose *Ramalina* and *Roccella* species, the cactus zone and the arid *Bursera* woodland seldom display, except for the odd *Acacia* whose bark may be especially adapted to hold moisture, many fruticose lichens, an occasional *Usnea* or the striking orange bushy *Teloschistes flavicans*.

Thalli of *Roccella babingtonii*, however, are sometimes so abundant on *Acacia* as to break moribund branches with their weight and their limp thalli lie in heaps upon the ground.

It is obvious that even the crustose lichens, colonizing as they do the harshest surfaces of lava blocks, are limited by intense drought and the strong impact of the sun's heat, to those faces of rock that are not directly exposed throughout the day. The most magnificent displays of lichens are to be found on vertical faces of the same rocks whose horizontal surfaces are barren. This of course is also true for the mosses. Mosses are usually quite lacking in the hottest, driest sites, but in the cactus forest and the transition zones, a few mosses begin to show up on vertical surfaces of rocks on talus slopes of the *barrancas*, in deep pits in the lava rock, and on heaps of lava where they enjoy the relatively greater protection afforded by vertical surfaces and crevices.

In the Transition Zone (50–200 m altitude), where the influence of the *garúa* produces for long periods of time a perpetual fog and drip, cactus trees begin to give way to a number of tropical hardwoods, and the tree growth is spindly. Here the fruticose lichen returns again in force, represented by the long pendent yellowish-green *Ramalina usnea*. The Transition Zone marks the beginning of tension between the aridity-adapted crustose lichens which rely on water vapor in the air, and the mosses and liverworts, which depend more on liquid water in their environment.

Figure 5.1. *Parmelia* sp. (Lichenes) and *Marchesinia brachiata* (Hepaticae), Transition Zone woodland, Santa Cruz. (Photograph by S.R. Gradstein).

In the Moist (subtropical forest) Zone that replaces the Transition Zone upwards (Fig. 5.2), bryophytes soon get the upper hand and cover the surfaces of trees and rocks ordinarily inhabited by lichens. Only certain large foliose lichens (*Pseudocyphellaria*, *Sticta*, and *Leptogium* species), erect-foliose types (*Everniastrum* and *Ramalina*) and erect ground lichens (*Cladonia*) compete effectively with the bryophytes.

The grassy tundra-like summit highlands support some curious lichens that recall far-distant places. Three species of reindeer lichens—yellow or white *Cladina* species, occur here, not covering the ground as they do in the arctic taiga, but as large round balls that by chance involvement with twigs of shrublets are prevented from rolling. These represent an Andean element. The essentially Australasian and South American *Cladia aggregata* forms similar red-brown balls.

Rocky tors of the summit highlands again support lichens in quantity on their arid surfaces, especially in the dry inversion zone on some of the highest peaks. Here two species of *Stereocaulon* occur, one of which, a new species, has its closest relative (*S. wrightii*) in the Arctic regions in the vicinity of Bering Strait.

Figure 5.2. Inside moss-covered woodland of *Scalesia pedunculata* on the north of Santa Cruz, at an altitude of about 650 m; the liverwort, *Bryopteris liebmanniana*, appears on the lower portion of the trunk in the foreground. (Photograph by S.R. Gradstein) See also Chapter 7, Figs. 1 and 4.

The identification of the species in the Galápagos lichen flora has been a very slow process because of the fact that on the western part of the South American mainland, lichenology is still without resident practitioners, and because lichen taxonomy in the tropics generally desperately needs generic monographers. Therefore, phytogeographical observations are preliminary and tentative. A few general and specific ones may safely be made. First, that the crustose lichens of the coastal rocks are mostly endemic and directly related to the assemblages of the Chilean mainland. The crustose lichens of the trees are probably in most instances widespread or widely disjunct species that have already been described but for the most part remain undetermined because of the lack of literary synthesis of subtropical and tropical lichen floras.

The following example dramatically illustrates our difficulty. A curious crustose lichen belonging to the very small family Cypheliaceae forms massive sheets on trees in the cactus forest and lower Transition Zone on Santa Cruz. It is characterized by having distinctive raised oblong fruiting structures. This lichen, *Schistophoron tenue*, belongs to a well-defined monotypic genus. If it has ever been collected on mainland South America it is not likely to have remained hidden among masses of unnamed lichens in herbaria. The unusual thing about *Schistophoron* is its distribution. Until its discovery on Galápagos, it was known only from three localities on the coast of West Africa! Most Galápagos lichens are not as clearly-marked or well-known, and they probably belong to species already described, but from widely-scattered areas of the world tropics. The resources required to identify them at the present time are clearly out of reach of anyone but a monographer.

Andean elements are few, but when they are present, as the *Cladina* species, and a number of species belonging to the parmelioid foliose lichens, they occur on the higher parts of the islands. The phytogeographic relationships of Galápagos lichens are, then, primarily with coastal Chile (as to the endemic coastal crustose types) and the subtropical and tropical forests of South America (bark lichens). While transport of the coastal rock lichens may be aided by birds, the bark lichens may be transported as fragments on bits of bark; many species are well-provided with soredia which are light enough to travel in the upper air.

In lichens (and bryophytes) there is no segregation of species between islands, no island endemism. I feel confident in stating that the same lichens will occur on any island that provides the proper habitat. Furthermore, in contrast to the situation in higher plants, racial differentiation between islands does not occur.

The occurrence of lichen colonies on the carapaces of Galápagos land tortoises (Hendrickson and Weber, 1964) captures the public imagination in much the same way as lichens did when, as alleged primitive plants—speculation arising through ignorance of biology—they were thought to be likely inhabitants of the planet Mars. Lichens are not primitive. They have arisen through an extremely slow and long process of coevolution involving the double sieve of natural selection requiring mutations of one host—the fungus—to be acceptable to the other host—the alga. Before lichens could arise, the evolution of special groups of fungi and algae had to be well-elaborated. The symbiosis between alga and fungus probably arose accidentally, involving first the epiphytism of algal scums on the surfaces of saprophytic fungi. The incorporation of the alga in a layer underneath the surface of the fungus, and replacement of the saprophytic fungal way of life by a parasitic one, in which the fungus destroyed some algal cells while affording others a stable microhabitat, probably originated independently in many unrelated lines of fungi and algae.

There is no special symbiotic significance in the occurrence of lichens on tortoise shells. The few species of lichens that have been found belong to the most common species of lichens. The thalli very rarely are well-enough developed to bear fruit and in many instances, therefore, certain identification is impossible. The tortoise carapace is simply another substrate, one likely to last for a long time and one not likely to be colonized by competitive bryophytes or vascular plants.

The habits of the tortoise restrict the geography of lichen thalli on the carapace. Tortoises habitually spend much of their time crashing through dense underbrush, so lichens cannot easily survive on the front, top, and sides of the carapace where abrasion is most likely to occur. Tortoises spend much of their time lying partly submerged in pools; lichens cannot survive prolonged immersion. The tortoise-lichens, therefore, commonly occur in a limited area on the upper rear of the carapace. This observation evoked a bit of doggerel for which I may hope to be excused:

> 'We who cannot grow lichens athwart us
> Should consider the case of the tortoise
> Who though scratched front and side
> Still has lichens that ride
> On his rump, in a crescent, of sort-is!

5.3. Bryophytes

Bryophytes are not as rare on the Galápagos as one might think. They are almost completely absent along the coastlines and on the desert islands where extremes of temperature and insolation are great and where water rarely falls as rain or accumulates on tree bark, in puddles or ponds. On the islands that attain heights of 400 m or more, however, relatively constant mesic conditions made possible by mist, drizzle, cloud cover, saturated air and occasional heavy rains, provide a variety of protective microhabitats for the flourishing of mosses and liverworts. To walk along fog-drenched trails through the upper moist zones is an eery experience, for the tree branches have become velvet ropes covered by massive colonies of reddish-brown liverworts which provide moist protective sheaths for the bases of other epiphytes such as mistletoe, ferns and orchids—all together giving a fairytale effect, lovely or frightening depending on one's preconditioning.

While our statistics on lichens were very premature because of the identification problem, the bryophytes on the other hand, are now well enough known to permit more solid analysis. What follows is a gleaning of some of the general and specific conclusions which was recently published in the full elaboration of bryogeography of the Galápagos (Gradstein and Weber, 1982).

As might be expected, species richness is highest in the evergreen zones with an optimum in the mossy upper woodlands and scrub (67 spp. of liverworts and 66 spp. of mosses). Many bryophytes of the summit pampa could also be added, since a large part of this grass-sedge-fern area is considered to be a formerly forested fire disclimax. The mossy woodland zone was previously called 'Brown Zone' because of the luxuriant brownish epiphyte vegetation, dominated by pendulous *Frullania* spp. (Figs 5.3 and 5.4) of the Sect. Meteoriopsis which grow in extensive mats or balls, as well as pendulous mosses of the genus *Squamidium*. Lejeuneaceae, which account for over a third of the total liverwort flora, are particularly well represented here.

Figure 5.3. *Frullania brasiliensis* (Hepaticae) in evergreen woodland; this is one of the commonest bryophytes of the islands. (Photograph by H.J. Sipman).

Thallose liverworts (Metzgeriales, Marchantiales and Anthocerotae) are well-represented on Galápagos (20% of the liverwort flora), which, for Marchantiales, seems to reflect the relatively dry climate. Thallose species are usually terrestrial, and in contrast to the foliose Jungermanniales, inhabit mainly the open, non-wooded regions. Most of them occur on saturated, packed bare soil in the pampa, but some species of *Riccia*, for example, the endemic, bluish *R. howellii*, inhabit the otherwise bryophytically poor Arid Lowland Zone.

Bryophytes are practically absent on the very hot and dry rocky coastal lowland. Only where rocks present prominent vertical surfaces to the moist trade winds and provide some protection from the sun (for example, the steep *barranco* on Santa Cruz a few hundred yards from the sea) do small colonies of *Campylopus galapagensis*, *Erpodium domingense*, and *Fissidens* share such sites with xerophytic ferns. Mosses first appear in some quantity in the Transition Zone on raised lava hummocks, an indication that the horizontal lava pavement still provides too little protection from desiccation. Here the weedy, pantropical xerophytic *Frullania ericoides*, the only foliose liverwort entering the Arid Zone woodland, occurs on rocks and on the trunks of smooth-barked trees. Ground mosses increase with altitude in the Transition Zone, particularly species of Pottiaceae. Soon, leaning tree-trunks are covered, near the ground, with mats of *Groutiella mucronifolia* and appearance of large brownish mats of *Frullania brasiliensis* on the spreading branches of large trees, and the ubiquitous pendant light-green *Zelometeorium patulum* (Fig. 5.5) and *Squamidium caroli* draping themselves over shrubbery, tree branches, and fences.

Figure 5.4. Pendulous mass of *Frullania darwinii* Gradst. (Hepaticae) in Psidium guava woodland, San Cristóbal. (Photograph by S.R. Gradstein).

The moist Evergreen Woodland Zone has already been mentioned as the richest for bryophytes. Because of the destruction of much of the original *Scalesia* forest (itself a rich habitat) and its replacement by extensively introduced exotic trees and cultivars, this zone probably will continue to yield new discoveries of bryophytes, and possibly some of them will have been accidentally imported in modern times with animals, fowl, provisions, shoes and pants-cuffs, just as have so many phanerogams. This area is rich in all forms of cryptogams and has not been sufficiently explored.

The closed evergreen forest more or less abruptly yields, on Santa Cruz at least, to the mossy evergreen scrub (*Miconia* Zone) which, because of its somewhat more open nature and abundance of small exposed twigs, harbors a number of interesting hepatics and ascending mosses, some of these extremely scattered and rare in their occurrence.

Figure 5.5. Garlands of *Zelometeorium patulum* (Musci) in upper Transition Zone woodland, Santa Cruz. (Photograph by S.R. Gradstein).

In the mesic pampa, which on Santa Cruz has been burned (ca. 1935, according to residents) the wet pot-holes, packed ground of trails, seasonal streams, occasional stands of shrubs and barren volcanic cones and plugs provide many rich and diversified habitats for bryophytes, particularly ground species (*Campylopus, Funaria, Ceratodon*), thalloid liverworts (*Marchantia, Riccia, Anthoceros*) and semi-aquatic mosses (*Sphagnum, Isopterygium*). On southern Isabela *Breutelia tomentosa, Entosthodon bonplandii, Herbertus pensilis, Anoectangium aestivum* and *Thuidium recognitum* have their unique stands on the islands in relatively wet pampa where persistent cloud veils may play a part. The very few permanent springs scattered over the islands in various zones support some very 'special' disjunct mosses, which occur practically nowhere else on Galápagos, and often in only one spring on a single island.

On Isabela (and possibly Fernandina), the only islands reaching higher than 1000 m, summit areas display a co-called 'inversion layer' above which rainfall decreases sharply, causing the development of a cool and dry summit zone. The pampa near and above the inversion layer, as on Volcán Cerro Azul, southern Isabela, supports several species otherwise unknown on the islands. Most of them are temperate and of southern origin. On Santa Cruz, where the inversion zone may possibly occur locally on the top of the barren exposed outcropping tors, the cosmopolitan *Polytrichum juniperinum* is the dominant moss.

As to individual species distributions it seems that almost 75% of the liverworts are restricted to a single altitudinal zone whereas only 25% have a wider vertical distribution. The latter category includes, in part, the weedy, ubiquitous species which are seen on most major islands. All of these species produce copious spores and/or asexual propagula (gemmae, cladulae) and thus seem to spread easily. In contrast, about 30 species of liverworts are still known only from a single island. Three causes may be applicable.

1. *Our insufficient exploration of their potential habitats.* For instance, some Arid Zone species are only to be seen after short periods of heavy rain when the porous ash soils are moistened enough to stretch the small, thin thalli. These species are known from single collections and most likely are overlooked for this reason.

2. *Ecological restrictions.* Some species occur in habitats which are rare in Galápagos, such as (a) the borders of the few extant springs (see above), (b) the single *permanent stream* on the island of San Cristóbal, where during our 1976 exploration about 10 species of liverworts new to the Galápagos Islands were discovered, including 4 new genera (Weber et al. 1977); (c) the *vertical Sphagnum-Cyathea bogs* on eroded moist crater edges (Santa Cruz, Cerro Azul on Isabela, Fig. 6) where single species of the high Andean genera such as *Herbertus* and *Bazzania* are found, and (d) the dry, cool *summit pampas above the inversion layer* found only on Isabela, where *Sauteria berteroana* and *Targionia stellaris* occur exclusively.

Figure 5.6. *Sphagnum-Cyathea* bog on eroded, moist crater edge in pampa on the southern slope of Volcán Cerro Azul, altitude 800 m. An area rich in bryophytes, several genera and species occur almost exclusively here: *Herbertus pensilis, Bazzania teretiuscula, Lophocolea trapezoidea, Plagiochila scabrifolia* and *Breutelia tomentosa.* (Photograph by S.R. Gradstein).

A special ecological group are the epiphyllous liverworts, mainly Lejeuneaceae, for which the native Galápagos vegetation hardly provides suitable habitats except for the macrophyllous evergreen leaves of *Miconia robinsoniana*, which forms mossy scrub vegetation on Santa Cruz and San Cristóbal. Since the colonization of the islands by man (about 150 years), cultivated trees and shrubs have been introduced and in some islands have largely eliminated the native vegetation of the moist zones. *Coffea arabica, Psidium guajava, Citrus aurantiaca* and *Eugenia jambos* provide habitats for epiphyllic bryophytes and lichens. Where these

Figure 5.7. *Plagiochasma rupestris* (Hepaticae) on rather dry rock in the summit pampa, Volcán Cerro Azul. (Photograph by S.R. Gradstein).

species have been planted (Santa Cruz, San Cristóbal, Floreana and southern Isabela's Sierra Negra) an epiphyllous vegetation has developed supporting about 10 species of Lejeuneaceae. The poverty of the epiphyllous flora as compared to tropical mainland areas is no doubt due to the poor representation, until recent time, of potential habitats—macrophyllous tropical rain-forest and evergreen cultivars.

3. *Dispersal capacity.* Loss of dispersability is a common phenomenon among island plants and animals. In unisexual bryophytes, plants of one sex may be absent, precluding the chances for dispersal by spores. Looking at the reproductive state of the liverworts on Galápagos, dispersability in general seems excellent: of the total flora about 85% produce spores and/or gemmae and about 40% of the species are bisexual. In comparison, the subantarctic Campbell Island, with an old and much richer liverwort flora (160 spp.) supports only 10% bisexual species and consequently many species there are considered relicts. While the excellent dispersal potential of the Galápagos liverworts argues for a young flora of recent arrival, it may also be significant that the majority of the species known thus far from a single Galápagos locality, albeit not of restricted ecology, are unisexual and only known in sterile condition here.

On the basis of preliminary observations we suggested earlier (Weber, 1966, Weber *et al.*, 1977) that the bryophyte flora of the Galápagos Islands is characterized by low endemism and high percentage of neotropical species, especially among the epiphytes. We are now able to give more precise figures, based on critical examination of over 95% of the collected species. Individual species ranges were taken from the most recent taxonomic revisions or, when lacking, from important floristic works. The following elements are distinguishable.

Endemics. While for seed plants, endemism amounts to about 50% of the indigenous Galápagos flora (Porter, 1979: 436 indigenous taxa of which 223 are endemic), for spore plants this percentage is, not unexpectedly, much lower. Of 108 fern taxa only 8 are considered endemic. In comparison, relatively many endemic taxa are still recognized among Galápagos liverworts (16%) but very few among the mosses (6%). Although most of the endemics have been examined by specialists and have proven distinct from species described from the mainland or other areas, it is nevertheless quite likely that some of them actually occur on the mainland but have yet to be collected there. A more intensive search of the bryophytically still very poorly known countries of Ecuador and Peru is certainly called for.

It is tempting to correlate the relatively higher hepatic endemism in the drier areas with similar findings, but much more suggestive, for vascular plants. According to Porter (1979), 67% of the endemic vascular plants occur in the Arid zone. It is a striking fact that the lichen flora exhibits its endemism almost completely outside the moist woodland areas, with a very high proportion of endemics (species of coastal Chilean relationships) occurring on the exposed rocks of the coast or rarely near or above the inversion zone.

Caribbean. This element comprises that group of Neotropical species found outside Galápagos only on Caribbean islands and adjacent coastal areas of North and Central America and northern South America. They might be considered coastal oceanic-Neotropical species. Their occurrence in Galápagos is usually at somewhat lower altitudes along the gradient, with optimal occurrence in the Transition Zone and the lower evergreen woodland zone. Caribbean liverworts belong mainly to the family Lejeuneaceae, a reflection of the prominent occurrence of the family on the lower tropical islands and coasts. Most of the species have excellent dispersal capacities, by gemmae or caducous leaves, spores or both.

The mosses show an extremely strong Caribbean relationship. The Galápagos moss flora was compared with the published record for Colombia, Puerto Rico and the Virgin Islands, Ecuador, Florida, and Guatemala. Even allowing for the imperfect record of the total Caribbean moss flora, it is very significant that 91% of the Galápagos mosses are found in the Caribbean area, and only 40% are known to occur in Ecuador. Virtually no species certain to have emanated from the Andes occur on the islands.

We do not know when mosses first reached the Galápagos, but it is very likely that most of them came from Central America (a very high correlation exists between Galápagos and Guatemala) or from the Caribbean region. Even today, the arrival of Caribbean taxa may be via the northeastern trade winds prevailing during the warm season. A small Caribbean element is also represented among the vascular plants (Svenson, 1946), and the Darwin finches have a close relative among the Caribbean avifauna (Lack, 1945). Very few of the Caribbean species found on the Galápagos Islands are represented on Cocos Island, which otherwise is located along the supposed migration route. However, this is probably explained by the extremely different highly tropical and extremely rain-drenched closed-forest and tall grass habitats not encountered anywhere on Galápagos.

Andean, Neo-tropical and Wide-tropical. These groups comprise essentially the 'mainland taxa' that, with the prevailing eastern winds, have direct access via aerial transport to the islands and would therefore be expected to be the prevalent groups of bryophytes. Indeed, among liverworts they comprise about 70% of the total flora, the majority of them being Neo-tropical. Andean species are those known thus far only from tropical Andean countries.

Neotropical and wide-tropical species mainly comprise common widespread tropical taxa. Among wide-tropical species are included those that enter oceanic-temperate regions where they are sometimes characterized as Tertiary tropical relics.

The number of wide-tropical taxa is still small as compared to those known only from the neotropics but their number is expected to increase as more serious efforts are undertaken to compare paleotropical with neotropical species.

A small group of 'tropical-montane' species are distinguished (32 liverworts) which, on the mainland, are mainly found above 1000 m in the mountain forests up to the *páramos*. Not surprisingly, these species occur in Galápagos only at the higher elevations and they are mainly restricted to the mossy evergreen woodlands and the pampa. Some of them have only restricted occurrence on the islands, whereas on the continent they are very common at high elevations. The causes may be ecological or lack of effective dispersal means on Galápagos.

Southern. The southern element comprises one moss—*Brachymenium fabronioides* (described from Argentina) and 4 species of Marchantiales which originate from southern subtropical or temperate regions and more or less disjunctly occur on Galápagos. On Galápagos these species were found exclusively at high altitudes on the pampa, two of them (*Sauteria berteroana, Targionia stellaris*) from the cool, dry pampa above the inversion layer on Isabela. Dispersability seems to be enhanced by copious production of spores (*Sauteria, Targionia, Riccia*) and gemmae (*Marchantia*). The occurrence of this element on Galápagos is not surprising; for vascular plants as well there is a relatively high percentage of temperate genera (*Pernettya, Aster, Salvia*) and as to animals there are the penguins and fur seals. As mentioned earlier there is a major element of southern South American coastal lichen genera and species vicariads on the Galápagos.

Cosmopolitan. Single collections have been made of the cosmopolitan *Marchantia polymorpha* and the subcosmopolitan *Anthoceros punctatus* and *Fossombronia pusilla*. They were mainly found in mesic pampa on Isabela. Several cosmopolitan mosses of a weedy nature are frequent: *Bryum argenteum, Ceratodon purpureus, Funaria hygrometrica,* and *Weissia controversa.*

While for vascular plants a vast floristic literature is available, allowing for whole-flora comparisons on a large scale for tropical regions, regional checklists for bryophytes are still severely lacking. In fact, it is only recently that professional bryologists have, in any numbers, begun seriously to collect in these areas on long-term thorough surveys, and the taxonomic problems of correlating disjunct floras are still very difficult. These factors limit the feasibility for a critical comparison of the Galápagos bryophytes with those of other islands or regions. Larsen and Holm-Nielsen's introductory statement at the Aarhus Symposium on Tropical Botany (1979) that tropical [vascular] floras are still poorly known, however true it may be, certainly holds much more for bryophytes than for vascular plants. Notwithstanding these limitations we will attempt to give a comparative characterization of the Galápagos bryophyte flora (for details see Gradstein and Weber, 1982). At least the mosses appear to belong to predominantly well-known species less likely to be overlooked in the field than lejeuneoid hepatics, and the statistics gain reliability overall by this fact.

Taking into account recent liverwort lists for Ecuador (Herzog, 1951, Arnell, 1963) and Colombia (Gradstein and Hekking, 1979) it appears that about two-thirds of the Galápagos liverwort flora occurs on the adjacent mainland. If endemics and disjunct temperate species are not taken into account, this figure rises to over 80%, which shows that the bulk of the liverwort flora, as for vascular plants, was derived from the mainland to the east. A smaller portion supposedly came from the north (Caribbean coastal species) and very few, if any, came from the south (Southern Temperate species). Arrival would have taken place by the prevailing eastern trade winds. As discussed elsewhere in this paper, this is not true of the mosses, an indication that liverwort and moss propagula are not equally efficient.

Biogeographic connections with the western Pacific seem to be almost entirely lacking for all Galápagos plants as well as animals (Thornton [1971] mentions a single example of a Pacific land snail that happens to occur on Galápagos), except of course for the common pantropical species. Mention should be made, however, of *Leptolejeunea elliptica* which, if delimited in a broad sense (Schuster, 1968), is amphi-Pacific with a vicariant subspecies (ssp. *acuta* [Steph.] Schuster) in tropical East Asia and Australasia. This is the only possible case of amphi-Pacific distribution among bryophytes.

5.4. Epilogue

Research on cryptogamic plants remains extremely imperfect so long as it is conducted from a distance and by the means of the occasional visit or brief expedition. While we have visited the islands four times we do not claim to have more than a glimpse of the extent of the flora. Real progress will come when the Galápagos has a full-time resident scientist concerned with these plants, after the science has developed resident scientists on the mainland, and when support of cryptogamic chairs in botanical institutions increases so as to breed the large number of monographers that is needed to make some sense of the vast literature and herbarium heritage of the tropics.

References

Farlow, W.G. (1902) Lichens, p. 83–89. In: B.L. Robinson, Flora of the Galápagos Islands. *Proc. Am. Acad. Arts Sci.*, 38.

Gradstein, S.R. and Hekking, W.H.A. (1979) Studies on Colombian cryptogams, IV. A catalogue of the Hepaticae of Colombia. *J. Hattori Bot. Lab.*, **45**, 93–144.

Gradstein, S.R. and Weber, W.A. (1982) Bryogeography of the Galápagos Islands. *J. Hattori Bot. Lab.*, **52**, 127–152.

Hendrickson, John R. and Weber, William A. (1964) Lichens on Galápagos giant tortoises. *Science*, **144**, 1463.

Herzog, T. (1942) Die foliosen Lebermoose der Juan Fernandez-Inseln und der Oster Insel. In *The Natural History of Juan Fernández and Easter Island*. Edited by C.S. Skottsberg. Vol. II, pages 699–752. Almquist & Wiksell, Uppsala.

Howell, J.T. (1942) Up under the Equator. *Sierra Club Bull.*, **1942**, 79–82.

Lack, David (1945) *The Galápagos finches (Geospizinae). A study in variation.* Occ. Pap. Calif. Acad. Sci., **21**, vii + 1–151, pl. 1–4.

Larson, K., and Holm-Nielsen, L.B. (1979) *Tropical Botany*, Academic Press.

Porter, Duncan M. (1979) Endemism and evolution in Galápagos Islands vascular plants. In *Plants and Islands*, edited by D. Bramwell. Pages 225–258. Academic Press.

Stewart, A. (1912) Notes on the lichens of the Galápagos Islands. *Proc. Calif. Acad. Sci.*, (4) **1**, 431–446.

Svenson, H.K. (1935) Plants of the Astor Expedition, 1930 (Galápagos and Cocos Islands). *Am. J. Bot.*, **22**, 208–227.

Svenson, H.K. (1946) Vegetation of the coast of Ecuador and its relation to the Galápagos Islands. *Am. J. Bot.*, **33**, 394–498.

Thornton, Ian (1971) *Darwin's Islands; a natural history of the Galápagos.* Natural History Press, Garden City.

Usinger, Robert Leslie (1972) *Autobiography of an entomologist.* Calif. Acad. Sci., San Francisco.

Weber, William A. (1964) Lichenology and bryology in the Galápagos Islands, with check lists of the lichens and bryophytes thus far reported. Chapter 25 in *The Galápagos*. Edited by Robert I. Bowman. Pages 190–200, Univ. Calif. Press, Berkeley.

Weber, William A., Gradstein, S.R., Lanier, Jeannine, and Sipman, H.J.R. (1977) Bryophytes and lichens of the Galápagos Islands. Noticias de Galápagos, **26**, 7–11.

CHAPTER 6

Endemism and Evolution in Terrestrial Plants

DUNCAN M. PORTER

Associate Professor of Botany, Virginia Polytechnic Institute and State University, Blacksburg, Virginia, USA

Contents

6.1.	Introduction	85
6.2.	The Vascular Plants	85
6.3.	The Endemics	90
6.4.	Endemism on Continental and Oceanic Islands	92
6.5.	Evolution of the Endemic Flora	93
	6.5.1. Adaptive radiation	94
	6.5.2. Endemism and island history	96
6.6.	Relationships of the Flora	98
6.7.	Acknowledgements	99
	References	99

6.1. Introduction

Essentially three types of organisms are to be found in any given area: (1) those that occur there naturally, and nowhere else; (2) those that occur there naturally, and also elsewhere; and (3) those that are native elsewhere, but which have been introduced into the area by man. These three types of organisms are called, respectively, endemics, natives, and weeds. More formally, natives may be called autochthones, or they may be said to be autochthonous. Of course, endemic species are also natives, but they are placed in a separate category to indicate their uniqueness from other natives which occur elsewhere as well. In this chapter, the term native refers to naturally occurring non-endemics.

6.2. The Vascular Plants

There are 229 endemic species, subspecies, or varieties of vascular plants (ferns, fern allies, and flowering plants) in the flora of the Galápagos Islands. There are also 312 natives, giving a total of 541 indigenous (naturally occurring) vascular plants. In addition, 195 weeds have been introduced by man over the past 450 years, arriving either as contaminants of crops, on or in domestic animals or man himself, or as garden plants which have escaped into the native vegetation and now successfully reproduce themselves. Thus, the total number of presently known vascular plants is 736.

As the flora has become better known and been more intensively studied, the number of species recognized also has risen. Since the publication of the first modern flora in 1971 by Wiggins and Porter, increased interest in the plants has resulted in the discovery of 4 new endemics (*Cranichis lichenophila* D. Weber, *Lycopodium setaceum* subsp. *galapagense* O. Hamann, *Scalesia microcephala* var. *cordifolia* Eliasson, and *Sisyrinchium galapagense* Ravenna), 29 new natives, and 27 new weeds. Indeed, as might be imagined, with increased exploration of the islands during the 19th and 20th centuries, increased knowledge of the plants resulted in the discovery of more and more species (Table 6.1).

In addition, as botanists learned more about the plants of adjacent South America, the percentage of endemics dropped (Table 6.1), as more presumed endemics were discovered on the mainland. Table 2 lists plants considered endemic in the *Flora of the Galápagos Islands* (Wiggins and Porter, 1971) which proved over the last decade to occur elsewhere as well, or which further study showed not to differ from other species. On the other hand, over the years the absolute number of endemics has risen. More recently, the number of introduced plants is rising.

The presently known vascular plant flora of the islands is summarized in Tables 6.3–6. Tables 6.3–5 list families of flowering plants, ferns, and fern allies that have no endemic species. Table 6 gives families of flowering plants, ferns, and fern allies that do contain endemics, and it indicates the taxonomic categories of

Figure 6.1. *Lecocarpus pinnatifidus*, Arid Zone, Floreana. In the background are *Macraea laricifolia* (the slender shrubs) and *Darwiniothamnus tenuifolius* (dense shrub to the left). (Photograph by Uno Eliasson).

Table 6.1. Numbers of species, subspecies, varieties, and forms of vascular plants reported from the Galápagos Islands in previous studies of the flora

Investigators	Number of taxa[1]	Endemics
Hooker (1847)	253	123 (49%)
Andersson (1855)	333[2]	179 (54%)
Robinson (1902)	590	239 (41%)
Stewart (1911)	615	252 (41%)
Wiggins and Porter (1971)	702[3]	228 (32%)
Johnson and Raven (1973)	635[4]	163 (26%)
Porter (1976)	703[3,5]	236 (34%)
	522[3,6]	236 (45%)
Porter (1979)	543[3,6]	231 (43%)

[1] Taxa (singular taxon) are taxonomic groups of any rank. Here they are species, subspecies, varieties, and forms, unless otherwise indicated.
[2] Only flowering plants were included in Andersson's flora.
[3] Forms are not included.
[4] Only species were included by Johnson and Raven.
[5] Total flora, including endemics, natives, and weeds.
[6] Only endemics and natives are included in this figure.

the endemics. These range from several families with only a single endemic species, subspecies, or variety, to the sunflower family (Compositae) with 4 genera, 29 species, 11 subspecies, and two varieties, all endemic to the Galápagos Islands. No vascular plant families are found exclusively in the archipelago, but 7 genera in three families are endemic: *Darwiniothamnus*, *Lecocarpus* (Figs 6.1 and 6.2), *Macraea*, and *Scalesia* of the Compositae; *Brachycereus* (Fig. 6.4) and *Jasminocereus* of the Cactaceae; and *Sicyocaulis* of the Cucurbitaceae.

Table 6.2. Plants listed as endemics in Wiggins and Porter (1971) that no longer are considered to be so

Monocotyledonae
Bromeliaceae
Tillandsia insularis var. *latilamina* Gilmartin = *T. insularis* Mez (van der Werff, 1977).
Orchidaceae
Erythrodes weberiana Garay also occurs in mainland Ecuador (L.A. Garay, personal communication).
Dicotyledonae
Amaranthaceae
Irisine edmonstonei Hooker fil. is a plant of mainland Ecuador (Porter, 1980).
Apiaceae
Hydrocotyle galapagensis Robinson = *H. umbellata* L. (G.P. Frank, personal communication).
Compositae
Jaegeria crassa Torres = *J. gracilis* Hooker fil. (van der Werff, 1977).
Euphorbiaceae
Acalypha parvula var. *chatamensis* (Robinson) Webster = *A. parvula* Hooker fil. (van der Werff, 1977).
A. parvula var. *reniformis* (Hooker. fil.) Mueller-Argoviensis = *A. parvula* Hooker fil. (van der Werff, 1977).
A. parvula var. *strobilifera* (Hooker fil.) Mueller-Argoviensis = *A. parvula* Hooker fil. (van der Werff, 1977).
A. sericea var. *indefessus* Webster = *A. sericea* var. *baurii* (Robinson and Greenman) Webster (van der Werff, 1977).
Menispermaceae
Cissampelos galapagensis Stewart = *C. glaberrima* Saint-Hilaire (Rhodes, 1975).
Solanaceae
Solanum edmonstonei Hooker fil. is a plant of mainland Ecuador (Porter, 1980).
Verbenaceae
Lippia rosmarinifolia var. *stewartii* Moldenke = *L. rosmarinifolia* Andersson var. *rosmarinifolia* (van der Werff, 1977).
Verbena galapagosensis Moldenke = *V. townsendii* Svenson (van der Werff, 1977).
V. glabrata var. *tenuispicata* Moldenke = *V. townsendii* Svenson (van der Werff, 1977).
V. stewartii Moldenke = *V. townsendii* Svenson (van der Werff, 1977).

Table 6.3. Families of flowering plants represented in the islands only by introduced weeds or naturalized garden escapes (species numbers in brackets)

Monocotyledonae	Capparidaceae (1)
Agavaceae (1)	Caricaceae (1)
Araceae (1)	Crassulaceae (1)
Dicotyledonae	Lauraceae (1)
Anacardiaceae (3)	Meliaceae (1)
Annonaceae (2)	Papaveraceae (1)
Bixaceae (1)	Polemoniaceae (1)
Bombacaceae (1)	Ulmaceae (1)
Brassicaceae (4)	Valerianaceae (1)
Callitrichaceae (1)	

Table 6.4. Families of ferns and fern allies in the islands which have no endemic members (native species numbers in brackets)

Psilophyta	Gleicheniaceae (1)
Psilophytaceae (1)	Grammitidaceae (2)
Equisetophyta	Gymnogrammaceae (5)
Equisetaceae (1)	Hymenophyllaceae (5)
Pteridophyta	Lomariopsidaceae (6)
Adiantaceae (5)	Oleandraceae (2)
Athyriaceae (1)	Ophioglossaceae (3)
Azollaceae (1)	Pteridaceae (1)
Blechnaceae (4)	Vittariaceae (1)
Dennstaedtiaceae (6)	

Table 6.5. Families of flowering plants in the islands which have no endemic members (native species numbers in brackets; a second number gives the number of species of introduced weeds or naturalized garden escapes also present)

Monocotyledonae	Goodeniaceae (1)
Cannaceae (1, 1)	Hydrophyllaceae (1)
Commelinaceae (1)	Hypericaceae (1)
Hypoxidaceae (1)	Lentibulariaceae (1)
Lemnaceae (1)	Loasaceae (2)
Najadaceae (2)	Lobeliaceae (1)
Potamogetonaceae (1)	Lythraceae (2)
Ruppiaceae (1)	Menispermaceae (2)
Dicotyledonae	Onagraceae (3)
Apiaceae (4, 2)	Oxalidaceae (2, 2)
Avicenniaceae (1)	Phytolaccaceae (1, 1)
Balanophoraceae (1)	Plumbaginaceae (2)
Basellaceae (1)	Ranunculaceae (1)
Batidaceae (1)	Rhizophoraceae (1)
Caesalpiniaceae (5)	Rutaceae (1, 1)
Celastraceae (1)	Sterculiaceae (2, 1)
Ceratophyllaceae (1)	Tiliaceae (1, 1)
Chenopodiaceae (2, 2)	Vitaceae (1)
Combretaceae (2)	

Table 6.6. Families of vascular plants in the islands with endemic taxa (native and endemic species number in brackets; the numbers and categories of endemic taxa also are given; a third number gives number of species of introduced weeds or naturalized garden escapes also present)

Lycophyta
Lycopodiaceae (8; 1 subsp.)
  Pteridophyta
Aspidiaceae (10; 1 sp.)
Aspleniaceae (8; 1 var.)
Cyatheaceae (1 sp.)
Polypodiaceae (10; 2 spp.)
Sinopteridaceae (8; 1 sp.)
Thelypteridaceae (16; 1 subsp.)
  Monocotyledonae
Bromeliaceae (1 sp.)
Cyperaceae (30; 2 spp., 1 subsp.; 6)
Iridaceae (1 sp.)
Orchidaceae (13; 2 spp.)
Poaceae (34; 10 spp., two with 2 vars. each; 28)
  Dicotyledonae
Acanthaceae (5; 1 sp.; 1)
Aizoaceae (3; 1 sp.)
Amaranthaceae (20; 16 spp., one with 7 vars., one with 3 subsp., one with 2 subsp.; 8)
Apocynaceae (1; 1 var.)
Asclepiadaceae (1 sp.; 1)
Boraginaceae (15; 10 spp.; 1)
Burseraceae (2; 1 sp.)
Cactaceae (2 gen., 8 spp., one with 5 vars., three with 3 vars. each)
Caryophyllaceae (3; 1 sp.; 1)
Compositae (35; 4 gen., 29 spp., one with 3 subsp., four with 2 subsp. each, one with 2 vars.; 26)
Convolvulaceae (12; 3 spp.; 5)
Cucurbitaceae (4; 1 gen., 2 spp., 1 var.; 2)
Cuscutaceae (2 spp.)
Ericaceae (1 sp.)
Euphorbiaceae (17; 15 spp., one with 4 vars., two with 2 vars. each; 5)
Fabaceae (15; 2 spp.; 12)
Lamiaceae (7; 4 spp.; 3)
Linaceae (2 spp.)
Malvaceae (12; 3 spp., 1 var.; 14)
Melastomataceae (1 sp.)
Mimosaceae (6; 1 sp.; 6)
Molluginaceae (5; 4 spp., one with 4 vars., one with 3 vars.)
Myrtaceae (1 sp. with 2 vars.; 1)
Nolanaceae (1 sp.)
Nyctaginaceae (5; 1 sp.; 2)
Passifloraceae (3; 1 sp., 1 var.)
Piperaceae (5; 3 spp., one with 2 vars.; 1)
Plantaginaceae (1sp.; 1)
Polygalaceae (3 spp. two with 2 vars. each)
Polygonaceae (4; 1 sp.; 2)
Portulacaceae (3; 2 spp.; 2)
Rhamnaceae (1 var.; 1)
Rubiaceae (10; 9 spp.; 7)
Sapindaceae (5; 1 sp., 1 var.)
Scrophulariaceae (8; 1 sp. with 2 subsp.; 2)
Simaroubaceae (1 sp.)
Solanaceae (12; 6 spp., one with 2 vars; 12)
Urticaceae (4; 1 sp.; 2)
Verbenaceae (12; 6 spp., one with 3 vars., two with 2 vars. each, 1 var.; 5)
Viscaceae (1 sp.)
Zygophyllaceae (1 sp.; 2)

Figure 6.2. *Lecocarpus pinnatifidus* (Compositae), at Black Beach, Floreana. (Photograph by Uno Eliasson).

6.3. The Endemics

At this point, one might ask: Why is so much emphasis put on the endemics? For a long time it has been known that study of the endemic organisms of an area may give some clues to the history of that area. This turns out to be particularly true for islands or archipelagoes. Sherwin Carlquist's *Island Life* (1965) and his later, more technical *Island Biology* (1974) provide many examples from around the world.

There are essentially two kinds of endemics, those which have recently evolved, and those which are quite old. The former probably have restricted distributions because they have not had time to colonize other areas. On the other hand, the latter presumably were more widely spread in the past, but their distributions are now more restricted. These are called relicts, and their distributions are termed relict as well.

Even if the biologist has no information on the geological history of an island or archipelago, he or she can predict their ages by studying the floras or faunas and their relationships. Even the percentage of endemics may be significant, for areas of higher endemism may be older and more isolated than those of a lower degree. In the case of the Galápagos Islands, the large percentage of endemic land vertebrates has caused some biogeographers in the past to estimate that the archipelago must be very old. The vascular plants, however, tell us a different story.

As is indicated above, there are 541 indigenous species, subspecies, and varieties of vascular plants, 229 endemics and 312 natives. This results in an endemism of 42%. However, there are a number of plant geographers who feel that to include anything but species in one's calculations gives a false impression of the situation. They feel that one should include only species to give a true picture, and also to make figures from different areas truly comparable. When only species are included in our figures for the Galápagos flora, we emerge with a total of 497 indigenous vascular plants, 170 endemics and 327 natives. At the species level, then, there is 34% endemism.

Refining these figures even further may be done by separating the flowering plants from the ferns and fern allies. This is a logical separation, not only because of the differences in reproductive structures used in classification, but also because of a basically different mechanism of dispersal. Fern allies and almost all ferns are dispersed by small spores which are carried aloft by winds. These are produced by the thousands and are resistant to desiccation. Only one fern was introduced into the Galápagos Islands by other means, the widespread water fern *Azolla microphylla* Kaulfuss, introduced by waterfowl.

Spore dispersal by ferns is so efficient that the distribution of a species should correspond closely to the geographic distribution of the habitat in which it potentially will grow. Given the speed at which dispersal takes place, the maximum distribution of a species should be reached in a relatively short time (Tryon, 1979). As dispersal from one area to another takes place more or less continuously, opportunities for evolution in isolation and speciation must be rather rare for ferns and fern allies. Relatively frequent dispersal to islands may take place to distances of about 800 km (Tryon, 1970), the minimum distance of the Galápagos from mainland Ecuador. Spores have occasionally reached the South Atlantic Island of Tristan da Cunha, 3200 km from their source area in South America. Consequently, the small amount of endemism in the pteridophyte flora of the Galápagos Islands (8%) is not surprising.

Although, like ferns, many flowering plants also are wind dispersed, this dispersal is effective only over short distances. Long distance wind dispersal to islands has a low probability of success (Wickens, 1976). this is reflected in the Galápagos flora, with the number of original introductions of flowering plants by wind being smaller than might be expected (see last section below). Unlike the situation in the ferns and fern allies, natural introductions of flowering plants must take place at a very low rate. Thus, the species endemism of flowering plants in the islands is 41%, and that for species, subspecies, and varieties is 51%.

The orchids (Orchidaceae) comprise a family of flowering plants which are all wind dispersed. Their minute seeds are as small as many fern spores, are produced in just as large numbers, and presumably are just as effective in dispersal. The endemism of the family in the archipelago reflects this, where only two out of 13 species (15%) are endemics. Orchids are quite common in tropical habitats, and one might expect a larger number in the Galápagos Islands, especially since they get around so easily. They are not to be expected in the lower, more arid zones, but there are plenty of habitats available to them on the higher, more mesic islands. Most orchids, however, are quite specific in their pollinators, and many potential members of the flora are not present because absence of their pollinators precludes their successful reproduction in the islands. The number of pollinators in the islands' insect fauna is quite small.

A more subtle reason for the small number of orchids, and perhaps a more important one, has to do with fungal symbionts. The roots and stems of orchids are invaded by a fungus which supplies organic compounds to the orchid through its breakdown of humus in the soil, or in the epiphytic cover in the case of orchids which grow on the surfaces of trees and shrubs. Fungal infection takes place early in the germination of the orchid seed. If the fungus is absent, the seed will not germinate or the young seedling will die. We know little about the fungi of the Galápagos Islands, still less about mycorrhizal fungi (those which invade the roots of plants such as orchids). It may well be that orchids are comparatively rare in their expected habitats in the archipelago because their fungal associates are rare as well.

The point of the two preceding paragraphs is that dispersal to an island is only half the story. The other half is establishment. In fact, establishment is more of a bottleneck to successful migration than is dispersal. No matter how often seeds of a species arrive, if conditions for their successful germination and growth are not present, the species will not become part of the island's flora.

6.4. Endemism on Continental and Oceanic Islands

Basically two kinds of islands can be recognized, continental and oceanic. Continental islands are those which were once connected to a continental landmass. Oceanic islands arose from the ocean depths and were never connected to the mainland. A good example of continental islands are the British Isles, Britain being severed from the continent of Europe only about 7000 years ago. On the other hand, the geological evidence indicates overwhelmingly that the Galápagos Islands are oceanic. In spite of much controversy in the past regarding their origin, today there is no question that they are not truly oceanic. They are a series of volcanoes which arose from the floor of the sea.

The histories of Great Britain and the Galápagos Islands are mirrored in their respective floras. Vascular plant endemism in the Galápagos is 34% at the species level, in Britain it is zero. Generally, it may be said that endemism in continental islands is lower than in oceanic islands. However, an 'old' continental island like New Caledonia, which severed its continental connections with Antarctica perhaps 100 million years ago, may harbor a number of relicts. Endemism in the native flowering plants of New Caledonia is perhaps 90%, and many of these are relicts. The only oceanic islands which approach this number are the Hawaiian Islands (94%) and the small Atlantic island of St. Helena (89%) (figures from Carlquist, 1974). Both the Hawaiian Islands and St. Helena are old and remote from areas from which natural introductions of seeds could take place. Those few that made it over the years proliferated and diversified, resulting in the evolution of their two highly endemic floras.

There are several other archipelagoes in the world, which because of their geographic positions might be compared with the Galápagos Islands. The comparisons should reveal to us similarities and differences which may assist in our understanding of endemism. These other island groups are chosen because they have certain similarities to the Galápagos. All are on the western sides of adjacent continents and consist of at least three islands each (Table 6.7).

What the figures in Table 6.7 reveal is that these four groups of islands are different in almost every respect. Further study shows that the easternmost Canary Islands are continental in origin, the others and the other archipelagoes are oceanic. Oceanicity is one of the few characteristics they all have in common. Likewise, in all cases their floras are closely related to those of the adjacent continent.

Table 6.7. A comparison of four archipelagoes and their endemic floras. Figures for the Canary and Cape Verde Islands are from Sunding (1979), for the Juan Fernández Islands from Carlquist (1974).

Archipelago	Number of larger islands	Location	Area (km²)	Height (m)	Nearest distance to mainland (km)
Galápagos	13	E Pacific, equatorial	7856	1707	800
Canaries	7	E Atlantic, 28°N	7273	3718	115
Cape Verdes	15	E Atlantic, 16°N	4033	2829	500
Juan Fernández	3	E Pacific, 33°S	144	1650	640

Archipelago	Number of Species		Endemics		
	Total Flora	Flowering Plants	Genera	Species	Endemism
Galápagos	496		7	170	34%
		390	7	162	42%
Canaries	1860		17	520	28%
Cape Verdes	650		0	92	14%
Juan Fernández		146	10	97	67%

The age of the Juan Fernández Islands is not known, but they presumably are Tertiary and probably post-Eocene, less than 38 million years old. The Galápagos Islands in contrast are at least 3 to 5 million years of age, the oldest rocks of the Canaries are about 80 million years old, and those of the Cape Verdes are about 150 million years old. One would think that these ages would be mirrored in their respective amounts of endemism, but this is not the case. Opportunities for the evolution of endemic species and for adaptive radiation (see below) probably are most dependent on two factors, ecological opportunity and low frequency of introduction. Ecological opportunity is mirrored in ecological diversity, the number of different habitats available to incoming species.

The Canary Islands are the richest of our islands in habitat diversity; they perhaps would have a higher endemism if they were not so close to Africa. In addition, overland dispersal to the easternmost islands was possible in the past. Although quite old, the Cape Verde Islands are poor in habitat diversity, which may help explain their low amount of endemism. The Juan Fernández Islands have low habitat diversity as well, but their high amount of endemism is surely related to low frequency of introduction. Habitat diversity in the Galápagos Islands is less than in the Canaries, but more than in the Cape Verde or Juan Fernández Islands. Likewise, rate of dispersal to the Galápagos appears to be intermediate between the rather low rate to Juan Fernández and the higher rates to the Canaries and the Cape Verdes.

6.5. Evolution of the Endemic Flora

Following the minimum of a single successful introduction in each case, a single endemic species has evolved in each of the following 53 genera: *Abutilon, Acacia, Acnistus, Baccharis, Brachycereus, Bursera, Calandrinia, Capsicum, Cardiospermum, Castela, Cenchrus, Chrysanthellum, Cranichis, Ctenitis, Cyathea, Dalea, Drymeria, Encelia, Epidendrum, Euphorbia, Exedeconus, Galium, Heliotropium, Hyptis, Jaegeria, Justicia, Kallstroemia, Lycium, Macraea, Miconia, Nolana, Notholaena, Pennisetum, Pernettya, Phaseolus, Philoxerus, Phoradendron, Physalis, Pilea, Pisonia, Plantago, Pleuropetalum, Polygonum, Portulaca, Sarcostemma, Sesuvium, Sicyocaulis, Sicyos, Sisyrinchium, Spilanthes, Tillandsia, Trisetum,* and *Urocarpidium.* Of these, the species most closely related to the endemics *Baccharis steetzii* Andersson, *Bursera malacophylla* Robinson, and *Sesuvium edmonstonei* Hooker fil. also occur in the archipelago. Whether each of the latter represents an independent introduction from that of its closest relative, or the endemic evolved following a single introduction, is not known. In addition, *Abutilon depauperatum* (Hooker fil.) Robinson and *Cardiospermum galapageium* Robinson and Greenman are questionably distinct from other, closely related species, while *Acacia rorudiana* Christopherson may not be truly endemic.

In other cases, the endemic taxon that has evolved following a single introduction is not reckoned to be different enough to warrant recognition as a separate species. Several such are ranked as subspecies (in *Lycopodium* and *Thelypteris*) or varieties (in *Asplenium, Clerodendrum, Dodonaea, Elaterium, Scutia,* and *Vallesia*). These endemic varieties in *Clerodendrum, Elaterium,* and *Vallesia* may not be distinct from the typical phases of their species, which also occur in the Galápagos. Those in *Dodonaea* and *Scutia* biologically are equivalent to subspecies, as are most endemic varieties in the islands, but the category variety traditionally is used in these genera to name taxa below the rank of species.

There are also some instances where more than one introduction took place in a genus in the past, each introduction giving rise to a single different endemic taxon. This has happened twice in *Cuscuta, Gossypium, Passiflora* (a variety is questionably distinct), and *Polypodium,* and three times in *Cyperus* and *Ipomoea.* However, one *Ipomoea, I. linearifolia* Hooker fil., is closely related to or identical with a mainland South American species. In *Cordia, Opuntia,* and *Verbena* two introductions gave rise to one or several endemics each, as did five in *Alternanthera.*

6.5.1. Adaptive radiation

In all the other cases which collectively make up the evolution of the endemic vascular plant flora, a single introduction has resulted in the evolution of two or more endemic taxa. There are 7 genera where a single introduction resulted in the evolution of 2 endemic species: *Delilia*, *Linum*, *Lithophila*, *Pectis*, *Psidium*, *Psychotria*, and *Tournefortia*. In addition, 1 species with 2 subspecies has been evolved in *Galvezia*, and 1 species with two varieties in *Lantana*, *Lycopersicon*, and *Trichoneura*. Two separate introductions in *Amaranthus* yielded 2 endemic species each, in *Lippia* 2 species (one with a questionably distinct variety), and in *Verbena* 3 species (one with two varieties questionably distinct from the typical variety).

The examples given in the foregoing paragraph are examples of a basic evolutionary phenomenon that is common on islands: adaptive radiation. Adaptive radiation is the evolution of divergent forms from a single ancestral form, each adapted to a different niche or different habitat. Darwin's finches serve as the classical example of adaptive radiation in the Galápagos Islands. Less well known, but equally as striking, are the adaptive radiations that have led to the evolution of three or more taxa in the tree composite genus *Scalesia* (Fig. 6.3) and 18 other vascular plant genera in the islands.

There are no examples of adaptive radiation in the ferns or fern allies. This is not at all surprising, recalling how they are so easily dispersed by their spores. In the flowering plants, on the other hand, there are over 20 genera in which adaptive radiation has occurred. In most of these cases, the evidence indicates that each radiation resulted following a single original introduction. In a few cases, one introduction led to adaptive radiation in a genus while a second or more led only to the evolution of a single endemic taxon.

Of the 7 endemic flowering plant genera, adaptive radiation has occurred in four. It has not taken place in *Brachycereus* (Fig. 6.4), *Macraea* (Fig. 6.1), or *Sicyocaulis*. Each of these genera is monotypic, that is each contains only a single species. Whether this is a reflection of the time they have been in the islands is unknown. In contrast, the other endemic genera contain the following numbers of taxa: *Darwiniothamnus* (Fig. 6.1), 2 species each with 2 subspecies; *Lecocarpus* (Figs 6.1 and 6.2), three species; *Scalesia* (Fig. 6.3), 14 species, 7 subspecies, and four varieties; and *Jasminocereus*, 1 species with three varieties.

In the monocotyledons, adaptive radiation has taken place only in 2 genera of grasses, in *Aristida* with 4 species, and in *Paspalum* with 2 species, one having two varieties. In the dicotyledons, on the other hand, it has occurred in several different families. In the Amaranthaceae *Alternanthera* (2 species, 1 with 7 subspecies) and *Froelichia* (2 species, one with 3 subspecies, one with two) have undergone adaptive radiation; in the Boraginaceae, *Cordia* (3 species) and *Tiquilia* (3 species); in the Euphorbiaceae, *Acalypha* (5 species, one with two varieties), *Chamaesyce* (8 species, one with two varieties), and *Croton* (2 species, 1 with four varieties); in the Lamiaceae, *Salvia* (3 species); in the Molluginaceae, *Mollugo* (4 species, one with 4 subspecies, one with three; Fig. 6.5); in the Piperaceae, *Peperomia* (3 species, one with two varieties); in the Polygalaceae, *Polygala* (3 species, two with two varieties each); and in the Rubiaceae, *Borreria* (6 species). Finally, in the prickly-pears, *Opuntia* (see Fig. 11, Chapter 19), we have the only known example of two original introductions leading to two separate adaptive radiations in the same genus. One radiation yielded 5 species, two with three varieties each. The second radiation yielded 1 species with five varieties.

Although we can recognize that adaptive radiation took place in each of these genera, and we can point to contemporary species in the Galápagos and elsewhere that are closely related to these species, little is known of the genetic relationships within each genus. Sometimes knowledge of chromosome numbers is useful in working out relationships. However, in the 1 genus where these are known for many taxa, *Scalesia*, they are all the same. Crossing experiments and study of the resulting hybrids also can prove useful in this regard. The only genera in which they have been reported are *Gossypium*, the endemic cottons, and *Lycopersicon*, the Galápagos tomatoes. Other than in these economically valuable genera, there is a wide open field for experimental studies of evolutionary relationships.

One of the most recent techniques in studying evolution is the use of comparative biochemistry. At its simplest, this involves looking for the same or different chemical compounds in different taxa. It was such a

Figure 6.3. Variation in leaf-shape in the endemic genus, *Scalesia* (Compositae). (Photograph by Uno Eliasson).

Figure 6.4. *Brachycereus nesioticus*, on barren lava headland, Fernandina. (Photograph by Roger Perry).

technique that supplied the evidence that *Opuntia* in the archipelago evolved from two independent introductions (Anderson and Walkington, 1968).

We have seen that genera in a number of families have undergone adaptive radiation in the Galápagos Islands. What they all have in common is that, like the rest of the flora, they are basically weedy. That is, they have the capacity to grow and prosper in disturbed habitats. The Galápagos Islands, being so volcanically active, constitute a mosaic of dry and wet, naturally disturbed habitats. These continually changing habitats have provided the opportunities for adaptive radiation to take place. Involved also is what Carlquist (1965) has called the archipelago effect. A series of islands allows more habitats and more isolation for evolution and adaptive radiation to take place than does a single island. Thus evolved the Galápagos endemics.

6.5.2. Endemism and island history

The figures in the preceding paragraphs tell us much about the history of the Galápagos endemics, even if they reveal little about their interrelationships. The most important thing they tell us is based on there being so much endemism at the level of subspecies and variety. In the absence of any information as to the age of the islands, the amount of endemism and adaptive radiation below the species level indicates that the islands are young. In addition, there is no evidence that any of the endemics are relicts. However, these would be only unproved hypotheses in the absence of corroborative geological evidence of age. In fact, the most recent estimates of the age of the archipelago, gained from accurate rock-dating techniques, reveals a maximum age of 3 to 5 million years (Chapter 2.3).

Figure 6.5. *Mollugo snodgrassii* growing on the caldera floor of Fernandina, March 1967. (Photograph by Uno Eliasson).

Another line of evidence as to the history of the Galápagos Islands comes from the study of fossil pollen and spores (Colinvaux and Schofield, 1976a, 1976b; Chapter 4.4). Colinvaux and Schofield's studies show that over the past 25,000 years there was first a dry period of 15,000 years, followed by a recent period of 10,000 years during which more mesic habitats were available for the plants. This is interpreted by many to mean that arid habitats were available for plants for longer than most mesic habitats have been.

This longer availability of arid habitats is shown when endemism by habitat is calculated. Roughly, we can recognize three types of habitats in the islands: arid, mesic, and littoral. The latter are at sea-level and contain such vegetation types as mangroves (Fig. 6.6), salt flats, beaches, and sand dunes. We find 67% of the islands' endemic taxa in arid habitats, 29% in mesic habitats, and 4% in littoral habitats (Porter, 1979). The figure for littoral habitats is so low because plants of such habitats tend to be widespread and to be easily dispersed. Constant introductions provide little opportunity for isolation and evolution of new taxa.

When we look at adaptive radiation, we find that almost all instances took place in arid habitats. The only examples where adaptive radiation appears to have taken place under mesic conditions are in the epiphytic *Peperomia* and the shrubby *Darwiniothamnus*. This again provides evidence that arid habitats have been available for a longer period of time than mesic habitats.

Figure 6.6. Mangroves trace tidal creeks in fissured lava at Punta Espinosa, Fernandina. (Photograph by Roger Perry).

6.6. Relationships of the Flora

With the publication of a modern flora for the islands (Wiggins and Porter, 1971) and a series of papers which followed it on new additions to the vascular plants (see Schofield, 1973, 1980 for references), it became possible to study in detail where the plants came from and how they arrived. We have already seen that 43% of vascular plant taxa are endemic, but where do the relationships of the rest of the native plants lie? Extra-Galapagean distributions of the non-endemic native plants are as follows: 48% Tropical American (distributed generally in the American tropics), 24% Pantropical (distributed in both the American and Old World tropics), 21% Andean (occurring only in western South America from Chile to Venezuela, throughout or in part), 5% Caribbean (occurring in the West Indies and often also in coastal parts of the surrounding continents), and 1% Mexican and Central American (occurring only in Mexico and/or Central America.

Distributions of the closest relatives of the endemics give us an accurate idea of where their progenitors might have come from. If we plot the percentages of original introductions by area from which they came, the results are as follows: 52% Andean, 27% Tropical American, 8% Pantropical, 5% Caribbean, 4% Mexican and Central American, 3% North American (occurring only in the United States and adjacent Mexico), and 1% South American (occurring only in extra-Andean South America). Since plants which are classed as Tropical American or Pantropical also occur in at least part of the Andean area, the latter in fact may have provided 94% of the non-endemic natives, and 87% of the endemic introductions!

How did these species or their ancestors arrive in the archipelago? An intensive study of fruits and seeds of

Galápagos species and their relatives, and how they are dispersed, provides the evidence to answer this question. The presently known vascular plant flora has probably arisen from a minimum of 607 original introductions, 413 by natural means, and 194 by man. For the whole flora, 40% arrived attached to the outsides or inside the alimentary canals of birds, 32% were brought by man, 22% glided in on the currents of the winds, and 6% floated in on oceanic currents. When we look only at natural introductions, we find that birds account for 59% of introductions, wind 32%, and oceanic drift 8%. Detailed evidence for these figures is given in another publication (Porter, 1983). Given a maximum age of 5 million years and a minimum number of 413 natural introductions, the present vascular plant flora of the Galápagos Islands accrued at an average rate of one successful introduction every 12,107 years!

6.7. Acknowledgements

Field studies in the Galápagos Islands in 1967 were made possible through the National Science Foundation, and in 1977, 1978, and 1981 through the Friends of the Museum of Comparative Zoology, Harvard University. The National Geographic Society, the American Philosophical Society, and the Virginia Polytechnic Institute and State University Education Foundation provided funds so that Galápagos specimens in England could be examined in 1976, 1977, 1979, and 1980–81. H. van der Werff, H. Adsersen, O. Hamann, U. Eliasson, W.G. D'Arcy, L.A. Garay, L.B. Smith, B.L. Turner, and G.P. Frank most kindly provided information on different endemics. S.H. Porter again helped make my prose more readable. All are gratefully acknowledged.

References

Anderson, E.F. and Walkington, D.L. (1968) A study of some neotropical opuntias of coastal Ecuador and the Galápagos Islands. *Notícias de Galápagos.*, **12**, 18–22.

Andersson, N.J. (1855) Om Galapagos öarnes vegetation. *Kgl. Svenska Vetenskapsakad. Handl.*, **1**, 61–256.

Carlquist, S. (1965) *Island Life.* Natural History Press, New York.

Carlquist, S. (1974) *Island Biology.* Columbia University Press, New York.

Colinvaux, P.A. and Schofield, E.K. (1976a) Historical ecology in the Galápagos Islands. I. A Holocene pollen record from El Junco Lake, Isla San Cristóbal. *J. Ecol.*, **64**, 989–1012.

Colinvaux, P.A. and Schofield, E.K. (1976b) Historical ecology in the Galápagos Islands. II. A Holocene spore record from El Junco Lake, Isla San Cristóbal. *J. Ecol.*, **64**, 1013–1028.

Hooker, J.D. (1847) On the vegetation of the Galápagos Archipelago as compared with that of some other tropical islands and of the continent of America. *Trans. Linn. Soc. Lond.*, **20**, 235–262.

Johnson, M.P. and Raven, P.R. (1973) Species number and endemism: The Galápagos Archipelago revisited. *Science.*, **179**, 893–895.

Porter, D.M. (1976) Geography and dispersal of Galápagos Islands vascular plants. *Nature, Lond.*, **264**, 745–746.

Porter, D.M. (1979) Endemism and evolution in Galápagos Islands vascular plants, in *Plants and Islands.* Edited by D. Bramwell. Pages 225–256. Academic Press, London.

Porter, D.M. (1980) The vascular plants of Joseph Dalton Hooker's *An enumeration of the plants of the Galápagos Archipelago; with descriptions of those which are new. Bot. J. Linn. Soc. Lond.*, **81**, 79–134.

Porter, D.M. (1983) Vascular plants of the Galápagos: Origins and dispersal, in *Patterns of Evolution in Galápagos Organisms.* Edited by R.I. Bowman, M. Berson and A. Leviton. Pages 33–96. American Association for the Advancement of Science, San Francisco.

Rhodes, D.G. (1975) A revision of the genus *Cissampelos. Phytologia.*, **30**, 415–484.

Robinson, B.L. (1902) Flora of the Galápagos Islands. *Proc. Amer. Acad. Arts.*, **38**, 78–270.

Schofield, E.K. (1973) Annotated bibliography of Galápagos botany. *Ann. Missouri Bot. Gard.*, **60**, 461–477.

Schofield, E.K. (1980) Annotated bibliography of Galápagos botany. Supplement I. *Brittonia.*, **32**, 537–547.

Stewart, A. (1911) A botanical survey of the Galápagos Islands. *Proc. Calif. Acad. Sci., ser. 4.*, **1**, 7–288.

Sunding, P. (1979) Origins of the Macaronesian flora, in *Plants and Islands.* Edited by D. Bramwell. Pages 13–40. Academic Press, London.

Tryon, R. (1970) Development and evoluton of fern floras of oceanic islands. *Biotropica.*, **2**, 76–84.

Tryon, R. (1979) Biogeography of the Antillean fern flora, in *Plants and Islands.* Edited by D. Bramwell. Pages 55–68. Academic Press, London.

van der Werff, H. (1977) Vascular plants from the Galápagos Islands: New records and taxonomic notes. *Bot. Not.*, **130**, 89–100.

Wickens, G.E. (1976) Speculations on long distance dispersal and the flora of Jebel Marra, Sudan Republic. *Kew Bull.*, **31**, 105–150.

Wiggins, I.L. and Porter, D.M. (1971) *Flora of the Galápagos Islands.* Stanford University Press, Stanford.

CHAPTER 7

Native Climax Forests

UNO ELIASSON

Department of Systematic Botany, University of Gothenburg, Sweden

Contents

7.1.	Introduction	101
7.2.	Vegetation Zones	102
7.3.	Definition of Climax Vegetation	103
7.4.	Classification of Vegetation	103
7.5.	Forest Formations in Closed Vegetation	104
	7.5.1. Evergreen *Scalesia* forests	104
	7.5.1.1. *Scalesia* forest on Santa Cruz	104
	Adaptations in *Scalesia pedunculata*	104
	Floristic composition	107
	Scalesia forest at its upper limit of distribution	109
	Scalesia forest as compared to tropical rain-forest	110
	7.5.1.2. *Scalesia pedunculata* on islands other than Santa Cruz	111
	7.5.1.3. *Scalesia microcephala*	112
	7.5.1.4. *Scalesia cordata*	112
	7.5.2. Evergreen forests not dominated by *Scalesia*	112
	7.5.3. Deciduous forests	113
7.6.	Steppe Forests	113
	References	114

7.1. Introduction

The Galápagos Islands are volcanic in origin and truly oceanic; they have never been connected to the mainland. As a consequence the flora is disharmonic, that is, in its composition very different from that of the nearest continent. Several plant families which are important and rich in species on the mainland are poorly represented or absent in the islands; such families are for example the monocotyledonous families Araceae, Bromeliaceae and Cyclanthaceae. As regards number of taxa (species, subspecies and varieties) the Galápagos flora is poor, a combined effect of remoteness, young age, and special geological conditions with vast areas covered by fresh lava. The supposedly indigenous flora of vascular plants comprises about 540 taxa, roughly 40% of these being endemic (Porter, 1979). The floristic affinity is with western South America, whereas there is no connection at all with other Pacific archipelagos, such as the Hawaiian Islands. As a result of improved communications with the mainland and the concomitant increase in visitors, the number of introduced species has grown in recent years and will inevitably continue to do so in settled areas. However, in vast areas of the archipelago, environmental conditions are so extreme that only indigenous well-adapted species can thrive. So far, a total of about 710 species has been reported as indigenous to or naturalized in the islands. A further, considerable number of introduced species—some of which are tall trees—occurs in conjunction with settlements (Black, 1974).

The Galápagos landscape is variable due to climatic and geological differences. Varying ground conditions and the fact that the amount of precipitation increases with altitude, have resulted in distinct types of vegetation, often restricted to special elevations. For an account of the climatic and geological conditions the reader is referred to Hamann (1979a) and McBirney and Williams (1969). Nomenclature of plants follows Wiggins and Porter (1971).

7.2. Vegetation Zones

In the Galápagos Islands the vegetation changes with altitude and moisture from sea level to the tops of the volcanoes at about 1600 m elevation (see Table on p. 4). Not only does the type of vegetation change, but also the species composition. Beyond the narrow *littoral zone*, there is an arid lowland, which on small islands may comprise the whole island. This *arid zone* has a predominantly xerophytic vegetation and extends to an altitude of 80–200 m or more depending on island and side of the island. Arborescent or shrubby species of *Jasminocereus* and *Opuntia*, on some islands also the low-growing *Brachycereus*, are characteristic of this zone. Although vast areas may be completely devoid of broad-leaved trees, low-growing specimens of *Croton scouleri* and *Bursera graveolens* are occasionally dominant. Other tree-forming genera are the leguminous genera *Acacia*, *Piscidia*, *Prosopis*, and, in the upper part of the zone, *Erythrina*. Above the arid zone a *transition zone* may be recognized. Here, trees are taller and more numerous than in the arid zone. As well as several trees that extend from the lowland, *Pisonia floribunda*, *Psidium galapageium* and *Zanthoxylum fagara* also occur in this zone. The undergrowth comprises several species that cannot endure the drought of lower areas. Above the transition zone there is a so-called *Scalesia zone*. This zone has the endemic composite tree *Scalesia* as its most characteristic and dominating member, but other trees occur. When well-developed the vegetation in this zone forms a forest with rich undergrowth, made possible by the increased moisture. The *Scalesia* zone occupies the summits of some islands or some volcanoes. The upper part of the *Scalesia* zone on the southern slope of Santa Cruz may look brown when viewed from a distance, and has been called the 'brown zone' (Bowman, 1961). The colour is due to clumps of epiphytic liverworts that drape the trees. On Santa Cruz, further belts are distinguishable. Thus, a *Miconia* zone, completely dominated by the endemic shrub *Miconia robinsoniana*, replaces the *Scalesia* forest on the south slope at an elevation around 450–550 m. *Miconia* may form almost pure stands of 3–4 m tall shrubs with an almost closed canopy. Epiphytic liverworts sheath the branches, but the undergrowth is sparse or lacking when the leaf canopy above is dense. At elevations over 550–650 m, *Miconia* is replaced by a *fern-sedge zone* which covers the top of the island. The vegetation mainly comprises sedges, grasses and ferns, among them the low, endemic tree-fern *Cyathea weatherbyana* (Chapter 5, Fig. 6).

Although differences are striking when representative parts of different zones are compared to each other there are, with few exceptions, no sharp boundaries between different zones, and the vegetation merges from one zone into another (Reeder and Riechert, 1975, Hamann, 1979a). Detailed descriptions of vegetation zones in Galápagos literature (see e.g. Wiggins and Porter, 1971) generally refer to conditions on Santa Cruz, but the vegetational zonation may be quite different on other islands. Due to local climatic conditions or other factors, the altitudinal extension of a particular zone may vary between island and island, and also from one side of an individual island to another. A particular zone may be characteristic and well developed on one island, but poorly represented or absent on another. Thus, on Volcán Cerro Azul, south-western Isabela, there is no arid zone as described above. Instead, local climatic conditions have created a type of vegetation which may be classified as 'dry season deciduous forest' at low elevation, whereas the vegetation at high altitudes is rather xerophytic evergreen scrub (van der Werff, 1978, Hamann, 1981).

7.3. Definition of Climax Vegetation

A 'climax vegetation' is normally defined as a stable vegetation in the sense that it has ceased to change and has reached a state of equilibrium with the environment. This term has sometimes been questioned from a theoretical point of view, as an absolutely stable vegetation scarcely exists. New immigrants may continually change the floristic composition. Although it may be difficult for immigrants to establish themselves in a well-balanced community aggressive newcomers occasionally succeed, and changes in the floristic composition result.

Provided the terrain is old enough and not covered by recent lava flows, the vegetation within any particular zone in the Galápagos may be regarded as a climax vegetation in that it comprises plants adapted to the special conditions pertaining to that zone; non-adapted plants simply would have failed to invade or to survive. In the long run, the vegetation on a lava field changes gradually as the lava weathers into gravel and soil, for more species are adapted to grow on gravel and soil than to pioneer fresh lava. Whether or not the two categories should be regarded as different degrees of climax vegetation is a question of definition. This chapter concentrates on certain kinds of forest vegetation. Although in this case, too, the term 'climax vegetation' must be treated with caution, these forests are restricted to particular elevations in the Galápagos and thus stable in the sense that they are adapted to the environmental conditions at present encountered.

7.4. Classification of Vegetation

There are different systems for classification of vegetation, and depending upon the criteria used different types of forests can be distinguished in the Galápagos. In the present review there will be no attempt at a detailed classification, nor at an analysis of the forest vegetation into phytosociological units. Instead, a general description will be given of some forests which comprise an important part of the vegetation in the Galápagos. Those interested in more detailed analyses are referred to the works of van der Werff (1978) and Hamann (1981).

Fosberg (1967) established a method of classification of vegetation based primarily on spacing and habit but also allowing the inclusion of other criteria. As regards spacing, three categories or primary structural groups were recognized; the vegetation could be closed, open, or sparse. In a *closed vegetation*, the crowns or peripheries of plants in one layer or in all of them taken together mostly touch or overlap. In an *open vegetation*, the plants do not touch but the crowns are separated by less than their diameter. In a *sparse vegetation*, the plants are more scattered and substratum dominates the landscape. Within each of these categories several types of formations can be distinguished, each formation being further subdivided into units of lower rank. At least one tree-containing formation may be recognized within each of the three primary structural groups, these being termed 'forest', 'steppe forest', and 'desert forest', respectively. The first two mentioned are common in the Galápagos, whereas the third formation may have extremely few or scattered trees, and hence is hardly deserving of the name 'forest' in the sense generally accepted.

Although the term 'forest' is normally well understood the concept is broad and subjective and the term accordingly diffuse. Fosberg (1967) defined 'forest' as an open or closed vegetation with the principal layer consisting of trees. This definition is adopted here. A 'tree' was defined as a non-climbing woody plant more than 5 m tall. This definition is not always strictly followed in this paper; single-stemmed woody plants with a well-developed crown are sometimes called trees even if only 2–4 m tall.

7.5. Forest Formations in Closed Vegetation

Forests in the Galápagos are either evergreen or dry season deciduous. Since moisture increases with altitude the evergreen forests are restricted to higher elevations, whereas vegetation with deciduous trees and shrubs occurs at lower altitudes, sometimes up to 500 m or more depending on island and side of the island.

7.5.1. Evergreen *Scalesia* forests

Scalesia is a composite genus endemic to the Galápagos and occurs on the majority of the islands. The genus is variable in habit as well as in morphological details (Eliasson 1974; see also Chapter 6, Fig. 3). Most species are shrubs 0.3–2 m tall. Three species form trees; *S. pedunculata* occurs on Santa Cruz, Santiago, Floreana and San Cristóbal, *S. cordata* is restricted to Isabela S of Istmo Perry, and *S. microcephala* inhabits Fernandina and the volcanoes N of Istmo Perry on Isabela.

7.5.1.1. Scalesia *forest on Santa Cruz*

Adaptations in *Scalesia pedunculata*. Although scattered specimens of *S. pedunculata* have been found at altitudes below 100 m on Santa Cruz, *Scalesia* increases in number with altitude and is the dominant tree in large areas of indigenous forests at 300–750 m elevation (Fig. 7.1). The altitudinal extension of the forest is variable, however. On the northern slope of Santa Cruz small parts of the *Scalesia* forest extend to almost 800 m elevation, on the southern slope to less than 650 m. *Scalesia* is the absolutely dominating tree in the well-developed *Scalesia* forest and reaches 5–15 m in height. Although free-standing specimens form rounded crowns, individuals in forest become flat-topped and assume a flat canopy, where individual crowns customarily fit into one another like pieces in a jigsaw puzzle (Fig. 7.2). The impression is that there is strong competition for space between the individual crowns. If a part of a crown falls to the ground the available space will soon be occupied by the further development of neighbouring crowns. As a consequence the *Scalesia* canopy is dense and the cover is high (Table 7.1). Under the closed canopy, seedlings of *Scalesia* are rare or absent. As soon as an opening in the forest appears, for example after a tree has fallen, permitting more light to enter, *Scalesia*-achenia on the ground germinate and usually several seedlings result. As documented by Hamann (1979b) in a demonstration of the dynamics of a stand of *Scalesia*, young plants grow very rapidly and may reach a height of 7–8 m in 3½–5½ years. This factor is important for the ability of *Scalesia* to exploit small clearings in the forest. On the other hand, as shown by Hamann, the mortality rate is very high during the first 4–5 years. Apparently a sudden opening in the closed canopy causes a veritable race among the seedlings. The winner may reach the opening and survive while competitors die. If neighbouring trees manage to fill up much of the opening before the new individual reaches this height, there may be so little space left for the new individual that it can develop only a very small crown with living leaves. Such stunted trees are often seen in the forest and are frequently destined to die.

The influence of light on the seed germination of flowering plants is a fascinating physiological question to which much attention has been devoted in recent years. The information is still fragmentary but apparently it is not so much the amount of light to reach the seed that is important but rather the quality. Light reaching a dormant seed directly through an opening in the canopy is different from that which has lost parts of its spectrum through the filter of a green canopy. *Scalesia* forest might be an interesting research subject for such a physiological study.

The flower-heads of *Scalesia* are produced near the ends of branches. These heads are upright and conspicuous against the green foliage. The most important pollinator is believed to be the endemic Galápagos bee, *Xylocopa darwinii*. After flowering, the heads become pendent on their long peduncles. The fruits have no

Figure 7.1. *Scalesia* forest: trees are *S. pedunculata*, their stems covered with epiphytic liverworts; shrubs are *Psychotria rufipes*; Los Gemelos, Santa Cruz.

adaptations for long-distance dispersal and normally fall to the ground over a prolonged period of time. Small larvae are often found in the phyllaries and other parts of the flower-heads. These larvae bore tunnels in the dense flower aggregates of the heads and their phyllaries. The injured heads secrete a sticky, gummy exudation, making achenes and other floral parts sticky. I have suggested (Eliasson, 1974) that, under rare circumstances at least, this may be of some importance for epizoic dispersal. Sticky achenes might adhere to

Figure 7.2. *Scalesia* canopy. The individual crowns fit into one another like the pieces in a jigsaw puzzle.

Figure 7.3. *Asplenium auritum* (erect) and *Nephrolepis cordifolia* (pendent) among liverworts on stem of *Tournefortia*; Los Gemelos, Santa Cruz.

the bill or plumage of Darwin's finches that regularly perch in the *Scalesia* canopy and search for insects hidden in the dead leaves that hang down under the green foliage—a characteristic of all plants in the genus. So far, however, this is a hypothetical possibility, and were it to be demonstrated to occur occasionally, there is little doubt that the normal mode of diaspore dispersal in all species of *Scalesia* is the gradual, passive dropping of fruits over extended periods of time.

Floristic composition. Undergrowth is rich in a luxuriant *Scalesia* forest (Fig. 7.1). Vegetation analyses summarized in Table 1 I made in Dec. 1980–Feb. 1981 on Santa Cruz, in the vicinity of Los Gemelos at an altitude of 600–620 m. Eighteen quadrats 10 m × 10 m were analysed to determine vascular plants present and the degree of cover of the different species. The precise sites of the quadrats were, so far as possible, chosen randomly, but areas obviously influenced by man or domestic animals were avoided. *Cover* is defined as the area of ground occupied by a vertical projection of all the epiterranean parts of individuals of a particular species. *Degree of cover* is the extent to which the quadrat is occupied by a particular species. Among the several methods of vegetation analysis available (Shimwell, 1971), the Hult-Sernander scale of degree of cover was chosen since it was easy to use under the conditions. In this scale the figure '5' indicates a cover range of 51–100%, '4' 26–50%, '3' 13–25%, '2' 6.5–12.5%, and '1' a cover of less than 6.25%. In Table 7.1 the vegetation in each of the 18 quadrats is shown separately. The *frequency* of a particular species is the number of squares in which it was present, expressed as a percentage of the total number of squares investigated.

Although there are floristic differences between different parts of the *Scalesia* forest and especially between forests from different elevations, certain generalized features appear clearly from Table 7.1. Thus, *Psidium galapageium* and *Zanthoxylum fagara* are characteristic tree elements in most parts of the *Scalesia* forest. Both are less frequent, however, and have lower cover values than *Scalesia*. In the shrub layer, *Psychotria rufipes* and 1 or 2 species of *Tournefortia* are likewise characteristic elements in the *Scalesia* forest on Santa Cruz. The same holds for *Alternanthera halimifolia*, *Borreria laevis*, *Commelina diffusa*, *Elaterium carthagenense* and *Pilea baurii* in the herb layer (Fig. 7.7). *Elaterium* is a vine but occasionally scrambles over the ground or among herbs. Several species of terrestrial ferns, e.g. *Adiantum henslovianum*, *Doryopteris pedata*, *Nephrolepis cordifolia*, *Polypodium phyllitidis* and *Thelypteris tetragona*, are normally found in the *Scalesia* forest, although the last-named species happened to be absent from all the quadrats examined.

In several cases there is some doubt as to whether a species should be regarded as a tree or a shrub. This was not a problem in this particular study, but, elsewhere, *Chiococca* may form a small tree and *Zanthoxylum* be shrubby.

Only terrestrial plants have been included in Table 7.1. However, there are several species growing as epiphytes. Besides impressive clumps of dark brown liverworts (Figs. 7.1, 7.4), especially species of *Frullania*, these include ferns (Figs 7.3, 7.4, 7.6) and some epiphytic angiosperms. Epiphytes may grow on various trees, with *Zanthoxylum* as an attractive host and, to a somewhat lesser extent, *Scalesia*. Common epiphytes are the ferns *Asplenium auritum*, *A. praemorsum*, *Nephrolepis cordifolia*, *Polypodium lanceolatum* and *P. steirolepis*. Common epiphytic angiosperms are the endemic orchid *Epidendrum spicatum*, and some endemic species of *Peperomia*. Certain ferns and angiosperms may be epiphytic as well as terrestrial. The parasitic endemic mistletoe *Phoradendron henslovii* grows on various woody species but in the *Scalesia* forest shows a preference for *Zanthoxylum*. Some species of vines, in particular *Cissus sicyoides*, *Elaterium carthagenense* and *Passiflora colinvauxii* (Fig. 7.5), also occur in *Scalesia* forest.

The undergrowth in a well-developed *Scalesia* forest may be very dense. Perennial herbs and subshrubs may form thickets with several-layered foliage, ½–1 m in thickness. In such cases the amount of light that reaches the ground is too small to permit growth of bryophytes, and a thin layer of litter covers the bare soil. This soil layer is several dm deep in the closed *Scalesia* forest on Santa Cruz.

Although areas with obvious signs of human disturbance were avoided when the analyses in Table 1 were made, it is difficult to judge to what extent the vegetation in 'seemingly natural' *Scalesia* forest might have been influenced either by man directly or, to a much larger extent, by animals introduced by man. The trees and shrubs in Table 7.1 are surely indigenous and the same probably holds for all the ferns. In the herb layer, however, there are some species the introduction and further dispersal of which might have been due to man and his animals. *Ageratum conyzoides* and *Eupatorium pycnocephalum* are probably relatively recent introductions to Galápagos. The two are difficult to separate when sterile—and the extensive sterile growth seen in my analyses could represent either species or both. Also, *Alternanthera halimifolia* (Fig. 7.7) is probably much more common in suitable areas in the Galápagos than it would have been had the islands not suffered

Table 7.1. Floristic composition and degree of cover of different species in *Scalesia* forest at Los Gemelos, Santa Cruz. Degree of cover according to the Hult–Sernander scale. Quadrat size $100\,\mathrm{m}^2$

		Number of quadrat																		Frequency (%)
		1	2	3	4	5	6	7	8	9	10	11	12	13	14	15	16	17	18	
Trees																				
Psidium galapageium	Myrtaceae	1	–	–	1	4	1	–	–	3	–	1	–	–	1	1	–	1	–	50
Scalesia pedunculata	Compositae	5	5	5	5	5	5	5	5	5	5	5	5	5	4	5	5	5	5	100
Zanthoxylum fagara	Rutaceae	2	3	1	1	3	–	2	1	–	1	1	1	2	2	–	1	2	1	83
Shrubs																				
Acnistus ellipticus	Solanaceae	–	–	–	–	–	–	1	–	–	–	–	–	–	–	–	–	–	–	6
Chiococca alba	Rubiaceae	–	1	1	1	–	–	–	–	1	1	–	–	1	–	–	–	–	–	33
Cordia leucophlyctis	Boraginaceae	1	–	2	–	–	–	–	–	–	–	–	–	–	–	–	–	–	1	17
Psychotria rufipes	Rubiaceae	2	2	2	3	3	3	2	2	1	2	3	1	3	3	3	2	1	3	100
Tournefortia rufo-sericea	Boraginaceae	1	1	–	–	–	1	–	–	–	–	–	–	–	–	–	–	–	–	17
Tournefortia sp.	Boraginaceae	1	1	1	2	–	2	1	1	1	1	1	1	1	1	1	1	–	1	89
Urera caracasana	Urticaceae	–	–	–	–	–	2	–	–	–	–	1	–	–	1	–	–	1	–	22
Herbs and subshrubs																				
Ageratum/Eupatorium (ster.)	Compositae	2	4	–	2	3	2	1	2	–	1	1	–	1	2	1	1	1	1	83
Alternanthera halimifolia	Amaranthaceae	1	2	4	–	3	2	1	1	2	1	2	3	1	1	1	1	1	1	94
Borreria laevis	Rubiaceae	3	1	1	3	–	1	1	1	1	2	3	1	–	–	4	–	–	4	72
Cissampelos pareira	Menispermaceae	–	–	–	–	–	–	–	–	1	–	–	–	–	–	–	–	–	–	6
Cissus sicyoides	Vitaceae	–	–	–	–	–	1	–	–	–	1	–	–	1	1	1	–	1	1	39
Commelina diffusa	Commelinaceae	1	1	1	1	1	1	–	–	–	–	–	1	1	1	1	1	1	1	72
Desmodium limense	Papilionaceae	1	–	–	–	–	–	–	–	–	1	1	–	–	–	–	–	–	–	17
Dichondra repens	Convolvulaceae	–	–	–	–	1	–	–	–	–	1	1	–	–	–	–	–	–	–	11
Drymaria cordata	Caryophyllaceae	–	–	–	–	–	–	–	–	1	–	1	1	–	–	–	–	–	–	17
Elaterium carthagenense	Cucurbitaceae	1	1	1	–	–	1	–	1	1	1	1	1	–	1	1	1	1	1	78
Galium galapagoense	Rubiaceae	–	–	1	–	–	–	1	1	1	–	–	–	1	–	–	–	–	–	28
Justicia galapagana	Acanthaceae	1	1	–	1	1	–	1	–	–	1	–	1	–	–	–	–	–	–	39
Parietaria debilis	Urticaceae	–	–	–	–	–	–	–	–	1	–	–	–	–	–	–	–	–	–	6
Passiflora colinvauxii	Passifloraceae	–	–	1	1	–	–	–	–	–	–	–	–	–	–	–	–	–	–	11
Peperomia sp.	Urticaceae	–	–	–	–	–	–	1	–	–	–	1	1	1	–	–	–	–	1	28
Pilea baurii	Urticaceae	1	1	1	–	1	2	1	1	2	–	1	1	1	1	1	1	1	1	89
Sida rhombifolia	Malvaceae	–	–	–	–	–	–	–	1	–	1	–	–	–	–	–	–	–	–	11
Solanum nodiflorum	Solanaceae	–	–	–	–	–	–	1	–	–	1	1	–	1	–	–	–	–	–	22
Grasses																				
Ichnanthus nemorosus	Gramineae	–	–	–	–	–	–	1	1	1	1	1	1	–	1	1	1	–	1	56
Paspalum sp. (sterile)	Gramineae	–	–	–	–	–	1	1	1	2	–	1	1	1	–	–	–	–	1	44
Ferns																				
Adiantum henslovianum	Polypodiaceae	–	1	–	–	1	–	1	–	–	–	1	–	–	–	–	1	–	1	33
A. macrophyllum	Polypodiaceae	–	–	–	–	–	–	–	–	–	–	–	1	–	–	–	–	–	–	6
Asplenium auritum	Polypodiaceae	1	–	–	–	–	1	1	1	–	–	–	1	–	1	–	–	1	–	39
A. cristatum	Polypodiaceae	–	–	1	1	–	1	1	–	–	1	1	–	1	1	–	–	1	1	56
A. feei	Polypodiaceae	–	–	–	–	–	–	–	–	–	–	–	–	–	–	–	–	–	1	6
A. formosum	Polypodiaceae	–	–	1	1	–	–	–	1	–	1	–	–	–	–	–	1	–	1	33
A. praemorsum	Polypodiaceae	1	–	–	–	–	–	1	–	–	1	–	–	–	–	–	–	–	–	17
Blechnum occidentale	Polypodiaceae	2	1	1	1	–	–	2	1	2	–	1	–	3	1	–	–	–	–	56
Dennstaedtia cicutaria	Polypodiaceae	–	–	–	–	–	–	–	–	2	–	–	–	3	–	–	–	–	–	11
D. globulifera	Polypodiaceae	–	–	–	–	–	–	–	–	–	–	–	–	–	–	–	–	1	–	6
Doryopteris pedata	Polypodiaceae	1	1	1	–	1	–	1	1	1	1	1	1	1	1	1	1	1	1	89
Hypolepis hostilis	Polypodiaceae	1	–	1	–	–	1	–	–	–	–	–	–	–	–	–	–	–	–	17
Nephrolepis cordifolia	Polypodiaceae	1	–	1	–	–	1	1	1	–	–	–	–	–	–	–	–	–	–	28
Polypodium aureum	Polypodiaceae	–	–	–	–	–	–	1	–	–	–	–	–	–	–	–	–	–	–	6
P. phyllitidis	Polypodiaceae	1	1	1	–	–	–	1	1	1	1	–	–	1	–	–	1	–	1	56
Pteris quadriaurita	Polypodiaceae	1	–	–	–	–	–	–	–	1	–	–	–	–	1	–	–	–	–	17
Thelypteris pilosula	Polypodiaceae	–	–	–	–	–	–	–	–	–	–	1	–	1	–	–	–	1	–	17

Figure 7.4. Stem of *Scalesia pedunculata* thickly covered with liverworts; *Peperomia* sp., *Polypodium lanceolatum*, and *Asplenium praemorsum* grow among the liverworts; Los Gemelos, Santa Cruz.

Figure 7.5. *Passiflora colinvauxii* climbing on stem of *Scalesia*; Los Gemelos, Santa Cruz.

disturbance. Of the 2 grass species, *Paspalum* at least is likely to be of recent introduction. *Ichnanthus* might have been overlooked in early investigations of the flora because of its close similarity with *Commelina* in the sterile stage.

It should be borne in mind that despite considerable taxonomic research on Galápagos plants during recent decades there are several taxa the delimitation and justification of which remain doubtful. Some of these occur in the *Scalesia* forest of Santa Cruz. Some specimens of *Cordia* are doubtful as to taxon, and some specimens of *Tournefortia rufo-sericea* tend toward the characteristics of *T. pubescens*. *Peperomia* species with several leaves at each node also show a pattern of variation that deserves a critical study.

Scalesia *forest at its upper limit of distribution.* The height of *Scalesia* and some other forest trees is dependent upon the climatic conditions at the altitude they grow. At around 400–500 m, *S. pedunculata* may reach 12 m or more in height. At higher elevations the trees decrease in height, despite the fact that moisture increases. Thus, the average height of *Scalesia* trees at Los Gemelos (alt. 600–620 m) is 6–7 m, even though the forest is well developed and *Scalesia* forms a closed canopy. Several factors have been suggested as possible reasons for reduced height in woody plants in certain environments (for further references see Byer and Weaver, 1977). Reduced transpiration rate has been proposed as likely to account for reduced height of *Scalesia* at high elevations on Santa Cruz (van der Werff, 1978). Due to the almost constantly saturated atmosphere, the

Figure 7.6. Epiphytes on *Scalesia; Asplenium praemorsum* (left), *Polypodium steirolepis* (center) and *Peperomia* sp. (right). *Peperomia* spp. with verticillate leaves need further critical study regarding delimitation as to species.

Figure 7.7. *Pilea baurii* (with serrate leaves) and *Alternanthera halimifolia* (with entire leaves) are among the most dominant terrestrial herbs in *Scalesia* forest; *Pilea baurii* is endemic to Galápagos; Los Gemelos, Santa Cruz.

transpiration rate is low. This is believed to hamper distribution of minerals within the plant, and a slow, stunted growth results.

Scalesia *forest as compared to tropical rain-forest.* In his classic work on the tropical rain-forest, Richards (1952) defined secondary rain-forest as the vegetation with the aspect of a forest that will occupy sites once a primary or virgin rain-forest has been destroyed. This secondary rain-forest remains a recognizable type of forest for considerable time. Among its characteristics are rapid growth, soft wood, non-tolerance of shade, and effective seed dispersal. Although *Scalesia pedunculata* meets all but the last of these criteria, I agree with Carlquist (1974) and van der Werff (1978) in asserting that such similarities are superficial. There is certainly no reason to regard *Scalesia* forest as being of a secondary nature. Since trees characteristic of primary rain-forest have poor dispersal mechanisms, they have never been able to reach the Galápagos. The ancestor of *Scalesia* is more likely to have been shrubby or herbaceous. Certain weedy characters appear in fact to be retained by present descendants. This would explain some of the wood-characters of *Scalesia*; for example, the pith is well-developed and occupies a large part of the transection area of the stem.

From an evolutionary point of view some plant families are more plastic than others and capable of radiating into different life forms adapted to particular environments. This holds for the Compositae. Some species of *Scalesia* grow on arid lava fields whereas others are adapted to moist habitats. *S. pedunculata* has developed tree-form to fit into an ecological niche the competition for which is weak in the Galápagos. The resemblances to mainland types of secondary rain-forests are superficial. The *Scalesia* forest is unique.

7.5.1.2. Scalesia pedunculata *on islands other than Santa Cruz*

When Alban Stewart, botanist to the expedition of the California Academy of Sciences to the Galápagos Islands, visited Santiago in 1905 and 1906 the interior of the island was covered by dense forests in which *Scalesia* was the most important member. Santiago lies NW of Santa Cruz and the two islands are roughly comparable as regards size and altitude. Large parts of the island, however, are covered with fresh lava fields and, in other ways, there are differences when compared to conditions prevailing on Santa Cruz. Notwithstanding these differences, the original *Scalesia* forest in the highland of Santiago had much the same floristic composition as that of Santa Cruz, and such species as *Psidium galapageium*, *Zanthoxylum fagara* and *Psychotria rufipes* seem to have had the same importance in tree- and shrub-layers. Unfortunately, the virgin *Scalesia* forest on Santiago has been ruined by introduced animals, in particular goats and pigs. Before the goat eradication programme started some years ago, the vegetation in the uppermost part of the island had been reduced to an open aspect with only scattered living trees. The few *Scalesia* trees surviving were all tall and there was no regeneration, as seedlings were immediately browsed by goats. Dead *Zanthoxylum* trees, their branches heavily sheathed by extensive growths of epiphytic liverworts, stood as monuments to the devastation of a unique forest. Today, with the numbers of goats reduced, several species are recovering.

The island of Floreana has been influenced by man, domestic animals, and introduced plants for a longer time than any other island in the archipelago. Although *Scalesia*-dominated forest still exists in the interior of the island, it is doubtful whether there is any significant piece of forest left that is representative of genuine, undisturbed vegetation. The introduced *Psidium guajava* is an aggressive invader into areas of indigenous vegetation, and scattered *Citrus* trees may be found where least expected. *S. pedunculata* grows from ca 250 m elevation to the top of the island at ca 560 m. It differs superficially from specimens on Santa Cruz and Santiago and has even been regarded as a distinct subspecies. It has a weaker appearance, the flower heads are smaller, and the trees seldom exceed 5 m in height. Depending somewhat on site and altitude, scalesias may be intermingled with small trees or shrubs of *Croton*, *Zanthoxylum*, *Chiococca*, *Clerodendrum*, *Cordia*, *Darwiniothamnus*, *Macraea* and *Psychotria*. The last-named genus is represented by *P. angustata*, endemic to Floreana. It is closely related to *P. rufipes*, the common species in the *Scalesia* forest on Santa Cruz and Santiago, and seems to be hardly more than a glabrous form of the latter. *Lippia salicifolia* may form trees 6 m tall with wide spacious crowns in open vegetation; it is rare, however, and endemic to the island.

On San Cristóbal, *S. pedunculata* has been collected only a few times. Apart from vast areas with lava, this island has been much changed by man and various introductions. Free-ranging cattle have destroyed indigenous vegetation and *Psidium guajava* has colonized vast areas. It is possible that there no longer remain significant areas in the highlands of San Cristóbal where *S. pedunculata* comprises an important element.

7.5.1.3. Scalesia microcephala

Scalesia microcephala is a small tree, mostly 2–4 m tall, and the most important member of the vegetation on the volcanoes of Isabela and Fernandina. It is common at altitudes of 1000–1600 m and rarely encountered at elevations below 300 m. In habit, it forms a tree, but a low height makes the vegetation it dominates fall within the definition of '*scrub*', rather than 'forest'. Nevertheless, the physiognomy of the *Scalesia*-dominated vegetation is that of a miniature forest.

In most places *S. microcephala* forms an open scrub with closed lower layers. Other woody species present are *Zanthoxylum fagara*, *Croton scouleri* and *Lippia rosmarinifolia*, with occasional *Macraea laricifolia*, *Duranta repens*, *Tournefortia rufo-sericea*, *Solanum erianthum*, *Acnistus ellipticus*, *Chiococca alba* and *Cordia* spp. A characteristic element in the vegetation of the crater rims is *Opuntia insularis*, a low-growing cactus with soft spines and often all pads oriented in one direction, giving the whole plant a flattened appearance. It is endemic to Isabela and Fernandina. Common species in the lower layers include *Acalypha* spp., the grasses *Paspalum galapageium*, *Trichoneura lindleyana* and *Aristida* spp., and the ferns *Pteridium aquilinum* and *Adiantum concinnum*. Common vines are *Galactia striata* and *Rhynchosia minima*, occasionally also *Ipomoea alba* and *Passiflora* spp. The epiphytic *Tillandsia insularis* is sometimes abundant. Epiphytic liverworts occasionally form impressive growths sheathing branches. Embedded in, or protruding from, such sheaths are the endemic orchid *Epidendrum spicatum*, some species of *Lycopodium*, and ferns of the genera *Hymenophyllum*, *Asplenium*, *Polypodium*, *Blechnum*, *Nephrolepis* and *Elaphoglossum*.

In some places *S. microcephala* forms dense vegetation with a closed canopy. This is the case in the southeastern part of the inner slope of the caldera of Volcán Alcedo on Isabela. There is a geyser in the vicinity and the steam from this saturates the air with moisture. This has created favourable local conditions for the growth of *Scalesia*.

7.5.1.4. Scalesia cordata

Scalesia cordata is taxonomically very close to *S. microcephala* and replaces this species S of Istmo Perry on Isabela. Although frequently 2–4 m tall, it has been reported to attain 10 m or more. It is a component of scrub near the rim of Cerro Azul and dominates evergreen forest at elevations of 150–250 m on the south slope. The detailed distribution of the species is poorly known and it seems to be diminishing due to free-ranging cattle and the concomitant spread of *Psidium guajava*.

7.5.2. Evergreen forests not dominated by *Scalesia*

There are few evergreen forests in the Galápagos in which *Scalesia* is not an important member. Below the *S. pedunculata* forest (or remains thereof) on Santiago, at an elevation of 300–400 m, an evergreen dense tree canopy is sometimes formed mainly by *Psidium galapageium* and *Pisonia floribunda*, both endemic to Galápagos. This is a true forest with the tallest trees (*Psidium*) reaching 10–12 m in height. *Zanthoxylum fagara* is common but normally forms a shrub, together with *Psychotria rufipes* and other species. As already mentioned, goats have greatly influenced the vegetation on Santiago and the absence of other species may be the result of browsing.

In certain areas of the Galápagos the physiognomy of the vegetation is that of a forest although the low height of the trees would categorize the vegetation as 'scrub' rather than 'forest'. *Scalesia microcephala* has been cited as one such example on Isabela. Some areas in the upper parts of Pinta receive a larger amount of moisture than other parts of the island. Here *Solanum erianthum* and *Zanthoxylum fagara* may form a closed canopy at a height of 2–4 m. Associated shrubs, mainly *Tournefortia rufo-sericea* and *Psychotria rufipes*, are low and hardly extend above the closed 0.5–1.8 m thick herb layer. Hamann (1981) categorized this vegetation as an evergreen forest. Whether or not it represents undisturbed vegetation in harmony with the environment is doubtful, however, since Pinta is another island that has been subjected to infestation by goats.

7.5.3. Deciduous forests

As already mentioned, there is generally no sharp delimitation of different vegetation zones in the Galápagos and one zone intergrades with another. Below the moist *Scalesia* zone on Santa Cruz there are forests, the dominating trees of which are deciduous. At an elevation of 500–600 m on the northern slope of Santa Cruz, *Psidium galapageium* and *Bursera graveolens* form an almost closed canopy up to 8 m above the ground. The shrub layer is composed of *Zanthoxylum fagara*, *Tournefortia psilostachya*, *Lantana peduncularis* and *Alternanthera echinocephala*, the latter reaching 2 m in height. The coverage of the herb layer varies considerably with the season, being very sparse during dry periods. By contrast, the southern slope of Santa Cruz is occupied by evergreen moist *Scalesia* forest at corresponding elevations.

At lower elevations on Santa Cruz, and elsewhere, the floristic composition in the forest varies with altitude, local conditions and to some extent with the island. Up to 100 m, the most important trees are *Bursera graveolens*, *Pisonia floribunda*, *Piscidia carthagenensis*, *Zanthoxylum fagara*, *Erythrina velutina* and *Psidium galapageium*. At altitudes below 50 m the four first-named dominate. Tall cacti also occur at low elevations. Occasionally *Bursera* may form true forests where the trees attain 5 m or more in height. This is a green and beautiful forest in the wet season, whereas in the dry season bone-white stems stand leafless and lower vegetation layers almost disappear.

7.6. Steppe Forests

With lower altitude, trees become progressively smaller and less numerous. Because of the aridity other plant layers are also poorly developed. The total cover of the vegetation decreases and the aspect becomes more open. These tree-containing formations in the Galápagos lowlands can normally be designated as steppe forest.

The vast majority of these steppe forests are deciduous. Such formations exist at low altitudes on most islands in the archipelago. *Bursera graveolens*, *Croton scouleri* and *Opuntia* spp. are the most important members in the tree layer but, depending on altitude and island, *Zanthoxylum fagara*, *Piscidia carthagenensis*, *Pisonia floribunda*, *Hippomane mancinella* and other species also occur. Evergreen shrub-forming species of *Scalesia* grow among otherwise predominantly deciduous woody species on e.g. Pinta and Pinzón. Formations designated as evergreen steppe forests were recognized by Hamann (1981) on Pinta, Santiago, Pinzón and Fernandina. Such formations generally occur at higher altitudes (300 m and more) where moisture allows the vegetation to be evergreen but where other conditions, such as the structure of the ground, prevent the development of true forest.

References

Black, J.(1974) *Galápagos, Archipiélago del Ecuador.* Imprinta Europa, Quito.

Bowman, R.I. (1961) Morphological differentiation and adaptation in the Galápagos finches. *Univ. Calif. Publ. Zool.*, **58**, 302 pp, pl. 1–22.

Byer, M.D. and Weaver, P.L. (1977) Early secondary succession in an elfin woodland in the Luquillo Mountains of Puerto Rico. *Biotropica*, **9**, 35–47.

Carlquist, S. (1974) *Island Biology.* Columbia University Press, New York.

Eliasson, U. (1974) Studies in Galápagos Plants. XIV. The genus *Scalesia* Arn. *Op. bot. Soc. bot. Lund*, **36**, 117 pp.

Fosberg, F.R. (1967) A classification of vegetation for general purposes. In G.F. Peterken, Guide to the Check Sheet for IBP Areas. Pp. 73–120. *IBP Handbook No 4.* Blackwell Scientific Publications, Oxford.

Hamann, O. (1979a) On climatic conditions, vegetation types, and leaf size in the Galápagos Islands. *Biotropica*, **11**, 101–122.

Hamann, O. (1979b) Dynamics of a stand of *Scalesia pedunculata* Hooker fil., Santa Cruz Island, Galápagos. *J. Linn. Soc. Bot.*, **78**, 67–84.

Hamann, O. (1981) Plant communities of the Galápagos Islands. *Dansk bot. Ark.*, **34**, 163 pp.

McBirney, A.R. and Williams, H. (1969) Geology and petrology of the Galápagos Islands. *Mem. geol. Soc. Am.*, **118**, 197 pp.

Porter, D.M. (1979) Endemism and evolution in Galápagos Islands vascular plants. In D. Bramwell (ed.), *Plants and islands.*, pp. 225–256, Academic Press, London.

Reeder, W.C. and Riechert, S.E. (1975) Vegetation along an altitudinal gradient, Santa Cruz, Galápagos Islands. *Biotropica*, **7**, 162–175.

Richards, P.W. (1952) *The tropical rain forest.* Cambridge University Press, Cambridge.

Shimwell, D.W. (1971) *Description and classification of vegetation.* Sidgwick & Jackson, London.

Werff, H. van der (1978) The vegetation of the Galápagos Islands. (Thesis, University of Utrecht) Zierikzee (Holland). 102 pp., pl. 1–15.

Wiggins, I.R. and Porter, D.M. (1971) *Flora of the Galápagos Islands.* Stanford University Press, Stanford.

CHAPTER 8

Changes and Threats to the Vegetation

OLE HAMANN

University of Copenhagen, Institute of Systematic Botany, Gothersgade, Copenhagen, Denmark

Contents

8.1.	Introduction	115
8.2.	The Galápagos Vegetation	116
8.3.	Impact of Colonization on the Vegetation	116
	8.3.1. The threats	117
8.4.	Recent Vegetation Changes	119
	8.4.1. Xerophytic vegetation	120
	8.4.2. Mesophytic vegetation	124
	8.4.3. Endangered vegetation types	129
8.5.	Endemic Ecosystems	129
	References	130

8.1. Introduction

An important consequence of the interactions between the organisms in any ecosystem and between the organisms and the environment is change. Man is now part of the Galápagos ecosystem and may be regarded as just another organism. But the uniqueness of the islands and the great national and international interest in preserving the Galápagos in as near a natural state as possible warrant special attention to those changes caused by man.

For over a century man has been modifying the ecosystems of the Galápagos Islands, with serious although not massive changes as a result. Following colonization many forest-covered areas on southern Isabela, San Cristóbal, Floreana and Santa Cruz were transformed into pastures, crop fields, fruit-tree plantations etc. Plants and domesticated animals were brought to the islands and some ran wild outside the colonized zones. This had a profound impact on the natural vegetation in some areas. Today the major threats to the indigenous ecosystems are feral mammals and introduced plants. However, in spite of the changes, large parts of the archipelago are still undisturbed and close to being in a pristine state.

8.2. The Galápagos Vegetation

Constant volcanic activity has caused abrupt changes to the local environment in many places in the archipelago. The sudden destruction or alteration of patches of vegetation has been (and remains) a common phenomenon, with new invasions, establishments and successions following. This is particularly the case on the islands of Fernandina and Isabela, where most of the present volcanic activity is centred. However, on geologically older islands, such as San Cristóbal, palaeoecological data suggest that only minor changes (fluctuations) have occurred in the mesophytic vegetation types of the highland during the last 9000 years (Colinvaux and Schofield, 1976a and b).

The present-day Galápagos vegetation has been divided into vegetation zones, each composed of a number of characteristic species and therefore to a certain degree also characterized structurally and physiognomically (Bowman, 1961, Wiggins and Porter, 1971). On southern Santa Cruz, seven principal vegetation zones represented are:

  Littoral Zone, at sea level;
  Arid Zone, to an altitude of about 80 to 100 m;
  Transition Zone, above the *Arid Zone*;
  Scalesia Zone, from about 180 to (in places) 5–600 m a.s.l.;
  Brown Zone, above the *Scalesia Zone* in certain places;
  Miconia Zone, from about 400 to about 700 m a.s.l.;
  Fern-Sedge Zone, above the *Miconia Zone* to the summit (864 m).

Gradual changes from one zone to another are often encountered, and vegetation types other than those represented in the zonation described above are present in the archipelago, notably on the western islands of Fernandina and Isabela (see van der Werff, 1978 and Hamann, 1979a and 1981 for comprehensive descriptions of Galápagos vegetation and also table on page 4).

8.3. Impact of Colonization on the Vegetation

After its discovery in 1535, the archipelago was frequently visited, first by buccaneers, then by whalers and hunters. The impact of these early visitors on the native fauna is well documented. Some of the serious conservation problems of today originated then: the early visitors removed a large proportion of the indigenous grazers, the giant tortoises, and left, in some cases, domesticated mammals instead (Black, 1974). Subsequent visitors continued this trend. For example, in 1813 four goats were set ashore on the uninhabited island of Santiago from the US frigate *Essex*; these escaped to the interior of the island and were later observed by other visitors (Slevin, 1959). This introduction presumably founded the population of feral goats now living on Santiago, although later introductions probably took place. In 1887, an expedition conducted by Agassiz visited Santiago when wild pigs were observed (Slevin, 1959). In 1905, when Stewart visited the island, feral goats and donkeys were numerous (Stewart, 1915). Today the estimated number of goats on Santiago is more than 100,000, and their grazing has changed and destroyed large areas of natural vegetation (Calvopiña and de Vries, 1975, de Vries and Calvopiña, 1977).

Some impact on the native vegetation invariably accompanied colonization. The first settlement was established on Floreana by General Villamil in 1832 when land was cleared in the highlands for farming and fruit plantations. Villamil also introduced domesticated mammals to then uninhabited islands as a prelude to future colonization (Black, 1974). In 1835, Floreana was visited by Darwin, who observed cultivated fields of sweet potatoes (*Ipomoea batatas*) and bananas (*Musa* spp.): he also noted that the colonists had no trouble in obtaining food: 'In the woods there are many wild pigs and goats; but the staple article of animal food is supplied by the tortoises. Their numbers have, of course, been greatly reduced in this island, but the people yet count on two days' hunting giving them food for the rest of the week'.

Some of the early settlements were abandoned after a few years, only to be followed by renewed attempts. In 1887, Floreana was visited by the French corvette *Decres*. The commander described the island, which at that time was without human inhabitants: 'The north side of Floriana (*sic*) is less arid than that of Chatham (San Cristóbal), and the central portion looks to me richer and more fertile. But none of us has found cane plantations or manioc stalks. To make up for it, orange and lemon trees (*Citrus* spp.) grow everywhere on the plain and on the hills. We have seen a large number of donkeys grazing on the hill-slopes and on the highest summits' (Slevin, 1959: 103).

Thus, already before settlement became permanent, Floreana displayed the now familiar picture of the four inhabited islands in the archipelago: the humid highlands were partly cleared of native forests, plants and animals were introduced, and some of these had spread into the wild.

8.3.1. The threats

The list of animals introduced to the Galápagos is very long (Chapter 16, Table 1). Some have failed to establish in the wild, e.g. sheep and guinea pigs (Duffy, 1981), while others have succeeded. Feral dogs, cats, rats and mice all create problems, as discussed in Chapter 16. But feral goats, pigs, donkeys, horses and cattle clearly have a profound influence on the vegetation. Eradication of goats has proven feasible on small and middle-sized islands: in 1961 they were eradicated on South Plaza, in 1971 on Santa Fé and Rábida, in 1978 on Española and in 1979 on Marchena (Anonymous, 1980). On Pinta, where an estimated 40,000 goats were shot during the 1970s, less than a hundred remain (Galápagos National Park personnel, pers. comm. 1981). However, large goat populations survive on Santa Cruz and Santiago and smaller populations on San Cristóbal, Isabela and Floreana. Similarly, some islands have large or small populations of feral pigs (Santiago, Isabela, Santa Cruz, Floreana). Wild cattle and horses are probably only a problem on southern Isabela; while small populations of donkeys are found on several islands.

Other animals may induce long-term changes in the ecosystems. Kastdalen (1965) reported that 2 species of introduced earthworms were changing the soil in the farm region on Santa Cruz. Such changes and the consequences thereof have yet to be investigated.

The general effect of the activities of feral mammals is an opening up of closed native vegetation (Fig. 8.1). When, for example, goats were introduced to Pinta around 1959 they soon multiplied. In a few years they destroyed much of the vegetation in the arid lowlands and so moved to the more humid highlands (Weber, 1971, Hamann, 1975, 1979b). Investigations on Santiago have shown that goats in particular are responsible for eating most seedlings of native woody plants (Calvopiña and de Vries, 1975, de Vries and Calvopiña, 1977). Since some Galápagos plants are relatively shortlived, e.g. *Scalesia* spp. (Hamann, 1979c), heavy grazing tends to remove woody species by impeding the naturally rapid turnover in their populations.

According to Colinvaux (1980), a closed cover in the mesophytic highland vegetation prevented further plant invasions once the cover was established. Therefore, when goats or other introduced mammals open or destroy the closed cover, invasion by new plant species is facilitated. The relatively recent spread of some introduced plant species into National Park Zones may thus have been prepared and facilitated by previous opening of the vegetation.

More than 200 plant species introduced by man occur in the Galápagos Islands (Black, 1974, Porter, 1979, Hamann, 1979d). A majority of these species are herbaceous weeds, many of which are naturalized. Weedy species are often characterized by advanced seeding and dispersal mechanisms, and by a considerable degree of adaptability to different climatic conditions and environments. Some of the weeds in the Galápagos are American or Pan-tropical species (*Ageratum conyzoides*, *Brickellia diffusa*, *Blainvillea dichotoma* and *Porophyllum ruderale*), while others have a European origin (*Coronopus didymus*, *Sonchus oleraceus* and *Plantago major*). Most of the naturalized weeds occur in mesophytic vegetation types.

The number of introduced weedy species is continually growing, thus representing possibly a subtle long-term threat to the indigenous vegetation. Essentially, the Galápagos flora is a 'weedy' flora: Porter (1976) argued that weedy plants, being adapted to open habitats, have been at an advantage when their disseminules reached the islands. The chance of immigrants surviving in any specific locality is greater initially than later when more closed communities have evolved. This is in accordance with Colinvaux (1980). It is therefore of no surprise that man-introduced weeds successfully compete with the native species once formerly closed vegetation has been opened up by introduced mammals. It is even possible that some of the new introductions are better adapted to the conditions prevalent today in many areas by being able to tolerate heavy grazing impact.

Figure 8.1. Characteristic open vegetation in the central part of Santa Fé in 1972, 6 months after goats had been eradicated on the island. Only old individuals of *Opuntia echios* var, *barringtonensis*, *Bursera graveolens* and (in centre) shrubs of *Cordia lutea* survive the long presence of goats.

Some introduced plants are spreading into National Park Zones (Table 8.1). Apart from the uninhabited island of Santiago, where *Persea americana* and *Citrus* spp. are remnants of abandoned settlements (Villa, 1971), these species are confined to the four large colonized islands. These islands have different histories of colonization, and to a certain degree are different in terms of environmental conditions. Consequently, the pattern of the spread of introduced plants is different from island to island. The National Park Service is therefore faced with a complex problem when dealing with introduced plants as a threat to indigenous vegetation.

Table 8.1. Ten introduced plant species considered as threats to indigenous vegetation of the Galápagos Islands

Family	Species	Local name	Use or useful product	Island(s) where the species is a problem[1]	Occurrence in vegetation zone(s)
Agavaceae	*Furcraea cubensis*	Cabuya	Hedge	Isabela Santa Cruz Floreana San Cristóbal	Arid to Fern-Sedge
Crassulaceae	*Kalanchoe pinnata*	–	Ornamental	San Cristóbal Floreana Isabela Santa Cruz	Arid & Transition
Lauraceae	*Persea americana*	Aguacate	Fruit	Santa Cruz Isabela Floreana San Cristóbal Santiago	Scalesia to Fern-Sedge
Myrtaceae	*Psidium guajava*	Guayaba	Fruit	Isabela San Cristóbal Floreana Santa Cruz	Transition to Fern-Sedge
Myrtaceae	*Eugenia jambos*	Poma-rosa	Fruit	San Cristóbal Santa Cruz Isabela	Scalesia and/or Miconia?
Poaceae	*Digitaria decumbens*	Pangola	Pasture	Santa Cruz	Scalesia
Poaceae	*Pennisetum purpureum*	Pasto elefante	Pasture	Santa Cruz	Scalesia to Fern-Sedge
Rubiaceae	*Cinchona succirubra*	Cascarilla	Quinine	Santa Cruz	Miconia and Fern-Sedge
Rutaceae	*Citrus* spp.[2]	–	Fruit	Floreana San Cristóbal Isabela Santa Cruz Santiago	Transition to Miconia
Verbenaceae	*Lantana camara*	Lantana	Hedge	Floreana	Arid to Scalesia

[1] This is not a full list of the distribution of species, but an indication as to the islands where their presence causes concern (the islands most affected appear first),
[2] Several species of *Citrus* now occur in the wild.
Data compiled from Kastdalen (1965), Villa (1971), Wiggins and Porter (1971), Black (1974), van der Werff (1979), Hamann (1979d), personal observations and Adsersen (pers. comm.).

8.4. Recent Vegetation Changes

Detailed information on vegetation changes in the Galápagos has recently been provided by investigations of permanent quadrats, established in various kinds of vegetation. But these investigations have only been carried out since 1966, so generalizations have to be made with caution. Another concern, common to many successional studies, is that evaluation of changes, induced or natural, have often to be made by comparing the vegetation of different sites thought to represent similar or different stages in the same successional series. In these particular cases, comparisons are made between undisturbed and disturbed areas in the assumption that the vegetation of the areas would be very similar, if no disturbance had occurred. This assumption is difficult to prove, because we have no detailed information on those areas prior to the disturbance. Nevertheless, some tentative generalizations and conclusions may be reached.

Today, permanent quadrats (ranging in size from 25 m^2 to 750 m^2) are established on Santa Cruz, Santa Fé, Pinta and Santiago. The study of these has elucidated the influence of introduced mammals and provided information on successional trends and dynamics of the vegetation (Hamann, 1975, 1979b and c, de Vries,

1977, Calvopiña and de Vries, 1975, de Vries and Calvopiña, 1977). The quadrats are in various vegetation types, ranging from very xerophytic to very mesophytic. In general, the Galápagos vegetation types may be characterized as either xerophytic or mesophytic, being dominated by species adapted to dry or to more humid conditions, respectively.

8.4.1. Xerophytic vegetation

The arid regions of the Galápagos are principally covered with xerophytic vegetation types such as dry season deciduous steppe forest and forest (Hamann, 1981) (most of the Arid Zone in the sense of Wiggins and Porter 1971). But further vegetation types are basically xerophytic, e.g. the Littoral Zone vegetation, and various evergreen and dry season deciduous types ranging from desert scrub to scrub. The latter types are predominant at high altitudes on some of the volcanoes of Isabela and on Fernandina.

On Santa Cruz, close to the Charles Darwin Research Station, two permanent quadrats were established in 1966. The vegetation in these quadrats is representative of the microphyllous dry season deciduous steppe forest (woodland) encountered at lower elevations on southern Santa Cruz (Fig. 8.2). Characteristic trees are *Opuntia echios* var. *gigantea*, *Jasminocereus thouarsii* var. *delicatus*, and *Bursera graveolens*. Smaller trees and shrubs are numerous, e.g. *Croton scouleri*, *Maytenus octogona*, *Scutia pauciflora*, *Castela galapageia*, *Parkinsonia aculeata*, *Prosopis juliflora* and *Clerodendrum molle*. Relatively few herb species occur as regular members of this vegetation; most conspicuous are the annual *Evolvolus glaber* and the perennials, *Cyperus elegans* ssp. *rubiginosus* and *Rhynchosia minima*.

No major change in the vegetation took place during the period 1966–1981: the number of woody species remained practically constant, and the density of individuals did not change much, although fluctuations occurred. Such fluctuations were caused by the appearance of seedlings of, for example, *Croton*, *Parkinsonia* and *Opuntia* at various times in the period, but few of these became established. To all appearances, the vegetation remained undisturbed.

Santiago is the island where feral mammals have been most destructive. In a study of the goat population and its impact on the vegetation, Calvopiña and de Vries (1975) observed the feeding behaviour and analysed stomach contents of the goats. In the Arid Zone vegetation at Buccaneer Bay young trees of *Bursera graveolens*, *Acacia* spp. and *Erythrina velutina* could no longer be found, and bushes of *Croton scouleri*, *Cordia lutea* and *Cryptocarpus pyriformis* were being browsed as far as goats could reach. Annual plants were completely removed in periods of drought, and at middle elevations, where *Psidium galapageium* dominates, the soil was a dust bowl between periods of rain.

Open permanent quadrats were established on Santiago in 1973 and 1974, and fenced quadrats in 1975. A 16-month study of changes in the vegetation subsequently showed, as expected, that differences between fenced and unfenced quadrats were great, both in species number and composition. For example, in September 1975, one fenced quadrat in the Arid Zone contained 35 species and had a closed herb layer; while two open quadrats close by contained 17 and 19 species, and had no closed herb layer present (de Vries and Calvopiña, 1977). The fenced quadrats on Santiago may, for the time being, serve as small, living seed banks, while a solution to the goat problem is sought (Chapter 16, Fig. 2).

On Santa Fé, dry season deciduous steppe forest (and transitions to steppe savanna) is the predominant vegetation type. Compared to the Arid Zone vegetation on Santa Cruz, the steppe forest has an open canopy and a low density of trees. *Opuntia echios* var. *barringtonensis* and *Bursera graveolens* are the only trees, and the mostly open shrub layer is formed by *Cordia lutea*, *Lantana peduncularis* and *Castela galapageia*. In some areas the semi-evergreen small shrub *Encelia hispida* dominates. In most places the herb layer is sparse, but grasses (e.g. *Aristida subspicata*) and sedges (e.g. *Cyperus elegans* spp. *rubiginosus*) are characteristic (Hamann, 1979b, 1981).

Until 1971, when goats were eliminated from Santa Fé, these animals had been on the island for at least 66

Figure 8.2. A permanent quadrat in dry season deciduous steppe forest, dominated by *Opuntia echios* var. *gigantea*, on Santa Cruz, October 1977. The three small *Opuntia* to the left, near the corner post of the quadrat, were then about 11 years old. Under natural conditions the growth of *Opuntia* appears to be very slow.

years (Stewart, 1915). The study of permanent quadrats, established in 1972, has shown that a certain regeneration of the vegetation is under way. However, it appears that not all woody species actually present on the island participate in this regeneration (Hamann, 1979b). This might be related to the importance of the floristic composition of the vegetation at the time when grazing stopped. The initial floristic composition (including surviving plants and all propagules) determines, to a large degree, the way a secondary succession starts; an initial pulse of establishment of species is often seen (Noble and Slatyer, 1980), but such an initial pulse is not encountered on Santa Fé. The number of plant species originally growing there was probably smaller than, for example, in Arid Zone vegetation on Santa Cruz, because Santa Fé is a small island with a relatively narrow range of habitats. Even so, only about half the woody species present appear to be extending their distribution on the island. Important factors influencing this could be selective seed predation (by finches, Abbott *et al.*, 1977), and the number and distribution of individuals of the remaining plants; it might be that so few individuals are left of certain species that it will take considerable time to build up new populations.

In a comparative study of *Bursera* populations on Isabela, northern Santa Cruz and Daphne Major, Grant (1981) found that goat-damaged populations of *Bursera graveolens* had a top-heavy age structure. Without the control of the goats, *Bursera* populations were foreseen eventually to collapse. All observations on Santa Fé indicate that the *Bursera* population there had a top-heavy age structure in 1971. Furthermore, the vegetation had been changed to a more open structure by grazing. This could facilitate invasion by new species; but in fact it appears to hinder the germination and re-establishment of *Bursera*, and perhaps *Opuntia* too. In 1977, de Vries marked and measured 55 *Bursera* seedlings, some of the first to appear after 1971. These seedlings were practically all growing in the shelter of rocks and boulders, or beneath the cover of other plants. No seedlings of *Bursera* (or *Opuntia*) were found on the open *Opuntia*-dominated plains, either in 1980 or in 1981, but several had appeared in sheltered places (pers. obs.). This indicates that the expected re-establishment of vegetation on Santa Fé has become difficult because of the change in vegetation structure caused by goat-grazing.

On Pinta a permanent quadrat was established in 1970 in typical Arid Zone vegetation, i.e. in dry season deciduous steppe forest. *Bursera graveolens* and *Opuntia galapageia* var. *galapageia* formed an open canopied tree

Figure 8.3. Seedlings of *Opuntia galapageia* var. *galapageia* in Arid Zone vegetation on Pinta, in 1980.

layer, and an equally open shrub layer was composed of *Castela galapageia*, *Scalesia baurii* ssp. *hopkinsii*, *Lantana peduncularis* and *Croton scouleri*. Many herbs consituted a rather open herb layer (Hamann, 1979b).

From 1970 to 1977, a notable regeneration of the vegetation took place, concurrent with the eradication of large numbers of goats (Fig. 8.3). Noteworthy was the appearance of seedlings of *Scalesia* and *Castela* during this period. Although some failed to establish, a steady increase in density of woody plants took place (Hamann, 1979b). In 1980 and 1981 seedlings of *Bursera* were also recorded. Figure 8.4 demonstrates this regeneration of *Scalesia* and *Castela* between 1970 and 1981.

The secondary succession in this area of Pinta, following the cessation of overgrazing, was characterized by an initial pulse of establishment of species—in contrast to the situation on Santa Fé. The main factor of importance here appears to be that most plants on Pinta survived the heavy, but relatively short duration of goat-grazing in sufficient numbers to enable them to multiply and so re-establish as soon as the goats had gone. This indicates that a relatively small goat population may damage the vegetation more, if left in the

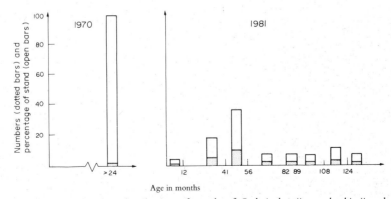

Figure 8.4. Age class distribution of stands of *Scalesia baurii* ssp. *hopkinsii* and *Castela galapageia* in a permanent quadrat on Pinta, recorded in 1970 and 1981. In 1970, 40 seedlings and 2 old individuals of *Scalesia* were recorded; in 1981 a more even distribution of various age classes was found (total number 51). In 1970 only two old individuals of *Castela* were found, while in 1981 a more even distribution of age classes was recorded (total number 27).

Arid Zone vegetation over a long period; while the vegetation is able to recuperate rapidly after even very heavy grazing, provided the grazing has not been too long sustained. On Santa Fé about 2–3000 goats were shot during a successful eradication campaign ending in 1971 (de Vries, 1977).

On Pinta about 40,000 goats have been shot so far, and less than a hundred are thought to remain; but goats have only been on the island a fraction of the time as compared to Santa Fé.

8.4.2. Mesophytic vegetation

Santa Cruz offers some good examples of upland, mesophytic vegetation types: microphyllous to mesophyllous evergreen forest (*Scalesia* Zone vegetation), mesophyllous evergreen scrub (*Miconia* Zone vegetation) and more or less seasonal meadows (Fern-Sedge Zone vegetation, or 'pampa' vegetation). Similar or comparable vegetation types are found on all the high islands, where the upper slopes receive more precipitation than coastal regions (Hamann, 1979a, 1981).

In 1970, a permanent quadrat was established in the evergreen forest (*Scalesia* forest) in the tortoise reserve in the southwest of Santa Cruz. The forest had a rather distinct stratification (see Chapter 1, Fig. 2), and epiphytes and vines were common. The tree layer formed a closed canopy at a height of 8–12 m, *Scalesia pedunculata* and *Psidium galapageium* being the dominants. Other tree species were *Pisonia floribunda*, *Zanthoxylum fagara*, and, at shallow pools, *Hippomane mancinella*. A mostly closed shrub layer was dominated by the evergreen *Psychotria rufipes* and *Tournefortia rufo-sericea*, and a closed herb layer, mainly composed of perennials, was a characteristic feature. The study of the vegetation in this quadrat has given information on the changes in mesophytic vegetation under conditions of very little or no disturbance, as well as on the growth and survival of *Scalesia pedunculata* trees (Hamann, 1979c).

The species composition of the vegetation changed little during the 7-year study, the most noteworthy being an establishment of individuals of *Psidium galapageium* and *Pisonia floribunda* and a change in dominants among the herb species. By contrast, the number of individuals of *Scalesia* in the quadrat fluctuated. It appeared that the growth and survival pattern of the *Scalesia* trees was an expression of an adaptive strategy fitted for a pioneer or early-successional tree. Simultaneously, the *Scalesia* trees were able to persist in the forest by means of a large reproductive effort and rapid population turnover, which enabled them to re-establish rapidly in gaps in the forest. The importance of gaps and natural disturbances for the dynamics of tropical forests has recently been emphasized (Bassaz and Pickett, 1980). Apparently, as explained in Chapter 7, gaps also play a major role in the dynamics of the *Scalesia* forest on Santa Cruz, although the number of species and structural diversity there is far lower than in tropical forests in general.

The *Scalesia* forest investigated appears to be in a 'dynamic but stable' stage: it is able to recuperate rapidly after temporary disturbance. *Scalesia* forest may be considered as a climax vegetation, but its diversity and complexity is not as great as tropical rain forest, for example, and the dominant species, *Scalesia pedunculata*, shows a pioneer or early-successional strategy for survival. This distinguishes *Scalesia* forest from most other tropical forests, where more complex and diverse vegetation is predominant, and where late-successional species dominate the climax-factors thus tending to make the vegetation less stable in the sense that it does not have the same ability to recuperate after temporary disturbance.

On San Cristóbal and Santiago, *Scalesia* Zone vegetation was formerly present. However, the influence of colonization has destroyed most *Scalesia* forest on San Cristóbal (van der Werff, 1979) and feral goats and pigs have had the same effect on Santiago (de Vries and Calvopiña, 1977). On those islands, only few individuals of *Scalesia pedunculata* are left. However, according to Kastdalen (1965), *Scalesia pedunculata* is an aggressive colonizer once grazing has stopped. Presumably it is still possible for *Scalesia* to re-establish in some areas on San Cristóbal and Santiago—if the right conditions are recreated, e.g. by eliminating the overgrazing on Santiago. However, the crucial factor may be time: goats eat all seedlings of *Scalesia pedunculata* in the highlands of Santiago, and the very short lifespan of *Scalesia* trees makes the remaining population very unstable. Only old individuals are left by the goats and in a few years they simply die of old age (de Vries and Calvopiña, 1977, Hamann, 1979c).

On Pinta, many different vegetation types are found, due to the high elevation and variations in local climatic conditions. Close to the summit, mesophytic low evergreen forest (Fig. 8.5) and evergreen scrub with scattered trees are predominant. Although these vegetation types do not contain *Scalesia*, they are comparable to the *Scalesia* Zone vegetation of Santa Cruz (Hamann, 1981). The dominant woody plants in this mesophytic vegetation were (in 1977) *Zanthoxylum fagara*, *Solanum erianthum*, *Tournefortia rufo-sericea* and *Psychotria rufipes*. A dense 'herb' layer, mostly dominated by ferns (e.g. *Pteridium aquilinum*), was conspicuous. After 1970, rapid changes in the vegetation occurred, at the same time as large numbers of goats were shot on Pinta. The cover changed in 2 years from open to closed (mainly caused by the re-growth and re-establishment of *Tournefortia*, *Psychotria* and *Solanum*) (Figs. 8.6A and B). It was suggested that much of the regeneration took place as regrowth from old stems and rhizomes which survived the grazing, in contrast to

Figure 8.5. The CDRS's invaluable field assistant, Camilo Calapucha, in dense evergreen forest close to the summit of Pinta in 1977. Old individuals of *Zanthoxylum fagara*, covered with epiphytes, dominate the vegetation. In this area a notable recovery of vegetation was recorded during the period 1970–1977.

Figure 8.6A. A permanent quadrat close to the summit of Pinta in 1970 with vegetation much destroyed by goats. (Photo: T. de Vries).

Figure 8.6B. Same quadrat as in Fig. 6A, in 1977. Dense vegetation covers the quadrat. Woody species are *Zanthoxylum fagara* (left centre), *Solanum erianthum*, *Psychotria rufipes* and *Tournefortia rufo-sericea*. The fern is *Pteridium aquilinum*.

the Arid Zone vegetation where the establishment of seedlings appeared to be most important (Hamann, 1979b).

It was foreseen that regeneration would lead to the formation of a low, closed, evergreen forest. It is questionable whether this will eventually be like the original forest described by Stewart (1915): the now very conspicuous *Solanum erianthum* was not listed by Stewart (1911, 1915). Perhaps this species was formerly rare on Pinta and, being largely avoided by goats, spread during the years of heavy goat infestation (Hamann, 1979b).

Miconia Zone vegetation on the upper slopes of Santa Cruz is a mesophytic, mesophyllous, evergreen scrub, dominated by *Miconia robinsoniana*. Other woody species, like *Psychotria rufipes*, are present, but not in great quantities. A dense ground layer, composed mainly of ferns and other pteridophytes is conspicuous (Hamann, 1981). Formerly *Miconia* Zone vegetation occurred on San Cristóbal, but today only scattered shrubs remain (van der Werff, 1979). Investigation of the *Miconia* Zone vegetation on Santa Cruz has shown that this has diminished in extent since colonization started in the 1920's, due to fires (natural and induced), grazing by cattle and perhaps climatic change (Kastdalen, 1965, Hamann, 1975). Apparently, *Miconia* regenerates slowly after disturbance. When shrubs were destroyed, it was therefore other species, mainly from the Fern-Sedge Zone, that invaded the area, thereby extending the total area of the Fern-Sedge Zone vegetation. Today, large parts of the upper slopes of Santa Cruz are covered with Fern-Sedge Zone vegetation (Fig. 8.7), which consists of a number of vegetation types: more or less seasonal meadows, dominated by ferns, sedges or grasses and herbs; heath-like vegetation dominated by the dwarf shrub,

Figure 8.7. View of the Fern-Sedge Zone in the highlands of Santa Cruz with a few trees of *Scalesia pedunculata* (at left).

Pernettya howellii; and bogs and fens dominated by *Sphagnum* (Itow and Weber, 1974, Hamann, 1981). In gulleys and on steep slopes of old craters the characteristic tree-fern *Cyathea weatherbyana* is found.

   Probably the entire summit region of Santa Cruz was originally covered by such Fern-Sedge Zone vegetation (Howell, 1942). However, today, the introduced tree, *Cinchona succirubra* (Table 8.1), has been able to establish in the Fern-Sedge Zone (Fig. 8.8). This tree grows in many places in the farm zone at lower elevation, where it fruits abundantly and from whence the light, winged seeds are easily carried up to the highland region. An intensive eradication campaign has been carried out by the Galápagos National Park Service, and, in the spring of 1981, it was estimated that virtually all *Cinchona* trees on eastern Santa Cruz had been destroyed (SPNG personnel, pers. com.). But as long as cattle are able to enter the highland region (e.g. in dry periods, Hamann, 1978), possibilities for the re-establishment of such species as *Cinchona* remain favourable. It is likely that the destruction of the otherwise closed and dense indigenous vegetation facilitates the establishment of species like *Cinchona*.

Figure 8.8. *Cinchona succirubra* growing in the Fern-Sedge Zone vegetation on Santa Cruz.

8.4.3. Endangered vegetation types

Vegetation types which originally had, or now have, a limited distribution in the archipelago are those that under certain circumstances will disappear quickly. *Miconia* Zone vegetation has already disappeared as a vegetation type from San Cristóbal. On Santa Cruz its extent has diminished due to colonization, cattle grazing, fires and perhaps climatic change, and the spread of introduced plants such as *Cinchona succirubra* threatens remaining *Miconia* vegetation. Also, the Fern–Sedge Zone vegetation types above the *Miconia* Zone are influenced by cattle grazing and introduced plants, although probably to a lesser degree.

Below the *Miconia* Zone on Santa Cruz, a 'Brown Zone' of vegetation was formerly found (Bowman, 1961). This vegetation was characterized by dwarfed *Scalesia pedunculata* and *Psidium galapageium* trees heavily draped with epiphytic mosses and ferns, which gave the vegetation a brown cast when viewed from a distance (page 77). The area where this Brown Zone occurred is now farmland; clearing for pastures and crop fields has removed this vegetation type almost completely (Hamann, 1979a, van der Werff, 1979).

Scalesia Zone vegetation formerly had a larger distribution in the islands. However, good examples of evergreen forest dominated by *Scalesia pedunculata* are still found on Santa Cruz and Floreana; but this vegetation has almost completely gone from San Cristóbal (due to colonization) and Santiago (where all vegetation types are threatened by feral mammals). The remaining *Scalesia pedunculata*-dominated forests are thus found on inhabited islands only, where the combined effects of grazing and the spread and establishment of introduced plants present a danger. The comparable evergreen forests on Isabela and Fernandina, dominated by *Scalesia cordata* and *Scalesia microcephala*, appear in most places to be relatively undisturbed, except on southern Isabela, where the effects of colonization are similar to those on Santa Cruz.

Arid Zone vegetation types, in the widest sense, are those which cover the largest area in the Galápagos Islands. Many parts of the Arid Zone have been seriously affected by the activities of introduced grazers, for example on Santa Fé, Pinta and Santiago. However, plants of the arid regions have adapted to harsh environmental conditions and are able to survive in extreme habitats. Even if the plant cover in Arid Zone vegetation is predominantly open, which could facilitate the invasion of new immigrants, recent introductions have much difficulty in establishing there as compared with mesophytic vegetation types (Haro, 1975). Furthermore, environmental changes in the form of volcanic events have presumably been a regular phenomenon throughout the history of the islands, whereby the creation of habitats suited for xerophytic vegetation in particular takes place. Therefore, the original members of the Arid Zone vegetation types are pioneer species: they are able to re-invade and re-establish on recently hardened lava flows and on ash fields, which during volcanic eruptions eradicate local vegetation. So, generally, Arid Zone vegetation types might be considered the most robust of Galápagos vegetation types, in the sense that they show the highest natural resistance to external perturbations.

8.5. Endemic Ecosystems

It is a common conception that endemic species are rare species. Endemic species occur, per definition, in a restricted geographical range, for example only in the Galápagos. Some endemic species are also rare in the sense that very few individuals of the species have existed, or do exist. This is the case for some Galápagos plants, such as *Calandrinia galapagosa*, which is only known to grow in two localities on San Cristóbal (J. Villa, pers. comm.), and also some *Scalesia* species only occur in small numbers within exceptionally limited areas (e.g. *S. stewartii*, *S. retroflexa*, *S. incisa*, see Eliasson, 1974). The endemic *Psychotria angustata* was presumably very rare originally: it was collected by Darwin (in 1835) and Andersson (in 1852), but has not been seen since (Wiggins and Porter, 1971). However, many endemic species in the Galápagos are extremely common; in fact the endemics are more often than not dominating and thereby determining the character of the vegetation.

Porter (1976) estimated that about 45% of the taxa in the Galápagos flora was endemic. It has been suggested that the number of endemic plants is far higher in arid regions than in moist (Svenson, 1957, Johnson and Raven, 1973, Porter, 1979). However, a recent analysis of the common plants that form the bulk of the vegetation showed that the percentage of endemic taxa also is very high in moist habitats, at least among woody plants (Hamann, 1981). It was also shown that habitats characterized as pioneer habitats in arid regions, i.e. relatively recently hardened lava flows etc., had a very high percentage of endemic plant taxa (Table 8.2). The 60 species treated in Table 8.2 are among the commonest in the most extensive Galápagos vegetation types. Conspicuous and often dominants in the four groups are:

Group I *Opuntia echios, Bursera graveolens, Castela galapageia*;
Group II *Pisonia floribunda, Clerodendrum molle, Piscidia carthagenensis*;
Group III *Scalesia pedunculata, Psidium galapageium, Psychotria rufipes*;
Group IV *Lippia rosmarinifolia, Borreria ericaefolia, Macraea laricifolia*

The fauna in each of these four kinds of habitat is also, to a large degree, composed of endemic species. The majority of Galápagos ecosystems is simply characterized by a very high proportion of endemic species—the ecosystems themselves are endemic and therefore literally unique. Thus, conservation in the Galápagos aims not only at saving threatened species, and not only at preserving ecosystems in which the endemic species live, but also at preserving unique, endemic ecosystems that are found nowhere else in the world.

Table 8.2. Proportions of endemic taxa among 60 common plants, which characterize 4 kinds of habitats in the Galápagos

	Group I. Arid zone[1]	Group II. Transition zone[1]	Group III. Scalesia zone[1]	Group IV. Pioneer habitats[2]
Number of taxa in group	13	10	25	12
Number of endemics in group	5 or 6[3]	2	11	10
Percentage of endemics in group (absolute)	39 or 46%	20%	44%	83%
Percentage of endemics in group in relation to the 60 taxa	8.3 or 10%	3.3%	18.3%	16.7%

[1] As defined by Wiggins and Porter (1971), e.g. on Santa Cruz.
[2] E.g. on Fernandina and Isabela.
[3] Endemic status of one taxon questionable.
Note that, in both absolute and relative terms, endemism appears to be as high or higher in Scalesia Zone vegetation and pioneer habitats as in Arid Zone vegetation. (Data from Hamann, 1981).

References

Abbott, I., Abbott, L.K. and Grant, P.R. (1977) Comparative ecology of Galápagos ground finches (*Geospiza* Gould): Evaluation of the importance of floristic diversity and interspecific competition. *Ecol. Monogr.*, **47**, 151–184.
Anonymous (1980) *Twenty years of conservation in the Galápagos. Assessment, lessons and future priorities.* Quito, Charles Darwin Foundation for the Galápagos Islands.
Bazzaz, F.A. and Pickett, S.T.A. (1980) Physiological ecology of tropical succession., *Ann. Rev. Ecol. Syst.*, **11**, 287–310.
Black, J. (1974) *Galápagos. Archipiélago del Ecuador.* Quito, Imprenta Europa.
Bowman, R.I. (1961) *Morphological differentiation and adaptation in the Galápagos finches.* Brussels, Palais des Académies.
Calvopiña, L.H. and de Vries, T. (1975) Estructura de la población de cabras salvajes (*Capras hircus* L.) y los daños causados en la vegetación de la isla San Salvador, Galápagos. *Revista Univ. Católica, Quito, Año*, **3**, (8), 219–241.
Colinvaux, P.A. and Schofield, E.K. (1976a) Historical ecology in the Galápagos Islands. I. A Holocene pollen record from El Junco lake, Isla San Cristóbal. *J. Ecol.*, **64**, 989–1012.
Colinvaux, P.A. and Schofield, E.K. (1976b). Historical ecology in the Galápagos Islands. II. A Holocene spore record from El Junco lake, Isla San Cristóbal. *J. Ecol.*, **64**, 1013–1028.
Colinvaux, P.A. (1980) Galápagos since 18K. *Not. Galápagos*, **31**, 11.

Darwin, C. (1907) *Journal of researches into the natural history and geology of the countries visited during the voyage round the world of H.M.S. 'Beagle' under command of Captain Fitzroy, R.N.* Page 380. London.

Duffy, D.C. (1981) Ferals that failed. *Not. Galápagos*, **33**, 21–22.

Eliasson, U. (1974) Studies in Galápagos plants XIV. The genus *Scalesia* Arn. *Opera Botanica*, **36**, 1–117.

Grant, P.R. (1981) Population fluctuations, tree rings and climate. *Not. Galápagos*, **33**, 12–16.

Hamann, O. (1975) Vegetational changes in the Galápagos Islands during the period 1966–73. *Biol. Conserv.*, **7**, 37–59.

Hamann, O. (1978) Recovery of vegetation on Pinta and Santa Fe. *Not. Galápagos*, **27**, 19–20.

Hamann, O. (1979a) On climatic conditions, vegetation types, and leaf size in the Galápagos Islands. *Biotropica*, **11**, 101–122.

Hamann, O. (1979b) Regeneration of vegetation on Santa Fe and Pinta Islands, Galápagos, after the eradication of goats. *Biol. Conserv.*, **15**, 215–236.

Hamann, O. (1979c) Dynamics of a stand of *Scalesia pedunculata* Hooker fil., Santa Cruz Island, Galápagos. *Bot. J. Linn. Soc.*, **78**, 67–84.

Hamann, O. (1979d) Taxonomic and floristic notes from the Galápagos Islands. *Bot. Notiser*, **132**, 435–440.

Hamann, O. (1981) Plant communities of the Galápagos Islands. *Dansk Bot. Arkiv*, **34**,(2), 1–163.

Haro, M. (1975) Grado de distribución de las plantas introducidas en la Isla Santa Cruz, Galápagos. *Revista Univ. Católica, Quito, Año* **3**, (8), 243–258.

Howell, J.T. (1942) Up under the Equator. *Sierra Club Bull.*, **27**, 79–82.

Itow, S. and Weber, D. (1974) Fens and bogs in the Galápagos Islands. *Hikobia*, **7**, 39–52.

Johnson, M.P. and Raven, P.H. (1973) Species number and endemism: The Galápagos Archipelago revisited. *Science*, **179**, 893–895.

Kastdalen, A. (1965) *Changes in the biology of Santa Cruz Island during the last thirty years.* Unpublished manuscript, Charles Darwin Research Station Library, Santa Cruz, Galápagos Islands, Ecuador.

Noble, I.R. and Slatyer, R.O. (1980) The use of vital attributes to predict successional changes in plant communities subject to recurrent disturbances. *Vegetatio*, **43**, 5–21.

Porter, D.M. (1976) Geography and dispersal of Galápagos Islands vascular plants. *Nature*, **264**, 745–746.

Porter, D.M. (1979) Endemism and evolution in Galápagos Islands vascular plants, in *Plants and Islands*. Edited by D. Bramwell. Pages 225–256. Academic Press, London and New York.

Slevin, J.R. (1959) The Galápagos Islands. A history of their exploration. *Occ. Papers Calif. Acad. Sci.*, **25**, 1–150.

Stewart, A. (1911) A botanical survey of the Galápagos Islands. *Proc. Calif. Acad. Sci.*, **4**, (1), 7–288.

Stewart, A. (1915). Some observations concerning the botanical conditions on The Galápagos Islands. *Trans. Wisconsin Acad. Sci.*, **18**, 272–340.

Svenson, H.K. (1957) Vegetation provinces of the Pacific-Galapagean. The Galápagos Islands. *Proc. 8th Pacific Sci. Congr.*, **4**, 162–166.

Villa, J. (1971) *Informe del programa de actividades llevados a cabo en la isla Santiago (San Salvador) del 12 de Agosto al 22 de Diciembre de 1970.* Charles Darwin Research Station Library, Santa Cruz, Galápagos, Ecuador.

de Vries, T. (1977) Como la caza de chivos afecta la vegetación en las islas Santa Fe y Pinta. *Revista Univ. Católica, Quito, Año* **5**, (16), 171–181.

de Vries, T. and Calvopiña, L.H. (1977) Papel de los chivos en los cambios de la vegetación de la isla San Salvador, Galápagos. *Revista Univ. Católica, Quito, Año* **5,** (16), 145–169.

Weber, D. (1971) Pinta, Galápagos: Une ile à sauver. *Biol. Conserv.*, **4**, 8–12.

Werff, H. van der (1978) *The vegetation of the Galápagos Islands.* Zierikzee.

Werff, H. van der (1979) Conservation and vegetation of the Galápagos Islands, in *Plants and Islands*. Edited by D. Bramwell. Pages 391–404. Academic Press, London and New York.

Wiggins, I.R. and Porter, D.M. (1971) *Flora of the Galápagos Islands.* Stanford University Press.

CHAPTER 9

The Inshore Fish Fauna of the Galápagos Islands

JOHN E. McCOSKER★ AND RICHARD H. ROSENBLATT†

★California Academy of Sciences, San Francisco, California; †Scripps Institution of Oceanography, La Jolla, California

Contents

9.1.	Introduction	133
9.2.	Early Ichthyological Explorations	134
9.3.	The Oceanographic Setting	136
9.4.	Faunal Composition	137
9.5.	Notable Galápagos Fishes	139
	9.5.1. The four-eyed blenny, *Dialommus fuscus*	139
	9.5.2. The vieja, *Bodianus eclancheri*	140
	9.5.3. The Galápagos batfish, *Ogcocephalus darwini*	141
	9.5.4. The garden eel, *Taenioconger* sp.	142
9.6.	Future Studies	142
9.7.	Acknowledgments	144
	References	144

9.1. Introduction

The mere suggestion of Charles Darwin, the enchanted Galápagos Islands, or the voyage of the *Beagle*, reminds most naturalists of large lumbering tortoises, beaver-tail cactus trees, and desert isles with little brown birds whose oddly-shaped bills were germinal stimuli for *The Origin of Species by Means of Natural Selection*. . . . Few naturalists appreciate the fact that Darwin, during his 1835 Galápagos visit aboard H.M.S. *Beagle*, was interested in aquatic life as well. His collections, preserved in spirits, represented the first ichthyological survey of Galápagos. This terrestrial bias in the mind of most 20th century naturalists is easily explained considering the ichthyological state of the art during Darwin's time. Each of the 15 fish specimens which he collected was new to science, and their relationships were then so poorly known that faunal comparisons were impossible. The uniqueness of the Galápagos terrestrial flora and fauna was apparent to Darwin and his contemporaries, but the marine fauna was not appreciated until the turn of this century.

The endemism of many Galápagos plants and animals demonstrated the theory that migrants to a desolate location could mutate, adapt, be selected upon, and evolve in isolation. But it was not until much later that marine biologists realized that a parallel condition exists underwater as well. A similar degree of Galápagos endemism exists among many groups of marine shorefishes, invertebrates, and plants.

9.2. Early Ichthyological Explorations

Nineteenth century ichthyological observations at Galápagos have, for the most part, been lost in history as a result of the excitement which accompanied the discoveries ashore. Slevin (1959), although possessing the bias of a land-locked herpetologist, prepared the most comprehensive account of early Galápagos explorations, and it is to his work that we direct the reader for further information.

A few specimens of aquatic animals were incidentally collected by various early explorers, yet it was clearly Charles Darwin who made the first significant collection of Galápagos fishes. His materials were described by the Reverend Leonard Jenyns in 1842. Jenyns was particularly appreciative of Darwin's painstaking care in the tagging of each specimen and making of careful journal entries of the fish's coloration in life. Although many of Darwin's fish collections were lost and the provenance of a few specimens was questionable, Jenyns noted that the Galápagos material returned intact and *in toto*. Jenyns described and illustrated all 15 specimens. Although each was a new form, only five are now considered to be Galápagos endemics, the remainder having been found elsewhere along the Central and South American coasts. Jenyns honored Darwin in naming a wrasse after him, *Cossyphus Darwini*.

Figure 9.1. The Galápagos sheephead, *Semicossyphus darwini*, named in 1842 by the Reverend Leonard Jenyns in honor of the collector. (Photograph by Leighton R. Taylor, Jr.).

The French Expedition aboard the frigate *La Venus* soon followed Darwin's visit, and stopped at several island localities between 21 June and 15 July 1838. Achille Valenciennes reported upon the fishes in 1855 and expressed his delight in completing the studies begun by the English aboard the *Beagle*. He described 13 new species (most of which were valid) from Galápagos and recognized the unique nature of the insular fish fauna. Although lacking considerable knowledge of the eastern Pacific fish fauna, he was able to observe that the Galápagos fauna was more closely related to that of 'Atlantic America' than to that of the Indian Ocean. The published lithographs of Valenciennes' new fishes were somewhat bizzare in color—probably a result of the condition of, and preservative used for, the specimens.

A variety of specimens, collected at Galápagos by New Bedford Whalers that came in for provisions, were brought back to American and European museums. It is probable that the few species which have never been subsequently collected at Galápagos, such as the sargassum anglerfish, *Histrio histrio*, or the banded moray, *Gymnothorax rueppelliae*, were actually collected by whalers in Hawaii or further west and misidentified as to the origin of the particular specimens. The first organized American expedition to Galápagos was conducted by Professor Louis Agassiz of Harvard aboard the steamer *Hassler*. Also aboard in 1873 were Dr. Franz Steindachner of Vienna and Count Louis François de Pourtales. Although only at Galápagos for 9 days, a number of specimens were collected and described. Expeditions aboard the U.S. Fisheries Service vessel *Albatross*, in 1888 and 1891, resulted in important aquatic and terrestrial collections. The most comprehensive collections made by zoologists were those of Edmund Heller and Robert Snodgrass who spent 6 months at Galápagos aboard the sealing schooner *Julia E. Whalen* during 1898 and 1899. Their results were published in two volumes (Heller and Snodgrass, 1903; Snodgrass and Heller, 1905) which listed 128 Galápagos species, of which 20 were new, and an analysis of the insular fauna of the tropical eastern Pacific.

Twentieth century expeditions slowly added to the Galápagos faunal list, as well as to the understanding of its zoogeographic significance. Ichthyology benefited from the fashionable practice of wealthy Americans who sent their yachts to Galápagos accompanied by a museum-associated scientist. William Beebe visited Galápagos in 1923 and 1925 and wrote popular volumes and scientific papers based on his brief visits. Allan Hancock sent his *Oaxaca* in 1928 and later the *Veleros I–III* during 1931–1935, which included ichthyologists Alvin Seale and George S. Myers. A.W.C.T. Herre, aboard the yacht *Illyria* in 1928, collected and later described several new species during the Crane Pacific Expedition, as did biologists aboard the *Mary Sachs*, *Mary Pinchot*, *Zaca*, Vanderbilt's *Cressida*, and the *Observer*.

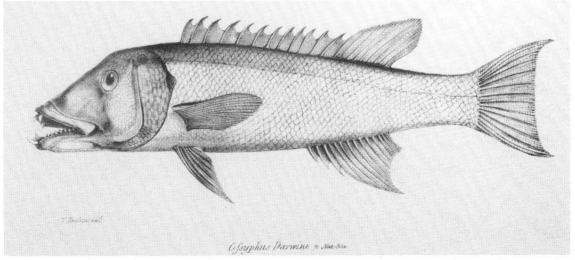

Figure 9.2. Drawing which accompanied the original description of the sheephead. The large white blotch on the male's flank is not shown; Darwin's specimens became discolored because of their preservation in alcoholic spirits.

The advent of modern Scuba techniques allowed the collection of small, reef-associated fishes, as well as the efficient subtidal usage of rotenone ichthyocides. Major collections by Edmund S. Hobson and Boyd W. Walker of the University of California at Los Angeles during the 1964 Galápagos International Scientific Project, and subsequent collections by the present authors have added significantly to our knowledge of deeper-living shore fishes of the Galápagos.

9.3. The Oceanographic Setting

The unique nature of the Galápagos marine fauna is a result of its geographic location. The archipelago rises abruptly from the intersection of the Cocos and the Carnegie submarine ridges, forming a platform separated from the mainland by deep oceanic water no shallower than 7000 ft. The closest island to the Archipelago is Malpelo, a small, mile-long rock that is 270 miles from the Colombian mainland and probably serves as a stepping-stone for some nearshore species to or from the mainland.

Fossil deposits are few on these relatively young islands, although Pleiocene vertebrate and late Miocene invertebrate deposits exist on Santa Cruz (McBirney and Williams, 1969). The oldest dating of the archipelago by paleomagnetic data and by potassium-argon aging techniques indicates that habitable submarine shallow water reef existed five to 15 million years ago (Tjeerd van Andel, pers. comm.). However, the dating of surface and shallow sub-surface volcanic terrain from various islands indicates that most of the surface rock has more recent origins (Chapter 2.3).

The aerial topography of most islands, namely sheer volcanic faces plummeting to the shoreline, extends underwater in many locations to depths of 100–200 ft, where the bottom slopes off along sand and shell bottoms. True coral reefs are absent in that hermatypic corals cannot tolerate the cool temperatures of most

Figure 9.3. A deepwater moray, *Muraena argus*, living along a vertical lava cliff face. Note the absence of corals and the extensive encrustation by algae and invertebrates, typical of this habitat. (Photograph by Carl Roessler at Gordon Rocks, Galápagos, at 150 ft).

islands, although extensive *Porites* and *Pocillopora* coral development and bank reefs exist at Darwin and Wolf, which lie 80 miles to the north of the main group of islands.

As reviewed by G. Houvenaghel in Chapter 3, the archipelago lies at the site of a complex ocean current system. The combined effect of the equatorial currents, localized currents, and the submarine profiles of each island result in great differences in surface water temperature within the archipelago. In general, the surface temperatures along the western shores of islands (primarily Fernandina and Isabela) are 5–10°F cooler than the eastern shores of other islands, and the associated lush algal growth and fishes are typical of the more temperate Peruvian and Chilean flora and fauna. Rosenblatt and Hobson's (1969) observations of parrotfishes, family Scaridae, at Española well exemplify this point. During February 1967, they recorded water temperature at 71°F at 15 ft along the south shore, the insular margin influenced by upwelling and the Peru Current. Along the north shore, they recorded water temperature of 79°F at the same depth and observed 4 species of tropical Pacific parrotfishes, genus *Scarus*, whereas only the eastern Pacific algae-eating form, *Nicholsina denticulata*, was present on the southern edge of this narrow island.

It is this combination of warm and cool, fresh and salty, nutrient-laden water which mixes at Galápagos, bringing its separate faunal elements from across the Pacific together to an isolated archipelago, that fascinates oceanographers and evolutionary biologists.

9.4. Faunal Composition

The recent analyses of the Galápagos fish fauna by Rosenblatt and Walker (1963) and by Walker (1966) have not been significantly modified by subsequent studies. This portion of our review is based for the most part on their discussions, and differs only slightly as new information has become available. A more comprehensive synoptic listing of the Galápagos fish fauna is in preparation by the authors.

The fish fauna of Galápagos is fairly well known, particularly along the shoreline to depths of 150 ft or more. The remaining areas which deserve further attention are the nearshore depths below 150 ft, benthic trawl surveys between islands, and the islands of Darwin, Wolf, and nearby Malpelo.

The Galápagos fish fauna is large when compared with those of other eastern tropical Pacific islands. As mentioned above, Heller and Snodgrass identified 128 species; Rosenblatt and Walker recognized 269 species from 88 families; and Walker identified 289 species (this includes the shorefishes, nearshore pelagic fishes, and the flying fishes). On the basis of recent literature and the deep water diving collections by McCosker, Taylor and Warner (1978), we now record 306 species representing 91 families. (This represents an actual increase of 2 families, the Callionymidae and Uranoscopidae, as well as the Grammistidae which were subsequently recognized as distinct from the Serranidae.) This is quite large, as compared to the fauna of Easter Island, which possesses 109 species, but less than that of the Hawaiian Islands, which has 471 inshore species (Randall, 1976, 1980). This faunal complexity is directly related to the variety of habitats available, such as rocky shore, sand, and mangrove, but limited in part due to the near absence of muddy substrates and the difficulty that many shorefishes have faced in reaching the distant archipelago.

The Galápagos fauna is considered to be a distinctive subunit of the Panamic province. It is actually a mosaic of elements from the Panamic and Chilean faunas, the western Pacific, and the Atlantic, as well as its own endemics. The fish fauna within the archipelago is best envisioned as an assemblage of various faunas, wherein either side of a single island can be inhabited by a different subfauna from largely separate provenances.

The shorefish fauna exhibits a high degree of similarity (nearly 60%) with that of the eastern tropical Pacific mainland. Nearly 8% are pantropical forms such as the large sharks, rays, spiny pufferfishes and dolphin fishes. A small but significant group of species is closely associated with the Peruvian and Chilean fauna, such as the large wrasses and certain groupers. Only 4 species are in common with the Atlantic (excluding the pantropicals), as well as with other eastern Pacific localities, and a single species, the porgy, *Archosargus pourtalesii*, is curious in that its closest relative is from the Atlantic but lacks a congener within the eastern

Pacific. An interesting group of 7 species is found only at Galápagos, Cocos, and Malpelo islands (McCosker and Rosenblatt, 1975).

The endemism of the Galápagos shorefish fauna is particularly striking, and not unlike that of the Hawaiian Islands or other oceanic outposts. We conservatively recognize 51 Galápagos endemics, of which seven are also at Cocos and Malpelo. This represents 16.7% of the 306 shorefish and nearshore pelagic species.

The degree of endemism varies between families of fishes and relates to the familial similarities within, and biological differences between, families. For example, the families showing a high degree of endemism are the: snake eels (Ophichthidae, three of 9 species); grunts (Pomadasyidae, four of nine); croakers (Sciaenidae, three of five); the gobies and eleotrids (Gobiidae and Eleotridae, each with three of five); sand stargazers (Dactyloscopidae, three of four); klipfishes (Clinidae, five of six); and the pike blennies (Chaenopsidae, three of three). Families with few endemic species are the morays (Muraenidae, none of 16); groupers (Serranidae, two of 18); jacks (Carangidae, none of 18); wrasses (Labridae, none of nine); and the true blennies (Blenniidae, none of three). It may at first seem odd that related families such as the snake eels and the moray eels, or the true blennies and the pike blennies, should display such differences. Yet the answer is demonstrated by the vagility, or transport ability, of the larval and/or adult stages and the duration of its larval stage. Those forms which are strong pelagic swimmers, such as the jacks or tunas, have no difficulty in crossing the 650-mile barrier between the archipelago and the mainland. Those with protracted larval stages which are well-suited to pelagic life, such as the serranids, some blennies, and moray eel leptocephali, or those with larval and adult forms that inhabit floating detritus, such as wrasses and blennies, are also able to cross the water gap. Only those forms with short larval lives which are unsuitable to open water transport, such as the croakers or grunts, have an opportunity to differentiate without continual genetic swamping, and only if they fortuitously arrive in the first place. The New World klipfishes, for example, are small, reef-associated blennies with a number of species of limited distribution. The adults are sedentary, their eggs are usually attached to a solid surface, and their larval life is short. This life history pattern makes them poor candidates for transport by currents. The single klipfish which is not a Galápagos endemic, *Labrisomus multiporosus*, has the widest geographic distribution among its Pacific congeners, and also appears to have an unusually long larval life (Hubbs, 1953; Rosenblatt and Walker, 1963). Thus, the combination of low vagility and the arrival of a suitable propagule will most likely result in an insular endemic.

Those forms that are endemic to Galápagos are usually well differentiated from their congeners. Although the degree of difference from their congeners makes it difficult to identify their ancestry, in many cases it is possible to locate their closest relative. The majority are most closely related to eastern tropical Pacific species, as one might expect from the distance separating the mainland or the central Pacific islands from the archipelago, as well as from the direction of the currents. Small reef associates such as pike blennies, klipfish, or stargazers are all related to genera endemic to the New World. Four species are related to species representative of the Peruvian-Chilean fauna. A burrowing snake eel, *Callechelys galapagensis*, is a sibling of a Hawaiian species (McCosker and Rosenblatt, 1972), and the porgy, *Archosargus pourtalesii*, finds its only congeners in the western Atlantic, probably a result of the inability of its congeners to survive elsewhere in the Pacific after the closure of the New World Panamic seaway.

Approximately 14% (43 species) of the shorefishes are shared with the Indo-Pacific. This comparison is based on external morphological characteristics (such as proportions and vertebrae, scale, and fin ray numbers) and has been supported by electrophoretic examination of isozymes (Rosenblatt and Waples, in preparation). The presence of Indo-Pacific species, such as the Moorish Idol (*Zanclus cornutus*) and the blue-chinned parrotfish (*Scarus ghobban*) at warm water localities is more conspicuous than it is along the mainland due to the relatively depauperate nature of the insular fauna (Rosenblatt *et al.*, 1972). Those Indo-Pacific species that successfully inhabited the Galápagos are particularly well adapted to transport by currents, either as pelagic larvae or by rafting under floating debris (Rosenblatt and Walker, 1963). It is likely, however, that a few individuals which are known from a single Galápagos specimen (such as the sharpnose pufferfish, *Canthigaster amboinensis*, or the sailfin leaf fish, *Taenianotus triacanthus*) are unable to colonize for lack of a satisfactory propagule, or may undergo occasional extinctions.

On the basis of the knowledge of the existing fauna and the recent geologic history of the archipelago, it is possible to hypothesize the paleogeographic conditions. The absence of several key mainland faunal elements strongly suggests that there has not been a closer land connection to Galápagos. Although islands such as Cocos and Malpelo may serve as stepping-stones or faunal bridges, the history of the Galápagos fauna is best explained as a result of long-distance dispersal.

9.5. Notable Galápagos Fishes

As described above, the unique origin of the Galápagos fauna and the uncommon oceanographic conditions which prevail have allowed the evolution of several remarkable species. Treated below are some of the more interesting life forms.

9.5.1. The Four-Eyed Blenny, *Dialommus fuscus*

At Punta Espinosa on Fernandina Island one is likely to observe a strange zoological procession wherein the Galápagos marine iguanas (*Amblyrhynchus cristatus*) may be seen crawling from their rocky perches into the sea, about to begin their search for the algae upon which they dine. At the same time, if you look carefully, you will observe small, mottled fishes either crawling ashore or alighting upon the volcanic rocks as a wave recedes. This endemic klipfish, called the Galápagos four-eyed blenny (*Dialommus fuscus*) has become amphibious in its search for the small shore crabs and insects upon which it feeds (Curio, 1968). Its terrestrial

Figure 9.4. The Galápagos four-eyed blenny, *Dialommus fuscus*, crawling across the shoreline in search of food. (Photograph by Earl S. Herald).

sojourns may take it as far as 100 ft from the shore, away from the groupers and snappers which are its normal predators, and into the habitat of the predatory herons and gulls. *Dialommus* is most closely related to *Mnierpes macrocephalus*, a species which lives along the mainland from Nicaragua to Panama and possesses a similar life style and morphological adaptations. Like the amphibious mud-skippers of the tropical Indo-Pacific, *Dialommus* has had to adapt to the problems of vision, locomotion, and respiration out of water. Its eye surfaces are most remarkable in that the corneas are laterally flattened and meet at an approximate 100° angle along the vertical midline. Studies by Graham (1970) and by Graham and Rosenblatt (1970) of the related *Mnierpes macrocephalus* show that the fish avoids myopia by equalling the refraction of light beams which strike the flattened corneal surface, so that the accommodation of the eye by the lens (as all bony fishes do) will result in a clearly focused image on the retina. To allow for movement on land, the fish has toughened skin pads along its head and its paired fins, and the anal fin is deeply intercut along the membrane that interconnects the fin rays. By curling its tail towards its head, bracing itself on its paired fins, and then extending its tail, it propels itself forward in leaps and spurts at a pace that leaves ichthyologists panting and cursing a safe distance behind. Gill modifications through thickening and filament enlargement, as well as behavioral adaptations, allow the fish to respire aerially for as long as 2 hours.

Figure 9.5. Preserved specimen of *Dialommus fuscus*, illustrating the vertical midline which divides the corneal surface. (Photograph by Earl S. Herald).

9.5.2. The Vieja, *Bodianus eclancheri*

A large colorful wrasse, *Bodianus eclancheri*, is the most spectacular fish seen in the shallow cool waters along the west coasts of Fernandina and Isabela. This labrid is especially apparent due to its harlequin coloration, reminiscent of a multicolored koi carp. Individuals may be all black, crimson, orange, or white, or a variable mixture of patches and splotches. Known locally as *Vieja*, this species is also found in Peruvian and Chilean coastal waters, but it is only the Galápagos population that has received even cursory observation (Warner, 1978; Hoffman, 1980). In that the coloration of a fish has a high survival and/or sexual signalling value, a possibly uncontrolled harlequin coloration would be at a distinct selective disadvantage. In examining the field behavior and sexual strategy of this species, Warner asked 'Why has natural selection not acted to produce a uniform, supposedly optimum coloration which conveys high fitness, in terms of either

Figure 9.6. A harlequin vieja, *Bodianus eclancheri*, swimming among black coral at 100 ft. (Photograph by Leighton R. Taylor, Jr.).

survival or reproduction?' He found no apparent correlation of coloration with size or sex, as well as an abnormal sexual pattern as compared to its congeners. Species of *Bodianus* are sequential protogynous hermaphrodites, whereby young fish are females which ultimately change sex to become males. Most species of *Bodianus* are sexually dimorphic (males are larger) and dichromatic, yet *B. eclancheri* sexes are not. Warner discovered that males of *B. eclancheri* exist in both the largest and the smallest size classes, however all male gonads appear to have been derived from ovarian structures.

The *vieja* is further distinct from its cogeners in having abnormally large gonads, equal activity budgets among sexes, and males which are not territorial. During mating, a female will enter a spawning site inhabited by many males and immediately rush to the surface and group spawn with several males. Hoffman (1980) has explained this seemingly unusual behavior, differing from its congeners in which males occupy and defend territories, to be a response to the predation pressures of Galápagos sea lions (*Zalophus californianus wollebaeki*) and Galápagos reef sharks (*Carcharhinus galapagensis*). In order to avoid the extraordinary predation found at Galápagos, the males of *B. eclancheri* have increased their feeding and reduced their time spent in reproductive activities, in a manner quite unlike their mainland congeners.

9.5.3. The Galápagos Batfish, *Ogcocephalus darwini*

The presence or absence of certain key predators within a depauperate insular fauna such as Galápagos may result in species and behaviors which do not survive along the mainland. An intriguing example is provided by 2 species of batfishes of the family Ogcocephalidae. Ogcocephalids are small, hand-sized, sedentary sand bottom fishes. Along the mainland, the spotted batfish, *Zalieutes elater*, lives commonly upon sand and mud bottoms to a depth of 370 ft. At Galápagos, this spiny but nearly immobile species is 'replaced' by

Ogcocephalus darwini, a smoother-skinned but equally sedentary, bottom dweller that is common below 30 ft and so incautious as to be hand-captured by a scuba diver. Species of *Ogcocephalus* are extremely rare along the eastern Pacific shoreline, however, and apparently limited by predators other than those at Galápagos.

Figure 9.7. The Galápagos batfish, *Ogcocephalus darwini*, resting over sand at 30 ft. (Photograph by Carl Roessler).

9.5.4. The Garden Eel, *Taenioconger* sp.

Another interesting example which exhibits a differential selection mechanism at Galápagos when compared with the mainland can be seen in the breadth of niches occupied by a single species. Whereas several congeneric mainland species, living sympatrically, may have finely divided a particular niche, the chance colonization by a fortuitous propagule at Galápagos may allow a significant niche expansion. An example is provided by a recently discovered species of Galápagos garden eel, *Taenioconger* sp., which appears to be very closely related to a species along the eastern Pacific mainland. Garden eels are extemely specialized, elongate congrid eels which live partially buried in the sand, and feed upon passing plankton. Whereas similar eastern tropical Pacific localities which we have studied (e.g., the Gulf of California, Costa Rica and Panama) are inhabited by 2 or 3 species of garden eels, which appear to be ecologically separated by water depth and/or substrate differences, the Galápagos is apparently inhabited by a single species living in depths of 15 to 180 ft (or more) and occupying a range of substrate types including sand, gravel, and broken shell. The absence of other garden eel species is perhaps indicative of the reduced larval vagility of garden eels as compared to other eels.

9.6. Future Studies

Ichthyologically speaking, the Galápagos are by no means adequately collected or understood. It is unlikely that many more species will be discovered between the surface and 100 ft along rocky shores, but the deep, nearshore steep slopes and unstudied islands of Darwin and Wolf are likely to contain interesting surprises. The difficulty in collecting specimens from the volcanic rubble-strewn bottom is partially responsible for the present lack of knowledge, but modern submersibles and mixed gas diving equipment allow mankind to

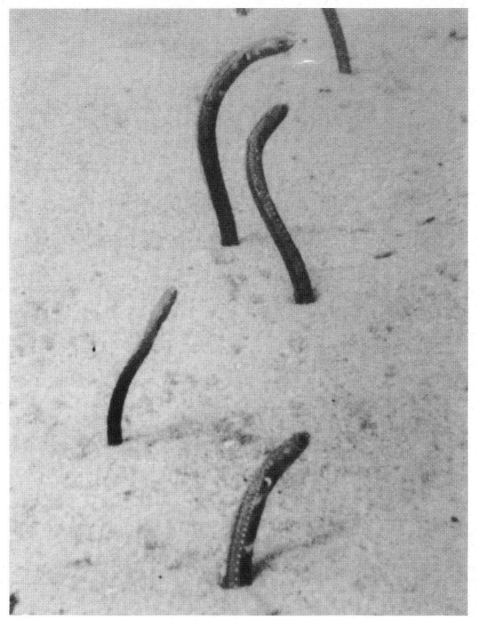

Figure 9.8. Garden eels, *Taenioconger* sp., feeding upon plankton in the passing current.

reach new depths. Equally interesting is the physiological research potential available from the adaptations which fish have made to the unique Galápagos environment.

Perhaps more significant is the concern over a developing fishery which is actively exporting to the mainland a variety of serranid groupers. Called *bacalao*, this dried and salted fish is in great demand and its fishery is expanding in the major bays and along the west coasts of Isabela and Fernandina. The primary study of the Galápagos fisheries (Quiroga and Armas, 1964) is incomplete and only recently has the Instituto Nacional de Pesca del Ecuador begun a program to investigate the biology and abundance of the target species. For example, the *norteño*, the third most abundant species captured, remains unidentified and is perhaps new to science.

Yet there is also reason for hope in that the Instituto Nacional de Pesca has begun teaching courses to educate local fishermen about conservation practices. The increase in tourism as well as skin and scuba diving activities has attracted an international interest in the submarine biota of the Galápagos, and the influence of the Charles Darwin Foundation for the Galápagos Isles will most certainly assist in the planned management of the unique aquatic life of the Galápagos.

9.7. Acknowledgments

We wish to thank: Earl S. Herald, Tom McHugh, Carl Roessler, and Leighton R. Taylor, Jr, for permission to use their photographs; Boyd W. Walker for allowing us to share the results of his studies of eastern Pacific fishes; the staff of the Charles Darwin Research Station, Fiddi Angermeyer, and Tui de Roy Moore for their assistance during our field studies; and the assistance and generosity of the Government of Ecuador in allowing us to carry out our studies at Galápagos.

References

Curio, E. (1968) Some observations on the 'Four-Eyed' blenny of the Galápagos Islands, *Dialommus fuscus* (Pisces: Clinidae). *Noticias de Galápagos*, **12**, 13–17.

Graham, J.B. (1970) Preliminary studies on the biology of the amphibious clinid *Mnierpes macrocephalus*. *Mar. Biol.*, Berlin, **5**, 136–140.

Graham, J.B. and Rosenblatt, R.H. (1970) Aerial vision: unique adaptation in an intertidal fish. *Science*, **168**, 586–588.

Heller, E. and Snodgrass, R.E. (1903) Papers from the Hopkins Stanford Galápagos Expedition, 1898–1899. XV. New Fishes. *Proc. Wash. Acad. Sci.*, **5**, 189–229.

Hoffman, S.G. (1980) *Sex-related social, mating, and foraging behavior in some sequentially hermaphroditic reef fishes*. Doctoral diss., Univ. Calif. Santa Barbara. 125 pp.

Hubbs, C. (1953) Revision of the eastern Pacific fishes of the clinid genus *Labrisomus*. *Zoologica*, **38**, 113–136.

Jenyns, L. (1842) Fish. *In* C. Darwin, Ed. Part IV. *The Zoology of the Voyage of HMS Beagle, under the Command of Captain Fitzroy, RN, during the Years 1832 to 1836*. Smith, Elder, and Co., London, 172 pp.

McBirney, A.R. and Williams, H. (1969) Geology and petrology of the Galápagos Islands. *Geol. Soc. Amer.*, Memoir, **118**, 197 pp.

McCosker, J.E. and Rosenblatt, R.H. (1972) Eastern Pacific snake-eels of the genus *Callechelys* (Apodes: Ophichthidae). *Trans. San Diego Soc. Nat. Hist.*, **17**, 15–24.

McCosker, J.E. and Rosenblatt, R.H. (1975) Fishes collected at Malpelo Island, in *The biological investigation of Malpelo Island, Colombia*. Ed. by J.B. Graham. *Smithsonian Contrib. Zool.*, **176**, 91–93.

McCosker, J.E. and Rosenblatt, R.H. (1975) The moray eels (Pisces: Muraenidae) of the Galápagos Islands, with new records and synonymies of extralimital species. *Proc. Calif. Acad. Sci., 4th ser.*, **40**, 417–427.

McCosker, J.E., Taylor, L.R. and Warner, R.R. (1978) Ichthyological studies at Galápagos. *Noticias de Galápagos*, **27**, 13–15.

Quiroga, D. and Armas, A. (1964) Apuntes e información sobre las pesquerías en el Archipiélago de Colón. *Bol. Inform. Inst. Nac. de Pesca del Ecuador*, **1**, 1–27.

Randall, J.E. (1976) The endemic shore fishes of the Hawaiian Islands, Lord Howe Island and Easter Island. *Colloque Commerson 1973 O. R. S. T. O. M. Trav. Doc.*, **47**, 49–73.

Randall, J.E. (1980) New records of fishes from the Hawaiian Islands. *Pac. Sci.*, **34**, 211–232.

Rosenblatt, R.H. and Hobson, E.S. (1969) Parrotfishes (Scaridae) of the eastern Pacific, with a generic rearrangement of the Scarinae. *Copeia*, **3**, 434–453.

Rosenblatt, R.H., McCosker, J.E. and Rubinoff, I. (1972) Indo-West Pacific fishes from the Gulf of Chiriqui, Panama. *Los Angeles Co. Nat. Hist. Mus., Contri. Sci.*, **234**, 1–18.

Rosenblatt, R.H. and Walker, B.W. (1963) The marine shore-fishes of the Galápagos Islands. *Occ. Pap. Calif. Acad. Sci.*, **44**, 97–106.

Slevin, J.R. (1959) The Galápagos Islands a history of their exploration. *Occ. Pap. Calif. Acad. Sci.*, **25**, 1–150.

Snodgrass, R.E. and Heller, E. (1905) Shore fishes of the Revillagigedos, Clipperton, Cocos and Galápagos Islands. *Proc. Wash. Acad. Sci.*, **6**, 333–427.

Walker, B.W. (1966) The origins and affinities of the Galápagos shorefishes. In *The Galápagos*, Ed. by R.I. Bowman. Pp. 172–174. U. C. Press, Berkeley.

Warner, R.R. (1978) Patterns of sex and coloration in the Galápagos wrasses *Bodianus eclancheri* and *Pimelometopon darwini*. *Noticias de Galápagos.*, **27**, 16–18.

CHAPTER 10

The Giant Tortoises: A Natural History Disturbed by Man

Tj. de VRIES

Departamento de Biología, Pontificia Universidad Católica del Ecuador, Quito, Ecuador

Contents

10.1.	Introduction	145
10.2.	The Historic Period	146
10.3.	Problems for the Future	147
10.4.	Natural History	149
	10.4.1. Mating and egg-laying seasons	149
	10.4.2. Natural predation and mortality	152
	10.4.3. Food and water	152
	10.4.4. Aggressive behaviour and symbiosis with finches	153
	10.4.5. Why are there distinct races on different islands?	154
	10.4.6. Age, growth and reproductive potential	155
	References	156

10.1. Introduction

Reptiles and seabirds form dominating elements of the Galápagos fauna. Amphibians do not occur, and native land mammals (bats and rats) are inconspicuous. Among the reptiles, a sea-going lizard is perhaps the most bizarre, land iguanas and the ubiquitous lava lizards the most eyecatching for tourists, but it was from the giant tortoises that the islands received their name. The Galápagos tortoises have also played a part in the discussion on the variability of species. Although Galápagos mockingbirds, and later the finches, became classic examples for evolutionary theory, Darwin wrote of the tortoises from the different islands, referring to their form and size: 'I must suspect they are only varieties'. Van Denburgh (1914) used binomials in describing the tortoises, giving the impression that he referred to different species from the various islands (and for four of the five main volcanoes of Isabela—the Alcedo tortoise awaited description). However, he consistently uses the term 'races' and concludes: 'The various races of tortoises of the Galápagos Islands differ from one another chiefly in shape. There are no real differences in structure, such as are found in the lizards and snakes of the archipelago. The relative values which should be attached to these differences in shape are

Table 10.1. The Galápagos tortoises *Geochelone elephantopus*, their
distribution and status.

Race	Island	Population size
G.e. elephantopus	Floreana	Extinct
not described	Santa Fé	Extinct
phantastica	Fernandina	Extinct
wallacei	Rábida	Extinct[1]
hoodensis	Española	15 (79)
abingdoni	Pinta	1
ephippium	Pinzón	200 (192)
chathamensis	San Cristóbal	700 (40)
darwini	Santiago	700 (115)
vicina	Volcán Cerro Azul, Isabela	600 (101)
güntheri	Sierra Negra, Isabela	500
vandenburghi	Volcán Alcedo, Isabela	5000
microphyes	Volcán Darwin, Isabela	1000
becki	Volcán Wolf, Isabela	2000 (14)
porteri	Santa Cruz	3000

Based on MacFarland *et al.* (1974) and CDRS files; numbers in
brackets refer to young reared at CDRS and returned to island of
origin.
[1] This race is only substantiated by one specimen collected in 1906,
most likely an artificial introduction; there is no further evidence that
a native race ever occurred.

extremely difficult to estimate'. At present, 15 subspecies are recognized as belonging to a single species, *Geochelone elephantopus* (for details see Table 10.1).

Representatives of the genus *Geochelone* survive in South America (medium-sized species and one small species, *G. denticulata*, *G. carbonaria*, *G. chilensis*), in the Galápagos (a giant species, *G. elephantopus*); in Africa (two medium-sized species, *G. sulcata*, *G. pardalis*); in Madagascar (two medium-sized species, *G. radiata*, *G. yniphora*); in Aldabra (a giant species, *G. gigantea*); and in Asia (seven medium to small-sized species, including *G. forsteni*, a small species from Celebes and Halmahera).

Giant tortoises were once common on all continents, with the exception of Australasia. Today, only the two species survive: those of Aldabra and the Galápagos. Their main differences lie in the rather more rounded head and in the presence of a nuchal plate in the Aldabra tortoise.

Recent papers that have summarized the systematics of these tortoises are Loveridge and Williams (1957, p. 220, advocating the possible subdivision of *Testudo* into several genera), Hendrickson (1966) and de Vries (1973).

In general, one can see from their distribution pattern that seawater has not been an insurmountable barrier to the dispersal of tortoises. Almost certainly they were carried to their island destinations by floating or having a ride on rafts of vegetation—the latter being by no means an unusual phenomenon on large tropical rivers. Clearly, it was one trial surviving to get to the Galápagos, but this was followed by the equally demanding problems of colonizing the islands and reproducing successfully. Whether just one advent from the American continent resulted in the present subspeciation within the archipelago remains of course a very open question. Ultimately, the colony grew to several hundred thousand tortoises, and these became the main herbivores on the islands (see Chapter 1, Fig. 1.2).

10.2. The Historic Period

Man arrived on the scene in 1535, but it was in the 16th and 17th centuries that the tortoises began to be seriously exploited for food. These reptiles provided an excellent source of fresh meat in days before refrigeration. So the animals were collected to fill the holds of ships, and there they had the ability to survive for several months without food and water. Predation on an even larger scale started in the 19th century with whalers collecting tortoises for oil and colonists killing the animals for both oil and meat. It is difficult to assess the scale of 3 centuries of plunder, but the total number of animals removed from the islands must have exceeded 100,000.

The most devastating effects of all were caused by the introduction of non-native mammals like pigs, dogs, cats, goats and black rats, all of which quickly ran wild. Goats were put ashore on several islands as a future meat source once tortoises became rare. But the arrival of most of these domestic animals followed the direct settlement of the various islands by man (Chapter 1).

As far as the tortoises are concerned, the effects of feral mammals differ in severity according to conditions on the different islands:

—Pigs dig up and destroy the eggs and kill young animals up to the age of 10–15 years (Santiago, Santa Cruz, southern Isabela).

—Dogs also dig up eggs and kill young under 10 years old (southern Isabela, Santa Cruz and, previously, San Cristóbal).

—Black rats kill and eat the newly hatched young (this is a major threat only on relatively dry islands, such as Pinzón).

—Goats are direct food competitors, mainly on small and arid islands (Española, until 1979 when goats were finally eliminated, Pinta, and parts of southern Isabela) but also on the large and more humid island of Santiago (Calvopiña and de Vries, 1975).

—Donkeys trample tortoise-nesting areas, crushing eggs, and change forested areas to open grassy pampas, at times causing extensive dust bowls (Volcán Alcedo, Isabela).

Man has continued to exploit tortoises in the 20th century. Salt-mine workers collected tortoises on Santiago, 1924–1930; ranch-hands eliminated tortoises from the lower southwestern slopes of Cerro Azul, Isabela, 1958–1960; and convicts of a penal colony on Sierra Negra, Isabela exploited tortoises for oil as late as 1959. On Santa Cruz, colonists killed many tortoises during the 1930s and 1940s (pers. comm. by an old settler, A. Rambech).

This was the picture up to the late 1950s with the giant tortoises having to struggle for survival against both man and feral mammals. It was ironic that mammals, a contributory cause of the disappearance of dinosaurs from Earth, were here causing the final demise of giant tortoises in a few short years. Two of the island races (Floreana and Santa Fé) had become extinct (around the mid-1800s), and all the others were seriously depleted in numbers.

Although not a direct part of this present story, it is interesting to relate what we know of the race of tortoise from Fernandina Island. Only one animal is known and this, a male, was found by Rollo Beck in 1906. Hopes rose in 1964 when droppings, supposedly from a tortoise, were found; but all subsequent searches have proved in vain. The late Eric Shipton, who took part in these searches on Fernandina and was also familiar with the Pamir Mountains, expressed his greater belief in the abominable snowman than in the survival of *G. e. phantastica*! If the one animal found was a true native of the island then this is the only instance of the extinction of a race by natural causes—presumably by volcanic activity, for Fernandina has no human settlement or feral mammals.

From the several hundreds of thousands of tortoises roaming the islands before the arrival of man, less than 15,000 survive today.

10.3. Problems for the Future

The 1960s were characterized by the first detailed surveys of surviving populations. Expeditions so far in the century had all painted a rather bleak picture for the future. This was based mainly on the absence or scarcity of tortoises from coastal areas of the larger islands (where these expeditions had tended to concentrate) and from the smaller islands generally. Many visiting groups collected tortoises simply 'to save the species' for breeding programmes in zoological gardens—a well intentioned precaution but one usually ending in failure. MacFarland *et al.* (1974) summarize the details of 14 scientific expeditions that removed some 661 tortoises during the years 1880 to 1930.

With the establishment of the Charles Darwin Research Station, the systematic marking, counting and mapping of tortoises began, with Miguel Castro, Oswaldo Chappy, Camilo Calapucha, Juan Black and José Villa as fieldworkers. Even then, to demonstrate the difficulties and delays in obtaining information in the rugged terrain of the Galápagos, it may be mentioned that it was the mountaineer, Eric Shipton, who, in 1965, discovered the large population of tortoises surviving on Volcán Alcedo, Isabela—despite the fact that Miguel Castro had climbed the mountain previously and reported no tortoises! Slowly, specific data became available. In 1969, Craig MacFarland started a long-term field study of the populations of Santa Cruz and Pinzón.

Today, 10 subspecies are regarded as no longer endangered, although all (except perhaps the three races of northern Isabela) require the helping hand of man. One subspecies, that of Pinta (*G.e. abingdoni*), is on the brink of extinction and is represented by a single old male, 'Lonesome George', found in 1972.

Figure 10.1. *Above:* The late Anders Rambech, first caretaker of the tortoise rearing programme. *Below:* Young tortoises in the rearing centre at the Charles Darwin Research Station. Growth rings can be seen on the horny scutes.

On Pinzón, black rats (*Rattus rattus*) attack and eat the hatching tortoises. Their depredations are so severe that very few young or juveniles survive. When studying hawks on Pinzón, and placing traps to assess information on rat densities, I once found a one-year old tortoise in front of the rat-trap, apparently attracted by the banana used as bait. Without the current tortoise-rearing programme, whereby eggs are transplanted from Pinzón to incubators at the Charles Darwin Research Station, and the young subsequently reared until they are of a size and age to be returned, the Pinzón race would very likely have been doomed to extinction. Since 1965, 192 tortoises have been reared and released on their native island to bolster the natural population of aging animals.

The Española race had been reduced by hunting to some two males and 13 females. In 1965, steps were taken to bring these survivors together in a breeding programme at the Darwin Station. Between 1970 and 1976, 79 young tortoises were hatched, reared and released; while a further 68 young (reared between 1976 and 1980) are still at the Station pending their return to Española (data from CDRS files, see Anonymous, 1981).

Other tortoise populations may yet be numbered in hundreds or even thousands (Santa Cruz, Isabela; Table 10.1), and have needed less help.

On Santiago, 115 young tortoises have been released, but pigs remain a major threat. From Cerro Azul, Isabela 101 young have been reared and returned, and 40 from San Cristóbal.

The crucial need for the survival of all these races is to eliminate the conflicting feral mammals.

10.4. Natural History

This story so far has centred on the non-natural predation by man and feral mammals. But what do we know about the life history of the tortoises under natural conditions? All the present populations are affected by conditions that have been changed to some extent by man. So what the factors were regulating populations in the past can only be conjectured. Probably a low fertility rate, deferred sexual maturity, limited areas for nesting, predation on hatchlings, and a high mortality of hatchlings in years of drought, were the most important factors controlling overall numbers. Patches of soft soil between lava rocks are limited, so females may dig and destroy eggs laid by other females. Egg loss, therefore, may have been considerable; with further instances when females deposited eggs in unsuitable rocky fissures. Darwin (1845, 1962, p. 384) commented: 'where the ground is rocky she drops them indiscriminately in any hole: Mr. Bynoe found seven placed in a fissure'. Few early accounts of egg-laying exist, so there is little way of judging if this was an abnormal instance.

10.4.1. Mating and egg-laying seasons

Tortoises mate from January to April, during the normally rainy season. On large and high islands, animals gather in the humid areas inland for this purpose. The hoarse roar of the male, emitted during copulation, can be heard up to a 100 m away. Its function is not clear; the sound may be without significance, simply being linked with airflow during the rhythmic movements of mating. It is the only sound made by a tortoise apart from hissing when it retracts abruptly into its carapace.

Male tortoises on the large islands tend to stay in the highlands; females, on the other hand, move down to the lowlands to find suitable patches of soil for nesting.

Tortoises use traditional trails which over the centuries become well defined, even among rugged volcanic terrain. At times, these 'tortoise highways' have offered pirates and scientists the best way to penetrate dense, bushy undergrowth. Such trails become more diffused on the smaller, lower islands, where less seasonal movements occur—although this topic has not been studied in detail (1500 individually marked tortoises on

Santa Cruz, and some 100 on Pinzón, would reveal information, with a patient student noting individual movements of the tortoises).

Digging the nest-hole is an elaborate task for such a ponderous and ungainly animal. This is achieved by the animal working blindly, rotating and using each hind-leg in turn. The female labours in this way for several hours to make a neat, cylindrical cavity, 30–40 cm deep. In breeding enclosures at the Darwin Station, females start digging one day, continue the next and, possibly, for several days more. Whilst digging, the female urinates frequently, thus softening and binding the loosened soil. Dropping the eggs is a matter of minutes, and filling the hole another hour's work. With the plastron, the damp soil is pressed down firmly over the nest. The female then departs and it is left to the heat of the sun to incubate the eggs. This may take from 4 to 8 months. MacFarland *et al.* (1974) demonstrated that the temperature in the centre of the clutch varies during the incubation period from 24–32.5°C (July–February) on Santa Cruz, and from 27–36°C (December–February) on Pinzón.

Figure 10.2. Tortoises mating in the crater of Volcán Alcedo; note difference in size between male and female.

Most eggs are laid between June and December (the *garúa* season, characterized by cloudy weather with occasional drizzling rains) with hatching and emerging from December until April. Females may lay 1–4 clutches per season, with possibly few or no clutches in consecutive dry years (but few data are available on this point). Clutch-size varies from 2–16 eggs. MacFarland *et al.* (1974) note that over a two-year period on Pinzón an averge clutch-size of five occurred (range 2–8 eggs for 26 nests), whereas on Santa Cruz this averaged nine (range 3–16 eggs, from 168 nests over 3 years). It is interesting that there exists this fair constancy in clutch-size over the years (for Pinzón on average 5.0 and 5.2; for Santa Cruz 9.1, 9.5 and 9.3).

On some Galápagos volcanoes, arid conditions extend to the highlands. In these areas nesting occurs high on the mountain (e.g. the southwestern part of Cerro Azul, at an elevation of 700–800 m, and in the crater of Volcán Alcedo).

Figure 10.3. Two males in *Psidium* forest with *Cassia* undergrowth; highlands of Santa Cruz.

Figure 10.4. A large male from Sierra Negra, Isabela; males can be distinguished by their large tail and concave plastron.

10.4.2. Natural predation and mortality

Under natural conditions, egg-predators do not exist and the only predators on hatchlings are the Galápagos hawk and, possibly, short-eared owl. Numbers taken by the hawk could have been considerable at times in the past when these birds were much more abundant. Darwin (1845) wrote of such predation: 'The young tortoises, as soon as they are hatched, fall a prey in great numbers to the carrion-feeding buzzard. The old ones seem generally to die from accidents, as from falling down precipices: at least several of the inhabitants told me, that they had never found one dead without some evident cause'. At present, hawks do not form a serious predator of tortoises (de Vries, 1976), except possibly on Volcán Alcedo where tortoises and hawks still occur in fair numbers. In their recent study, MacFarland *et al.* (1974) suggest 'that the natural mortality rates of tortoises of 3–4 years of age and older are apparently very low, when based on the population censuses. . . . Mortality is probably very great for younger animals, especially hatchlings, during those years when forage is very scarce in the lowland nesting zones, due to lack of heavy rains during the wet season.'

Some hatchlings may be trapped in their nests when conditions are dry and the encasing soil becomes hard. In other years, animals drown when nesting areas are flooded. However, studies by MacFarland on Santa Cruz and Pinzón revealed in all years (1969–1972) a high escape rate of hatchlings (80.5–95.7%). Additionally, fertility and hatching rates were high (77.9–85.7% and 73.2–84.6%, respectively). Although there were marked differences in rainfall in those 4 years (1969 and 1972 being wet, 1970 very dry, and 1971 intermediate; for further rainfall data see de Vries, 1975, p. 42), it is interesting to note that hatching and emerging rates were similar, indicating that severe conditions seem to have a less dramatic effect than might be imagined.

MacFarland reported 57 hatchlings emerging in a certain area on Santa Cruz in 1970 (rainfall 26.6 mm during the wet season, January–March), none of which could be found after April. By contrast, in the same area in 1971 (rainfall 255 mm), 47 hatchlings emerged of which 21 were marked; many of these were subsequently found, e.g. 10 of the marked tortoises on 12 November 1971, all weighing 3–4 times their weight at emergence. Although a small sample, these instances suggest that survival of hatchlings is related to the humidity of conditions in their first year.

10.4.3. Food and water

Tortoises living on small arid islands subsist on cactus pads and fruits and a variety of grasses and herbs. They search for water collected in small depressions in the lava rock and also benefit from the moisture of dew falling on vegetation. In the rainy season, when vegetation may become luxuriant, tortoises build up their reserves of fat. Such reserves may be one of the reasons why there is little fluctuation in clutch-size between seasons.

On the other hand, tortoises living on large, humid islands generally have little trouble finding food. Here, one encounters the largest and heaviest tortoises, notably on Santa Cruz and Volcán Alcedo, Isabela. Animals graze for hours at a time, cutting mouthfuls of grasses with their horny mandibles. The food thus enters the digestive tract without much chewing and is rather poorly digested. Evidence for this lies in droppings, which contain much coarse material.

A person can approach a grazing tortoise very closely from behind without disturbing it, an observation made by Darwin and which led him to comment on their bad hearing. Tortoises depend primarily on smell and eye-sight for information about their environment.

Tortoises like freshwater and frequently visit, and submerge themselves in, seasonal pools. This not only insulates them against the relatively cool nights of the highlands but provides effective protection against mosquitos, which might otherwise draw blood from the soft, growing tissue between the horny plates of the carapace.

During the nesting season, females rely on cactus and dry grasses and herbs for food. Young tortoises remain in the lowlands during their first years of life. The reason for their remaining in regions less favourable for feeding may be attributed to the colder conditions of the highlands. As is well-known, tortoises survive long periods without drinking. This is achieved by utilizing fat stored in their tissues (in metabolic processes 100 g of fat produce some 107 g of water).

10.4.4. Aggressive behaviour and symbiosis with finches

Most of the time tortoises live solitary lives, congregating peacefully when water is available. Nowadays, one rarely finds groups of 50 or more tortoises together. Volcán Alcedo is an exception, and on one occasion there I could have walked twenty paces or so simply by stepping on the backs of the tortoises that had assembled around a geyser pool. Galápagos tortoises are not known to defend a territory, but disputes arise over food, and sometimes, for no apparent reason, two males rear up on their legs with open mouths and outstretched necks. Rarely does this resort to biting, as one of the contestants (usually the smaller) backs away in retreat.

MacFarland has reported an interesting behavioural pattern between tortoises and finches. Finches will remove ticks from the tortoise while they stand high on their legs, with outstretched neck, so that the birds

Figure 10.5. Different island races of tortoise: Above left: *G.e. hoodensis*; Above right: *G.e. ephippium*; Below left: *G.e. vandenburghi*; Below right: *G.e. darwini*.

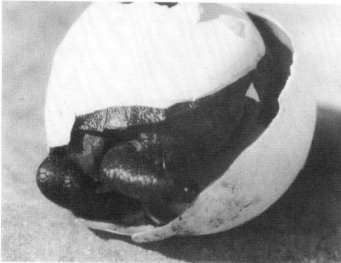

Figure 10.6. Hatching tortoise; the egg is the size of a tennisball.

can reach soft parts of the skin where the ectoparasites lodge. Finches will provoke this posing response by hopping in front of a tortoise. Two species are involved, the small groundfinch (*Geospiza fuliginosa*) and the medium groundfinch (*G. fortis*), and the behaviour parallels similar responses in the land iguana (*Conolophus*) described by I. Eibl-Eibesfeldt in the next chapter.

10.4.5. Why are there distinct races on different islands?

Tortoises on small, dry islands (Española, Pinzón), and those confined to arid regions of the larger islands (Pinta, Volcán Wolf of Isabela), are of the 'saddle-back type': the front part of the carapace is elevated, allowing the neck to be stretched higher and enabling the animal to browse on leaves of bushes and cactus pads.

Tortoises of the humid highlands (Santa Cruz, Volcán Alcedo of Isabela) have a 'dome-shaped' shell, short neck and short legs. Here vegetation is lush for most of the year and food is thus available to the tortoises close to the ground; the carapace, neck and legs became adapted accordingly. Since all islands have rather different conditions in climate and a different floral composition, distinct island races have resulted. Figure 10.5 demonstrates these differences: two saddle-back tortoises (from Española and Pinzón), a dome-shaped tortoise (from Volcán Alcedo), and an intermediate form (from Santiago).

10.4.6. Age, growth and reproductive potential

There has been much speculation about the life-span of Galápagos tortoises. Although the scutes clearly show growth rings, these do not refer to annual growth, but reflect periods of differing food conditions. In any case, in older animals these rings often become abraded and indiscernible. None the less, all the evidence suggests that the tortoises can reach great ages, very likely of 100 years or more.

One historically documented case is that of a Galápagos tortoise given by Captain James Cook (either 1774 or 1777) to the King of Tonga. This animal was still alive in 1927, so must have been at least 160 years old; and if it was an adult when donated this tortoise might well have been over 200 years old when it died. The year 2060 will be the first occasion when presently documented tortoises can be verified as reaching a century!

At hatching (Fig. 10.6) a young tortoise weighs some 80 g. Subsequently, it may reach a weight of 300–400 lbs (see Fig. 10.7). MacFarland estimates that a Galápagos tortoise reaches sexual maturity at an age of 30–40 years. He found females on Santa Cruz with a curved carapace length of 90 cm already laying. In a population of 3000 animals there would be a maximum of 450 females of this size or over, and these could produce some 5600 tortoises per year.

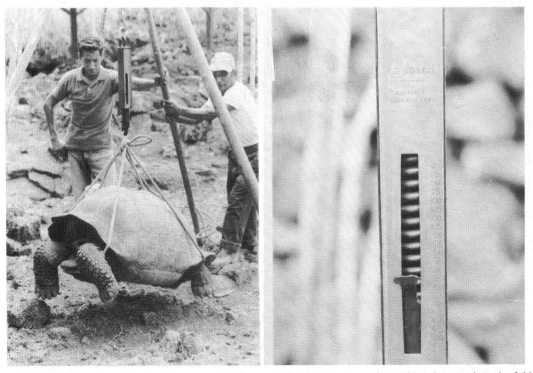

Figure 10.7. A large male of Santa Cruz tipping the scales at 325 lbs. It is no easy task weighing the animals in the field.

Potentially then, over a period of 60 years, a female, laying two clutches of 10 eggs per year, could produce 1200 young. Thus, under optimum conditions, there would seem to be no hurry for a tortoise to reach maturity.

References

Anonymous (1981) News from Academy Bay. *Noticias de Galápagos*, **33**, 1–6.

Calvopiña, L. and de Vries, Tj. (1975) Estructura de la población de cabras salvajes (*Capra hircus* L.) y los daños causados en la vegetación de la isla San Salvador, Galápagos. *Revista Universidad Católica Quito*, **3**,(8), 219–241.

Darwin, C. (1845) *The Voyage of the Beagle*. Natural History Library, Doubleday, 1962.

de Vries, Tj. (1973) Opmerkingen over taxonomie en ecologie van de reptielen van de Galápagos eilanden I. De reuzenschildpadden. *Lacerta*, **32**,(1), 3–15.

de Vries, Tj. (1975) The breeding biology of the Galápagos Hawk, *Buteo galapagoensis*. *Le Gerfaut*, **65**, 29–57.

de Vries, Tj. (1976) Prey selection and hunting methods of the Galápagos Hawk, *Buteo galapagoensis*. *Le Gerfaut*, **66**, 3–43.

Hendrickson, J.R. (1966) The Galápagos tortoises, *Geochelone* Fitzinger 1835 (*Testudo* Linnaeus 1758 in part). In: R.I. Bowman (ed), *The Galápagos* pp. 252–257. Univ. Calif. Press, Berkeley.

Loveridge, A. and Williams, E.E. (1957) Revision of the African Tortoises and Turtles of the Suborder Cryptodyra. *Bull. Mus. Comp. Zool.*, **115**, 115–557.

MacFarland, C. and Reeder, W.G. (1974) Cleaning symbiosis involving Galápagos tortoises and two species of Darwin's finches. *Z. Tierpsychol.*, **34**, 464–483.

MacFarland, C.G., Villa, J. and Toro, B. (1974) The Galápagos Giant Tortoises (*Geochelone elephantopus*). Part I. Status of the surviving populations. *Biol. Conservation*, **6**, 118–133. Part II. Conservation Methods. ibid., **6**, 198–212.

Van Denburgh, J. (1914) The gigantic land tortoises of the Galápagos Islands. *Proc. Calif. Acad. Sci.* series 4, **2**, 203–374.

CHAPTER 11

The Large Iguanas of the Galápagos Islands

IRENÄUS EIBL-EIBESFELDT

Forschungsstelle für Humanethologie, Max-Planck-Institut für Verhaltenphysiologie, Seewiesen, West Germany

Contents

11.1.	Marine Iguana (*Amblyrhynchus cristatus*)	157
	11.1.1. Description	158
	11.1.2. Habitat, distribution and island subspeciation	159
	11.1.3. Marine adaptations and feeding habits	160
	11.1.4. Territoriality and breeding behaviour	162
	11.1.5. Copulation, egg-laying and hatching	164
	11.1.6. Relations to other animals	165
11.2.	Land Iguana (*Conolophus subcristatus*)	165
	11.2.1. Description	166
	11.2.2. Ecology and feeding habits	166
	11.2.3. Home range and territoriality	168
	11.2.4. Egg-laying and hatching	171
	11.2.5. Interspecific relations	171
11.3.	Acknowledgements	172
	References	173

11.1. Marine Iguana (*Amblyrhynchus cristatus*)

At the height of the Mesozoic, the seas were abounding with reptiles. Today, only a few species of turtles, lizards, sea-snakes and estuarine crocodiles survive, and, of these, the marine lizards are particularly rare and limited in distribution. In the Philippines, the gecko, *Lepidodactylus woodfordi*, has been reported to hunt crabs in the supralittoral zone, and on the Californian island of Cerralvo an iguanid lizard, *Ctenosaura hemilopha*, has been observed to feed in a similar way during the dry season, when vegetation is sparse. On the Colombian island of Malpelo, *Anolis agassizi* lives partly, and the skink (*Diploglossus hancocki*) entirely, upon crustaceans caught in the tidal region. These islands are barren remnants of once larger landmasses and it is easy to imagine how their inhabitants were forced into this way of life, even though it is a difficult one for lizards to

Figure 11.1. Marine iguanas at Punta Espinosa, Fernandina. (Photograph by I. Eibl-Eibesfeldt)

follow. Fricke (1970) describes similar behaviour for the skink (*Cryptoblepharus cognatus*), living on the harsh volcanic island of Nossi Bé near Madagascar. These lizards descend daily into the intertidal region to feed on insects crustaceans and fish—again, an arid hinterland leaves them with few alternatives.

The only example of a truly marine lizard is the marine iguana (*Amblyrhynchus cristatus*) of the Galápagos Islands. These are large lizards and can be seen literally by the hundreds covering lava rocks of the shorelines. Their staple diet consists of marine algae which are taken by diving to submarine pastures or by browsing the plants on rocks exposed at low tides.

11.1.1. Description

The marine iguana varies widely between the different islands of the archipelago. Adult males range from 60 to 140 cm in length and from 1.5 to 12.5 kg in weight. The snout is short (Fig. 11.2) and is the feature from which the generic name (*amblys* = short, *rhynchos* = snout) has been derived. This shortened form of the skull facilitates the foraging on marine algae attached to rocks. The jaws are lined on each side with a row of tricuspid teeth. The head is covered with pyramid-shaped scales, which are particularly prominent in adult males and serve as interlocking devices during head-butting tournaments (see below). The tail is laterally compressed and rather longer than the body. Nuchal, dorsal and caudal crests are well-developed. The feet are armed with very long claws, which allow animals to cling on to surf-beaten rocks.

The basic colouration is black to dark grey becoming brownish or light grey on the belly. During the breeding season, and in some subspecies (Table 11.1) throughout the year, the sides of the body and the mid-dorsal parts of the head and legs acquire red and greenish colouration (11.1.4 below).

Figure 11.2. Male with several female marine iguanas in elevated basking posture. (Photograph by I. Eibl-Eibesfeldt)

11.1.2. Habitat, distribution and island subspeciation

Marine iguanas inhabit rocky shores and have in fact a patchy distribution in the archipelago. There is a clear preference for southern shorelines, which are more exposed to wave action and where algae appear to grow more prolifically than they do along sheltered northern coasts. The animals are often abundant in the vicinity of shallow reefs and along extended intertidal zones. A further factor affecting distribution is the proximity of nesting sites for the females.

Table 11.1

Subspecies	Island(s)	
A.c. cristatus (Bell)	Fernandina	Largest in size; form a closely related group of the central and western islands
A.c. hassi (Eibl)	Santa Cruz	
A.c. albermarlensis (Eibl)	Isabela	
A.c. mertensi (Eibl)	San Cristóbal; Santiago	
A.c. sielmanni (Eibl)	Pinta	
A.c. venustissimus (Eibl)	Española	Most brightly coloured
A.c. nanus (Garman)	Genovesa	Small, dark coloured

Subspecies of the Galápagos Marine Iguana (*Amblyrhynchus cristatus*) (Eibl-Eibesfeldt, 1956, 1962.)

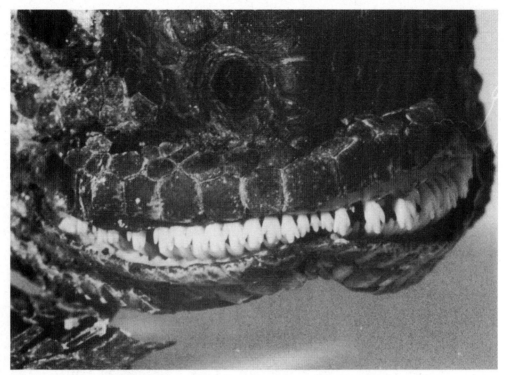

Figure 11.3. Three-cusped teeth form a sharp cutting edge. (Photograph by R. Krell).

Laurie (1982) was the first to undertake a careful census of marine iguana populations in the Galápagos Islands. He visited and circumnavigated all the main islands except for Darwin and Wolf. He classified the major colonies into three classes: 500–1000 iguanas/km, 1000–3000 iguanas/km and 3000 iguanas/km. From his results and taking into consideration the smaller island colonies, I would estimate the total number of marine iguanas in the archipelago at between 200,000 and 300,000. Laurie's findings also revealed important differences in age structure and recruitment between populations. This has been related in some areas to predation of the young iguanas by cats and dogs, a particular problem that is discussed further by H. Hoeck in Chapter 16.

S. Garman (1892) first drew attention to differences between marine iguanas on the different islands of the archipelago. Seven subspecies have been recognized, differing significantly in size and colouration. A revision by the present author forms the basis of the classification appearing in Table 11.1.

11.1.3. Marine adaptations and feeding habits

Marine iguanas are adept at both swimming and diving. Diving times have a duration of usually a few minutes, but instances extending beyond half-an-hour have been recorded. Large iguanas dive to depths of at least 15 m for their food (Eibl-Eibesfeldt, 1964a, Hobson, 1965). Among morphological adaptations to facilitate swimming is the laterally compressed tail; marine iguanas swim with their legs held tightly back, pressed against their sides. Another adaptation to marine life lies in salt glands which allow the excretion of surplus salt taken into the body. These glands open into the nose and their secretion is ejected (rather like blowing our nose) with a jet of air through the nostrils (Dunson, 1969, Schmidt-Nielsen and Fänge, 1958).

Carpenter's (1966) analysis of stomach contents yielded 9 species of algae taken by marine iguanas as food: *Tylotus ecuadorianus, Bryopsis indica triseriata, Plocamium pacificum, Prionitis abbreviata, Glossophora galapagensis, Lophosiphonia villum, Ptersosiphonia paucicorticata, Blossevillea galapagensis* and *Gelidium hancocki.*

In addition to algae, marine iguanas will occasionally eat animal matter, such as the after-birth of sea lions and freshly moulted crab. I have also seen young iguanas chasing and catching grasshoppers. In the settlements and in captivity they accept a variety of food, ranging from bread, raw and cooked meat, fish and vegetables.

Feeding times and requirements vary with age. Juveniles feed in the upper littoral zone, with animals of 120–200 gms only beginning to venture into the intertidal zone. So young animals are restricted in their feeding to a state of the tide low enough to expose algae; adult animals swim out and dive to submarine pastures. Feeding may become very irregular during the breeding season, with territorial males fasting for many days at a time.

The dark pigment in the skin of marine iguanas helps shield the animals from the effects of ultraviolet rays in sunlight. It also aids at times in warming the body. In the early morning and after diving, when body

Figure 11.4. Marine iguana feeding underwater. (Photograph by I. Eibl-Eibesfeldt).

temperatures are less than 25°C, the iguanas assume a prostrate basking posture, lying flat on the substrate with their legs spread on either side. Conversely, at temperatures above 37°C, they prevent overheating by assuming an elevated basking posture, exposing less surface to the sun and benefiting from the cooling effects of the wind; if this fails, the animals retreat to lava cracks, caves or to the shade of mangroves. By behavioural adaptations, they thus control body temperature, maintaining this normally between about 35 and 37°C.

Experiments by Bartholomew (1966) suggest that cardiovascular adjustments assist in reducing heat loss during diving. He further attributes the often reported avoidance of the sea when chased to a reluctance by marine iguanas to chill in the water.

11.1.4. Territoriality and breeding behaviour

Marine iguanas usually start to breed during the months of November and December, although on Española breeding commences about a month later. During the breeding season the males try to establish territories. They occupy a few square metres of lava, which they defend by display and by fighting rivals. Females enter the territory, where mating usually occurs.

According to Trillmich (1979) and Rauch (1982), the siting of the territory is of paramount importance in determining reproductive success. A good territory lies above the intertidal zone and remains dry; it is also advantageous that it lies suitably close to a nesting site. By contrast, males with their territories in wet intertidal regions attract fewer females, and hence have less chance of successfully breeding.

On Santa Cruz males set up their territories from early October to mid December; these territories are not necessarily in the same areas where iguanas congregate outside the breeding season. Initially the males leave regularly for feeding, and they also often bask outside their territories; later they remain constantly in their territories.

During this season, the males assume a breeding colouration, which differs in intensity between subspecies (Table 11.1). The Española subspecies has a brilliant red mottling on the sides and malachite green on the head

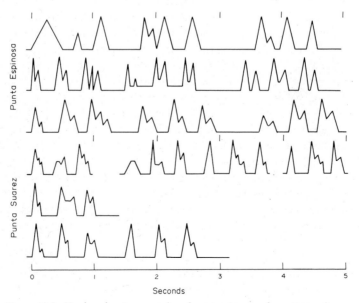

Figure 11.5. Head nod pattern graphs of marine iguanas from Fernandina (Punta Espinosa) and Española (Punta Suárez). (After Carpenter, 1966).

Figure 11.6. Head-butting during ritualized fighting between marine iguanas at Fernandina. (Photograph by I. Eibl-Eibesfeldt).

and back; the Floreana and Santa Fé races are also significantly red; while those of Fernandina and particularly Genovesa are comparatively dull-coloured.

Males constantly check their territory by touching the substrate with their tongues, thus taking samples into their Jacobson's organ. Recognition is also by scent, visual and probably other clues. Excrements may serve as markings as well as secretions from femoral glands, which are enlarged during the breeding season.

Fighting is highly ritualized, but damaging fights also occur. This ritualized fighting starts with display. Intruder and defender place themselves laterally to each other, walking with stiff legs, their bodies raised above the ground, crests erect and gular regions expanded. Mouths are often held agape, displaying a red spot on the tongue. Head-bobbing movements accompany this display, occurring as single, double or multiple nods, the later nods usually being less vigorous than the first (Fig. 11.5).

The lateral display is followed by a frontal display, during which the rivals stand facing each other while gaping and nodding. Attack amounts to rushing at one's opponent. Instead of biting, however, the animals clash with their lowered heads, when the horn-like scales on top interlock. In the ensuing *mêlée*, each tries to push the other away. The pushing back and forth may last for half-an-hour or more, followed by a pause during which the animals repeat the frontal display. Fights sometimes last for 4 or 5 hours altogether, with pauses and intermittent retreats until one animal is finally driven away or assumes a submissive posture flat on his belly. This attitude is recognized by the victor who stops fighting and waits in the threat posture until his rival retreats.

Biting occurs when intruders enter without display. The attacker rushes at his opponent and takes hold of the side of the body, nape of the neck, or one of the extremities and shakes violently. Wounds are seldom inflicted and the animal attacked usually retaliates in a similar fashion.

Rauch (personal communication) observed that as a rule fighting between neighbouring iguanas is ritualized, each tending to respect the other's territory, even when it is temporarily abandoned.

11.1.5. Copulation, egg-laying and hatching

In mating, the male approaches a female from the rear or from the side. As noted by Carpenter (1966), head-nodding by the male during courtship is at high speed and low amplitude, appearing more as a vertical vibration or shudder of the head. If the female does not move away, the male mounts her, throwing one front leg over her back, thus pinning her down. At the same time he attempts to grasp her by the nape of the neck. If the female does not resist, he carries her in this way; a female ready to copulate allows herself to be carried, either assisting with her own legs or leaving her forelegs dangling passively. This manoeuvre last perhaps for a minute or more, during which the male nods and shakes the female. Mating then occurs.

Egg-laying takes place about 5 weeks later. On Santa Cruz, this is from about mid February to mid March (Rauch, 1982). Females on this island move from the areas where they spend most of the year to traditional locations for nesting. On Española, females compete fiercely for laying sites, which are scarce on the predominantly rocky coasts. Furthermore, the nests are subsequently guarded (Eibl-Eibesfeldt, 1966a,b)—a behavioural trait which has now been reported from populations on Fernandina and on Coamaño on the south coast of Santa Cruz (Trillmich, 1979). The egg-laying period on Española is accompanied by a remarkable change in colouration of the females, which become almost as brightly coloured as the males; linked with this assumption of masculine colouring is an increased aggression of the females.

The nest is a hole dug obliquely into the ground. Digging itself evidently carries some risk, for Carpenter (1966) found individuals trapped in collapsed burrows on Fernandina; on Santa Cruz Rauch (personal communication) came across three accidents of this sort in some 300 complete nests examined. Once a shallow depression has been made, the female digs with alternate forelegs and shoves the excavated soil backwards with her hindfeet. When the burrow has a depth of 30 to 80 cm, the female emerges to the entrance from time to time to look around for approaching sea lions (which might otherwise crush her) and rival females.

Female marine iguanas excavating their burrows are often challenged by others searching for an egg-laying site. Such challenges may result in contests recalling the ritualized posturing and fighting of rival males.

During the actual egg-laying females face towards their burrow entrance. Normally, two or three eggs are laid, each about 8 cm long and 4 cm wide, and with shells the texture of parchment. The average weight of an egg of the Santa Cruz subspecies is 90 gm. When laying is completed the female leaves the cache, scratching the sand or earth backwards with her fore- and hindlegs. Finally the cache entrance is sealed and the ground levelled. The duration of the egg-laying season varies from 3–4 weeks on Santa Cruz (during 1981, from 10 February until 7 March) to over 6 weeks on Española.

It is a strange sight observing female iguanas spaced on rocks 2 or 3 metres apart and guarding their nests. They continue this vigil for several days before leaving the area to feed. Trillmich has observed a female on Coamaño guarding her eggs for 10 days. On Española, the egg-laying area I was once watching became a resting venue for sea lions during the night. The iguanas left their stations in the evening and took refuge under nearby rocks. In the morning, when the sea lions had left, they returned, each touching the ground with her tongue to locate the nest site. Fresh sand was scratched over each position and then the females continued their guard.

Rauch (1982) found that the incubation period on Santa Cruz varied from 89 to 120 days. Temperature in the egg chambers (at a depth of about 18 cm), during 3 days observed, ranged from 27.7 to 29.8°C. As the egg-laying season is of fairly short duration most eggs at a given site hatch over a short interval of time.

Upon emergence, newly-hatched marine iguanas look around for a few moments and then run, often bipedally at high speeds to the nearest cover—not necessarily in the direction of the shore (Laurie, 1982). Groups of four or five hatchlings start at the same time, followed by a pause before the next batch leaves. Young iguanas thus show an early adaptation in their behaviour to predators; eventually they make their way to the shore.

11.1.6. Relations to other animals

The ground finches (*Geospiza fuliginosa* and *G. fortis*) remove ticks from marine iguanas; the iguanas allow this to occur but, in contrast to land iguanas (*Conolophus*), do not adopt a special posture (page 172) (Eibl-Eibesfeldt, 1964b, 1977). The crab (*Grapsus grapsus*) forages on their bodies and Beebe (1923) observed ticks being removed in this way.

Mockingbirds, snakes and rats prey on the eggs of marine iguanas. The Galápagos hawk (*Buteo galapagoensis*), great blue heron (*Ardea herodias*) and lava heron (*Butorides sundevalli*) all prey upon young and half-grown iguanas, and (according to Krisztina Trillmich) the hawks even take adults. The snake (*Dromicus*) is another predator of the young. In the water, sharks feed on both young and adults (Heller, 1903), and Laurie (1982) found the remains of young marine iguanas in stomachs of the hawkfish, *Cirrhites rivulatus*; this helps explain the apparent isolation and subspeciation within *Amblyrhynchus*.

In recent times, animals introduced to the Galápagos Islands have become a threat to marine iguanas. Among the more significant of these are feral cats, rats, dogs and pigs (Chapter 16). Adult marine iguanas are not adapted to predation by land mammals; they have a short flight distance and move only reluctantly when chased. On Pinzón, introduced rats constitute a menace to eggs and young. Thus, the future of marine iguanas on all the islands with these alien predators must be a cause for concern.

11.2. Land Iguana (*Conolophus subcristatus*)

The land iguana is the terrestrial counterpart of the marine iguana. The genus is endemic to the Galápagos Islands and appears to be related to *Amblyrhynchus*.

Two species of *Conolophus* have been described: *C. subcristatus* (from Fernandina, Isabela, Santiago, Santa Cruz, Baltra and South Plaza) and *C. pallidus* (from Santa Fé). The differences between these two are small, however, and it seems reasonable to look upon them as subspecies. The fine systematics of the genus remains to be determined. H. Snell (personal communication) considers there to be at least two taxonomically distinct *forms* of *C. subcristatus*; one inhabiting Santa Cruz, Baltra and South Plaza, the other Isabela and Fernandina.

Land iguanas exist today on Fernandina, Isabela, Santa Cruz, South Plaza, *Seymour* and Santa Fé. On Santiago—where they were once so abundant permeating the ground with their burrows that Charles Darwin could scarcely find space to pitch his tent—none has been seen in recent years. On Baltra, they disappeared during the Second World War when the island was used as a military base; but the Baltra form survived as a result of William Beebe having transplanted some fifty individuals previously to the neighbouring island of Seymour (which had no native land iguanas).

Table 11.2

Differences between Marine and Land Iguanas	
Marine Iguana	Land Iguana
essentially gregarious in habit	solitary in habit
feed on algae in littoral zone	feed on terrestrial arid zone plants
burrows not dug	burrows dug for shelter
ritualized fighting by head-butting	no ritualized fighting by head-buttings
submissive posture by collapsing flat on the belly	no clear submissive posture
no appeasement display by 'sky-pointing'	appeasement display by raising head vertically ('sky-pointing')
no posturing when cleaned by finches	stilt posturing to incite cleaning response
few but large progeny per female	progeny in larger number but smaller per female

Figure 11.7. Land iguana (with mockingbird), caldera of Fernandina. The largest population of these iguanas exists today on Fernandina, with many females making the long journey to traditional nesting sites in the crater (Fig. 11.8). The picture was taken before the eruption of June 1968. (Photograph by Alan Root/courtesy Charles Darwin Foundation).

11.2.1. Description

Land iguanas are stout-bodied lizards with typical iguanid snouts (not shortened as in *Amblyrhynchus*). The jaws are strong and the teeth are adapted for biting and tearing plant material. The dorsal part of the head is covered with elevated scales, but these are less pronounced than in the marine iguana (Table 11.2 lists the principal differences between the 2 genera). Overall length of the largest males is 1.20 m. The tail is rounded and shorter than the body. The colour of the head, legs and belly is usually yellow, with the back a dark to rusty brown—either uniformly or in patches, depending on age and island. The Santa Fé land iguana is more of a pale yellowish-grey.

Land iguanas show marked sexual dimorphism, with the males two to three times heavier than the females. Differences between island populations are also marked. Males from South Plaza rarely exceed a weight of 5 kg; on Fernandina they average 7 kg and the females 3.5 kg (Werner, 1982); while on Baltra a specimen has been recorded at over 12 kg.

11.2.2. Ecology and feeding habits

The habitats of the different island populations vary considerably. Basically, dry areas are preferred. On Santa Cruz, where vegetation ranges from desert to moist evergreen forest, land iguanas are found in the arid belt below 200 m. They are however confined to the northwestern part of the island, near Conway Bay; formerly they extended into the south—as witnessed by skeletal remains found in lava tunnels at Academy

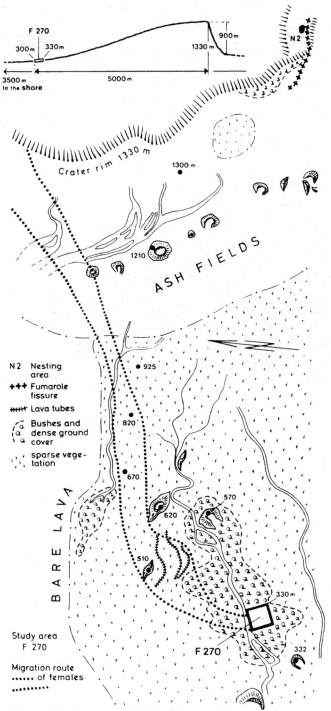

Figure 11.8. Survey area (F 270) of Dagmar Werner on the western flank of the central volcano of Fernandina. 12 out of 13 females used the outlined route on their way to the rim; depending on weather conditions they needed 3–10 days for the journey. A nesting area (N 2) is shown where the nests are heated by fumarole activity. (From Werner 1982).

Bay. On Fernandina, an island that is dry even in the upper regions, land iguanas inhabit the summit area at altitudes from 1200 to 1500 m, but there are also resident populations at lower altitudes—wherever in fact segments of vegetation have established between lava flows.

In contrast is the restricted range of the population on South Plaza. This small island off the east coast of Santa Cruz is about 1 km in length, 250 m at its broadest, and rises to a flattened ridge of lava barely 20 m above the sea. The land area is 11.7 ha, of which a third is covered with shrubs and *Opuntia*. The islet supports about 330 land iguanas; and a population has evidently survived in this meagre environment for countless generations.

Land iguanas are herbivorous, feeding on many different plants according to season and occurrence. On Fernandina, Dagmar Werner found that, during a particular period, 90% of the food intake of iguanas in her study area (330 m altitude) consisted of the buds and flowers of the morning glory (*Ipomoea alba*). Carpenter (1969) collected 50 scats of iguanas near the coast of this island and these contained principally cactus remains. On Plaza, *Opuntia* constitutes the main diet. In addition to this vegetarian diet, land iguanas are opportunistic feeders on animal remains, such as the afterbirth of sea lions and dead birds. I have seen young iguanas catch grasshoppers—and even a half-grown one prey upon a newly-moulted crab; animals seen repeatedly in the tidal region I have assumed to feed there.

The prickly pear and candelabra (*Jasminocereus*) cacti have spines which easily penetrate the gums and tongues of iguanas. The lizards try to remove these by scraping or rolling pads and fruits on the ground, or they may simply try to bite away the larger spines. Despite the precautions spines often become embedded in their mouths, but these appear not greatly to inconvenience the animals. The fruits and pads that are taken are usually those that have fallen to the ground; only occasionally do land iguanas attempt the difficult task of climbing a cactus tree.

11.2.3. Home range and territoriality

Studies by Dagmar Werner (in print), on Fernandina, and by the Snells (personal communication), on South Plaza, have provided an interesting and informative picture of the social life of land iguanas.

The social habits of these iguanas change throughout the year, with two main phases being distinguished: a reproductive phase during the warm season (January to July on Fernandina) and a non-reproductive season during the colder months. In her study area on the western side of Fernandina (Fig. 11.8), Werner found that both sexes congregate at the outset of the reproductive season and then, as egg-laying time approaches, the females move up the slope of the central volcano and down inside the caldera. Some of the males remain on their territories, while others wander away to other feeding areas.

The territories on Fernandina range in size from 250 m² to 1600 m². When food is scarce these may be even larger, but at such times the boundaries are less well-defined and burrows (rather than the peripheries of territories) are defended. When moving around in their territories the males touch the ground with their tongues in a manner recalling marine iguanas and suggesting olfactory probing.

Females return to the same mating areas each year. Within these broad areas they may inspect several territories before selecting a mate. These 'inspection tours' may last several days or even weeks. It is the female who chooses, and once she has made her choice she will remain with 1 male and share his territory and burrow during the night. As many as 7 females have been found associated together with 1 territorial male (Werner, 1982).

By a specific 'submissive display' females appear to inhibit aggression by the males. The female raises her head so that the snout points to the sky (Fig. 11.9a–c). Her mouth may be slightly opened and she may remain motionless in this position. Sometimes this is accompanied by low amplitude head-bobbing. Finally, she will slowly strut away, sky-pointing and nodding.

In the centre of their territories (Fig. 11.10) the males may dig several burrows—a habit not encountered in

Figure 11.9a–c. Female land iguana 'sky pointing' at the approach of a male: South Plaza Island. (From 16 mm ciné film by author).

marine iguanas. Ownership is marked by patrolling, assertion displays and guarding from elevated spots within the territory. This assertion display is a low intensity threat display, during which the body is slightly raised from the ground and the head bobs with low amplitude.

Challenging displays are of higher intensity. Males raise themselves on all legs and walk stiff-legged, their gular regions expanded, nuchal and dorsal crests erected, and bodies bloated. The mouth may be slightly opened and the head is shaken. Carpenter (1969) noted differences in the head movement pattern between the Santa Fé and South Plaza iguanas (Fig. 11.11).

The fighting behaviour of the land iguana is less ritualized than that of the marine iguana. Attacks are directed against the sides or nape of the neck of the opponent, but these often result in no more than simply butting the opponent with the snout. Serious damage rarely occurs. Tail slashing occasionally takes place during defensive display, when one individual is approached by another.

When food is abundant, males remain in their territories after mating. Besides feeding they do little except move between sun and shade for thermoregulation, walking in some cases no more than 5 m (Werner, 1982). Other males leave on feeding excursions which take them up to several kilometres away in the higher parts of the island, from where they return from time to time to their territories. During this period, males defend their burrows and they continue to keep their individual distances.

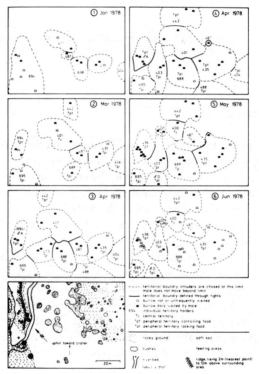

Figure 11.10. Ecological setting (left, bottom) and distribution of territories in Werner's study area (F 270, Figure 8) on Fernandina during 1978. Successive changes in territories follow the onset of breeding activity: (1) January. A loose agglomeration of territories with no females yet present; (2) late March. Two further males and most of the females have arrived; (3) mid April. Tightly packed territories with frequent fighting; (4) late April. Situation at beginning of mating; (5) mid May. A period of conflict with territory gains and losses; (6) early June. Most females have left the area for egg-laying. Few fights and displays now occur and males occupy single burrows in their territories. (From Werner, 1982).

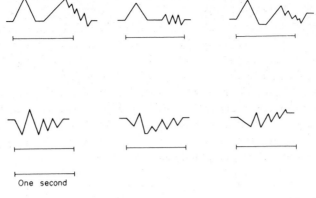

One second

Figure 11.11. Head nod pattern graphs of *Conolophus subcristatus* (top)
and *C. pallidus* (below). Lines represent up and down movements of
the head through time. (From Carpenter, 1969).

11.2.4. Egg-laying and hatching

About 95% of the female population observed by Werner in the breeding area on the western side of Fernandina migrate to the top of the island and descend into the caldera (Fig. 11.8). The distance involved may be up to 15 km, with an ascent of 1000 to 1300 m to the rim, followed by a descent of some 900 m. The initial part of the journey to the rim takes each female 4–14 days (average of 9 days); from there, to the egg-laying site, to dig the nest, lay eggs and return again to the rim takes another 20–33 days (with an average of 23 days). The round trip for nesting thus averages about 32 days. The small remaining proportion of the population nests on the outer slope of the volcano.

Inside the crater females seek places where the ground has a constant temperature of around 31.5–33°C. Digging the nest is undertaken in a similar way to that of the marine iguana. Egg-laying is spread over a period of about 6 weeks, with a peak during the first 2 weeks of July. Seven to twenty-three eggs are laid by each female. These eggs are smaller than those of the marine iguana, with an average weight of 50.7 g and a mean length of 6 cm. After a nest is closed it is guarded by the female for several days.

On Fernandina, hatching takes place about 3½ months after laying. Upon emergence as (observed by Werner on Santa Cruz and Santa Fé) the young immediately race for cover—a response to predation by hawks and snakes.

Many aspects of the land iguana's reproductive behaviour remain to be investigated. Howard and Heidi Snell are currently studying the population on South Plaza to see if reproduction is effected through a wide section of adults or by a limited few. There are indications that such a subset of breeding 'elite' exists.

11.2.5. Interspecific relations

A symbiotic relationship exists between the land iguana and small and medium ground finches (*Geospiza*) and, on Fernandina (Dagmar Werner, personal communication), between the land iguana and mockingbird (*Nesomimus*). In this 'cleaning symbiosis' the iguana adopts a special posture which facilitates the bird in removing ticks. Upon seeing a finch (Fig. 11.12a–d), a land iguana will ostentatiously raise itself off the ground and so expose ventral surfaces for inspection. The mutual interest depends upon the degree of infestation by ticks. Such a symbiosis also occurs in the Galápagos tortoises (MacFarland and Reeder, 1974).

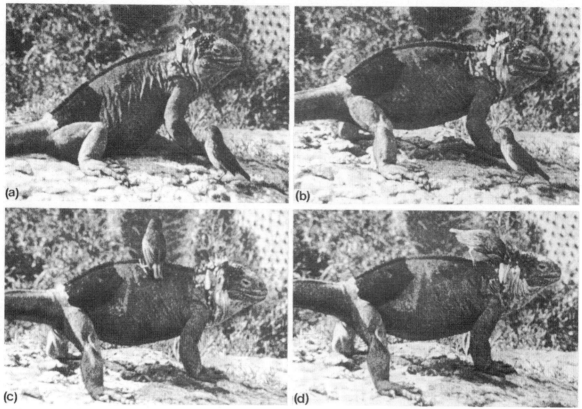

Figure 11.12. Cleaning symbiosis between the small ground finch (*Geospiza fuliginosa*) and South Plaza land iguana. The finch lands near the iguana (a), which then raises into a stilting posture (b); the finch mounts (c) and begins inspecting the iguana for external parasites. (Photographs from ciné-film by I. Eibl-Eibesfeldt).

Natural predators of the land iguana are the land snake (*Dromicus*) and the Galápagos hawk (*Buteo galapagoensis*). Both take juveniles and hatchlings. Adults defend themselves effectively (see Fig. 19.9, Chapter 19). If approached by man, iguanas which have not been previously molested retreat with haste; if caught, they lash out with their tails and can give a severe bite. In general their flight and defence responses to mammalian predators appear to be inadequate. Thus on islands where cats, pigs and dogs have been introduced they are threatened with extinction. On Santiago and Baltra populations have already disappeared. On both Santa Cruz and Isabela land iguanas are endangered and so breeding nuclei have been transferred to enclosures at the Charles Darwin Research Station, where the hatchlings are raised in captivity for subsequent release.

11.3. Acknowledgements

For information and helpful comments, I wish to thank Andrew Laurie, Norbert Rauch, Howard and Heidi Snell, Krisztina Trillmich and Dagmar Werner. I would also like to thank Polly Wiessner for her help with the English text and for numerous suggestions.

References

Bartholomew, G.A. (1966) A Field Study of Temperature Regulation in the Galápagos Marine Iguana. *Copeia*, **2**, 240–250.

Beebe, W. (1923) Galápagos Reptiles and Birds of the Zoological Parks. *Zool. Soc. Bull., N.Y.*, **26**, 99–106.

Carpenter, C.C. (1966) The Marine Iguana of the Galápagos Islands: Its Behavior and Ecology. *Proc. Calif. Acad. Sci.*, **4**, 329–376.

Carpenter, C.C. (1969) Behavioral and Ecological Notes on the Galápagos Land Iguanas. *Herpetologica*, **25**, 155–164.

Dunson, W.A. (1969) Electrolyte Excretion by the Salt Gland of the Galápagos Marine Iguana. *Am. J. Physiol.*, **216**, 995–1002.

Eibl-Eibesfeldt, I. (1956) Neue Rasse der Meerechse. *Senck. Biol.*, **43**, 177–199.

Eibl-Eibesfeldt, I. (1962) Neue Unterarten der Meerechse, *Amblyrhynchus cristatus*, nebst weiteren Angaben zur Biologie der Art. *Senck. Biol.*, **37**, 87–100.

Eibl-Eibesfeldt, I. (1964a) *Amblyrhynchus cristatus* (Iguanidae): Nahrungserwerb an Land und unter Wasser. Beiheft zu Film E 581/1964, *Encycl. Cinemat. Gottingen*, 293–295.

Eibl-Eibesfeldt, I. (1964b) *Geospiza fuliginosa* (Fringillidae): Säubern von Meerechsen. Beiheft zu Film E 576/1964, *Encycl. Cinemat. Göttingen*, 327–329.

Eibl-Eibesfeldt, I. (1966a) Das Verteidigen der Eiablageplötze bei der Hood-Meerechse (*Amblyrhynchus cristatus venustissimus*). *Zeitschr. Tierpsychol.*, **23**, 627–631.

Eibl-Eibesfeldt, I. (1966b) *Amblyrhynchus cristatus* (Iguanidae): Kampf der Weibchen. Beiheft zu Film E 582/1964, *Encycl. Cinemat. Göttingen*, 675–680.

Eibl-Eibesfeldt, I. (1977) *Geospiza fuliginosa* (Fringillidae): Putzsymbiose mit *Conolophus subcristatus* (Freilandaufnahmen). Beiheft zu Film E 2283/1976, *Encycl. Cinemat. Göttingen*, 3–9.

Fricke, H. (1970) Die ökologische spezialisation der Eidechse (*Cryptoblepharus butoni cognatus* Böttger) auf das Leben in der Gezeitenzone (Reptilia, Skinkidae). *Oecologia (Berl)*, **5**, 380–391.

Garman, S. (1892) The Reptiles of the Galápagos Islands. *Bull. Essex Inst.*, **24**, 73–87.

Heller, E. (1903) Papers of the Hopkins Stanford Galápagos Expedition 1898–99, Reptiles. *Proc. Washington Acad. Sci.*, **5**, 39–98.

Hobson, E.S. (1965) Observations on diving in the Galápagos Iguana *Amblyrhynchus cristatus*. *Copeia*, **2**, 249–250.

Laurie, A. (1982) Marine Iguanas: A Report from Galápagos. *Oryx* (in press).

MacFarland, C.G. and Reeder, W.G. (1974) Cleaning Symbiosis Involving Galápagos Tortoises and Two Species of Darwin Finches. *Z. Tierpsychol.*, **34**, 464–483.

Rauch, N. (1982) Reproductive Strategies of Male and Female Marine Iguanas. Report to the Charles Darwin Foundation.

Schmidt-Nielsen, K. and Fange, R. (1958) Salt Glands in Marine Reptiles. *Nature*, **182**, 783–785.

Trillmich, K. (1979) Feeding Behaviour and Social Behaviour of the Marine Iguana. *Noticias de Galápagos*, **29**, 17–20.

Werner, D. (1982) Social Organisation and Ecology of Land Iguanas, *Conolophus subcristatus* in *Iguanas of the World*. Edited by G.M. Burghardt and A.S. Rand. Garland Press, New York.

Werner, D. (in press) Reproductive Effort in the Iguana *Conolophus subcristatus*: clutch size and migration costs. *Am. Naturalist*.

CHAPTER 12

The Endemic Land Birds

P.R. GRANT

Division of Biological Sciences, The University of Michigan, Ann Arbor, Michigan, USA

Contents

12.1. Introduction   175
12.2. The Species   176
12.3. Distributions   178
12.4. Breeding Ecology   180
    12.4.1. Introduction and breeding systems   180
    12.4.2. Breeding seasons   180
    12.4.3. Breeding characteristics and success   181
    12.4.4. Population fluctuations   182
12.5. Feeding Ecology   185
    12.5.1. Feeding habits   185
    12.5.2. Seasonal variation in food supply   186
12.6. Evolution   186
12.7. Conservation   188
12.8. Acknowledgements   188
    References   188

12.1. Introduction

Birds are the most conspicuous element of the Galápagos fauna. The resident land birds are of special interest because of the part they played, and continue to play, in the development of our understanding of evolution. When Charles Darwin visited the archipelago in 1835 he was impressed by the fact that different species of mockingbirds replaced each other on different islands; likewise tortoises differed markedly in their appearance from one island to another. Exactly what he thought of the finches is more difficult to make out from his notes and publications (Sulloway, 1982), but he must surely have been confused by them as everyone visiting the islands is today. It is difficult if not impossible to identify all the finches you see because the largest members of some species are almost indistinguishable from the smallest members of others. Such a confusion must have been a stimulus to this perceptive naturalist. Taken together, his observations on tortoises, mockingbirds and finches set in motion a train of thought on the plasticity of species which eventually led him to propose a comprehensive theory of evolution based on that great organizing principle of biology, the principle of natural selection.

In this Chapter I will discuss the land bird fauna as a whole, giving particular emphasis to biological peculiarities exhibited by the species, and concluding with some remarks on their future conservation. I omit all those species usually associated with water, that is the seabirds, shore birds, ducks and herons.

12.2. The Species

Twenty-eight species of land birds breed on the Galápagos (Table 12.1). One of them, the Paint-billed Crake, was only discovered in 1953 and therefore might have immigrated recently, but the rest were present on Darwin's visit. The majority are endemic, i.e. they are unique species found only on the Galápagos. The remaining five, excluding the Crake, differ in less substantial ways from their relatives in South America but one of them, the Vermilion Flycatcher, has distinctive populations on different islands and these are recognized as three different subspecies.

The two groups which have undergone speciation on the islands are the mockingbirds and the finches. Both groups pose taxonomic problems. There are four groups of mockingbirds, (Fig. 12.1), but they are allopatric (live on different islands) so it is not known whether they would interbreed if living on the same island. Should they be called 4 species, or 4 subspecies of the same species? They certainly differ conspicuously in plumage patterns around the face and chest, in eye colour and in size. For example, the adult

Table 12.1. The land birds. Endemic species are indicated with an asterisk.
Based on Harris (1973, 1974).

English Name	Local (Galápagos) Name	Scientific Name
Galápagos Hawk	Gavilán	*Buteo galapagoensis
Galápagos Rail	Pachay	*Laterallus spilonotus
Paint-billed Crake	Gallareta	Neocrex erythrops
Galápagos Dove	Paloma	*Zenaida galapagoensis
Dark-billed Cuckoo	Cuclillo	Coccyzus melacorhyphus
Barn Owl	Lechuza blanca	Tyto alba
Short-eared Owl	Lechuza de campo	Asio flammeus
Vermilion Flycatcher	Brujo	Pyrocephalus rubinus
Large-billed Flycatcher	Papamoscas	*Myiarchus magnirostris
Galápagos Martin	Golondrina	*Progne modesta
Galápagos Mockingbird	Cucuve	*Nesomimus parvulus
Charles Mockingbird	Cucuve	*Nesomimus trifasciatus
Hood Mockingbird	Cucuve	*Nesomimus macdonaldi
Chatham Mockingbird	Cucuve	*Nesomimus melanotis
Yellow Warbler	Canario	Dendroica petechia
Small Ground Finch	Pinzón	*Geospiza fuliginosa
Medium Ground Finch	Pinzón	*Geospiza fortis
Large Ground Finch	Pinzón	*Geospiza magnirostris
Sharp-beaked Ground Finch	Pinzón	*Geospiza difficilis
Cactus Ground Finch	Pinzón	*Geospiza scandens
Large Cactus Ground Finch	Pinzón	*Geospiza conirostris
Vegetarian Finch	Pinzón	*Platyspiza crassirostris
Small Tree Finch	Pinzón	*Camarhynchus parvulus
Medium Tree Finch	Pinzón	*Camarhynchus pauper
Large Tree Finch	Pinzón	*Camarhynchus psittacula
Woodpecker Finch	Pinzón	*Cactospiza pallida
Mangrove Finch	Pinzón	*Cactospiza heliobates
Warbler Finch	Pinzón	*Certhidea olivacea

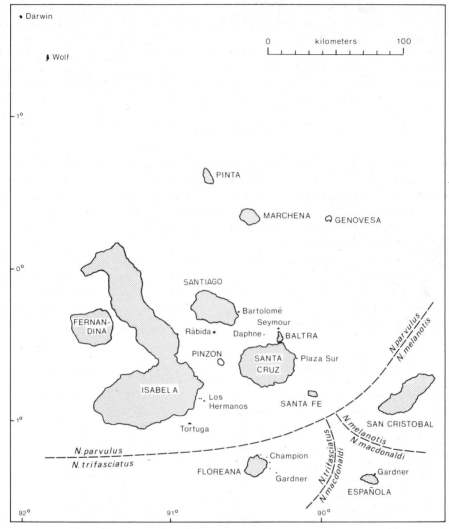

Figure 12.1. The Galápagos Islands and the distribution of the 4 species of mockingbirds (see also Table 12.2 and Chapter 19, Fig. 19.1).

Charles mockingbird has a dark red-brown eye, whereas the eyes of the three others are different shades of yellow or green. The Hood mockingbird has a much longer beak (Chapter 19, Fig. 19.1) and longer legs than the others, and is about 25% heavier than the Galápagos mockingbird. Such differences are equivalent to differences between species in mainland regions, which is why 4 species of mockingbirds are currently recognized. They all differ from the mockingbird species *Mimus longicaudatus* on the Ecuadorian mainland in size, proportions and plumage patterns, but a recent study has shown that these mainland-island differences are not so large as to justify automatically placing the island mockingbirds in a separate genus (Abbott and Abbott, 1978). Possibly, therefore, they should all be grouped together in the genus *Mimus*.

Darwin's Finches present similar problems at the same two taxonomic levels. Is the Large Cactus Ground Finch (*G. conirostris*) on Genovesa really a particularly large form of the Cactus Ground Finch (*G. scandens*), in view of their morphological similarity (Lack, 1947)? If so, are the remaining populations of *G. conirostris* a unique species, or are they unusual forms of the Large Ground Finch (*G. magnirostris*)? Similar problems prevail with populations of the Sharp-beaked Ground Finch (*G. difficilis*); the largest birds, on Wolf and Darwin, are almost twice as heavy as the smallest birds, on Genovesa (Grant, 1981a)! Since the problematical populations are allopatric and well differentiated (Grant, 1983) their taxonomic status is uncertain; they may represent 1, 2 or 3 species. Likewise there is uncertainty and no general agreement on whether there are 3 genera of tree finches (Bowman, 1961), as shown in Table 12.1 (Harris, 1974) or a single genus (Lack, 1947).

Although these are taxonomic headaches, the different levels of differentiation are rich material for making inferences about the evolutionary history of the groups.

12.3. Distributions

Distributions of breeding populations of the 28 species are listed in Table 12.2. Doves occur on all major islands and many of the smaller ones such as Daphne Major, Champion, Bainbridge Rocks and other satellites of the large islands. The Medium Tree Finch occurs only on Floreana. The remaining species are distributed in ways that lie between these two extremes. Most species occur on the five largest islands: Isabela, Santa Cruz, Fernandina, Santiago and San Cristóbal. These are also the highest and have the greatest number of habitats. Few species occur on the northern islands, especially on the remote islands of Wolf and Darwin, and few species occur on low, arid, small islands. Viewed the other way around, the number of bird species breeding on any one island is a function of the size of that island, its elevation, number of plant species and distance to the next large island. Elevation is the most important determinant of the number of plant species, and this in turn is the most important determinant of the number of land bird species, with island size and degree of isolation being of secondary importance (Harris, 1973, Abbott *et al.*, 1977).

Why are some species widely distributed throughout the archipelago and others restricted to one or a few islands? Some may be restricted because they are relatively recent arrivals, like the Crake, and have not had enough time to disperse. But birds have been seen flying between islands fairly frequently, and small numbers of some species are found periodically on islands where they do not breed (Grant *et al.*, 1975), so this does not seem to be a major reason. Others are restricted because their requirements are not met on all the islands. Thus the Barn Owl is dependent on mammals for prey, the Vegetarian Finch is dependent on green vegetation and fleshy berries, the Mangrove Finch is dependent on mangroves, and the crake and rail are dependent on moist, thick, ground vegetation which is found almost exclusively at moderately high elevations. None of these requirements are met on all islands: none of these species occurs on more than 10 islands. In contrast, the dove's requirements of small and large seeds (P.R. Grant and K.T. Grant, 1979) are met on all islands, and this species is ubiquitous.

The distribution of requirements does not explain all distributions of species. Small seeds are present on Genovesa, Wolf and Darwin but the Small Ground Finch, which exploits small seeds elsewhere in the archipelago, is not present on these three islands. Has it simply never arrived? No, a few were encountered by visitors to Wolf in 1906. These three islands that lack the Small Ground Finch have breeding populations of a similar species, the Sharp-beaked Ground Finch. This correspondence led David Lack (1947) to suggest that the Small Ground Finch is outcompeted, whenever it arrives on these islands, by the Sharp-beaked Ground Finch. Our recent studies of the diets and food supply of the two species support Lack's suggestion (Grant and Schluter, 1984). Other distributional patterns in the archipelago can be interpreted in a similar way.

Distributions are not static. Changes have taken place since Darwin's visit, and since the California Academy of Sciences' year-long expedition to the Galápagos in 1905–06. We can be certain, for example, that the Large Ground Finch became extinct on San Cristóbal and Floreana some time after Darwin's visit, and that the Sharp-beaked Ground Finch became extinct on Santa Cruz some time after the visit of H.S. Swarth in 1932. But in other cases we cannot be sure that breeding populations of certain species occurred on particular islands, even though they were recorded there in small numbers in the past and are no longer present. For

Table 12.2. Distribution of breeding populations of the land birds on the 16 islands larger than $2.0\,km^2$ and on some smaller islands. Based on Harris (1973, 1974).

Species	Islands
Galápagos Hawk	All major islands except San Cristóbal (extinct), Genovesa, Wolf and Darwin
Galápagos Rail	Santa Cruz, Santiago, Pinta; possibly also Isabela, Fernandina and Floreana
Paint-billed Crake	Santa Cruz and Floreana
Galápagos Dove	All major islands and many small ones
Dark-billed Cuckoo	Isabela, Santa Cruz, Fernandina, Santiago, San Cristóbal, Floreana and Pinzón
Barn Owl	Isabela, Santa Cruz, Fernandina, Santiago and San Cristóbal
Short-eared Owl	All major islands except Wolf and possibly Rábida
Vermilion Flycatcher	All major islands except Española, Baltra, Santa Fé, Genovesa, Rábida, Wolf and Darwin
Large-billed Flycatcher	All major islands except the northern Darwin, Wolf and Genovesa
Galápagos Martin	All major islands except the northern Darwin, Wolf, Pinta, Marchena and Genovesa
Galápagos Mockingbird	All major islands except Floreana, Española, San Cristóbal and Pinzón
Charles Mockingbird	Extinct on Floreana (Charles), now only on its satellites Champion and Gardner
Hood Mockingbird	Española (Hood) and its satellite, Gardner near Española
Chatham Mockingbird	San Cristóbal (Chatham)
Yellow Warbler	All major islands and several small ones
Small Ground Finch	All major islands except Genovesa, Wolf and Darwin, and several small ones
Medium Ground Finch	All major islands except Española, Genovesa, Wolf and Darwin
Large Ground Finch	All major islands except Española; extinct on San Cristóbal and, probably, on Floreana and Santa Fé
Sharp-beaked Ground Finch	Fernandina, Santiago, Pinta, Genovesa, Wolf, Darwin; extinct on Santa Cruz, probably once resident and now extinct on San Cristóbal, Isabela and Floreana
Cactus Ground Finch	All major islands except Fernandina, Pinzón (extinct), Genovesa, Wolf and Darwin
Large Cactus Ground Finch	Española and Genovesa; possibly formerly on Wolf and Darwin
Vegetarian Finch	All major islands except Española, Baltra, Santa Fé, Genovesa, Wolf and Darwin
Small Tree Finch	All major islands except Marchena, Española, Genovesa, Wolf and Darwin
Medium Tree Finch	Floreana
Large Tree Finch	All major islands except Española, Genovesa, Wolf and Darwin, possibly also San Cristóbal, Santa Fé and Pinzón
Woodpecker Finch	Isabela, Santa Cruz, Fernandina, Santiago, San Cristóbal and Pinzón
Mangrove Finch	Isabela and Fernandina
Warbler Finch	All major islands and some small ones

example, the Academy exhibition collected 6 specimens of the Small Ground Finch on Wolf and 14 specimens of the Medium Ground Finch on Española. Because none were in the black plumage that adult males usually acquire, and because most vagrants to islands are immature birds, we assume these were immigrants.

Recent field studies on Daphne Major have shown that as many as 50 or more Small Ground Finches and Large Ground Finches immigrate after the breeding season, presumably from nearby Santa Cruz (Grant, et al., 1975). Most are immatures, they stay for several months, then depart (or die) at the beginning of the next breeding season. This type of inter-island movement makes it very difficult to assess the status of a species on an island, when perhaps 2 or 3 specimens were collected on an island at the turn of the century but no individuals have been seen since. These specimens could be the remnants of a population close to extinction, or could be vagrants. Most are probably the latter, and most have not been included in Table 12.2.

The other reason for our uncertainty is that breeding of the land bird species has been rarely studied directly; it has usually been reported from casual observations or inferred from the number of birds present. The breeding of rare birds can easily be overlooked. A visitor to Santa Fé in the period 1966 to 1970 would probably not have recorded the Large Ground Finch but Tjitte de Vries, who spent many months there studying hawks, observed a single pair—the only pair on the island—breeding in each year. Other species which are cryptic in their breeding habits, like the Galápagos Rail and the Cuckoo, may have small breeding populations on islands where they have been seen only a few times. Thus further research may necessitate a revision of Table 12.2, although the vast majority of breeding populations are certainly known.

12.4. Breeding Ecology

12.4.1. Introduction and breeding systems

Modern ecological studies of land birds began in 1966–70 with an investigation of the feeding and breeding habits of Galápagos Hawks on two islands, Santiago and Santa Fé (de Vries, 1975, 1976). By colour ringing many individuals, de Vries discovered several interesting features of the breeding of these birds. First, their breeding was rather erratic. Some birds bred for 3 years in a row, then stopped for a year and resumed the next year; others bred every other year; and so on. Second, a breeding female was often accompanied by 2, 3 or 4 males, rather than just one, and all these males mated with her. Polyandry such as this is rare in birds, but not unknown in hawks elsewhere.

Young male hawks are driven out of the territory they were born on and spend a few years in the highlands before joining a female and, with her, taking over a territory to breed (Faaborg *et al.*, 1980). The mixing of the birds in the highlands makes it extremely unlikely that the 2 to 4 males that join a female are related to each other. Yet they co-operate in helping her to raise offspring, by feeding separately in different areas and bringing different prey to the nest for the nestlings. This cooperation is surprising because the female often lays fewer eggs than the number of consorts she has, so they cannot all be fathers of the nestlings. However, the system works to the benefit of both female and males; females raise more offspring by having several males helping, and males gain from having a chance of being a father of at least one nestling, and in having a greater chance of surviving to the next breeding season than if they had stayed in the highlands.

Only some finch and mockingbird species have been studied in comparable or greater detail. In contrast to these species, virtually nothing is known about the breeding and feeding ecology of the 2 flycatcher species, the martin and the cuckoo.

Mockingbirds, like hawks, are cooperative breeders, but unlike them they are monogamous; the helpers at the nest are invariably sons of the breeding pair, and they may be 1 to 3 years old. Typically one or two brothers help their parents, and the breeding success of the pair is enhanced by the help received. In turn, one possible advantage to the young males in staying on their territory of birth is the chance to secure that territory when the parents die, or to secure a neighbouring territory. This is important because territories become vacant infrequently. On Genovesa, where a continuing study was begun in 1978, it appears that all suitable space on the island is usually occupied as breeding territories (P.R. Grant and N. Grant, 1979).

The difference between the hawks and the mockingbirds can be explained by a combination of different ecological and intrinsic factors. There is no suitable unoccupied space for young mockingbirds to assemble in while waiting for an opportunity to breed as there is for hawks, and mockingbirds do not have the same abilities possessed by hawks to patrol large areas in search of vacancies.

As far as is known all other land birds are usually monogamous and do not regularly breed cooperatively. Male Cactus Ground Finches and Medium Ground Finches have been observed helping at the nest of unrelated birds on Daphne Major, but this seems to be a case of misdirected parental care precipitated by the presence of an excess of males.

12.4.2. Breeding seasons

The breeding season of all land birds except the Galápagos Rail is strongly influenced directly or indirectly by rainfall. Heavy rains fall from late December or January through to April or May, but are unpredictable in occurrence and duration. In some years there may be virtually no rain, in other years (the *El Niño* years) the rainy season may be prolonged. In the drought year of 1977, when less than 25 mm of rain fell on Daphne Major, the resident Medium Ground Finches did not breed at all. In *El Niño* years breeding may continue for a large part of the year, perhaps for all of it: so far, no continuous studies of breeding have been made in an *El Niño* year. We know from a moderate wet year on Genovesa that individual finches successfully produced five successive broods of young, so it seems plausible that breeding of individuals would be more extensive in an *El Niño* year.

Not all birds are so closely tied in their breeding to rainfall. On Daphne Major some pairs of the Cactus Ground Finch start to breed in December before the rains begin, and in the drought year of 1977 many pairs bred. The reason is that their breeding is influenced by their diet of pollen and nectar from the flowers of *Opuntia* cactus. This is available in large quantities as early as December. Perhaps some of the tree finches, such as the Woodpecker Finch and the Vegetarian Finch, start to breed before the rains come in response to the availability of particular foods, but so far the breeding of the tree finches has not been studied.

In contrast to the Cactus Ground Finch, a few other species start to breed distinctly later than the onset of the rains, and in each case the reason lies in the availability of food. The breeding of doves follows about 3 weeks after the first rains fall. On Genovesa, the hatching of the first eggs coincides with the ripening of seeds of *Croton scouleri*. These are the principal food of the nestlings there (P.R. Grant and K.T. Grant, 1979). Hawks and owls breed even later, when young finches, doves and mockingbirds are out of the nest and available as prey for their own young. Nests of these 2 species have been found in every month of the year (Harris, 1974).

It is a reasonable guess, but only a guess, that the cessation of breeding is also determined by the food supply. Different species have different diets and stop breeding at different times. While finches may rear four or five broods in a row, mockingbirds and doves rear one or two and then stop at a time when finches are continuing. Doves may start again after a hiatus of 1 or 2 months. This happened on Genovesa in 1980 but not in 1979; climatic and food conditions were similar in the 2 years except that the fruiting season of *Bursera graveolens* (a food plant) was prolonged in 1980. Doves have been recorded breeding in all months of the year except December, but not in the same year.

In general old finches start breeding earlier and cease breeding later than young birds breeding for the first time. This suggests that in addition to the food supply itself, age-related skills at exploiting the food supply can influence breeding in finches, and probably other species as well.

The Galápagos Rail is exceptional in breeding between June and February, with a peak in the cool season and not when the heavy rains fall (Harris, 1974). It is a ground-nesting bird, so it might suffer from flooding if it nested then.

12.4.3. Breeding characteristics and success

Unpredictability in the arrival, quantity and duration of the rainfall, and hence the production of plants and of the insects that feed on them, places a premium on rapid and in many cases repeated breeding. Darwin's Finches show these characteristics (Grant and Grant, 1980a). Eggs are laid as early as the end of the first week after the rains. Compared with other finch species on the mainland of Ecuador, Darwin's Finches lay large clutches of small eggs (up to six per clutch). Total clutch weight is a relatively small fraction of the mother's body weight, and the incubation period is relatively short at about 12 days (Grant, 1982). Nestling growth is not especially fast or slow, and young tend to stay in the nest (13–16 days) longer than their mainland counterparts. But the mother often lays another clutch of eggs in another nest before the first brood have fledged, and this overlapping of broods may be repeated several times within a breeding season, with the result that as many as 20 offspring or more are produced in a period of about 5 months.

Breeding success on Genovesa was greatest in the Sharp-beaked Ground Finch and least in the Large Ground Finch and the Warbler Finch. The difference between the species can be partly attributed to disturbance of nesting activities of the Warbler Finch by mockingbirds and predation of Large Ground Finch nestlings by Short-eared Owls. This interference factor varies from island to island however; owls do not prey on nestlings on Daphne Major, and mockingbirds are not present, so a high proportion of nestlings fledge.

12.4.4. Population fluctuations

Once out of the nest small birds are especially vulnerable to predators. In addition to hawks and owls, predators include three types of heron: the Lava Heron (*Butorides sundevalli*), the Night Heron (*Nyctanassa violacea*) and the Common Egret (*Casmerodius albus*). More importantly, how many young birds survive and for how long is determined by the feeding conditions after the breeding season. These vary greatly, so does survival. In 1973, the second of two successive wet years and a time of plentiful food supply, survival of all Medium and Cactus Ground Finches (adults and young) exceeded 90% on Daphne Major during the 8 months after the breeding season (Grant *et al.*, 1975, and revised calculations). By contrast, all but one of the 388 Medium Ground Finch nestlings ringed in 1976 died before or during the drought of 1977; scarcely any Cactus Ground Finch nestlings survived either.

As a consequence of annual variation in food conditions, population sizes fluctuate substantially. For example, the net result of the 1977 drought was a reduction in the Daphne Major population of Medium Ground Finches of 85%, from about 1200 individuals or more to less than 200 (Fig. 12.2): the Cactus Ground Finch population declined from about 300 to 100 individuals (Grant and Grant, 1980b). The effective population sizes after the drought were much smaller than these numbers indicate, because females fared worse than males. The numbers of breeding pairs in 1978, the year after the drought, were 35 Medium Ground Finches and 25 Cactus Ground Finches. Since that time the population of Medium Ground Finches has increased slowly, but by the end of 1981, 4 years after the drought, it had reached less than 50% of pre-drought sizes. In contrast, the Cactus Ground Finch population was almost back to its pre-drought size.

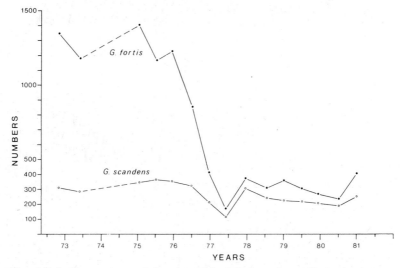

Figure 12.2. Changes in population sizes of the 2 finch species on Isla Daphne Major. *G. fortis* is the Medium Ground Finch and *G. scandens* is the Cactus Ground Finch. Broken lines span a period of more than 1 year when the populations were not censused, but observations of previously ringed birds in the breeding season of 1974 suggest that the populations did not change appreciably in size then (Grant *et al.*, 1975). On the horizontal axis numbers are placed at the middle of each year.

In addition to these short-term changes in population size, there appear to be long-term changes that are similarly associated with a varying pattern of rainfall. For example, the population of Cactus Ground Finches on I. Daphne Major seems to have been much smaller formerly than now. There are only 3 specimens in museum collections, all collected in the first 40 years of the century, whereas there are 42 specimens of the

Figure 12.3. Isla Daphne Major in January 1939 (above) and November 1977 (below). This island has never been disturbed by human settlement or by introduced mammals such as goats, yet the area covered by *Opuntia echios* cactus is greater now than formerly, perhaps as a result of a change in rainfall. Notice the grassy vegetation in the upper crater in the upper illustration but not in the lower one. Earlier and later photographs which might document how and when the vegetation changes took place are, unfortunately, not available. L.S.V. Venables took and kindly supplied the upper photograph; the lower one was taken by the author.

Medium Ground Finch, all collected during the same period. The relative scarcity of Cactus Ground Finch specimens is all the more striking in view of the collector's eye for the unusual. Forty years ago there was less *Opuntia* cactus than now, at least on one slope (Fig. 12.3), and this may be the reason for the previous scarcity of Cactus Ground Finches. In turn, the smaller amount of cactus and perhaps smaller amount of flower and fruit production may have been due to a different rainfall regime. Exactly what that regime was we will never know because rainfall on the Galápagos was not measured then. All we can say is that before the 1939 photograph in Figure 3 was taken there had probably been heavy rains. This is inferred from the presence of grass in the upper crater (unlike now); heavy and persistent rains are associated with warm seawater, the blue-footed boobies (*Sula nebouxii*) which normally breed in the crater cannot obtain sufficient fish to breed then, and in their absence grass grows without being trampled.

Populations of doves and cuckoos also appear to fluctuate greatly in size, but whether the observed changes are brought about by birth and death processes, or whether the birds just move from one place to another on an island is not known. A short study of mockingbirds on Genovesa suggests that they fluctuate in numbers less dramatically.

In all the species studied, most birds die before breeding. Those that survive the critical first year of life typically do not breed for another one (finches) or more (mockingbirds and hawks) years, and then live a long life. Some of the Medium and Cactus Ground Finches we ringed as adults on Daphne Major in 1973 were still alive in 1981, and a Large Ground Finch lived 20 years in the San Diego zoo (R.I. Bowman, pers. comm.).

Figure 12.4. Woodpecker Finch (*Cactospiza pallida*), Santa Cruz Island. (Photograph by Roger Perry).

12.5. Feeding Ecology

12.5.1. Feeding habits

Galápagos land birds feed generally in ways typical of their mainland relatives. The outstanding exception is Darwin's Finches. Collectively they feed on a remarkable diversity of foods: insects, spiders, seeds, fruits, nectar, pollen, cambium, leaves, buds, the pulp of cactus pads and the blood of seabirds and of sealion placentae.

Not all birds feed on all things, and specialization in diet is facilitated by a specialization in beak form and associated behaviour. Here are a few examples. The Woodpecker Finch (Fig. 12.4) uses a twig, cactus spine or leaf petiole as a tool, gripped in the beak, to pry insect larvae out of cavities in the dead branches of trees in

Figure 12.5. Cactus Ground Finch (*Geospiza scandens*), Santa Cruz Island. (Photograph by Alan Root/ Courtesy of the Charles Darwin Foundation).

arid zone habitat. When the prey is close to the entrance of the cavity, the finch drops the tool or braces it against the perch with a foot and reaches in with its elongated beak to extract the prey. The Mangrove Finch performs similar manoeuvres in mangroves (Curio and Kramer, 1964). The Large Tree Finch is equipped with a stronger and blunter beak which it uses in a different way to extract prey from similar positions: it crushes or tears the twigs or branches. Small, Medium and Sharp-beaked Ground Finches remove ticks from tortoises and iguanas, responding, in some instances, to ritualized soliciting behaviour of the reptiles (MacFarland and Reeder, 1974; Chapter 11, Fig. 11.12). Perhaps the most bizarre feeding habit is shown by Sharp-beaked Ground Finches on the northern islands of Wolf (Bowman and Billeb, 1965) and Darwin (D. Schluter, pers. comm.). They perch on boobies (*Sula* spp.), peck around the base of the tail where new feathers are developing and drink the blood from the wounds they inflict. Bowman and Billeb (1965) speculate that this peculiar habit is derived from the more widespread behaviour of removing ticks from animals.

12.5.2. Seasonal variation in food supply

One can appreciate how the acquisition of unusual feeding habits such as these was driven by necessity, when one compares the supply of food available to birds at different times of the year. After the rainy season much of the green vegetation at low altitude dies. With few exceptions, there is no further production of fruits, seeds or arthropods until the next rainy season. Therefore birds have to survive largely on what has been produced during the rainy season, and in fact many die. From the end of one wet season to the end of the following dry season, birds reduce the total amount of fruits and seeds by as much as one order of magnitude (Smith *et al.*, 1978).

During this time of diminishing food supply, feeding becomes restricted to those food types which can be most efficiently exploited. Thus all species change from a common, wet season, diet of easily dealt with foods, mainly caterpillars, to different diets reflecting their beak size and shape specializations. As new foods become available, such as pollen and nectar in the flowers of *Opuntia* cactus at the end of the calendar year, those species capable of exploiting them switch their feeding to them (Grant and Grant, 1981). An individual in a population who, unlike the others, can take advantage of a new food at a time of generally low food availability has a potentially great advantage over the rest, and should survive and subsequently reproduce better than the others. The new feeding trait could rapidly increase in frequency in the population, either because the trait is copied by others or because it has a genetic basis and is favoured by natural selection.

12.6. Evolution

Being well isolated, the Galápagos receive very few bird immigrants from South America. This fact, together with a floristic diversity among islands and along altitudinal gradients within islands, has facilitated adaptive changes and speciation by the few land birds that have managed to reach the islands. Not all immigrants have undergone these changes however, partly because they have not had the ecological opportunity, partly because they have not been there long enough: the islands are only 3 to 5 million years old (Bailey, 1976), and in their present aspect many are only about 1 million years old.

Presumably the ancestral Darwin's Finch species was an early immigrant. There are now 13 species of Darwin's Finches on the Galápagos, and one more on Cocos Island off the coast of Costa Rica. David Lack (1947) was the first person to offer a comprehensive account of how the 13 species could have been derived from the single ancestor, based largely upon the reasoning of Darwin. The following is a summary of a modern version of Lack's theory (Grant, 1981b).

One of the Galápagos islands was colonized from the mainland, or possibly from Cocos Island. The population of colonists increased in size. Some adaptive change to the local conditions took place during this time, facilitated by the scarcity or even absence of other land bird species. Eventually some individuals dispersed to another island and founded a new (second) population. Since the two islands did not offer identical ecological opportunities, further adaptive change took place on the second island. It is possible that random genetic changes occurred as well. In combination these changes gave rise to small differences between the populations. This is the stage of differentiation reached by the Vermilion Flycatcher today. The colonization of new islands occurred repeatedly, followed by adaptation to local conditions. Members of the most different populations would be quite dissimilar in appearance. In the extreme case they would be different species, or close to that degree of difference. Such a stage exists today with the mockingbird populations.

In the next stage of evolution some individuals of one of the derived populations flew to an island already occupied by a moderately different population. This probably happened several times, on several islands. The newcomers and residents interbred when not very different from each other. They did not interbreed, or interbred only rarely, when they perceived each other as different, furthermore the offspring produced by interbreeding were less fit than those produced from residents breeding with residents and newcomers breeding with newcomers. Therefore natural selection favoured those that bred 'true', and differences between the two groups in signals and responses involved in pair formation and reproduction became enhanced. In a similar way natural selection favoured members of the two groups which fed in different ways from each other and which, as a result, did not compete severely with each other at times of food shortage. At this point we may speak of 2 species living in sympatry having evolved from a single ancestor, partly by changes occurring in allopatry and partly by changes in sympatry.

This process of evolutionary diversification was repeated many times. Each time there were changes in beak structure and associated changes in feeding skills and feeding niches. The culmination of many such events is the present variety of finch species with different modes of feeding (Chapter 19, Fig. 19.12). They differ conspicuously in their songs too (Bowman, 1983). This is partly a reflection of different adaptation to the sound transmitting properties of the environment on different islands (Bowman, 1979; Chapter 19, Fig. 10). But the different patterns of songs, which are sung by males, serve to identify the singers to females as potential mates (same species) or not (different species). In addition beak size and shape, the character by which species are adapted to exploiting different foods, is also used by females to distinguish between acceptable and unacceptable males (Ratcliffe, 1981). Evidently species discrimination by finches is usually successful because hybridization is rare. Thus the adaptive radiation of Darwin's Finches has involved primarily beak form and song structure.

The above outline is not the only way that speciation can occur. It is theoretically possible for a population to split into two non-interbreeding segments on a single island, providing that the environment is heterogeneous enough, and providing that like types which mate with each other are favoured over those which mate randomly. The conditions for sympatric speciation to occur are severe and are unlikely to be met commonly in nature, but they have been explored in a potential subject, the Large Cactus Ground Finch on Genovesa (B.R. Grant and P.R. Grant, 1979, and unpublished).

As in all historical reconstructions of evolutionary processes there is inevitable uncertainty about exactly how, why, where and when the crucial events occurred. Nevertheless Darwin's Finches are important to evolutionary biologists because they provide a relatively clear pattern of differentiation and speciation. They can be used as a model for other groups of species elsewhere in the world which are less well known or difficult to investigate. The recent discovery of fossils (Steadman, 1981) and the application of electrophoresis to the assessment of systematic relationships among the species (Yang and Patton, 1981) has helped to place the evolutionary interpretation of those patterns on a sounder foundation.

A third recent development is the investigation of micro-evolutionary processes, i.e. small evolutionary changes in the characteristics of finch populations. It has been found that a large amount of genetic variation underlies the beak size variation within populations (Boag and Grant, 1978). This variation is subject to natural selection, as happened in the drought of 1977 on Daphne Major (Boag and Grant, 1981). Large-beaked members of the Medium Ground Finch population survived better than small-beaked members because they were able to exploit the large and hard seeds that were left after most of the small seeds had been consumed. Studies like this should be able to provide a better understanding of why some finch populations are much more variable than others in beak characteristics (Grant et al., 1976, Grant and Price, 1981). Eventually it may be possible to use this knowledge to explain how one species is transformed into another, i.e. to understand the process of speciation in terms of genetics, ecological factors and natural selection.

12.7. Conservation

The largest Darwin's Finches disappeared from San Cristóbal and Floreana in the last century. The single most important causal factor was probably human activities, ranging from the cutting and clearing of vegetation to the introduction of goats, cats, rats, etc (see Chapter 16). Unless these birds were a distinct species, as opposed to a particularly large form of the Large Ground Finch, no *species* of land bird has gone extinct on the Galápagos in historical times. This is gratifying but no cause for complacency. It is populations which are important because they are unique even if only in subtle ways and hence are, strictly speaking, irreplaceable. We will never be able to see the indigenous hawks on San Cristóbal because the population has been eliminated by human hunting (Harris, 1974). Hawks may be reintroduced from another island one day, but they will not be the same as the original occupants of that island.

There are three important requirements for the optimal conservation of the landbird fauna. First is the prevention of any new destruction of natural habitat and, where possible, encouragement of the recovery of partly disturbed habitat. Second is the elimination of introduced species, principally the mammals, and where that is not possible then at least their control. Third is the acquisition of base-line data on bird populations. This does not mean that every bird population needs to be studied. Instead it means that questions about the breeding status of particular species on certain islands should be resolved; that small and possibly endangered populations should be regularly censused; and that certain carefully selected populations should be intensively studied so that the normal fluctuations of populations and their causes can be established and understood.

12.8. Acknowledgements

I thank Sonja Eklund of Uppsala University for typing the manuscript and B.R. Grant for helpful comments.

References

Abbott, I. and Abbott, L.K. (1978) Multivariate study of morphological variation in Galápagos and Ecuadorian mockingbirds. *Condor*, **80**, 302–308.

Abbott, I., Abbott, L.K. and Grant, P.R. (1977) Comparative ecology of Galápagos ground finches (*Geospiza* Gould): evaluation of the importance of floristic diversity and interspecific competition. *Ecol. Monogr.*, **47**, 151–184.

Bailey, K. (1976) Potassium-Argon ages from the Galápagos Islands. *Science*, **192**, 465–467.

Boag, P.T. and Grant, P.R. (1978) Heritability of external morphology in Darwin's finches. *Nature*, **274**, 793–794.

Boag, P.T. and Grant, P.R. (1981) Intense natural selection on a population of Darwin's finches (Geospizinae) in the Galápagos. *Science*, **214**, 82–85.

Bowman, R.I. (1961) Morphological differentiation and adaptation in the Galápagos finches. *Univ. Calif. Publs. Zool.*, **58**, 1–302.

Bowman, R.I. (1979) Adaptive morphology of song dialects in Darwin's Finches. *J. f. Ornithol.*, **120**, 353–389.

Bowman, R.I. (1983) The evolution of song in Darwin's Finches. In *Patterns of evolution in Galápagos organisms*. Edited by R.I. Bowman, M. Berson and A. Leviton. Special Publ., Amer. Assoc. Adv. Sci., Pacific Division, in press.

Bowman, R.I. and Billeb, S.I. (1965) Blood-eating in a Galápagos Finch. *The Living Bird*, **4**, 29–44.

Curio, E. and Kramer, P. (1964) Vom Mangrovefinken (*Cactospiza heliobates*). *Zeits. f. Tierpsychol.*, **21**, 223–234.

de Vries, Tj. (1975). The breeding biology of the Galápagos Hawk, *Buteo galapagoensis*. *Le Gerfaut*, **65**, 29–57.

de Vries, Tj. (1976) Prey selection and hunting methods of the Galápagos Hawk, *Buteo galapagoensis*. *Le Gerfaut*, **66**, 3–42.

Faaborg, J., de Vries, Tj., Patterson, C.B. and Griffin, C.R. (1980) Preliminary observations on the occurrence and evolution of polyandry in the Galápagos Hawk (*Buteo galapagoensis*). *Auk*, **97**, 581–590.

Grant, B.R. and Grant, P.R. (1979) Darwin's finches: Population variation and sympatric speciation. *Proc. Nat. Acad. Sci. USA*, **76**, 2359–2363.

Grant, B.R. and Grant, P.R. (1981) Exploitation of *Opuntia* cactus by birds on the Galápagos. *Oecologia (Berl.)*, **49**, 179–187.

Grant, P.R. (1981a) Patterns of growth in Darwin's Finches. *Proc. Roy. Soc. Lond. B.*, **212**, 403–432.

Grant, P.R. (1983) The role of interspecific competition in the adaptive radiation of Darwin's Finches. In *Patterns of evolution in Galápagos organisms*. Edited by R.I. Bowman, M. Berson and A. Leviton. Special Publ., Amer. Assoc. Adv. Sci., Pacific Division, in press.

Grant, P.R. (1981b) Speciation and the adaptive radiation of Darwin's Finches. *Amer. Sci.*, **69**, 653–663.

Grant, P.R. (1982) Variation in the size and shape of Darwin's Finch eggs. *Auk*, **99**, 15–23.

Grant, P.R. and Grant, B.R. (1980a) The breeding and feeding characteristics of Darwin's Finches on Isla Genovesa, Galápagos. *Ecol. Monogr.*, **50**, 381–410.

Grant, P.R. and Grant, B.R. (1980b) Annual variation in finch numbers, foraging and food supply on Isla Daphne Major, Galápagos. *Oecologia (Berl.)*, **46**, 55–62.

Grant, P.R., Grant, B.R., Smith, J.N.M., Abbott, I.J. and Abbott, L.K. (1976) Darwin's finches: Population variation and natural selection. *Proc. Nat. Acad. Sci. USA*, **73**, 257–261.

Grant, P.R. and Grant, K.T. (1979) Breeding and feeding ecology of the Galápagos Dove. *Condor*, **81**, 397–403.

Grant, P.R and Grant, N. (1979) Breeding and feeding of Galápagos mockingbirds, *Nesomimus parvulus*. *Auk*, **96**, 723–736.

Grant, P.R. and Price, T.D. (1981) Population variation in continuously varying traits as an ecological genetics problem. *Amer. Zool.*, **21**, 795–811.

Grant, P.R. and Schluter, D. (1984) Interspecific competition inferred from patterns of guild structure. In *Ecological communities: conceptual issues and the evidence*. Edited by D.R. Strong, D.S. Simberloff, A.B. Thistle and L.G. Abele. Princeton Univ. Press.

Grant, P.R., Smith, J.N.M., Grant, B.R., Abbott, I.J. and Abbott, L.K. (1975) Finch numbers, owl predation and plant dispersal on Isla Daphne Major, Galápagos. *Oecologia (Berl.)*, **19**, 239–257.

Harris, M.P. (1973) The Galápagos avifauna. *Condor*, **75**, 265–278.

Harris, M.P. (1974) *A Field Guide to the Birds of Galápagos*. Collins, London.

Lack, D. (1947) *Darwin's Finches*. Cambridge Univ. Press, Cambridge.

MacFarland, C. and Reeder, W. (1974) Cleaning symbiosis involving Galápagos tortoises and two species of Darwin's Finches. *Zeits. f. Tierpsychol.*, **34**, 464–483.

Ratcliffe, L.M. (1981) Species recognition in Darwin's Ground Finches (*Geospiza* Gould). Ph.D. thesis, McGill Univ., Montreal.

Smith, J.N.M., Grant, P.R., Grant, B.R., Abbott, I.J., and Abbott, L.K. (1978) Seasonal variation in feeding habits of Darwin's Ground Finches. *Ecology*, **59**, 1137–1150.

Steadman, D.W. (1981) Vertebrate fossils in lava tubes in the Galápagos Islands. *Proc. Eight. Internat. Congr. Speleology*, pages 549–550.

Sulloway, F.J. (1982) Darwin and his finches: the evolution of a legend. *J. Hist. Biol.*, **15**, 1–53.

Yang, S.Y. and Patton, J.L. (1981) Genic variability and differentiation in Galápagos finches. *Auk*, **98**, 230–242.

CHAPTER 13

The Seabirds

M.P. HARRIS

Institute of Terrestrial Ecology, Hill of Brathens, Banchory, Kincardineshire, Scotland

Contents

13.1.	Background	191
	13.1.1. Food	195
	13.1.2. Ecological separation	195
	13.1.3. Seasonal changes in food	196
	13.1.4. Food shortages	197
13.2.	Breeding Seasons	199
	13.2.1. Annual breeding cycle	200
	13.2.2. Shorter than annual breeding cycle	201
	13.2.3. Other species	202
	13.2.4. Factors influencing breeding seasons	202
13.3.	The Future	204
	References	205

Although not as famous as Darwin's finches, the seabirds have attracted considerable attention during the last 20 years because 5 of the 19 breeding species are endemic and many species breed at less than annual intervals. A list of species, their scientific names and approximate population sizes are given in Table 13.1 and source references to most species in Tables 13.1–3.

13.1. Background

The oceanographic setting is complex and is discussed in detail in Chapter 3. The main points must, however, be restated here as they are crucial to the understanding of seabird ecology. The Galápagos area is influenced by three sea currents—the Humboldt or South Equatorial Current which flows westwards across the Pacific bringing relatively cold water, the North Equatorial Current which brings 'blue' warm and appreciably less productive water from the north, and the deep, eastward flowing Cromwell Current which upwells where it meets the eastern flanks of Fernandina and Isabela bringing cold and nutrient-rich water to the surface. The coolest period is from June to December when surface temperatures are 5°C lower than during other months. As well as this predictable seasonal change there are occasional years when warm sea conditions prevail (Chapter 4.2). During this *El Niño* phenomenon much of Galápagos is surrounded by water 3–4°C warmer than normal. This results in failure of breeding of some Galápagos seabirds, but not the massive mortality as occurs in Peruvian birds. Galápagos seabirds appear to be better adapted to such happenings.

Figure 13.1. Galápagos penguin (*Spheniscus mendiculus*) (Photograph by M.P. Harris).

This meeting of waters allows the co-existence of seabirds from different backgrounds. Species typical of the Humboldt Current are the endemic penguin (Fig. 13.1), wedge-rumped and white-vented storm petrels; those typical of warmer waters include brown pelican, two frigatebirds, three boobies, Audubon's shearwater, dark-rumped petrel, red-billed tropicbird, band-rumped storm petrel, brown noddy and sooty tern. The last is an 'indicator' species of unproductive, blue, oceanic water; it nests only on Darwin and is rarely seen within the archipelago. The waved albatross (Fig. 13.2), swallow-tailed gull, lava gull and flightless cormorant are endemic, if one excludes a few pairs of the former gull on Malpelo Island, Colombia and of albatrosses on Isla de la Plata, Ecuador; these species have evolved so far that their affinities are uncertain. The Cromwell Current is a submarine current, so, not surprisingly, has brought no species with it, but its upwelling does allow the existence of penguins on the equator and the only flightless member of the Pelecaniformes.

Published estimates of the numbers of some species, augmented by my 'guesstimates' of the remainder, are given in Table 1. All these are of low accuracy but altogether they do suggest that there may be some three-quarters of a million pairs of seabirds breeding in the islands. This is far less than many seabird populations, e.g. that of Britain and Ireland is probably in the order of three million pairs (Cramp *et al.*, 1974), that of Peru may reach 16 million birds (Jordan and Fuentes, 1966). It is, however, among the largest by tropical standards. As well as 5 endemic species, the Galápagos Islands have maybe 30% of the world's blue-footed boobies, the largest red-footed booby colony (on Genovesa) and perhaps the largest concentration of masked boobies (Nelson, 1978).

When they are not breeding, individuals of some species leave the area, e.g. waved albatrosses and swallow-tailed gulls all move east and south down the Humboldt Current to Peruvian seas. Other species are sedentary, the extreme being the flightless cormorant, most individuals of which rarely move more than 10 km from their birthplace. In species which breed both on the islands and the South American mainland it is difficult to know whether Galápagos individuals migrate. However, three young blue-footed boobies ringed in Galápagos have been recovered off mainland Ecuador. One was old enough to breed when found, which indicates either that it had moved to one of the small mainland colonies or that adults migrate. Similarly some magnificent frigates migrate, as one Galápagos-ringed bird was later recovered in Costa Rica. The more pelagic red-billed tropicbirds range widely when they are not breeding and ringing recoveries have come from the Gulf of Panama and well west of Peru. Surprisingly, only one migrant seabird, the red-necked (= northern) phalarope (*Lobipes lobatus*), occurs in any numbers in Galápagos waters. About 30 other seabirds have been recorded showing that the area is not isolated. Perhaps the lack of a regular seasonal increase in food does not allow incomers to compete successfully against the resident experts. This is a challenging problem for future students.

Figure 13.2. Waved albatross (*Diomedea irrorata*): Isla Española (Photograph by T. de Vries).

Table 13.1. Breeding seabirds of the Galápagos Islands.

Species	Observed distribution at sea	No. of colonies	Approximate total population	Source
Galápagos penguin *Spheniscus mendiculus*	Inshore	Many	6–15,000 birds	Boersma, 1977
Waved albatross *Diomedea irrorata*	Pelagic	1	12,000 pairs	Harris, 1973
Audubon's shearwater *Puffinus lherminieri*	Inshore	29+	(10,000 pairs)	
Dark-rumped petrel *Pterodroma phaeopygia*	Pelagic	5 islands	(10–50,000 pairs)	Baker, 1980, personal observations
Band-rumped storm petrel *Oceanodroma castro*	Pelagic	15	(15,000 pairs)	
Wedge-rumped storm petrel *Oceanodroma tethys*	Pelagic/between islands	3	200,000 pairs	Harris, 1969a
White-vented storm petrel *Oceanites gracilis*	Inshore	none found	many thousands of birds	
Red-billed tropicbird *Phaethon aethereus*	Pelagic	30	few thousand pairs	
Brown pelican *Pelecanus occidentalis*	Inshore	Many	few thousand pairs	
Blue-footed booby *Sula nebouxii*	Inshore	35+	at least 10,000 pairs	Nelson, 1978
Masked booby *Sula dactylatra*	Between islands	23	25–50,000 pairs	Nelson, 1978
Red-footed booby *Sula sula*	Pelagic	5	250,000 pairs	Nelson, 1978
Flightless cormorant *Nannopterum harrisi*	Inshore	112+	700–800 pairs	Harris, 1974
Great frigatebird *Fregata minor*	Pelagic	12	(few thousand pairs)	
Magnificent frigatebird *Fregata magnificens*	Inshore/between islands	12	(1000 pairs)	
Swallow-tailed gull *Creagrus furcatus*	Between islands	55+	10–15,000 pairs	Harris, 1970
Lava gull *Larus fuliginosus*	Coastal	Solitary nester	300–400 pairs	Snow and Snow, 1969
Brown noddy *Anous stolidus*	Inshore	Many	few thousand pairs	
Sooty tern *Sterna fuscata*	Pelagic	1	enormous numbers	Fosberg, 1965

Notes: (1) Population figures are all of unknown accuracy. Those in brackets should be treated with the greatest reserve. (2) Where no source is given, estimates are based on my own experience.

13.1.1. Food

As yet, the only systematic survey of the food of Galápagos seabirds is that brought to young waved albatrosses. A full survey of the food of all species is highly desirable but to be meaningful this should also include some measures of the abundance and availability of the prey species. The practical difficulties are obvious and daunting and for the present we must make the best of what we have—that is, records collected during breeding biology studies over limited periods. Despite these limitations it is clear that each species has its own distinctive diet. That of the waved albatross, based on 259 food samples regurgitated by young during two seasons (Harris, 1973), gives an indication of the range of food taken by these seabirds. The commonest prey were squid (from 137 individuals) representing 7 of the 8 families found in the east Pacific, but over 80% (of 299 beaks) belonged to only 2 families—Histioteuthidae and Octopodoteuthidae. Fish, which occurred in 40% of samples, were mostly surface living species, including flying-fish (Exocoetidae), a carangid, *Decapterus*, and a clupeid, *Etrumeus*, but there were also bottom-dwelling forms, such as the frogfish, *Antennarius*. Pelagic crustacea occurred in almost half the samples, the commonest being a euphausid up to 120 mm long, *Benthophausia* (usually found below a depth of 1000 m), and krill, *Thysanopoda*. Some pelagic crabs and isopods parasitic in the mouths of fish were also eaten. The wide range of prey of this large ungainly bird, which takes its food in the top 50 cm of the sea, is unexpected.

Generally the largest seabirds eat the largest prey. Pelicans and albatrosses can cope with fish at least 340 mm long, whereas Audubon's shearwater often eats larval fish barely 10 mm long. There are, however, exceptions, pelicans sometimes filter small fish from the water, and lava gulls catch small fish in tide-pools. The same holds for squid—those eaten by storm petrels weigh only a few grams, whereas the mean weight (calculated from the measurements of chitinous beaks) of those regurgitated by albatrosses is 260 g—8% the weight of the adult albatross. However, 16 Ommastrephidae had a mean weight of 2.1 kg. These must have been swallowed piecemeal and the largest, 11 kg, must surely have been found dead. Swallow-tailed gulls also eat Ommastrephids heavier than themselves.

13.1.2. Ecological separation

Despite the various species having rather distinctive food preferences there is still considerable overlap in diet so that different species could well compete for food. There are several ways in which this competition could be reduced (Harris, 1977).

There are great differences in the methods used by different species to catch the same prey. For instance, a masked booby catches a flying-fish well below the surface using momentum gained by a spectacular dive from high above the water; the albatross catches it just below the surface either by crashing into the sea or when swimming; a frigatebird picks it from the surface without landing, whereas a red-footed booby can catch a flying fish in the air. Associated with differences in feeding method are differences in beak form (Ashmole and Ashmole, 1967): the masked booby has a stout stream-lined dagger-shaped beak with a serrated edge with which it holds its prey; the albatross has a massive hooked beak and a powerful grasp; the frigatebird has a rather more delicate, but still hooked, beak to pick fish from the surface. Furthermore, most species have well-defined feeding areas (Table 13.1), which gives spatial separation. For example, competition between the boobies is reduced by the blue-footed booby feeding inshore, the red-footed booby well away from the islands, the masked booby between the islands. The dispersion of breeding colonies and many aspects of the breeding biology of the species fits in with this (Nelson, 1978). The blue-footed booby (Fig. 13.3) breeds in numerous small colonies scattered through the archipelago, lays two or three eggs, has short incubation stints and feeds the young several times a day. If conditions are good it can sometimes successfully feed and fledge two young because the food is near. The far more numerous red-footed booby (Fig. 13.4) is restricted to five colonies on the peripheral islands. It lays a single egg, has long incubation stints (mean length

Figure 13.3. Blue-footed booby (*Sula nebouxii*): Isla Daphne (Photograph by T. de Vries).

60 hours) and the chick is fed less than once a day. This species feeds so far away that a pair cannot hope to feed more than a single young, even if food is abundant. The masked booby is again intermediate.

Finally, a few species feed at night when plankton, fish and squid are more abundant near the surface than they are by day. The swallow-tailed gull (Fig. 13.5) is a specialized nocturnal feeder and virtually never feeds by day. When it does it is ruthlessly persecuted by frigatebirds trying to steal its food. The swallow-tailed gull and the red-billed tropicbird have very similar diets, but the gull catches squid and fish at the surface at night, fairly close to a colony, whereas the tropicbird feeds by day, by plunge-diving well away from the colony. The band-rumped and wedge-rumped storm petrels also seem to be separated by feeding time: the former visits its colonies only at night and feeds by day; the latter is diurnal on land and feeds at night. Surprisingly, only a few seabird species have been recorded feeding at night.

13.1.3. Seasonal changes in food

The marked seasonal fluctuations in water temperatures might result in a change in marine productivity, but plankton samples taken over an eighteen-month period in 1965–67 failed to detect any regular changes; instead they showed an extremely patchy distribution both in time and place. The non-annual breeding of many Galápagos seabirds (discussed later) suggests that there is no regular seasonal fluctuation in food supply. There are, however, quite marked temporal differences in diet. Between December 1965 and February 1966, swallow-tailed gulls ate mainly squid (22/29 regurgitations), whereas during the succeeding 7 months fish (50/53 samples) were the staple food. Long term differences must also occur, for flying-fish were commonly seen in Galápagos and figured prominently in the diet of all the larger seabirds during 1965–67, whereas very few were seen in 1970–71.

Figure 13.4. Red-footed booby (*Sula sula*), a tree-nesting species: Isla Genovesa (Photograph by R. Perry).

13.1.4. Food shortages

Seabirds of temperate regions usually manage to rear young each season, suggesting that food is predictably abundant, in contrast to total breeding failure which is not uncommon in tropical seas. Galápagos seabirds often fail to rear young, apparently because food becomes very short.

The failures fall into two, perhaps arbitrary, classes—those of short duration and not obviously related to changes in sea temperature, and those associated with the *El Niño* phenomenon. The former have been recorded in Audubon's shearwater (including four in a 21-month period), blue-footed and red-footed booby, tropicbird, pelican and frigatebirds. Also, Nelson (1978) found evidence of food shortage in masked boobies, and I have recorded brown noddies returning to the colonies as though to breed but deferring laying. Thus, probably all warm water species are affected, but the data are too scattered to decide whether food shortages occur simultaneously in different species.

Figure 13.5. Adult and juvenile swallow-tailed gull (*Creagrus furcatus*): South Plaza. The large eye is associated with nocturnal feeding. (Photograph by M.P. Harris).

An *El Niño* has the greatest impact on typically cold-water species, especially those in the cold upwelling of the Cromwell Current. The effect of the 1972 *El Niño*, when the water temperature at Punta Espinosa was 23–28°C instead of the normal 18–22°C, was well-documented. Galápagos penguins lost weight, those with eggs deserted them. Breeding ceased with the sea temperature above 25°C, and subsequently became so upset that many pairs nested three times within 15 months, but only one recorded nest started between December 1971 to October 1972 was successful. Boersma (1978) attributed her above findings to the lack of feeding frenzies which contribute to the normal feeding activity of penguins and other diving seabirds. These are infrequent when the sea temperature is above 23°C. Pelicans take part in these frenzies and their breeding attempts in the same year also failed. Flightless cormorants suffered only marginally less. Breeding success and survival rates of juveniles after they took to the water were only 23% and 32% of the normal; no cormorants bred for the first time and probably many other pairs failed to nest. Cormorants feed in the Galápagos on bottom-living reef fish and octopuses and it is difficult to see how the change in water temperature would effect numbers of prey. It might, however change their behaviour or make them move into deeper water.

The waved albatross, nesting well away from the Cromwell Current, has also suffered periodic breeding failures—the most spectacular being in 1965, another *El Niño* year, when no young at all were reared. However, even in normal years birds in some colonies abandon their eggs, and in 1972 some colonies did well—even though the *El Niño* was just as dramatic as in 1965. The reason for the success of some colonies, when others only a few hundred metres away fail completely, is totally obscure. Warm water, however, is not deleterious for all species, and both frigatebirds in the islands raised far more young than normal in 1972. I would predict that sooty terns are also favoured in such years.

The overall picture is of regular but unpredictable food shortages and of adults abandoning breeding before conditions get too difficult. The survival rates between cycles of adults of all the species studied are extremely high e.g. waved albatross (96%), Audubon's shearwater (93%), swallow-tailed gull (>90%). The individual's strategy seems to be not to weaken itself by trying to raise a young in difficult conditions but to abandon the attempt, the chances being that it will survive until the next breeding cycle when conditions will probably be better.

13.2. Breeding Seasons

Compared to those of temperate regions, marine conditions in the tropics are often fairly uniform. However, in most tropical areas there are seasonal fluctuations in temperature, salinity and productivity brought about by changes of currents or winds. Many tropical seabirds have well-defined seasonal breeding, although laying occurs over several or many months compared to 6–8 weeks in temperature regions and 2–3 weeks in boreal regions. In a few areas, e.g. Ascension Island (8°S) in the Atlantic and Christmas Island (2°N) in the Pacific, species of seabirds can be found nesting in all months of the year. In the Galápagos Islands between 12 and 15 species have been found nesting in each month although there is a slight peak of breeding during the colder part of the year. This apparent uniformity has to be qualified, however, by stating that some annual breeding species nest in different months on different islands. Other species breed at less than annual intervals (Table 13.2).

Table 13.2. Breeding cycles of Galápagos seabirds.

Species	Cycle	Source
Galápagos penguin	Less than annual[1]	Boersma, 1978
Waved albatross	Rigidly annual, restricted laying	Harris, 1973
Audubon's shearwater	Shorter than annual	Snow, 1965a, Harris, 1969c
Dark-rumped petrel	Annual	Harris, 1970
Wedge-rumped storm petrel	Annual	Harris, 1969a
Band-rumped storm petrel	Annual, two breeding populations	Harris, 1969a
White-vented storm petrel	(Breeding not proved, probably annual)	Harris, 1969a
Red-billed tropicbird	Annual or shorter than annual	Snow, 1965b
Brown pelican	Shorter than annual[1]	Harris, 1969b
Blue-footed booby	Shorter than annual	Nelson, 1978, Harris, 1969b
Masked booby	Annual	Harris, 1969b
Red-footed booby	Slightly longer than annual[2]	Nelson, 1978
Flightless cormorant	Males annual, females non-annual	Harris, 1979
Magnificent frigatebird	Longer than annual[2]	Nelson, 1968
Great frigatebird	Longer than annual[2]	Nelson, 1967
Lava gull	Less than annual	Harris, 1969b
Swallow-tailed gull	Shorter than annual	Snow & Snow, 1967, Harris, 1970b
Brown noddy	Shorter than annual[1]	Harris, 1969b
Sooty tern	Unknown, non-annual in some areas	Harris, 1969b

[1] Possibly annual if successful
[2] Annual if unsuccessful

13.2.1. Annual breeding cycle

The simplest cycle is that of the waved albatross where 50% of the eggs are laid during the first two weeks of May and all within a two-month span. The masked booby also has an annual cycle, but eggs are laid September–November on Genovesa, November–February on Española. Similar out-of-phase annual nesting has recently been found in the dark-rumped petrel (Tomkins, 1980). These constant differences are probably associated with the seasonal movement of the northern boundary of the Humboldt Current. Both magnificent and great frigatebird populations have annual breeding with eggs being found in up to 7 months each year; again there is great variation between colonies. These breeding cycles are difficult to interpret because adult frigatebirds feed fledged young for several months so that a successful breeding cycle takes more than a year. Unsuccessful birds can lay at the same month the next year; successful birds cannot, but they could, hypothetically, breed twice in every 3 years, either by laying early in the first season, late in the second and missing out the third, or by changing colony. Or, like the magnificent frigatebird in the Lesser Antilles, males could breed every year, successful females every other year (Diamond, 1973).

A further variation of annual breeding occurs in the band-rumped and wedge-rumped storm petrels. The former has two breeding seasons a year but there are two completely separate populations, each breeding annually, one in the hot season (eggs April to June), the other, smaller population laying December to January (Fig. 13.6). During 1965–74, 2363 full grown birds were handled and no interchange between the two

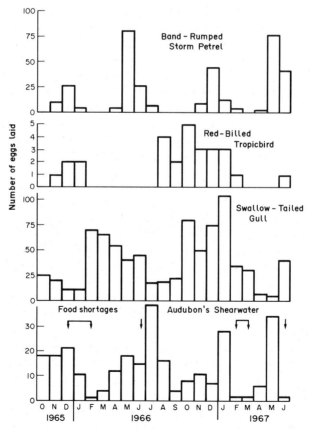

Figure 13.6. The monthly distribution of egg laying of 4 species of seabirds on South Plaza Island, 1965–67. The times of four food shortages for Audubon's shearwaters are also shown.

populations was noted. Even nonbreeders retained allegiance to their season. The factors preventing nesting throughout the year are unknown, but presumably there is some advantage to a pair in breeding when the majority of individuals do so which more than compensates for competition for food and nest-sites. Perhaps it reduces significantly the chance of predation by short-eared owls. The bulk of wedge-rumped storm petrels lay May to July, but, at Genovesa a few eggs are laid January–February. This does not happen at Punta Pitt on San Cristóbal. Possibly the situation on Genovesa is the first stage in the development of two breeding seasons a year. A final complication occurs in the red-billed tropicbird which has an annual breeding cycle on South Plaza Island but not elsewhere (later).

13.2.2. Shorter than annual breeding cycle

A wide selection of species have been found to lay more than once a year but only a few have been studied in detail.

The most straightforward cycle is that of the swallow-tailed gull. A single visit to an area finds gulls at all stages of breeding from pre-nuptial display to birds feeding fledged young. However, breeding is not continuous and frequent checks show that there is a regular pattern (Fig. 13.6). Birds in each small area, e.g. a cove, have their breeding synchronized and peak laying occurs at some of these even when there is a trough of laying in the colony as a whole. Each successful pair breeds about every 9 months (mean interval between laying of 92 pairs = 277 days), unsuccessful pairs about every eight (mean of 78 = 242 days). After breeding, individual gulls leave the colonies, moult, and return some 5 months later. With this overall difference and the great individual variation in length of the cycle (extremes 195–365 days), the synchrony would soon break down unless birds about to breed actively came together. This does not happen, and, as in most seabirds, adults remain faithful to their nest-site; the only reasonable explanation is that the group synchrony is caused by the birds themselves, perhaps by their noisy displays. Such local synchrony of breeding is widespread in seabirds. Presumably it has some definite advantage, perhaps by reducing predation, but the advantage to swallow-tailed gulls with no serious predators is unclear. At any time there is likely to be a peak of laying in some colony and breeding remains at a fairly constant level. This suggests that there is no seasonal increase in food. Such a system prevents undue strain being placed on food resources, but what stops the most efficient birds breeding when they want, rather than waiting for the mass, is unclear.

Superficially, the same occurs in Audubon's shearwater for eggs are laid in all months and there are major 'peaks' and 'troughs' of breeding (Fig. 13.6). However, detailed studies (Snow, 1965a, Harris, 1969) have shown that the situation is very different. Although much individual variation exists, successful breeders lay on the average every 9 months (range 7.5–10.5) after the first laying, those which lose a chick after 8 months (6–9.5), and birds losing an egg after about 6.5 months (4.5–8). Surprisingly, even pairs which lose an egg the day it is laid do not relay for 5–8 months, even when conditions are suitable for others to lay. This inability to relay is typical of the Procellariiformes; though it seems wasteful for such a resident species as Audubon's shearwater. Although variable, the time between the end of a breeding attempt (i.e. loss of an egg or chick or fledging) and relaying does not depend on the success of the first attempt. This strongly suggests that the birds are breeding as quickly as possible.

As in the swallow-tailed gull, the time Audubon's shearwaters are away from the colony is taken up by moult of the main wing feathers. The synchrony of breeding is far less marked than in the gull and seems to be caused by external factors. Thus when food becomes scarce there is a set series of events. First, the size of feeds brought to young decrease (from 40 to 10 g), as adults return to the colonies even if they cannot collect much food, and this is followed by a reduction in feeding frequency (70% fed per day to 18%). Next, the mean time each adult spends on the egg is prolonged (from 2.5 days to 6.3 days) and young are left immediately after hatching. If conditions deteriorate further, adults rarely spend any time in the burrows except when incubating. No new eggs are laid and, finally, eggs and even young are deserted. When conditions improve birds return and take part in noisy, aerial display. This is followed by a burst of laying when birds which would otherwise have laid over several weeks lay at the same time. Thus food shortages tend to synchronize birds which otherwise would have laid asynchronously. A prolonged period of good feeding conditions would inevitably result in a fairly constant level of breeding. The increase in display just prior to a peak of breeding is probably a result and not the cause of establishing a synchrony of laying. Thus, the situation appears to be very different to that in the swallow-tailed gull.

The Galápagos penguin and some populations of red-billed tropicbirds also have their breeding upset, and the timing of laying of pairs apparently synchronized, by periodic food shortages. Boersma (1978) noted that the breeding of penguins is commonest between May and December, but that in a 15-month period spanning the 1972 El Niño, 55 out of 75 pairs bred twice and 15 pairs three times. Probably the penguin is normally an annual nester. Blue-footed boobies also suffer from food shortages but it is unclear if these synchronize their breeding. Breeding of this booby is non-annual, with pairs nesting every 9–10 months.

Like frigatebirds, red-footed boobies in Galápagos take more than a year to raise a chick and only unsuccessful birds can breed every year. However, it is far from clear whether or not there is even an annual peak of laying in the islands. For the present it seems best to consider the species a non-annual breeder. Brown noddy, lava gull, brown pelican all appear to have cycles of less than a year. Probably the same holds for sooty tern but the only colony on the remote island of Darwin is so far removed from the rest of the archipelago that there are only scattered records of even when the birds are present in the area.

13.2.3. Other species

The red-billed tropicbird has a variable breeding regime. On Plaza there is a well-defined breeding season, pairs nest annually and eggs are laid August–February (with one record in June). At large colonies elsewhere in the islands breeding occurs throughout the year and pairs lay at less than annual intervals, e.g. intervals between successful breedings on Daphne (only 20 km from Plaza) were 10 months (Snow, 1965b). As mentioned earlier, breeding synchrony can quickly break down, yet annual breeding has persisted for 20 years on Plaza, and non-annual breeding on other islands for at least 60 years. Presumably both regimes are about equally efficient so that neither has selective advantage.

Flightless cormorants (Fig. 13.7) breed throughout the year, although many fewer clutches are laid November–March. Some birds breed several times within a year, e.g. a male bred seven times within 24 months, and a female laid eight clutches within 36 months. As usual, the interval between successive attempts is longest for successful breeders. The male feeds the young for much longer than the female. This results in successful males breeding every 13 months, whereas successful females lay every 9–10 months. Associated with this is a lack of mate fidelity; it is rare for a bird to breed twice with the same mate even if they lose their clutch.

13.2.4. Factors influencing breeding seasons

Timing of avian breeding is influenced by two kinds of factors—ultimate and proximate (Baker, 1938). The most important ultimate factor appears to be availability of food; either for the young (Lack, 1954) or for the female when she is forming the eggs (Perrins, 1966). The critical point is that birds which breed at the optimum time leave more young which survive to join the breeding population than pairs breeding at other times. Often it appears as though pairs try to breed as early in the season as possible. However, females which lay too early may produce nonviable eggs, or even reduce their own chances of survival and hence that of their genotypes through the young. In temperate regions the proximate factor controlling the initiation of breeding, i.e. the clue which tells birds that conditions will be suitable for rearing young some weeks ahead, appears to be increasing day-length. In other areas it may be rainfall or the availability of food.

Figure 13.7. Flightless cormorant (*Nannopterum harrisi*) (Photograph by M.P. Harris).

Non-annual breeding of seabirds is only common near the equator where day length and sea conditions are relatively constant. There are, however, subtle changes which birds are certainly capable of detecting; so birds are presumably choosing to breed throughout the year. Indeed, most seem to breed as frequently as possible and periodic food shortages produce the synchrony. The situation in the swallow-tailed gull is unexplained as this species does not seem to experience food shortages. Even when food is obviously plentiful there is still a period between cycles when birds of all species, except the flightless cormorant, are away from colonies. Something is preventing continuous breeding. The most likely explanation is that birds need time to replace their main wing and tail feathers. During this moult, flight efficiency is reduced by gaps in the wing and tail, and as birds often have trouble feeding their young even when they are at maximum efficiency, it seems unlikely they could breed when in wing moult. Although moult occupies the whole time between breeding it is conceivable that the moult itself is adapted to the food supply; if this supply is poor it might be advantageous to spread moult over as long a period as available. It is also conceivable that the gonads need time to recuperate after breeding, but females of many of the species lay only a single egg (swallow-tailed gull, Audubon's shearwater), or a clutch of small eggs in relation to the adult's weight (pelican, blue-footed booby). Also, many do not re-lay if the clutch is lost but moult and then start another cycle. This seems unlikely to cause any great strain on the ovary. In Audubon's shearwater nesting success does not influence the interval between the end of one cycle and the next laying; again this suggests that there is sufficient time for the gonads to recover.

It is harder to explain why some breed annually. The waved albatross, dark-rumped petrel and storm petrels are pelagic feeders whose breeding is probably influenced by factors acting well away from the islands. The other annual breeders have breeding out of phase on different islands which suggests that their activities are controlled by the regular movement of the Humboldt Current.

13.3. The Future

All the evidence suggests that there are now at least as many seabirds in Galápagos as there ever have been. No species of bird has become extinct in recent times and only the dark-rumped petrel has become noticeably scarcer. The rarer species may once have been even rarer, for Darwin failed to record the flightless cormorant and penguin in 1835, even though he visited areas where they now breed, and the former species was not described to science until 1897. The lava gull and magnificent frigatebird have possibly gained from the increase in human population bringing fish waste and garbage to the islands.

The rapid expansion of tourism in the islands from a few hundred people a year in the mid-1960s to 25,000 visitors per annum in 1981, resulted in the realization that wildlife was a major resource which attracted many people and much money to the islands. Concern in case these developments unduly disturbed the birds in particular resulted in the setting up of studies to monitor the impact of tourism. It is, as yet, too early to be complacent but the indications are that an adequate standard of guiding of the tourists and the extreme tameness of animals have resulted in minimal damage to populations.

Introduced animals (treated in detail in Chapter 16) pose much greater threats, especially to seabirds on the main islands. The most obvious damage is caused by a few hundred feral dogs on the southern half of Isabela (details in Kruuk, 1979). Although marine iguanas (*Amblyrhynchus cristatus*) were the preferred prey (122 of 156 prey remains examined), seabirds were also taken including blue-footed boobies (10), penguins (6), pelicans (3), swallow-tailed gulls (1). At Elizabeth Bay penguin remains were found in a third of 88 droppings collected from about 15 dogs resident there. Kruuk suggested that the dogs killed *c.* 450 penguins annually, even though only 200 individuals were thought to occur in the area (Boersma, 1974). Penguins often roost ashore, and spend most time under rocks when moulting. Presumably many of those killed were not breeding; if they were transients in the area the penguin population as a whole was unlikely to be affected. If the dogs manage to cross Istmo Perry and colonize northern Isabela, they could have a serious effect on the penguins there and would almost certainly eliminate flightless cormorants. This would leave Fernandina as the only safe breeding area for these 2 species.

Dark-rumped petrels have so many problems that the depressing tale is worth telling in some detail. The species occurs in the humid highlands but most is known of the birds on Santa Cruz. A few pairs nest in caves and among rocks but the majority dig burrows in areas of moist soil with thick vegetation. Unfortunately for the birds these areas are also the best agricultural land and a large proportion of the habitat used by petrels has been cleared for cattle grazing. Many birds have been displaced, others killed by flying into fences. Even where the habitat has remained unaltered the birds suffer from introduced animals. Originally the petrel had only two serious predators—short-eared owl (*Asio flammeus*) and the endemic hawk (*Buteo galapagoensis*), which catch birds in flight and on the ground. Once in the burrow a petrel was probably safe as the native rats (*Oryzomys spp.* and *Nesoryzomys* spp.) are mainly vegetarian. Pigs, introduced after the settlement of Santa Cruz in the 1920s, soon became abundant. In the ensuing years the pigs rooted out burrows and ate petrels with the result that the pig's flesh became so tainted as to be inedible. The increase in pigs coincided with the major land clearances and petrel numbers declined. Although pigs were certainly once the main threat to the petrels, they are not at present common on Santa Cruz, though still cause havoc on Santiago. Now it is difficult to know whether dogs or rats pose the greatest threat. Seven (9%) of 78 adults I ringed at a colony at Media Luna on Santa Cruz were found killed by dogs in 1967, as were 10 (18%) of 126 breeding birds in 1978 (Tomkins, 1980). This is about double the normal total annual mortality of seabirds of this family. It represents a minimum estimate as more birds would have died undetected among vegetation and during the 6 months or so the birds spend at sea. Breeding success is extremely low (Table 13.3), apparently because black rats (*Rattus rattus*) eat eggs and small young. The number of young reared is quite inadequate to balance the normal mortality of adults, let alone the losses caused by dogs. The Media Luna colony is obviously doomed and the number of occupied burrows declined from 120 in 1967 to less that 20 in 1981 (R. Harcourt pers. comm.). In 1979, Tomkins found that breeding success was slightly higher on Santiago (39%) and Floreana (49%). Hopefully, this is typical and the situation found at Media Luna abnormal. If it is not, then the future of the species in Galápagos is in jeopardy. It is similarly threatened at the only other breeding place, in Hawaii, by introduced mammals, including mongooses and rats.

Table 13.3. Nesting success of dark-rumped petrels at Media Luna, Santa Cruz.

Year	Burrows checked	Eggs laid	Young fledged	Success per egg laid	Source
1966	62	41+	4	0.10	Harris, 1970a
1967	30	26+	0	0	Harris, 1970a
1971	37	7+	1	0.14	Jacobs, 1972
1978	87	64	0	0	Tomkins, 1980
1979	95	39	2	0.05	Tomkins, 1980
1980	99	32	3	0.10	Bass, 1980

Many *Pterodroma* or 'gad-fly' petrels have had their numbers reduced by man directly (for food) or indirectly (susceptibility to introduced predators) (Bourne, 1965). Several are close to extinction, e.g. the black-capped petrel (*P. hasitata carribbaea*) of Jamaica, Cook's (*P. cooki*) and mottled petrels (*P. inexpectata*) on some New Zealand Islands and Solander's petrel (*P. solandi*) on Lord Howe Island. The cahow (*P. cahow*) of Bermuda was thought to be extinct but a few tens of birds have been rediscovered. All species of the genus appear to be very resilient to ill-fortune. The low annual mortality rates result in an average life expectancy for an adult of probably about 25–30 years, so that a population can survive even a prolonged period of poor reproductive output. However, low recruitment coupled with an increased adult mortality, such as that caused by alien predators, can only result in a rapid decline in numbers. Time must be running out for the dark-rumped petrel on Santa Cruz and perhaps elsewhere. The species has recently been added to *IUCN Red Data Book* of endangered species. Every effort must be made now to control dogs and rats at these colonies otherwise the dark-rumped petrel could be the first bird species to become extinct in Galápagos.

References

Ashmole, N.P. and Ashmole, M.J. (1967) Comparative feeding ecology of sea birds of a tropical oceanic island. *Bull. Peabody Mus. Nat. Hist.*, **24**, 1–131.

Baker, A.R. (1980) Breeding distribution and population size of the dark-rumped petrel (*Pterodroma phaeopygia*) on Santa Cruz Island, Galápagos. Unpubl. report to Charles Darwin Research Station.

Baker, J.T. (1938) The evolution of breeding seasons. In *Evolution*, Edited by G.R. de Beer, Pages 161–177. Oxford University Press, London.

Bass, F. (1980) Report of the Dark-rumped Petrel (*Pterodroma phaeopygia*) monitoring program on Santa Cruz, Galápagos 1980. Unpubl. report, C.D.R.S.

Boersma, D. (1974) The Galápagos Penguin. PhD. thesis, Ohio State University.

Boersma, D. (1977) An ecological and behavioral study of the Galápagos Penguin *Living Bird*, **1976**, 43–93.

Boersma, D. (1978) Breeding patterns of Galápagos Penguins as an indicator of oceanographic conditions. *Science*, **200**, 1481–1483.

Bourne, W.R.P. (1965) The missing petrels. *Bull. Brit. Ornithol. Club*, **85**, 97–105.

Cramp, S., Bourne, W.R.P. and Saunders, D. (1974). *The Seabirds of Britain and Ireland*. Collins, London.

Diamond, A.W. (1973) Notes on the breeding biology and behavior of the Magnificent Frigatebird. *Condor*, **75**, 200–209.

Fosberg, F.R. (1965) Natural bird refuges in the Galápagos. *Elepaio*, **25**, 60–67.

Harris, M.P. (1969a) The biology of storm petrels in the Galápagos Islands. *Proc. Calif. Acad. Sci.*, **37**, 95–166.

Harris, M.P. (1969b) Breeding seasons of sea-birds in the Galápagos Islands. *J. Zool., Lond.*, **159**, 145–165.

Harris, M.P. (1969c) Food as a factor controlling the breeding of *Puffinus lherminieri*. *Ibis*, **111**, 139–156.

Harris, M.P. (1970a) The biology of an endangered species, the Dark-rumped Petrel (*Pterodroma phaeopygia*), in the Galápagos Islands. *Condor*, **72**, 76–84.

Harris, M.P. (1970b) Breeding ecology of the Swallow-tailed Gull *Creagrus furcatus*. *Auk*, **87**, 215–243.

Harris, M.P. (1973) The biology of the Waved Albatross *Diomedea irrorata* of Hood Island, Galápagos. *Ibis*, **115**, 483–510.

Harris, M.P. (1974) A complete census of the Flightless Cormorant (*Nannopterum harrisi*). *Biol. Conserv.*, **6**, 188–191.

Harris, M.P. (1977) Comparative ecology of seabirds in the Galápagos Archipelago. In *Evolutionary Ecology*. Edited by B. Stonehouse and C.M. Perrins, pages 65–76. Macmillan, London.

Harris, M.P. (1979) Population dynamics of the Flightless Cormorant *Nannopterum harrisis*. *Ibis*, **121**, 135–146.

Jacobs, B. (1972) A progress report on the survey and study of the Dark-rumped Petrel in the Galápagos Islands. Unpubl. report, C.D.R.S.

Jordan, R. and Fuentes, H. (1966) Las poblaciones de aves guaneras y su situación actual. Publication Institute del Mar del Peru, No. 10.

Kruuk, H. (1979) Ecology and control of feral dogs in Galápagos. Unpubl. report, Institute of Terrestrial Ecology, Scotland.

Lack, D. (1954) *The Natural Regulation of Animal Numbers*. Oxford University Press, London.

Nelson, J.B. (1967) Etho-ecological adaptations in the Great Frigate bird *Nature, Lond.*, **214**, 318.

Nelson, J.B. (1968) *Galápagos, Islands of Birds*. Longmans, London.

Nelson, J.B. (1978) *The Sulidae*. Aberdeen University Press, Oxford.

Perrins, C.M. (1966) Survival of young Manx Shearwaters *Puffinus puffinus* in relation to their presumed date of hatching. *Ibis*, **108**, 132–135.

Snow, B.K. and Snow, D.W. (1969) Observations on the Lava Gull *Larus fuliginosus*. *Ibis*, **111**, 30–35.

Snow, D.W. (1965a) The breeding of the Audubon's Shearwater (*Puffinus lherminieri*) in the Galápagos. *Auk*, **82**, 591–597.

Snow, D.W. (1965b) The breeding of the red-billed tropicbird in the Galápagos Islands. *Condor*, **67**, 210–214.

Snow, D.W. and Snow, B.K. (1967) The breeding cycle of the Swallow-tailed Gull *Creagrus furcatus*. *Ibis*, **109**, 14–24.

Tomkins, R.J. (1980) A study of the conservation of the Dark-rumped Petrel (*Pterodroma phaeopygia*) considered to be an endangered species in the Galápagos Archipelago. Unpubl. report to C.D.R.S.

CHAPTER 14

The Galápagos Seals
Part 1. Natural History of the Galápagos Sea Lion (*Zalophus californianus wollebaeki*, Sivertsen)

I. EIBL-EIBESFELDT

Forschungsstelle für Humanethologie, Max-Planck-Institut für Verhaltensphysiologie, Seewiesen, West Germany

Contents

14.1.	Natural History of the Galápagos Sea Lion	207
	14.1.1. Introduction	207
	14.1.2. Habitat and locomotion	208
	14.1.3. Feeding and daily activity	209
	14.1.4. Territoriality and reproduction	209
	14.1.5. Care of young	211
	14.1.6. Play	213
	14.1.7. Relations with other animals	214
	14.1.8. Population size	214
	References	214

14.1. Natural History of the Galápagos Sea Lion (*Zalophus californianus wollebaeki*, Sivertsen)

14.1.1. Introduction

E. Sivertsen (1953) described the Galápagos sea lion as a distinct species and named it *Zalophus wollebaeki* in honour of the Norwegian zoologist, Alf Wollebaek, who visited the islands in 1924. However, the species is so similar and apparently so closely related to the Californian sea lion that it seems reasonable to consider it as a subspecies of the latter. From outward appearances, it is hardly distinguishable from the Californian sea lion, but in behaviour the Galápagos sea lion exhibits some remarkable peculiarities.

The Galápagos sea lion is the more conspicuous of the 2 seals of the archipelago. In contrast to the Galápagos fur seal, which rests during daytime, often hidden in the shade of rocks, and fishes during the night, the sea lion is most active during the day and is usually encountered in larger numbers (Table 14.1.1). Sea lions are amongst the most conspicuous inhabitants of these shores. They are active, playful and easy-to-observe, since they show no fear of man. Detailed studies of the ecology and ethology of this species are still lacking, however, but observations carried out by a number of visitors give a general picture with some interesting details.

Figure 14.1.1. Male sea lion sleeping while drifting in his territory. Flippers under the water are held downwards, presumably to help stabilize the animal's floating position. (Photograph by I. Eibl-Eibesfeldt).

14.1.2. Habitat and locomotion

The Galápagos sea lion is found throughout the archipelago. It prefers rocky coasts, which are not too steep and thus provide opportunities for rest and shade provided by lava boulders, caves or shore vegetation. Shade must normally be available, particularly for the young; sandy beaches without shade may be used for resting, but seldom as pupping grounds. Favoured areas are those with tide-pools and which are not exposed to pounding surf. The pools provide playgrounds for the young, while adults rest there during the hot hours.

Around steep cliffs, one may find groups of adults fishing or drifting on the surface in a resting position—either floating sideways, one rear and one front flipper held vertically above the water (Fig. 14.1.1.), or floating on their backs with both front flippers above them. Such clusters of fins are a curious and by no means unusual feature of the Galápagos.

On land, sea lions employ the two basic mammalian quadruped modes of locomotion. Firstly, with the

Table 14.1.1

Comparison between Galápagos Sea Lion and Galápagos Fur Seal	
Galápagos Sea Lion (*Zalophus californianus wollebaeki*)	Galápagos Fur Seal (*Arctocephalus galapagoensis*)
mainly diurnal feeding	nocturnal feeding
territorial in the water	territorial on shore
extended breeding season	short breeding season
nursing usually less than a year	protracted nursing, often extending to 2 years
no large intervals between nursing	nursing often interrupted for 1–3 days ('spaced nursing')

hind flippers brought forward beneath them to support the rear of the body, a cross-gait is employed for climbing and slow locomotion. Secondly, when moving fast, i.e. when chasing away a rival, the animal progresses by a series of galloping jumps.

In the water, sea lions move with grace and astounding manoeuverability. Due to the flexibility of their bodies, they can practically turn on the spot, even at great speeds. Propulsion during normal swimming is achieved by means of the front flippers. The synchronous down and backward beating visibly accelerates the body within fractions of a second. Their hind-flippers are held backwards and are used more for steering than for acceleration. During fast locomotion on the surface of the water, sea lions move in a series of jumps. Even when very small, pups can propel themselves in the water by means of their front flippers, as has been observed when pups have been accidentally washed from cliffs.

14.1.3. Feeding and daily activity

Sea lions are basically diurnal with two activity peaks, one in the morning and the other in the late afternoon. Cephalopods and fish constitute the main diet. They thrash large octopi violently against the surface of the water, apparently to stun them before swallowing them. While fishing, sea lions dive to considerable depths; Kooyman *et al.* (1980) recorded dives of over 100 m.

Sea lions have more heat tolerance than fur seals. They do not avoid the sun, except during the hottest hours of the day, when they retreat either into the shade of rocks or bushes, or into the tidal region to cool in the water. Patterns of self-grooming reflect their land mammalian heritage. They scratch themselves with the toe nails of their hindlegs like dogs, wipe their noses with their front flippers and comb their fur by nibbling with their incisors. Rubbing the fur with the head or chin is a pattern peculiar to seals, and one to my knowledge that has not yet been investigated. It is somewhat reminiscent of the movements by which waterbirds oil their feathers, and it may have a similar function.

14.1.4. Territoriality and reproduction

The breeding season is longer than for the fur seal. Except for the months of April and May, when pupping rarely occurs, young are born throughout the year, with a peak during August, September and October. There seem to exist local variations, however, since Howard Snell (pers. comm.) recorded a peak of pupping in January on South Plaza Island.

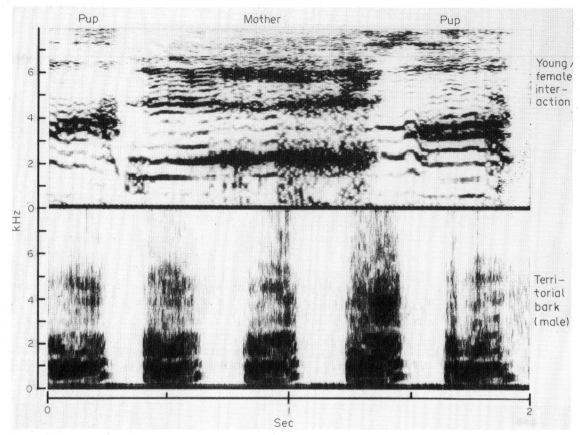

Figure 14.1.2. Sonagrams of (top) mother/pup exchange greeting calls and (bottom) territorial bark of male Galápagos sea lion. Sonagrams taken by F. Trillmich; for further information, see Trillmich (1981).

Due to this extended breeding season, territorial males can be observed practically throughout the year. These males mark off a stretch of shore line as their territory. Such defended territories vary in length, usually ranging from 40 to 100 m, but sometimes even larger areas are occupied (Eibl-Eibesfeldt, 1955). The males patrol by swimming up and down the coastline uttering a loud territorial bark, which can be described as *ou ou ou* (Fig. 14.1.2, bottom). At the borders of their territories, they pose in the shallow water calling to the neighbour, who responds in the same fashion. As a rule, no fights result from this ceremonial territory-marking behaviour.

When fighting does occur, males raise their necks in front of each other, utter trumpeting sounds and show their teeth. Pushing each other, chest against chest, they try to bite and slash their opponent with heavy sideways blows of their necks. These encounters may result in deep gashes and adult males are often covered with scars on the sides of their heads and necks. The wounds, however, seldom seem to be serious and much of the fight consists of wrestling during which the rivals try to push each other away or press each other's neck to the ground. Before one gives up, he may assume what appears to me as a submissive posture. He collapses to the ground with a flattened outstretched neck, uttering a greeting call accompanied by a rapid sideways swaying of the head. Thereupon he usually turns to flee, often chased by the victor for some distance into the water.

Each territorial male tries to acquire a harem ranging from a few to as many as 30 females. Should a female start to stray into another territory, her mate may cut her off and so keep her inside his own territory.

Another means by which the male keeps his group together involves the appeasement of conflict. Females keep their individual distances, even though these are small, avoiding bodily contact with others and defending their resting places when they have pups. Should a disturbance break out, the bull climbs the shore, approaches the cows, greeting both combatants, even squeezing himself between them; this separates the females and allows them to calm down.

Males without territories often congregate in bachelor groups. On the small island *lobería* in front of Bahía del Correo on Floreana, I once counted 5 bachelor groups, with a total of 250 males. In addition to these there was a territorial male on the island with a harem of 5 females. Whether or not there exist traditional 'bachelor beaches' needs to be investigated, but on repeated visits I have always found the same stretch of sandy beach occupied by bachelor sea lions.

Sometimes bachelors stay close to, or even within, the borders of a territorial male, keeping silent and unobtrusive. If the territory owner encounters such a male, he will give chase, but perhaps not as fiercely as one would expect. On the other hand, an *intruder* is not tolerated at all.

Territorial bulls are mainly occupied with patrolling and territorial defence, and so have little time for feeding. Once they do leave to feed, other males may come and occupy the territory. Usually males keep their territory for up to 2 weeks and are then replaced. The females meanwhile, seeming not to attach themselves to any particular bull, accept the change. Later, the original male may attempt to win back his territory. (In the Californian sea lion territorial maintenance lasts on average about 27 days (Odell, 1975)).

14.1.5. Care of young

Immediately after birth a phase of intensive interaction between mother and pup can be observed. The young and the mother greet each other with nosing, headshaking and bleeting like sheep, the mother in a deeper voice, the pup in one very similar to a young lamb (Fig. 14.1.2, top). The mother also rubs the newborn with her chin. I assume that during this phase of interaction a strong individual bond is created, similar to that observed in some other mammals which live in herds and give birth to young in a fairly advanced stage of development. It has been known for a long time that mother and young recognize each other individually by smell and by their individual calls (Eibl-Eibesfeldt, 1955). The matter was investigated in more detail by Trillmich (1981) who confirmed that individual recognition by sound occurs for both sea lions and fur seals.

Mothers stay with their pups ashore for a substantial part of the day and during the night. During feeding excursions the pups remain ashore. How mother and pup find each other after her return from a fishing excursion can be observed with particular ease late in the afternoon, when the young are already ashore and the females return one by one. Each mother approaches the shore uttering her greeting call; as a rule only one pup will bleet in response. Alternately bleeting, they approach each other and a frantic greeting with nosing and calling takes place. Once the mother slumps down on her resting place, the young feeds. If her mammae are not accessible, the young will bite the mother and thus cause her to shift position in such a way as to allow nursing.

Only occasionally a pup errs and approaches a female which is not its mother. In most cases it realizes the mistake and soon retires. In those rare instances when it approaches a strange mother, it is threatened and perhaps attacked and bitten. On the other hand, pups are quite fierce when their mother is approached by another pup. They attack and bite the intruder, and even fairly small pups may chase away larger young. Orphans therefore have no chance of survival.

Young are groomed by their mothers who comb their fur with the teeth and stroke it with their chins and sides of the head. If a small pup is carried away by the sea, the mother will rescue it by holding it between her teeth by the nape of the neck. In this way she may also transport a small baby whilst swimming and diving.

Figure 14.1.3. Female/young interaction: the pup approaches its mother and is inspected by nose-to-nose contact. (Photograph by I. Eibl-Eibesfeldt).

In contrast to other seals, which seem to ignore other pups to the extent of trampling those in their path, sea lions acknowledge young by sniffing and greeting. Whilst diving, I have observed bull sea lions herding young which are swimming into deep water and bring them towards the shore. They also position themselves between the young and a diver, uttering their territorial call underwater. Territorial males on such occasions may attack a diver. I have also observed this herding towards the shore in the presence of sharks and therefore interpret the behaviour as protective. This means that males defend not only their young, but all young within their water territory (Eibl-Eibesfeldt, 1955). Nelson (1968) observed this behaviour and Barlow (1972) watched bull sea lions intervening when sharks were in the vicinity of a rookery near Champion Island: 'When a shark approached to 5–10 m of the edge of the dark reef, one or two, sometimes three bulls swam toward it. Each sea lion's approach was rapid and initially on the surface. When 5–7 m away the bull slowed and coasted under water on an intercept course. At the leading bull's approach, the shark started to turn away. The bull then adjusted course to parallel that of the veering shark. The bull thus deflected the shark away from the rookery. The closest bull, and often one or two others, followed the shark 10–30 m. Once a bull bit (at) a shark's tail but apparently missed. The sea lions behind the bulls responded to the sharks only when they entered the dark reef. Then the smaller animals dashed shoreward, pausing in water about 30 m deep with land 1–5 m distant.'

It is interesting to note that in these cases, several males cooperated to bring about collective mobbing.

Figure 14.1.4. Female Galápagos sea lion greeting her grown-up pup: (a) by nosing and (b) sniffing by snout/skin contact. (Photographs by I. Eibl-Eibesfeldt).

14.1.6. Play

Sea lions are notoriously playful animals. The young engage in playful fighting, wrestling, pushing and mock-biting, but with clear inhibition towards any biting that would break the skin. In particular, when they grasp each other's snout or jaws the inhibition becomes very apparent, since in this situation they both keep their mouths open.

In the water, young chase each other, with subadults and females occasionally joining in. Adult females play with objects. They catch drifting sticks, and throw them into the air. They may also dive for pebbles and in a similar fashion play with them. Once in a while, an unfortunate marine iguana may be caught on its way back to the shore and have its tail pulled. These inquisitive animals once even stole my flippers and played tug-of-war with them!

One favourite game of young and old is surfing. They dive into the crest of a wave and with it are carried towards the shore until the wave breaks. With a skilful turn they dive under the wave, swim out again and repeat the performance.

14.1.7. Relations with other animals

I have occasionally observed sea lions and fur seals together on the same shore, apparently ignoring each others presence. The fur seals in these cases were higher up and hidden among rocks. Hostilities between the 2 species are rare but do occur (see 14.2.5, below).

Sea lions suffer heavy predation by sharks. Many animals bear the typical scars which result from such attacks, and on every visit to South Plaza I have seen half-grown and adult females lacerated from fresh shark attacks. Sea lions show no primary fear of man, but soon learn to flee from him once they are persecuted. The males will occasionally attack people who intrude into their territory—both on land and in the water; but usually they are content to be curious and inquisitive, milling around divers in company with their females and pups.

14.1.8. Population size

Estimates concerning the number of sea lions in the Galápagos range from 20,000 to 50,000 (Brosset, 1963). There are, however, frequent fluctuations. During the last 15 years epidemics of seal pox have severely reduced numbers of these animals in the islands.

References

Barlow, G.W. (1972) A Paternal Role for Bulls of the Galápagos Islands Sea Lions. *Evolution*, **26**, 307–308.
Brosset, A. (1963) Mammifères des Iles Galápagos: Statut actuel des mammifères des Iles Galápagos. *Mammalia*, **27**, 323–338.
Eibl-Eibesfeldt, I. (1955) Ethologische Studien am Galápagos Seelöwen. *Zeitschr. Tierpsychol.*, **12**, 286–303.
Eibl-Eibesfeldt, I. (1977) *Galápagos*. Piper, Munich.
Kooyman, G.L., Trillmich, F. and Arnold, W. (1980) Diving Characteristics of Galápagos Fur Seals and Sea Lions at Fernandina Island. *Ann. Report Charles Darwin Foundation*, 159–161.
Nelson, B. (1968) *Galápagos: Islands of Birds*. Longmans, London.
Odell, D.K. (1975) Breeding Biology of the California Sea Lion, *Zalophus californianus. Cons. Int. Explor. Mer.*, **169**, 374–387.
Sivertsen, E. (1953) A New Species of Sea Lion, *Zalophus wollebaeki*, from the Galápagos Islands. *Konigelige Norske Videnskabers Forhandlinger*, **26**,(1), 1–3.
Trillmich, F. (1981) Mutual mother-pup recognition in Galápagos fur seals and sea lions: Cues used and functional significance. *Behaviour*, **78**, 21–42.

Part 2. Natural History of the Galápagos Fur Seal (*Arctocephalus galapagoensis*, Heller)

FRITZ TRILLMICH

Abteilung Wickler, Max-Planck-Institut für Verhaltensphysiologie, Seewiesen, West Germany

Contents

14.2.	Natural History of the Galápagos Fur Seal	215
	14.2.1. Introduction	215
	14.2.2. Systematics	216
	14.2.3. Abundance and distribution	217
	14.2.4. Food and feeding	218
	14.2.5. Habitat	218
	14.2.6. Thermoregulatory behaviour	218
	14.2.7. Reproductive biology	219
	14.2.7.1. Seasonality of reproduction	219
	14.2.7.2. Reproductive cycle of females	220
	14.2.7.3. Territorial behaviour of males	221
	References	223

14.2. Natural History of the Galápagos Fur Seal (*Arctocephalus galapagoensis***, Heller)**

14.2.1. Introduction

In the southern fur seal genus, *Arctocephalus*, the Galápagos fur seal (*Arctocephalus galapagoensis*) occupies a unique position: it is the only tropical species of a basically subantarctic genus. Furthermore, it is the smallest of all these species, and sexual size dimorphism (Table 14.2.1) is least not only among fur seals but in all Otariidae, the family of sea lions and fur seals.

As most southern fur seals are aquatic most of the year, their primary adaptations are aquatic, not terrestrial. But the Galápagos fur seal, being non-migratory, spends about 30% of its adult life on land, exposed to an equatorial desert climate. How has the Galápagos fur seal come to terms with this demanding

Table 14.2.1. Size of adult Galápagos fur seals.

		Minimum	Maximum	Average ± s.d.	N
♀♀	body length (cm)[1]	106	129	120 ± 7	10
	weight (kg)	21.5	33.0	27.3 ± 3.3	10
♂♂[2]	body length (cm)[1]	151	154	——	2
	weight (kg)	60.0	68.0	63.7	3

[1] Curvilinear length.
[2] Territorial males only.

land habitat? It can escape thermal stress only by seeking out a favourable microclimate in caves or talus slopes composed of massive boulders, a behavioural response which Bartholomew (1966) compared with that of a fossorial desert rodent. But how does this solution of the thermal problem affect the highly polygynous breeding system for which fur seals are famous? Some other fur seals have similar difficulties (see Bonner, 1981 for a natural history of the genus), but in Galápagos, so aptly called the 'laboratory of evolution', the problems are thrown into sharp relief. After only a short habituation period Galápagos fur seals are easy to observe and become ready subjects for experimental investigation (Fig. 14.2.1). I will here describe the natural history of the species emphasizing how the animals have succeeded in adapting to their hostile environment. Although some speculation is necessary, this may help focus on the interesting questions posed by the biology of this fur seal.

14.2.2. Systematics

The Galápagos fur seal was first described in 1904 by Heller. Its closest relative is found on the mainland, where colonies of the South American Fur Seal (*Arctocephalus australis*) occur as far north as southern Peru. Presumably fur seals crossed to the Galápagos from Peruvian or Ecuadorian coastal colonies at a time when

Figure 14.2.1. Galápagos fur seals habituate rapidly to the presence of an observer; even the territorial male (foreground) appears undisturbed.

watermasses even colder than today's Peru current facilitated the journey and the survival of immigrants once they had arrived at the Galápagos. Although the Galápagos fur seal has been described as a subspecies of the South American fur seal (King, 1964), skull dimensions show a clear distinction. It is now considered a valid species (see Repenning *et al.*, 1971 for a discussion of *Arctocephalus* systematics).

14.2.3. Abundance and distribution

By the time Heller described the Galápagos fur seal, relentless slaughter by sealers from various countries had made it very rare. It was probably near extinction early in the 20th century, when sealing ended as it had become totally uneconomic (see Townsend, 1934 and Slevin, 1959 for accounts of the exploitation of the species). Recovery seems to have begun slowly in the 1930s, with fur seals coming gradually to be found on more and more islands of the archipelago (Eibl-Eibesfeldt, 1959, Levêque, 1963). The total fur seal population is at present estimated as between 30,000 and 40,000 animals. It now appears to be stable, except on Isabela, where predation by introduced feral dogs threatens the local population of Cerro Azul. If dogs were to cross the Perry Isthmus into northern Isabela, about one-third of the fur seal population of the Galápagos would be threatened.

Today, fur seals breed on almost all islands, except Santa Fé, Floreana, Española and perhaps San Cristóbal. The densest populations are found in the northwest of the archipelago on Marchena, Pinta, Isabela and Fernandina (Fig. 14.2.2). The distribution along island coasts is closely linked with areas of upwelling (see Chapter 3). Upwelling brings phytoplankton nutrients towards the surface, causing high local primary productivity. This presumably results in great abundance of the fur seals' prey organisms and provides the necessary food resources for thriving seal colonies.

Figure 14.2.2. Distribution of Galápagos fur seals. Dots: breeding colonies; Lines: very dense breeding colonies; Arrows: small non-breeding groups.

14.2.4. Food and feeding

Galápagos fur seals feed mostly at night on small squids (mainly *Onychoteuthis banksi*: Clarke and Trillmich, 1980), schooling fish (*Engraulis* sp.) and occasionally mackerel (*Scomber* sp.). This information was obtained from vomit analyses and is certainly not exhaustive; nor is it possible to quantify the relative importance of individual prey species for the energy budget of the seal. Clearly fur seals do no harm whatever to local commercial fishing, which specializes in large bottom-dwelling fish of the family *Serranidae*.

Work with diving recorders (Kooyman and Trillmich in prep.) showed that fur seals are essentially surface feeders, only rarely diving deeper than 30 m and never exceeding 100 m. Presumably many of their food species show a daily vertical migration, staying too deep to be within easy reach during the day (and during nights with full moon) and approaching the surface on dark nights. This could explain why fur seals feed predominantly at night and avoid being at sea during full moonlit nights.

Furthermore, sharks are a hazard—even adult seals are regularly observed with shark bite wounds—and bright moonlight aids the sharks. It silhouettes the fur seals against the surface of the sea, and allows sharks to approach undetected from the shadows below (Trillmich and Mohren, 1981). Thus night feeding and avoidance of the water at full moon can be explained as adaptations of Galápagos fur seals to poor feeding conditions at sea (compared with conditions for other fur seals), and perhaps to high shark predation pressure in Galápagos waters.

14.2.5. Habitat

Fur seals prefer wave-battered rocky coastlines where heaped boulders, cliffs and tunnels provide shade from the sun. Piled rocks compel the fur seals to climb a lot, which they do with amazing dexterity. Only in a few sites, where rough rocky coast and smooth lava flats or sand beaches border each other, do fur seals and sea lions compete for space. In such areas males of the 2 species may give boundary displays and actually fight. In the highly-structured habitat, fur seal bulls are able to defy sea lion bulls weighing about four times their weight.

14.2.6. Thermoregulatory behaviour

Pinnipeds, because of their aquatic adaptations for heat retention, cannot regulate their body temperature by physiological means alone when exposed to a hot-dry land environment. Galápagos fur seals must endure particularly severe conditions; the high equatorial solar radiation heats them directly, and rock surface temperatures sometimes exceed 50°C. As the sun rises, or cloud cover breaks in the morning, the animals react by altering postures, increasing the surface contact of the highly vascular flipper sole (Fig. 14.2.3). This allows better conduction of heat to wet substrate or to rock surfaces that are still cool. But with increasing heat load these adjustments of posture soon become insufficient, and the animals begin to sweat, seen most clearly on the naked parts of the flippers. At this stage at the latest the seals begin to move—into the shade, on to wet rock or into the water (Fig. 14.2.3). This produces a typical morning thermoregulatory shift away from the hot dry land down to the tide-line, a shift reversed late in the afternoon when conditions again become tolerable for a dry fur seal.

As pups under 10 days old are in acute danger of being washed away by waves, their mothers stay on dry land as much as possible and try to find a shady retreat where they can spend the hot noon hours together with their pups. Females with dependent young of all ages forage predominantly at night; they must therefore spend the hot daytime ashore nursing their young. As all females with young prefer shady spots for nursing,

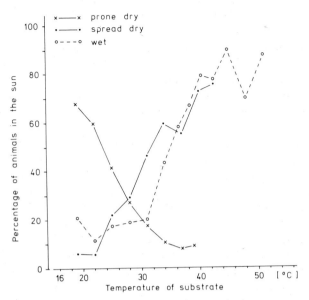

Figure 14.2.3. Thermoregulatory behaviour: in the *prone* posture, all four flippers are tucked away under the belly; in the *spread* posture, soles of all flippers are in contact with the substrate; at high temperatures all animals in the sun may actually be wet (100%), as even those judged dry by the visible areas of fur probably had wet bellies.

there is strong resting site competition and many aggressive interactions ensue between females. Those unable to defend such a retreat must move to and fro between land and water or wet rock. The particularly strong competition between females around the peak of the pupping season causes females with older offspring to move away from the most frequented pupping sites. Females with yearlings often move to the wilder parts of the coast too dangerous for newborns, and so avoided for pupping. Thus the limited number of sites offering thermoregulatory relief appears to dictate the unusually low seal density. In a dense Galápagos fur seal colony there are only about 6 adult fur seals per 100 m^2, while density in other species is about one order of magnitude higher.

14.2.7. Reproductive biology

14.2.7.1. Seasonality of reproduction

Fur seals reproduce during the cool *garúa* season, which lasts from about June to December. Food is most plentiful then, because of the intense upwelling bringing to the surface the essential nutrients for phytoplankton growth. Also thermoregulatory problems are least during this season, as a cool, sea wind blows almost constantly, and the regular, if light, cloud cover partly shades solar radiation. On Fernandina and Santiago the reproductive season lasts from August to November; no data are available for other islands. During this time females pup, and come into oestrus about a week later and copulate. Females without pups, and virgin females, come into oestrus spontaneously. Although this reproductive season is long for a fur seal, it is short compared with that of the sympatric Galápagos sea lion. We do not yet understand why these 2 species differ in this respect, nor is it clear why the peak of pupping in fur seals regularly lies at the beginning of October.

14.2.7.2. Reproductive cycle of females

The youngest known-age female seen copulating was three-years-old. Most females estimated (by their size) to be 5 years or older appear to copulate once every year. Only 3 females were observed to copulate twice within one season. Fur seals delay the implantation of the fertilized egg and thus pup at yearly intervals, although actual development of the embryo lasts only about 7 months.

Females come ashore 1 or 2 days before giving birth to a single pup, weighing between 3.0 and 4.5 kg. They then remain with the pup for about a week before leaving it alone for the first time. During this time mother and young come to recognize each other by smell and by voice characteristics (Trillmich, 1981). A female guarding her pup after parturition loses about 2% of her body weight per day. Much of this is transferred as milk to the pup, which can gain up to about 1 kg in its first week of life.

After the post-partum oestrus, about a week after parturition, females routinely leave the pup to go on foraging excursions of 1–4 days, with intervals on land of a few hours to about 2 days, resting near the pups or nursing them. They stay on land longest around full moon, and spend most time away from their pups around new moon. The young are cared for in this way until they are two to three years old. Their milk demand increases drastically during the first year, so that yearlings are nursed about 70% of their mothers' time ashore; unweaned two-year-olds require less, about 40–50% of their mothers' time ashore. These long nursing times indicate that milk still forms a significant share of their total diet. Yearlings and two-year-olds gain 1–2 kg in weight at each of their mothers' visits, but lose most of this again before the next visit.

The young moult their pup fur when about six months old. At about a year they occasionally forage for themselves, but are still largely dependent. First year mortality is low, only about 20%. So a new pup may be born while its mother is still accompanied by a yearling or two-year-old. But, although all females copulate in post-partum oestrus, only the biggest (presumably oldest) and healthiest-looking give birth next year (about 15%) if they are still accompanied by their previous offspring; of females without young about 70% pup. Food may be a limiting resource, which a female must apportion between her own needs, the developing embryo and the milk demands of an older pup. Only the strongest females seem able to get enough food to satisfy all these demands.

In cases where a newborn pup has an older sibling, a yearling or a two-year-old, strong competition for the mother's milk develops, or outright aggression. Although the mother usually defends the newborn against the older sibling (Fig. 14.2.4), the newborn in this situation invariably becomes a runt and almost always dies within its first month of life if the sibling is a yearling, or in about 50% of the cases if it is a two-year-old. The effect of the longer dependence of the young is that females of this species—unlike all other fur seals—can at best raise a pup every other year. If a female survives until the age of 15, and has her first pup when she is 5, she can raise only about 5 offspring. As the fur seal population at present appears to be stable, and has increased in the past from near extinction, survival of young to reproductive age must be high. One factor, or two factors combined, could explain this lengthening of the reproductive cycle of Galápagos fur seal females: (1) Food limitation could cause the unusually low growth rate of young, and thus longer dependence. If females are unable to obtain enough food for themselves and a fast-growing young, natural selection will decrease juvenile growth rate. The speculation that food is limiting is supported by a first analysis of milk samples showing unusually low fat (about 23%) and protein (about 4%) content for fur seal milk. The low protein content in particular may reflect the strain upon the female to gather enough food for herself and her young, consequent upon her limited diving abilities, restricting her feeding niche. This could also explain why only the biggest and the healthiest females have successful pregnancies while still feeding an earlier young, as these females are the best divers.

(2) Shark attacks on animals of all ages are a regular phenomenon. Very few adult females disappeared during observations made over four reproductive periods; but many adults are seen with more or less serious shark bite wounds. So shark predation on them seems not particularly efficient. However, sharks may be a much greater danger for the small and inexperienced young. Increased maternal care reduces the necessity for young

to forage for themselves, and so also considerably reduces the risk of mortality from sharks. Thus predation pressure may select for prolonged maternal investment.

But why should a female with an older young develop an embryo and give birth to a pup with such a slim chance of survival?

One possible explanation is that it is advantageous for her to have a replacement ready if the older young dies during her pregnancy: she does not lose a whole year of her reproductive lifetime, but can start raising a new pup immediately.

Figure 14.2.4. Female defending a pup against its one-year-old sibling.

14.2.7.3. Territorial behaviour of males

During the course of the whole year males haul out at the colony, where they become territorial during the reproductive season. Territory establishment begins in late July/early August before any pups are born. The bulls leave less frequently for foraging and gradually establish territorial boundaries which at first encompass very large areas. As more and more bulls move in, pieces are split off these huge territories, but average territory area remains enormous for such a small fur seal bull of about 65 kg. Whereas other much larger fur seal species have territories between 10 and 100 m², the average Galápagos fur seal territory is about 200 m² (as large as the area claimed by a Steller's sea lion bull (*Eumetopias jubata*) weighing 1000 kg). Bulls can claim such huge territory areas because the density of competing full-grown males is low. This territory size compensates for low female density: males have access to about as many females as fur seal bulls of other species defending much smaller areas in their much denser colonies. These larger territories in such a structured habitat are harder to defend, as they rarely contain a vantage point from which the whole perimeter can be surveyed; non-territorial (usually small) males can intrude more easily, and may sometimes remain on a territory for long periods, occasionally even copulating undetected by the territorial male. Another drawback is that bulls have to do a lot of walking and climbing to keep check on females, and defend the territory boundaries against neighbours.

All territories have access to the water, so that bulls can cool off in the sea during the noon hours. The rare exceptions only emphasize the vital need of these seals for behavioural thermoregulation: inland territories always possess large caves or lava tunnels, providing shade where bulls and females can rest during the hottest hours.

Once a male becomes established on his territory he no longer leaves to forage. Drinking of seawater, however, can regularly be observed. They live on the energy stored in their subcutaneous blubber, which normally serves to retain body heat during swimming and diving. During tenure of their territories males may lose up to about 20–25% of their original body weight. As this tremendous weight loss means a dramatic decrease in their ability for heat retention, they may face grave thermoregulatory problems at the end of their tenure when they return to the aquatic environment. Fasting is occasionally interrupted towards the end of very long tenure periods, when a bull may leave overnight to forage. The bigger and fatter a male when he takes over a territory, the longer he will be able to remain on it and defend it without feeding. He is challenged frequently and can repel rivals only while he is still in reasonable body condition. Tenure may last up to 51 days. Most males cannot defend a territory for such a long time, but even so this is only about half of the reproductive period. Median time of first tenure is 27 days. Most males are ousted by challenging males, but some manage to stay until they are too exhausted to copulate. The long reproductive period, and the comparatively short time on territory of the average bull, allow 'early' bulls to spend about a month at sea between an initial and a second period of territory tenure. In 1980, 10 of 36 territorial bulls (28%) followed this strategy. Second tenure tends to be shorter than the first, maximum time was about 24 days and the median 15 days.

Shortly after the peak of the pupping season territorial structure begins to disintegrate, as most of the big bulls leave exhausted, although there are still many females in oestrus. This gives smaller bulls and even half-grown males a chance to copulate, as females will copulate with any male dominant at the moment in their area.

Towards the end of the season, as oestrous females become rare, males begin to leave their territories overnight to forage. They may even absent themselves for a day or two. The risk of losing a territory during such an absence is low, as competition is minor at this stage of the reproductive season. Even loss of territorial status would be less serious than continuing to fast, as only very few copulations can now be expected on a given territory. Clearly, then, tenure times very late in the season cannot compare with earlier tenures.

The most successful males follow one of two strategies:
(1) They come early, before the first pups are born, and remain as long as possible. With luck this may be until peak pupping-time. They then spend 3–6 weeks at sea fattening up, and return to their territories towards the end of the season. Chances to reconquer a territory at this time are surprisingly high.
(2) They claim a territory when the main pupping activity has already begun, and stay for the whole peak period.

Males following either of these strategies may have over 20 copulations within one season. But most males have lower reproductive success and quite a few territorial bulls are ousted by a rival before they copulate at all.

The female biannual reproductive cycle strongly affects copulation value. Copulation with a female which has just pupped has a very low probability of resulting in a surviving young (only about 20%). Chances are much higher with females with older young or none. As females without young or with yearlings or two-year-olds come into oestrus early in the season, it is advantageous for males to become territorial early too: copulations at this time are most likely to produce surviving offspring. This may explain the curious observed partial breakdown of territorial organization soon after the peak of pupping, when many oestrous females are still available.

Males were found to return to their territories for up to 3 years in a row. But only a small percentage return this often, as mortality of territorial males is very high (about 30% per year). Recognized returning males always reoccupied exactly the same territories and at about the same time of the season.

This information on territoriality of the males may help to understand why sexual size dimorphism is reduced in this fur seal. The large territories, and the consequent tremendous climbing and walking effort required of territorial males, may exert strong selective pressure to decrease the size of fully adult bulls, as the cost of climbing decreases with decreasing body weight. Further, loss of heat is much easier for a smaller animal, with a relatively larger body surface to radiate or conduct heat to the environment. This must be material, as males produce a lot of heat while running, copulating or fighting; a smaller bull will certainly find it much easier to avoid overheating, and may show more endurance in these strenuous activities. But of course reduced body size lowers fighting power and the fat reserves needed during territory tenure. Through natural selection, working on this parameter complex, the reduced size of Galápagos fur seal bulls must have evolved as a compromise in response to this exceptional environment.

References

Bartholomew, G.A. (1966) Interaction of physiology and behavior under natural conditions. In: *The Galápagos*, R.I. Bowman ed., 39–45, Univ. Calif. Press, Berkeley and Los Angeles.

Bonner, W.N. (1981) Southern fur seals – *Arctocephalus*. In: *Handbook of marine mammals*. Vol. I, S.H. Ridgway and R.J. Harrison eds., 161–208, Academic Press, London, New York, Toronto, Sydney, San Francisco.

Clarke, M.R. and F. Trillmich (1980) Cephalopods in the diet of fur seals of the Galápagos islands. *J. Zool. (London)*, **190**, 211–215.

Eibl-Eibesfeldt, I. (1959) Survey on the Galápagos islands. *Unesco Mission Report 8*, Paris.

Heller, E. (1904) Mammals of the Galápagos archipelago, exclusive of the Cetacea. *Proc. Calif. Acad. Sci. Ser. 3*, **3**, 233–250.

King, J.E. (1964) *Seals of the world*. Brit. Mus. (Natural History), London.

Levêque, R. (1963) Le statut actuel des mammifères rares et menacés de l'archipel des Galapagos. *Terre et Vie 4*, 397–430.

Repenning, C.A., Peterson, R.S. and Hubbs, C.L. (1971) Contributions to the systematics of the southern fur seals, with particular reference to the Juan Fernández and Guadalupe species. In: Antarctic Research Series. Vol. 18. W.H. Burt, ed., 1–34, Antarctic Pinnipedia. Am. Geophys. Un. Washington, D.C.

Slevin, J.R. (1959) The Galápagos islands. A history of their exploration. *Occ. Papers, Calif. Acad. Sci.*, San Francisco.

Townsend, C.H. (1934) The fur seal of the Galápagos islands. *Zoologica, N.Y.*, **18**, 43–56.

Trillmich, F. (1981) Mutual mother-pup recognition in Galápagos fur seals and sea lions: Cues used and functional significance. *Behaviour*, **78**, 21–42.

Trillmich, F. and W. Mohren (1981) Effects of the lunar cycle on the Galápagos fur seal, *Arctocephalus galapagoensis*. *Oecologia*, **48**, 85–92.

CHAPTER 15

Native Land Mammals

DEBORAH A. CLARK

Organization for Tropical Studies, Universidad de Costa Rica, Ciudad Universitaria, Costa Rica

Contents

15.1.	Introduction	225
15.2.	Bats	226
15.3.	Native Rats	226
	15.3.1. Species and distribution	226
	15.3.2. Demise of native rats	229
	15.3.3. Ecology of the native rats	230
15.4.	Conservation	231
	References	231

15.1. Introduction

Given the isolation of the Galápagos Islands, it is easy to understand why the fauna is poor in terrestrial mammals. What kinds of non-marine mammals could be expected to make the trip to a group of islands 1000 km from the nearest continent? Bats are logical candidates, and 2 species of bats are known from Galápagos. For the non-fliers the only means of access would be as hitch-hikers on debris carried from South America by the ocean currents. Robert Orr (1966) noted that floating rafts of debris are often swept to sea when Ecuador's Guayas River is in flood. He also calculated that the currents which head toward the Galápagos from Ecuador, coupled with the southeast trade winds, could enable such a raft to drift the 1000 km in less than 2 weeks. The only mammals able to survive such a trip would be small ones, those which could find enough food, water, and shelter on the floating debris to sustain themselves. And, in fact, the only known native land mammals in Galápagos (except for bats) are rats. The Galápagos native rats hold the world record for sea crossings by terrestrial mammals (Thornton, 1971).

Important by their absence from the native mammalian fauna of Galápagos are medium to large grazer/browsers (such as deer) and predators (such as cats or foxes). The absence of such mammals over evolutionary time has meant that the native plants and animals did not maintain protective features against these groups. Thus Galápagos organisms are especially vulnerable when exposed to exotic mammals such as the introduced goats and dogs.

15.2. Bats

Two species of bats are known to have reached the Galápagos Islands and apparently established there. Both are in the genus *Lasiurus*, a group including migratory species which have colonized other oceanic islands.

The first Galápagos bat specimen, taken in 1891, was described as an endemic species (Allen, 1892), now named *Lasiurus brachyotis*. Although it was very similar to the red bat (*L. borealis*) of the South American mainland, Allen believed its smaller size and shorter ears and wings justified assigning this individual to its own species. Until the early 1960's all bats from the Galápagos were thought to belong to this species. Then Robert Orr discovered that 5 specimens collected since the early 1950's were all hoary bats (*L. cinereus*), a larger species present on the mainland. When Niethammer (1964) examined a series of owl pellets collected in 1962–3 on Santa Cruz, he found bat skulls of two sizes. One was a hoary bat, and the other was a smaller *Lasiurus* fitting the measurements of *L. brachyotis*, the Galápagos red bat.

The most recent summary of the distribution of bats in Galápagos was published by Brosset (1963). He reported having sighted *Lasiurus* bats (species not determined) on Floreana, the west coast of Isabela (in mangroves) and on the coast and in the highlands of Santa Cruz. He also noted that bats were abundant on San Cristóbal, the island where the Galápagos red bat was originally discovered. For the remaining islands of the archipelago Brosset could find no report of bat sightings.

Only anecdotal information exists on the bats' ecology. At Academy Bay on Santa Cruz, Brosset observed bats roosting in mangroves, in the crown of a large *Opuntia* (cactus) tree, in the foliage of an introduced ornamental tree (*Terminalia catappa*), and under a roof overhang next to mangroves. David Clark and I twice flushed a bat from a hollow trunk of a guayabillo (*Psidium galapageium*) in the mid–altitude Transition Zone on Santa Cruz. The only data regarding reproduction come from Brosset's captures of three pregnant females, each with two young. These were caught in January, March, and April, thus all in the Galápagos 'hot season'.

This fragmentary information leaves a very uncertain picture of the Galápagos bats. First, does the endemic bat still exist? The owl pellets Niethammer examined included bones of mammals which had been extinct on Santa Cruz for over 25 years. The bat skulls he found could represent prey killed by Galápagos owls decades or more previously. Apparently no Galápagos red bats have been caught and identified in this century. Are they really different enough from the mainland red bat to be considered an endemic species? More than one museum skin and one skull will be necessary to resolve this question. If this bat is still present in the Galápagos, on which island(s) does it occur? Does it coexist with the hoary bat? A careful study of the distribution, identity, and ecology of the bats currently in the archipelago would be extemely interesting.

15.3. Native Rats

15.3.1. Species and distribution

Although the Galápagos native rodents have received scientists' attention ever since Darwin collected the first specimen, until recently big gaps existed in the information available on this diverse island fauna. It is likely that some surprises still remain. However, recent studies have greatly broadened our understanding of the origin and radiation of these endemic Galápagos mammals. To date seven islands are known to have each harbored 1 to 3 species of native rats. Researchers agree that these taxa belong to three distinct groups, each with its own history.

The native rats found on San Cristóbal and Santa Fé were initially classified as 2 endemic species of the genus *Oryzomys*, an extremely diverse group of small rats occurring in North, Central, and South America. The question of whether or not the two forms were actually separate species can not now be resolved by means of breeding tests, because one of the two, *O. galapagoensis* (San Cristóbal), is extinct. However, Patton and Hafner (in press) used a large set of quantitative characters to compare the two. Because the holotype of *O. galapagoensis* (a specimen in the British Museum) fell well within the range occupied by *O. bauri* (Santa Fé), these researchers concluded that the two Galápagos *Oryzomys* were probably different island populations of the same species.

Because the Santa Fé *Oryzomys* still survives, it has been possible to follow several lines of evidence in order to deduce the nearest relative of this endemic Galápagos mammal. Gardner and Patton (1976) found a mainland *Oryzomys* (*O. xantheolus*) whose chromosomes very closely matched those of *O. bauri*. Patton and Hafner (in press) found a genetic similarity of 86% between these 2 species, based on an electrophoretic analysis using 22 loci. They also found the 2 species to be hardly distinguishable morphologically. These workers have therefore concluded that the Galápagos *Oryzomys* stem from a relatively recent colonization of the islands, perhaps even from an introduction of *O. xantheolus* by aboriginal sailors within the last several hundred years!

A second group of Galápagos rodents, while clearly related to *Oryzomys*, are distinctive enough to have prompted the naming of a new endemic genus, *Nesoryzomys*. The chromosomal studies of Gardner and Patton (1976) and the genetic and morphological analyses by Patton and Hafner (in press) have provided overwhelming support for classifying these species as a genus endemic to the archipelago. Seven island populations of *Nesoryzomys* rats have now been found (Table 15.1). Two of these are very recent discoveries. In 1980, D.W. Steadman found remains of a small, apparently-undescribed species of *Nesoryzomys* in two lava tubes on Isabela. This exciting find clears up the long-standing mystery of how *Nesoryzomys* rats could have apparently reached Fernandina from the central islands without first establishing on the intervening island of Isabela. Meanwhile, in 1979, Hutterer and Hirsch described a new species of *Nesoryzomys* from a large series of small rat skulls found in fresh owl pellets on Fernandina. This evidence of a small *Nesoryzomys* coexisting with the larger *N. narboroughi* (paralleling the *N. darwini*/*N. indefessus* pair on Santa Cruz) prompted Hutterer and Hirsch to hypothesize that other *Nesoryzomys* species pairs are yet to be found (on Santiago, for example, where only *N. swarthi* is known).

It may be that the entire *Nesoryzomys* complex involves populations of just two species. Patton and Hafner's analysis (in press) of the 4 taxa known before 1979 demonstrated the distinctiveness of *N. darwini*, but showed a close similarity among the remaining three named species. Patton and Hafner therefore recommended that these large *Nesoryzomys* be considered island races of a single species (which receives the name *N. indefessus*). It would be very interesting to determine the relationships of the two most recently-discovered *Nesoryzomys* by a similar morphological analysis.

Also resulting from Patton and Hafner's study of oryzomine relationships was evidence suggesting the origin of the *Nesoryzomys* group. One morphological analysis indicated a link between the four *Nesoryzomys* and the *Oryzomys xantheolus*-*O. bauri* pair. Based on this similarity, Patton and Hafner hypothesized that the ancestral stock for *Nesoryzomys* was related to *O. xantheolus* and existed on the arid coast of Peru and Chile. While they hypothesize the same origin for the Galápagos *Oryzomys*, their evidence points to a much earlier immigration to Galápagos for *Nesoryzomys*. The genetic difference between *N. narboroughi* and *O. xantheolus* suggests that *Nesoryzomys* diverged from *Oryzomys* stock approximately 3–3.5 million years ago.

The third kind of endemic Galápagos rat, perhaps best described as the 'giant rat', was only discovered very recently. Among the bones found in a cave in the Santa Cruz highlands, Niethammer (1964) discovered a jawbone, scapula, and legbone of a muskrat-sized rodent. This rat has subsequently been named *Megaoryzomys curioi* (Lenglet and Coppois, 1979, cited in Steadman and Ray, in press), a member of a new rodent genus endemic to Galápagos. Since 1962 much more material, including several excellent skulls, has been collected from owl caves and collapsed lava tubes on Santa Cruz in sites ranging from the coast to about 200 m altitude. In addition, remains of a *Megaoryzomys* (species not yet determined) have been found on Isabela. After comparing *M. curioi* to members of many neotropical genera, Steadman and Ray (in press) concluded that the closest relative to *Megaoryzomys* is the South American cricetine genus *Thomasomys*, which

Table 15.1. Summary of existing historical records for the native rodents of the Galápagos Islands.

Species	Island	History	Current Status	Black Rats on Island?
Oryzomys bauri[1]	Santa Fé	First collected in 1891 (Allen, 1892).	Abundant 10,000–100,000 (D.B. Clark, 1980)	NO
Oryzomys galapagoensis[1]	San Cristóbal	First collected by Darwin (in 1835), who found it abundant along the coast (Waterhouse, 1839, cited in Orr, 1966); not reported since.	EXTINCT	YES First collected in 1898 (Heller, 1904).
Nesoryzomys indefessus[2]	Baltra	Collected in 1898–9 (Heller, 1904) and 1905 (Slevin, 1931).	EXTINCT	YES Probably present during World War II, and possibly earlier (no records).
	Santa Cruz	Collected in 1897 (Thomas, 1899, cited in Orr, 1966), 1898–9 (Heller, 1904), 1929 (Osgood, 1929, cited in Orr, 1966), and 1934 (1 specimen; Patton and Hafner, in press).	EXTINCT Very few left by late 1934 (Rambech, 1971—see text).	YES Abundant in late 1934 (Rambech, 1971—see text). Collected in 1935 (Chapin, 1935).
Nesoryzomys darwini	Santa Cruz	Collected in 1906 (Orr, 1938), 1929 (Osgood, 1929, cited in Orr, 1966), and 1930 (collected by Chapin; see Patton and Hafner, in press).	EXTINCT Apparently very few or none left by late 1934 (Rambech, 1971—see text).	YES Abundant in late 1934 (Rambech, 1971). Collected in 1935 (Chapin, 1935).
Nesoryzomys swarthi[2]	Santiago	Collected only in 1905–6 (Orr, 1938).	EXTINCT	YES First collected by Darwin in 1835 (Waterhouse, 1839, cited in Orr, 1966).
Nesoryzomys narboroughi[2]	Fernandina	First collected in 1899 (Heller, 1904).	At least locally abundant. No population estimate for the island.	NO
Nesoryzomys fernandinae	Fernandina	Known only from remains in fresh owl pellets (Hutterer and Hirsch, 1979).	No data.	NO
Nesoryzomys sp.	Isabela	Never trapped or seen alive. Known only from subfossil remains discovered in 1980 (Steadman, 1981).	EXTINCT	YES (Possibly not relevant).
Megaoryzomys curioi	Santa Cruz	Never trapped or seen alive. Known only from subfossil remains recovered since 1962–3 (Niethammer, 1964; Steadman and Ray, in press).	EXTINCT	Probably not relevant.
Megaoryzomys sp.	Isabela	Never trapped or seen alive. Known only from subfossil remains found in 1968 and 1980 (Steadman and Ray, in press).	EXTINCT	Probably not relevant.

[1] These two forms probably belong in a single species (Patton and Hafner, in press).
[2] These three forms are considered a single species by Patton and Hafner (in press).

belongs to a different tribe from that of the other Galápagos rodents. Thus this Galápagos rat genus must have originated from yet a third invasion of the archipelago by a mainland rodent.

How recently did the giant rats live in Galápagos? No one has ever seen one alive, even though it would have been difficult to miss. Scientific expeditions have collected on Santa Cruz since the late 1800's. Even if *Megaoryzomys* were shy, nocturnal, and too big for any of the collectors' traps, it is difficult to believe such an animal could have been left undiscovered by the colonists, who arrived in the early 1900's. Similarly, Isabela has been inhabited since the late 1800's. Thus, it seems likely that the Galápagos giant rats have been extinct for quite some time. It would be very interesting to obtain radio-carbon age determinations for deposits containing *Megaoryzomys* remains. Meanwhile, more work will be needed to resolve such questions as whether the Isabela *Megaoryzomys* were of a different species, and whether this genus once occurred on other islands.

15.3.2. Demise of native rats

Most of the Galápagos native rodents are now extinct. Five of the nine known island populations of *Nesoryzomys* and *Oryzomys* have disappeared since 1835 (four were lost in this century). Brosset (1963) and Niethammer (1964) both noted the strong circumstantial evidence linking these extinctions to the introduction of black rats (*Rattus rattus*), which were brought into the Galápagos on ships. Black rats are present on all islands which have lost native rats, and they have not yet reached the two islands (Fernandina and Santa Fé) where native rats remain (Table 15.1).

The most detailed information exists for the species replacement on Santa Cruz, where two *Nesoryzomys* species were lost. Both *N. indefessus* and *N. darwini* were collected in Conway Bay and Academy Bay as late as 1929. An early Santa Cruz settler, Anders Rambech, recalled that the native rats were abundant from the coast to the wet summit during the time between his arrival on Santa Cruz in 1926 and his departure from Galápagos in early 1930; he saw no black rats during this period (unpublished interview by C. MacFarland, 1971). In April 1930 J.P. Chapin collected 14 *N. darwini* in the highlands of Santa Cruz. When Rambech returned to Santa Cruz in November 1934, he began to see black rats all over, from the coast to the highlands, and he never saw native rats again (the last known specimen of a Santa Cruz native rat is an *N. indefessus* collected in December, 1934). Brosset was told by early Santa Cruz settlers that black rats immediately became incredibly abundant and provoked the organization of anti-rat campaigns by the populace. When Chapin returned to Santa Cruz in March 1935, he caught only black rats at Conway Bay (on the uninhabited northwest coast), where both *Nesoryzomys* species had been caught just 6 years previously (Osgood, 1929, cited in Orr, 1966).

Why did the Galápagos native rats succumb after introductions of black rats? Brosset (1963) noted three possibilities: the black rats could have outcompeted the endemic rats for their food, they could have simply attacked the (generally smaller) native rodents, or they could have brought with them a disease or parasite to which the native rats had never been exposed. This third explanation would most reasonably account for the rapidity with which the Santa Cruz *Nesoryzomys* completely disappeared. An interesting anecdote comes from Brosset, who brought 14 captive *Oryzomys bauri* from Santa Fé to the Darwin Station on Santa Cruz, where black rats were abundant. Within a week of their arrival, all the native rats had died of an unidentified illness.

On Santiago the situation must have been more complicated. Darwin found black rats already on the island in 1835. Nevertheless, both *Nesoryzomys* and black rats were caught on the island 70 years later. Although this indicates that native rats could co-exist for decades with the introduced rats, the Santiago *Nesoryzomys* did disappear completely. None has been found since 1906. In 1974, David Clark and I ran traps from the coast to the top of Santiago, and we caught only black rats at all sites. Two years later we trapped on two small islands just off Santiago (Sombrero Chino and Bartolomé), in the hopes of encountering a remnant population of native rats. We found only black rats.

15.3.3. Ecology of the native rats

Although many of the Galápagos rats have disappeared, the persistence of 2 species has left an opportunity to study the ecological results of rodent evolution in these simple communities. Most information is available on the Santa Fé rat, *Oryzomys bauri*, largely from a long-term study by D.B. Clark (1980) and initial observations by Rosero Posso (1975) and Brosset (1963). *O. bauri* is a small reddish-brown rat, with the males about 30% bigger than females. Two remarkable qualities of this species, in the opinion of anyone who has stayed on Santa Fé, are its fearlessness towards humans and a tendency to gnaw any unfamiliar object within reach—plastic, tents, and people included (these features of *O. bauri* behaviour make camping on the island an exercise in human ingenuity).

The Santa Fé rat is primarily crepuscular/nocturnal, venturing out from under shrubs and other cover as dusk approaches. Occasionally individuals are out and active during the day. Tjitte de Vries (1976) found *O. bauri* to be a fairly frequent prey item brought to the nest by Galápagos hawks, which hunt diurnally. After dark, the rats fall prey to Galápagos Short-eared Owls. Several times David Clark and I saw these owls come into our camp, catch a rat, and fly off with it.

Like their mainland relatives, the Santa Fé *Oryzomys* are omnivorous, eating a variety of plant and animal foods. From direct observation and a few stomach and fecal analyses, we found them eating principally grass seeds (*Cenchrus* and *Panicum*). Also eaten were fleshy fruits and their seeds (*Castela, Opuntia, Physalis, Cordia, Lantana*), stems of the coastal shrub, *Cryptocarpus*, and arthropods (caterpillars, grasshoppers, and others). Brosset observed them eating remains of fish left by fishermen; scavenging along the shore could provide an important part of the diet for the coastal rats.

In his study of *Oryzomys bauri*'s population ecology, D.B. Clark (1980) found that the rats are closely tied to the seasonal rains. They breed for only a few months a year, after the hot season rains have caused the island to become green and comparatively lush. The rats also seem to adjust their litter size to the amount of rainfall, which is probably closely related to food availability. During the months of more abundant food, *O. bauri* build up fat reserves. These reserves must increase the rats' ability to survive the ensuing months of the *garúa* season, when most Santa Fé woody plants are dry and leafless, and the annuals are dead. D.B. Clark found most adult rats lost weight during these months. Nevertheless, this species must have adapted well to its desert island. Two of the rats in the study lived to be at least two-years-old, and over a third of the individuals lived at least a year. In population studies of *Oryzomys* species elsewhere, almost no rats were found alive after a year. The Santa Fé native rat also turned out to be exceptional for the stability of its populations, in spite of the high inter-year variability in hot season rainfall. Using the population numbers obtained from different habitats on the island, D.B. Clark estimated that the total population size of *O. bauri* was between 10,000 and 100,000 in 1976.

As D.B. Clark (1980) noted, it is likely that this species' numbers are now increasing. He found that the rats' population levels in different habitats were correlated with the density of vegetation present. Since 1971, when goats were exterminated from Santa Fé, the vegetation has been increasing (the goats had devastated the island's plant cover). Thus, the outlook for *O. bauri* is quite good.

Because nearly all the *Nesoryzomys* island populations are extinct, little information exists on their biology. It is likely that all of them exhibited the apparent fearlessness and curiosity toward humans that characterizes *O. bauri*. Present-day campers on Fernandina often give up and leave their tent doors open, in order to keep the rats from chewing their way in. Because they are the only remaining *Nesoryzomys*, the Fernandina rats afford the only chance for an intensive study of any member of this endemic group. Fortunately, such work has begun. C.W. Eshelman has studied a coastal population of *N. narboroughi* for an eight-month-period, and has obtained data on longevity, home range, and breeding. He also has observed these rats being taken by Galápagos Hawks and by a Barn Owl (Eshelman, pers. comm.). Now that evidence exists of the presence of a second species on Fernandina, further intensive study of the island's *Nesoryzomys* will be particularly interesting.

15.4. Conservation

By introducing black rats to Galápagos, humans have caused the demise of most of the archipelago's endemic rodents. It is imperative that the surviving species be protected from a similar fate. Thus, all necessary safeguards should be maintained against the accidental introduction of any exotic animals, particularly black rats, on Fernandina and Santa Fé.

References

Allen, J.A. (1892) On a small collection of mammals from the Galápagos Islands, collected by Dr. G. Baur. *Bull. Amer. Mus. Nat. Hist.*, **4**, 47–50.

Brosset, A. (1963) Statut actuel des mammifères des îles Galapagos. *Mammalia*, **27**, 323–338.

Chapin, J.P. (1935) Unpublished journal, Astor Expedition and Templeton Crocker Expedition. Original at American Museum of Natural History, New York.

Clark, D.B. (1980) Population ecology of an endemic neotropical island rodent: *Oryzomys bauri* of Santa Fé Island, Galapagos, Ecuador. *J. Anim. Ecol.*, **49**, 185–198.

de Vries, Tj. (1976) Prey selection and hunting methods of the Galápagos Hawk, *Buteo galapagoensis*. *Le Gerfaut – De Giervalk*, **66**, 3–42.

Gardner, A.L., and J.L. Patton. (1976) Karyotypic variation in oryzomyine rodents (Cricetinae) with comments on chromosomal evolution in the neotropical cricetine complex. *Occas. Papers Mus. Zool., Louisiana State Univ.*, **49**, 1–48.

Heller, E. (1904) Mammals of the Galapagos Archipelago, exclusive of the Cetacea. *Proc. Calif. Acad. Sci. ser. 3*, **3**, 233–249.

Hutterer, R., and U. Hirsch. (1979) Ein neuer *Nesoryzomys* von der Insel Fernandina, Galápagos (Mammalia, Rodentia). *Bonner Zoologische Beiträge*, **30**, (3–4), 276–283.

Niethammer, J. (1964) Contribution a la connaissance des mammifères terrestres de l'île Indefatigable (= Santa Cruz), Galápagos. *Mammalia*, **28**, 593–606.

Orr, R.T. (1938) A new rodent of the genus *Nesoryzomys* from the Galapagos Islands. *Proc. Calif. Acad. Sci. ser. 4*, **23**, 03–306.

Orr, R.T. (1966) Evolutionary aspects of the mammalian fauna of the Galápagos. In *Proc. Symp. Galápagos International Scientific Project*. Edited by R.I. Bowman. Pages 276–281. University of California Press.

Patton, J.L., and M.S. Hafner. (in press). Biosystematics of the native rodents of the Galápagos Archipelago, Ecuador. In *Patterns of Evolution in Galápagos Organisms*. Edited by R.I. Bowman, M. Berson and A.E. Leviton. San Francisco. American Association for the Advancement of Science, Pacific Division.

Rosero Posso, E. (1975) Peso, longitudes de cola y perineo y forma de vida de la rata endémica de la Isla Santa Fé, *Oryzomys bauri* (Cricetidae). *Revista de la Universidad Católica (Quito, Ecuador)*, **3**,(8), 185–217.

Slevin, J.R. (1931) Log of the Schooner 'Academy' on a voyage of scientific research to the Galápagos Islands, 1905–1906. *Occas. Papers Calif. Acad. Sci.*, **17**, 1–162.

Steadman, D.W. (1981) Vertebrate fossils in lava tubes in the Galápagos Islands. In *Proceedings of the Eighth International Congress of Speleology, Volume II*. Edited by B.F. Beck. Pages 549–550. Americus. Georgia Southwestern College.

Steadman, D.W. and C.E. Ray. (in press) The relationships of *Megaoryzomys curioi*, an extinct cricetine rodent (Muroidea, Muridae) from the Galápagos Islands, Ecuador. *Smithsonian Contributions to Paleobiology No. 51.*

Thornton, I. (1971) *Darwin's Islands*. The Natural History Press, Garden City, New York.

CHAPTER 16

Introduced Fauna

H.N. HOECK

Formerly Director, Charles Darwin Research Station, 1978–80. Universität Konstanz, Fachbereich Biologie, Konstanz, West Germany

Contents

16.1.	Introduction	233
16.2.	Introduced Mammals	234
	16.2.1. Cattle	234
	16.2.2. Goats	237
	16.2.3. Donkeys and horses	238
	16.2.4. Pigs	239
	16.2.5. Dogs	239
	16.2.6. Cats	241
	16.2.7. Black rats	241
	16.2.8. Sheep, guinea pig and house mouse	242
16.3.	Introduced Birds	242
16.4.	Introduced Invertebrates	242
16.5.	Conservation Policy	243
16.6.	Acknowledgements	244
	References	245

'We may infer ... what havoc the introduction of any new beast of prey must cause in a country, before the instincts of the indigenous inhabitants have become adapted to the stranger's craft of power' (Charles Darwin in *The Voyage of the Beagle*).

16.1. Introduction

In a famous lecture to the British Association in 1866, Sir Joseph Hooker compared the flora and fauna of oceanic islands with those of continents (Turrill, 1964) and related the differences mainly to differences in the dispersal abilities of species. The organisms found on islands are usually those whose dispersal capabilities have allowed them to cross large stretches of water. Organisms which colonize islands are therefore protected from those species which are less adapted for transoceanic dispersal.

Since terrestrial mammals are very poorly adapted for crossing large expanses of water they are generally under-represented among insular faunas. New Zealand, for example, has only two native terrestrial mammals (both species of bat) but a wide variety of marine mammals (Gibb and Flux, 1973). In the Galápagos archipelago the native terrestrial mammal fauna consists of two bats and a small but interesting group of rodents (see Chapter 15). Thus, on islands, native plant and animals species have evolved without competition and predation pressure from most terrestrial mammals—a group which, on continents has successfully occupied all ecological niches. The abundance of seabirds breeding on islands, and the loss of dispersal ability among many insect and bird species living on islands, are largely due to the corresponding absence of ground predators (Holdgate, 1967, Williamson, 1981). Thus islands are extremely vulnerable to the effects of almost all introduced species.

Although man has always travelled with plants and animals, it is only in recent centuries that there have been large scale introductions, particularly of mammals, into oceanic islands. So far 33 different species of terrestrial mammals have been introduced into New Zealand, with devastating consequences for the native flora and fauna (Gibb and Flux, 1973). This is perhaps best illustrated by the sad story of the flightless bush wren (*Xenicus lyalli*) from New Zealand's Stephen Island (Carlquist, 1965). In 1894, the lighthouse keeper's cat brought to him all specimens of the wren, a previously unknown species. The cat thus discovered the species and, at the same time, exterminated it! Today, there are at least 15 mammal species living in a wild state in Hawaii, and about 40% of the islands' endemic birds are believed to be extinct (Berger, 1972).

The Galápagos Islands have a comparable record of species introductions, followed by habitat alteration and destruction on the major islands. In this chapter, I will discuss the introduced fauna and its effects, as well as the efforts that are being made to protect indigenous species.

16.2. Introduced Mammals

So far as we know 11 different mammal species have been introduced by man into the Galápagos Islands (Table 16.1). The two rodents were probably the first to reach the islands as 'tramp' species on board pirate and whaling ships. Seven of the other nine species, which were mainly introduced by the first settlers as domestic animals, have become feral. (Feral animals are descendents of domestic ancestors which exist in the wild as free-roaming and self-sustaining populations.)

The sudden influx of such continental animals as mammalian herbivores, omnivores and carnivores, which had behind them a long evolutionary history of successful exploitation of different niches, had a drastic and dramatic effect on the autochthonous biota of the major islands. Unfortunately, little so far has been recorded of these effects that introduced species have had (and still have) on the ecology of individual islands.

The only extensive long-term studies carried out have been on black rats and feral goats. More cursory studies have been made on feral dogs, and research is in progress on feral cats and on donkeys; no studies have been made on pigs, cattle, horses and house mice.

I will now summarize the information available about each species and, when possible, mention the effects that the species has had on other oceanic islands, such as New Zealand, Hawaii and Tristan da Cunha.

In Table 16.2 is given the general distribution of the introduced mammal species, their numbers when known, and the approximate dates of introduction and eradication.

16.2.1. Cattle

Domestic cattle together with other domestic mammals were introduced by the first settlers into Floreana in 1832 (Larrea, 1960). Settlements followed on San Cristóbal, southern Isabela and Santa Cruz, thus bringing domestic animals additionally to these islands. Cattle evidently became feral soon after their introduction, for

Table 16.1. The introduced fauna. Based on Black (1973) and Simkin
et al. (1972).

English Name	Mammals Spanish Name	Scientific Name
	Herbivores:	
Cow	Ganado vacuno	*Bos taurus*
Goat	Cabra, chivo	*Capra hircus*
Guinea pig	Cuy, cobayo	*Cavia porcellus*
Donkey (burro)	Burro, asno	*Equus asinus*
Horse	Caballo	*Equus caballus*
Sheep	Oveja, borrego	*Ovis aries*
	Omnivores:	
Black rat	Rata	*Rattus rattus*
House mouse	Ratón	*Mus musculus*
Pig	Chancho, cerdo, puerco	*Sus scofra*
	Carnivores:	
Dog	Perro	*Canis familiaris*
Cat	Gato	*Felis catus*
	Birds	
Fowl	Gallo	*Gallus domestica*
Pigeon	Paloma	*Columba livia*
	Insects	
Fire ant	Hormiga colorada	*Wasmannia auropunctata*

Rollo Beck of the 1905 California Academy of Sciences Expedition saw 'thousands' roaming wild on southern Isabela (Koford, 1966).

Within the last 10 years, feral cattle have disappeared from San Cristóbal, Santa Cruz and Floreana as a result of hunting and because of law enforcement by National Park authorities. Today, large domestic stocks are maintained on farms and some 200 to 500 animals are exported alive every other month to continental South America. On southern Isabela, there are between 10,000 and 30,000 head of cattle on the slopes of Volcán Cerro Azul (J. Gordillo and A. Tupiza, pers. comm.) (Fig. 16.1). In the 1960s, feral cattle were herded down to Iguana Cove and from there shipped to the continent. However, this enterprise soon failed, and today animals are only killed sporadically by fishermen and park wardens. Feral dogs have been reported to prey on the young cattle (Kruuk, 1979).

Figure 16.1. Feral cattle on Volcán Cerro Azul, Isabela.
(Photograph by H. Hoeck).

Table 16.2. Distribution of introduced mammals. Abbreviations are as follows: Island names with * are inhabited by man; − = absent; + = present; f. = feral; d. = domestic; i. = introduced (*the dates of introduction are approximative*); er. = eradicated (dates are exact); ? = unknown. Information on introduced mammals is based on Berg (1980); Black (1973); Clark and Clark (1976); Clark (1978); Clark (1980); Calvopiña and de Vries (1975); Eckhardt (1972); Hoeck (Annual Reports to the CDRS); Koford (1966); Kruuk (1979); R. Perry (pers. comm.).

Islands	Cattle	Goat	Guinea pig	Donkey	Horse	Sheep	Black rat	Mouse	Pig	Dog	Cat
Baltra*	−	f.(~200) i.1900	−	−	−	−	+	+	−	d	d
Bartolomé	−	−	−	−	−	−	i.? er.1976	−	−	−	−
Española	−	i.before 1905 er.1978	−	−	−	−	−	−	−	−	−
Floreana*	d. i.1832	f. i.1832	−	d,f i.1832	d.	−	+	+	d,f i.1832	d i.1832	d,f i.1832
Isabela (Northern)	−	f. i.after 1968	−	f.(~500) i.mid 1800	−	−	+	+	−	−	f.
Isabela (Southern)*	d.,f. i.after 1890	f. i.after 1897	−	d.,f. i.?	d.,f. i.after 1897	?	i.1891	+	d.,f. i.after 1897	d.,f. i.1868	d.,f.
Marchena	−	i.1967 er.1979	−	−	−	−	−	−	−	−	−
Pinta	−	i.1959 (~200)	−	−	−	−	−	−	−	−	−
Pinzón	−	−	−	−	−	−	i.1880	−	−	−	−
Rábida	−	i.1971 er.1971	−	−	−	−	−	−	−	−	−
San Cristóbal*	d. i.1847	f. i.1847	?	d.,f. i.1847	d. i.1847	?	+	+	d.,f. i.1847	d. i.1847	d.,f.
Santa Cruz*	d. i.after 1923	d.,f. i.after 1925	d. i.?	d.,f. i.?	d. i.?	d. i.?	i.prior to 1934	+	d.,f. i.late 1920s	d.,f. i.f.in 1868	d.,f. i.?
Santa Fé	−	i.1905 er.1971	−	−	−	−	−	−	−	−	−
Santiago	−	f. i.1813 (~100,000)	−	f. i.?	−	−	+ i.1835	+	f. i.before 1930	−	−
South Plaza	−	i.? er.1961	−	−	−	−	−	−	−	−	−

There has been no study of the impact of this large herbivore population on the vegetation of Cerro Azul. However, on Tristan da Cunha, Nouvelle Amsterdam and Auckland Islands, where cattle have also been introduced and become feral, population size is limited by food resources. As a result, vegetation has been greatly modified, with bush and tussock grasslands being replaced by low growing swards of aliens; this has led to substantial soil erosion (Holdgate, 1967). It is reasonable to assume that the feral cattle are having a similar effect on the vegetation and soils of Cerro Azul, and that they compete for food especially with the tortoises. In years of extreme drought, domestic cattle populations on various Galápagos Islands have been reduced, suggesting that in the feral population mortality is highest probably also in these dry years.

There are large domestic and semi-feral herds on Sierra Negra, Isabela, where the sale of cattle is second only to tourism as a source of income. The breed is likely to improve as a result of an artificial insemination programme begun in 1979. Also, since cattle on Galápagos do not carry most of the diseases and parasites found in continental herds, they might become an even more important source of income for local farmers.

16.2.2. Goats

The first report of goats in the Galápagos dates from the 17th century when the Viceroy of Peru ordered that dogs be released on Santiago to kill animals that it was believed were providing a source of meat for British pirates (Hagen, 1949). However, there is no mention of goats in ships' logs of the period, so there must be some doubt as to the authenticity of this account. In 1813, Captain D. Porter of the U.S. frigate *Essex*, released goats on Santiago, and, in 1906, Rollo Beck transferred four animals from Baltra to the same island (Slevin, 1931 and 1959). On Floreana, San Cristóbal, southern Isabela and Santa Cruz goats were probably introduced, together with cattle, by the first settlers. When Charles Darwin visited Floreana in 1835 he observed large numbers of feral goats and pigs.

The 1905 California Academy of Sciences Expedition reported feral goats on the small islands of Baltra, Santa Fé and Española (Slevin, 1931). Although it is usually believed that goats were introduced to Pinta about 1959, some fishermen have reported introducing them as early as 1954 (M. Cifuentes pers. comm.). Goats were taken to Marchena and Rábida in 1971. A small number of feral goats from southern Isabela succeeded in crossing the rugged lava fields of Istmo Perry to reach Volcán Alcedo sometime after 1968.

The impact of goats on island vegetation is well-documented. According to Holdgate (1966), they have been the primary cause of destruction of vegetation on subtropical islands (whereas sheep have been the most destructive on temperate islands). St. Helena is a good example. In the 16th century, this island was covered with luxuriant forest, whereas today only small patches survive around the highest summits. Much of the native fauna has vanished, and soil erosion is a continuing problem.

On several New Zealand islands, forests have been converted into grasslands because of the catholic feeding behaviour of goats (Gibb and Flux, 1973). On Santa Catalina Island, off the Californian coast, feral goats are reported to be seasonally opportunistic feeders. Because they travel typically in single file, 1% to 2% of the land is occupied by trails and thus eroded (Coblentz, 1977 and 1978).

In New Zealand, goats breed continuously throughout the year. Females begin breeding at the age of 6 months, and 52% of all conceptions are twins (Rudge, 1969). Rudge and Smith (1970) calculated that if a goat population were reduced by 80% it could still reach 90% of its original size in just 4 years, and double in size every second year.

Similar observations have been made on the feral goats of several Galápagos islands. L.H. Calvopiña, who spent the period February 1974 to February 1975 studying the feeding and breeding ecology of goats on Santiago, reports that there are about 100,000 animals on the island and that their browsing has turned highland forests into pampalike grasslands (Fig. 16.2). *Scalesia pedunculata*, *Zanthoxylum fagara* and *Acnistus ellipticus* have been prevented from propagating, and such trees as remain are very old.

On small islands, such as Española and Santa Fé, the effects of goats on the vegetation are particularly noticeable because cactus (*Opuntia*) stands have been widely destroyed. Weber (1971) described vividly the gradual destruction of the vegetation of Pinta caused by the descendants of one male and two female goats: by 1970 these 'were common all over the island, invading even the humid zone; previously this area had dense undergrowth but it now resembles English parkland'. In 1968, the population was estimated to number between 3000 and 5000, and by 1973 this had increased to about 30,000. However, intensive hunting during the 1970s brought the population down to about 200 individuals (Berg, 1980).

Dunson (1974) observed feral goats on Española drinking sea water when fresh water was not available, suggesting that the animals are exceptionally adaptable under adverse conditions. Because they cause the deterioration of woody plant communities, they have a marked impact on indigenous fauna. Invertebrates and birds, which are dependent on this vegetation disappear, and native herbivores such as tortoises and land iguanas have to compete for food. Feral goats are believed to have contributed to the extinction or reduction of some races of tortoise and land iguana (MacFarland *et al.*, 1974).

Although feral pigs prey on new born kids, goat numbers are regulated mainly by food availability, as has been recorded for a number of ungulate species elsewhere (Sinclair and Norton-Griffiths, 1979). Goats are

Figure 16.2. The effects of goats on the vegetation of Santiago. Fenced area has remained ungrazed for about 3 years; vegetation there is dense and composed mainly of *Scalesia*. (Photograph by H. Hoeck).

regularly hunted by the inhabitants of Santa Cruz, San Cristóbal, Floreana and southern Isabela; park wardens, fishermen and boat crews also hunt them on Santiago. Because feral goat populations are so large on these islands, hunting has only a limited effect on overall numbers. However, the eradication programme run by the National Park Service and the Charles Darwin Research Station succeeded in eliminating goats from the small island of South Plaza in 1961, from Santa Fé and Rábida in 1971, and from Española and Marchena in 1978 and 1979 respectively.

16.2.3. Donkeys and horses

There are large feral donkey populations on Floreana, Santa Cruz, San Cristóbal, Santiago, southern Isabela and on Volcán Alcedo, northern Isabela. Although donkeys are found in all vegetation zones, in the drier months of the year they concentrate in the highlands where conditions are more humid. Fowler (1980) estimated the population of Volcán Alcedo to be between 500 and 700, and there is probably a similar number of animals on each of the other islands. Flying over Alcedo in 1978, I observed a dense trail pattern—evident signs that donkeys open up the vegetation and contribute considerably to soil erosion. Tortoises and land iguanas probably have to compete for food with donkeys, and their nesting areas may be trampled or used as wallowing places.

The only predator of feral donkeys is man, who, on the inhabited islands, captures young animals for domestication. The park wardens hunt donkey irregularly.

Domestic horses are found on all settled islands but there is only one feral herd, on Sierra Negra in southern

Isabela. This herd, which consists of 300 to 500 individuals (A. Tupiza pers. comm.), is concentrated on the open grassy pampas in the highlands. During dry months the animals become extremely thin, when mortality may be high due to starvation. Farmers herd the feral horses regularly and catch juveniles for domestication.

16.2.4. Pigs

Because pigs are omnivorous they not only damage vegetation but devastate bird populations by preying on their eggs. Mauritius dodos (*Raphus cucullatus*) became extinct in 1681, partly because feral pigs (introduced into the island by convicts) destroyed their eggs (Frankel and Soulé, 1981). Unfortunately, nothing is known about the biology of feral pigs in Galápagos. None the less, the damage they have caused to the native flora and fauna is obvious enough. Pigs regularly dig up and eat the eggs of tortoises and land and marine iguanas on Santa Cruz, San Cristóbal, southern Isabela and Santiago. Together with feral dogs, they are probably responsible for the extermination of land iguanas, and for reducing the numbers of tortoises, on Santiago. A particularly striking example of their destructive tendencies can be observed every year on the sandy beaches of Santiago, southern Isabela and Santa Cruz, where green turtles (*Chelonia mydas*) come to lay their eggs. On some beaches pigs dig up every single nest and consume the eggs. Some individuals have been observed eating the eggs as they are laid (Hurtado, 1979)!

Feral pigs uproot plants and prey on insect larvae and the eggs of lizards and snakes. Research in New Zealand has shown that pigs are relatively sedentary, and that they are more likely to be vectors of contagious diseases than other feral mammals (Martin, 1972 and 1975). On Santiago, feral pigs are heavily infested with jigger fleas (*Tunca penetrans*), which also infect man.

Although feral pigs are hunted in various areas by farmers, fishermen and wardens, there has yet to be a systematic eradication campaign. Pigs are surprisingly intelligent, have a high reproductive rate, and, in contrast to goats, are crepuscular to nocturnal in habit, thus making eradication extremely difficult, if not impossible, to achieve (Berg, 1980).

16.2.5. Dogs

Dogs have been introduced into many oceanic islands, but it is only in Galápagos that feral populations have been reported to cause problems for native fauna. Here dogs have adapted to the harsh environment of bare lava fields, and they continue to contribute to the decline of several endemic animal species. Feral dogs have recently been studied (Kruuk, 1979, Kruuk and Snell, 1981), and the following summarizes what we know of their biology.

Domestic dogs were brought by the first settlers to Galápagos and are found on all inhabited islands. Most farms have two or more and in the villages of Puerto Ayora and Villamil nearly every second household has a dog. Farm dogs are used for hunting pigs and goats.

Dog populations became feral following the abandonment of settlements and convict colonies. Today, animals are found on Santa Cruz (where there are between 25 and 70 individuals) and southern Isabela (200 to 500 animals). They have been present continuously on southern Isabela since the last century, but on Santa Cruz they disappeared around 1930 and re-established about 1970.

Farmers eliminated populations on San Cristóbal and Floreana by poisoning and shooting in the early 1970s.

The Santa Cruz dogs are similar in many ways to the domestic population, but on southern Isabela they differ markedly from the domestic stock in colour and size. Animals of coastal populations are mostly white with some dark brown or black patches (Figs 16.3 and 16.4), while dogs in the highlands of Cerro Azul and Sierra Negra are predominantly dark in colour.

Coastal dogs move in packs with a mean size of 2.6 animals, while in the highlands a pack size averages 7.7 animals; this difference is probably related to prey type and size. Highland dogs prey mainly on feral cattle, while coastal dogs feed mostly on marine iguanas, but also on fur seals, blue-footed boobies and penguins. Feral dogs also dig up nests of the marine iguana and eat their eggs.

Coastal dogs are most active after sunset and before sunrise, spending the hot hours of the day sheltering in lava holes (Fig. 16.4). In certain places feral dogs consume more than 15% of the marine iguana population. They prefer animals larger than 90 cm, most of which are males. This preference can be explained by the behaviour of iguanas: large animals allow predators to approach closely before they turn to flee. Furthermore, at night they usually do not hide in crevices as smaller iguanas do, but sleep on open lava rocks where they are easy prey. In parts of southern Santa Cruz, feral dogs have completely eradicated marine iguanas over the past few years. In the mid 1970s, the land iguana populations of Santa Cruz and southern Isabela declined rapidly due to dog predation; a few individuals were saved by maintaining a captive breeding population at the Darwin Station.

On Santa Cruz, feral dogs are found in coastal regions, not in the highlands. This is probably because of the presence of domestic dogs in the highlands (where they destroy nests of the dark-rumped petrel; see page 204).

Experiences on Floreana and San Cristóbal has shown that feral dog populations can be eliminated. Recently an eradication campaign was started in southern Isabela, because of the danger that dogs will succeed—as goats have—in crossing the lava fields of Istmo Perry and thus spread into northern Isabela. It is worth underlining here the importance of northern Isabela (20% of the area of the national park), with its large populations of tortoises, land iguanas, flightless cormorants, penguins and fur seals; it is a key area that has received too little attention in the past.

Figure 16.3. Feral dogs at Caleta Webb, southern Isabela. (Photograph by H. Hoeck).

Figure 16.4. Adult and half grown feral dog on southern Isabela. Animals seek shelter in caves and holes in the lava during the day. (Photograph by H. Hoeck).

16.2.6. Cats

On oceanic islands where they have become established, feral cats have caused damage to populations of insects and small birds (Aarde, 1979, Gibb and Flux, 1973, Holdgate, 1966). Very little is known of the effects cats have had on the fauna of Santa Cruz, San Cristóbal, Floreana and Isabela, although they are widespread on these islands.

Preliminary faecal analysis studies by Kruuk (1979) have shown that black rats are by far the most important source of food for feral cats, followed by small birds, insects, crustaceans and lizards.

16.2.7. Black rats

Formerly the Galápagos archipelago had a number of native rodent species (see table on page 228). Today, endemic rat species survive on Santa Fé and Fernandina—both islands into which the black rat has not been introduced; on San Cristóbal, Santa Cruz, Santiago and Baltra endemic rats disappeared soon after black rats were introduced.

The most detailed information so far available for an introduced mammal is on the black rat. Drs. D.A. and D.B. Clark studied several aspects of its ecology, mainly on Santa Cruz and Santiago. Rats are omnivores, feeding on a wide variety of plant and animal foods, with plant material averaging 83% of the diet by volume. Dietary composition varies however with age. Young, growing rats consume more than 30% animal material, whereas adults eat less than 20% animal matter. There are also different food preferences between the sexes.

Rats have had a devastating effect on the Pinzón race of giant tortoise. They were established on this small island around 1880 and each year since then have killed almost every tortoise hatchling that emerges from its nest. MacFarland *et al.* (1974) calculated that in a period of 10 years between 7000 and 19,000 hatchlings were produced, but only a single one-year old tortoise was found on the entire island!

Black rats have also contributed to the decline of the dark-rumped petrel in the Galápagos Islands.

Black rats are found in all vegetation zones. On smaller islands (with an area less than 2 km^2), population densities tend to be higher than in similar habitats on large islands. This is probably because marine organic material washed on to beaches provide an additional food source. Population size is dependent mainly on the availability of plant material, which depends in turn on rainfall. Breeding, too, is dependent on rainfall, and is thus restricted to the wet season. The main predators of black rats are the Galápagos hawk, barn and short-eared owls and cats. It is very unlikely that black rat populations will ever be controlled, let alone eliminated. However, on the small island of Bartolomé just off the coast of Santiago, rats were successfully exterminated in 1976 by a concentrated trapping and poisoning campaign.

16.2.8. Sheep, guinea pig and house mouse

There are a few domestic sheep on Santa Cruz and possibly also on isolated farms on San Cristóbal and southern Isabela. Sheep are unlikely to become feral and thereby pose a problem for the native biota; feral sheep have only been successful on southern ocean islands with a cold climate (Holdgate, 1966).

Domestic guinea pigs are maintained on farms on Santa Cruz, and possibly also on San Cristóbal and southern Isabela. It is likely that some animals have become feral, in which case they must compete with black rats.

Nothing is known about the population densities of the house mouse or their effects on native biota.

16.3. Introduced Birds

Two domestic bird species, the fowl and the pigeon (see Table 16.1 for scientific names), have been introduced. There are fowl on all settled islands, but these have become feral only on Floreana. The effects of this population on the vegetation, fauna and soil is unknown. Puerto Ayora has several flocks of pigeons but so far these have shown no tendency to spread to other islands and become feral.

16.4. Introduced Invertebrates

Tourist and cargo ships regularly bring to the islands the foodstuffs and building materials that an increasingly wealthy population demands. Along with these goods so called tramp species reach the islands. For example, several frogs have been caught on Santa Cruz and southern Isabela. At least 3 species of alien earthworms have been present in soils on cultivated islands during the past 30 years. Arthropods, such as flies, cockroaches, moths and spiders, which hide in the cracks of timber or among clothes, slip in regularly. In addition, man is a good vector for several endo- and ectoparasites. These modes of introduction are extremely difficult to control and seldom documented.

Because it is such a pest and because its effects are so conspicuous, the fire ant is the only introduced invertebrate that has so far been studied in detail. These ants were introduced some time between 1910 and 1920 and are now found on all the cultivated islands. On Santa Cruz, their density increases with altitude, though they are not at present found in either the driest or wettest parts of the island. An indication of density figures has been given as from about 190 workers/m² in lowland areas to over 1150 workers/m² in Humid Zone vegetation (Guayasamín, 1977). Fire ants feed mostly on invertebrates, such as snails, insect larvae, grasshoppers, spiders, isopods and beetles as well as on native ants (Pazmiño, 1977). They are therefore probably responsible for the displacement of some native ant species. Unfortunately, fire ants are easily transported between islands with domestic foodstuffs. In 1975, a small population was discovered close to the landing beach on Santa Fé, but, thanks to a quick and effective poisoning and burning campaign, their establishment on this island was thwarted. Studies have been under way to find possible ways of reducing fire ant numbers and of preventing their dispersal to further islands.

16.5. Conservation Policy

'. . . nothing but incisive action by *this* generation can save a large proportion of now-living species from extinction within the next few decades' (O.H. Frankel and M.E. Soulé, 1979).

The Galápagos Islands provided the source of man's understanding of evolution, but if they are to provide an arena for continuing scientific endeavour in the future efforts must be intensified to conserve their unique biota.

Conservation work in the islands began in 1934 with the enactment by the Ecuadorian government of the first laws protecting certain native animal species from hunting or capture, and by declaring the islands of Española, Santiago, Pinzón, Santa Fé, Rábida, Seymour, Genovesa, Marchena, Pinta, Daphne, Wolf and Darwin 'Reserves and National Parks'. Two years later, a further law called for the protection generally of the flora and fauna of these islands and of Santa Cruz and northern Isabela. However, it was not until much later that the first technical officers arrived to manage the National Park (Chapter 18.1.5).

Detailed aspects of conservation work are discussed elsewhere and an attempt is made here only to underline the importance of programmes and studies aimed at elucidating the dangers of introduced species. Without such analyses it is impossible to assess fully the impact these aliens have on the Galápagos biota. Even then, alas, it has to be accepted that there are not ways of really ensuring that ships and aircraft do not bring new organisms to the islands. Ever present, for instance, are the fears of the spread of such species as the black rat and fire ant.

This being said, one can yet look back on some considerable successes in the fields of applied conservation and preservation. (By *conservation*, I mean those programmes aimed at the long-term maintenance of native communities under conditions which allow for their continuing evolution; while *preservation* programmes are aimed at individuals or groups which are so small that evolutionary changes are uncertain (see Frankel and Soulé, 1979)). For example, goats have been eradicated from five of the smaller islands, and their numbers on Pinta reduced sufficiently for native plant and animal communities to recover.

Another notable success has been saving races of giant tortoises by captive breeding programmes (page 149) and subsequently restocking populations in the wild. Where the population of an endemic race or species is reduced to a few individuals, as are the tortoises of Española and the land iguanas of Santa Cruz and southern Isabela, prolonged breeding programmes seem to be indicated—certainly at least until the present threats are removed. The unknown factor then becomes the extent to which genetic diversity is being limited and so impair the chances of long-term survival. Many long and careful studies are awaited to assess the true impact of man and his introduced animals on the native Galápagos biota. The conservation of these islands is an arduous and also a challenging enterprise, and one from which man can not only learn more about the past, but demonstrate his ability to live in harmony with a fragile and unique environment.

Figure 16.5.   Tree cacti (*Opuntia echios barringtonensis*) in the coastal zone of Santa Fé. Goats were successfully eliminated on this small arid island in 1971. (Photograph by T. de Vries).

16.6. Acknowledgements

I would like to thank Professor Dr. H. Markl for many helpful suggestions and for providing conducive atmosphere in which to write this paper. The writing of this chapter was made possible through a grant from the Alexander von Humboldt-Stiftung, for which I am most grateful. My thanks also go to Anne Moffat for revising the English and making useful comments and to my wife, Pia, for typing parts of the manuscript.

References

Aarde, R. van (1978) The cats of Marion Island; friend or foe? *Afr. Wildlife*, **32**,(6), 30–32.

Berger, A.J. (1972) The present status of the birds of Hawaii. Edited by E.A. Kay. *A Natural History of the Hawaiian Islands*. Pages 432–445. Univ. Press of Hawaii, Honolulu.

Berg, F.C. von (1980) Concise Report on GOATEX '80. Unpublished report. Inst. f. Wildbiologie u. Jagdkunde, Göttingen.

Black, J. (1973) *Galápagos Archipiélago del Ecuador*. Imprenta Europa, Quito.

Calvopiña, L.H. and de Vries, T. (1975) Estructura de la población de cabras salvajes (*Capra hircus L.*) y los daños causados en la vegetación de la Isla San Salvador, Galápagos. *Revista Univ. Catolica*, **3**,(8), 219–241.

Carlquist, S. (1965) *Island Life, a Natural History of the Islands of the World*. The Natural History Press, New York.

Clark, D.B. and Clark, D.A. (1976). Informe sobre el programa de control de la introducida rata negra, *Rattus rattus*, en la isla Bartolomé. *Noticias de Galápagos*, **24**, 2–23.

Clark, D.A. (1978) Black rat (*Rattus rattus*) feeding ecology in the Galápagos Islands, Ecuador. Unpublished Ph.D. Thesis, Univ. of Wisconsin, Madison, Wisconsin.

Clark, D.B. (1978) Population biology of two rodents of the Galápagos Islands, *Rattus rattus* and *Oryzomys bauri*. Unpublished Ph.D. Thesis. Univ. of Wisconsin, Madison, Wisconsin.

Clark, D.A. (1980) Age- and sex-dependent foraging strategies of a small mammalian omnivore. *J. Anim. Ecol.*, **49**, 49–563.

Coblentz, B.E. (1977) Some range relationships of feral goats on Santa Catalina Island, California. *J. Range. Manage.*, **30**, 415–419.

Coblentz, B.E. (1978) The effects of feral goats (*Capra hircus*) on island ecosystems. *Biol. Conserv.*, **13**, 279–286.

Darwin, C. (1845) *Journal of Researches into the natural history and geology of the countries visited during the voyage of H.M.S. Beagle round the world*. 2nd. edition, Ward, Lock Co, London.

Dunson, W.A. (1974) Some aspects of salt and water balance of feral goats from arid islands. *Amer. J. Physiol.*, **226**, 662–669.

Eckhardt, R.C. (1972) Introduced Plants and Animals in the Galápagos Islands. *Bio Science*, **22**,(10), 585–590.

Fowler, L. (1980) Donkey-work on Alcedo. *Noticias de Galápagos*, **32**, 20–22.

Frankel, O.H. and Soulé, M.E. (1981) *Conservation and Evolution*. Cambridge Univ. Press, Cambridge.

Gibb, J.A. and Flux, J.E.C. (1973) Mammals. G.R. Williams Ed. *The Natural History of New Zealand*. Pages 334–371. Reed, Wellington.

Guayasamin, C. (1977) Distribución de la hormiga colorada *Wasmania auropunctata* en la Isla Santa Cruz, Galápagos. *Revista Univ. Católica*, **5**,(16), 45–57.

Hagen, V.W. von (1949) *Ecuador and the Galápagos Islands*. Univ. Okla. Press, Norman.

Holdgate, M.W. (1967) The Influence of introduced species on the ecosystems of temperate oceanic islands. In: *Towards a new Relationship of Man and Nature in Temperate Lands*. Part III, Changes due to introduced species. Pages 151–176. *IUCN Publication New Series*, **9**, 259 pp.

Hurtado, M. (1979) Ecological study of the Green Turtle *Chelonia mydas agassizi* in the Galápagos Islands. Annual Report, Charles Darwin Research Station.

Koford, C.B. (1966) Economic Resources of the Galápagos Islands. In: *The Galápagos: Proceedings of the Symposia of the Galápagos International Scientific Project*. Edited by R.I. Bowman. Pages 286–290. Univ. Calif. Press, Berkeley and Los Angeles.

Kruuk, H. (1979) Ecology and control of feral dogs in Galápagos. Unpublished report, pp. 44. Institute of Terrestrial Ecology, Scotland.

Kruuk, H. and Snell, H. (1981) Prey selection by feral dogs from a population of marine iguanas (*Amblyrhynchus cristatus*). *J. of Appl. Ecology*, **18**, 197–204.

Larrea, C.M. (1960) *El Archipiélago de Colón (Galápagos)*. Casa de la Cultura Ecuatoriana, Quito.

MacFarland, C.G. *et al.* (1974). The Galápagos Giant Tortoises (*Geochelone elephantopus*). Part I: Status of the Surviving Populations. *Biol. Conserv.*, **6**,(2). 118–212.

Martin, J.T. (1972) Wild pigs, potential vectors of foot and mouth disease. *N.Z.J. Agric.*, **125**, 18–23.

Martin, J.T. (1975) Movement of feral pigs in North Canterbury, New Zealand. *J. Mammal.*, **56**, 914–915.

Pazmiño, O.E. (1977) Alimentación y actividad diaria de la hormiga colorada *Wasmannia auropunctata* en la Isla Santa Cruz, Galápagos. *Revista Univ. Católica*, **5**,(16), 59–70.

Rudge, M.R. (1969) Reproduction of feral goats (*Capra hircus L.*) near Wellington, New Zealand. *N.Z.J. Sci.*, **12**, 817–827.

Rudge, M.R. and Smith, T.J. (1970) Expected rate of increase of hunted populations of feral goats (*Capra hircus L.*) in New Zealand. *N.Z.J. Sci.*, **13**, 256–259.

Sinclair, A.R.E. and Norton-Griffiths, M. (1979) *Serengeti: Dynamics of an Ecosystem*. Chicago University Press, Chicago.

Simkin, T. *et al.* (1972) Galápagos science: 1972 status and needs. Report of Galápagos Sci. Conf. 87 pp. Washington D.C.

Slevin, J.R. (1931) Log of the schooner 'Academy'. *Occas. Papers Calif. Acad. Sci.*, **17**.

Slevin, J.R. (1959) The Galápagos Islands. A history of their exploration. *Occas. Papers Calif. Acad. Sci.*, **25**.

Turrill, W.B. (1964) *Joseph Dalton Hooker*. Nelson, London.

Weber, D. (1971) Pinta, Galápagos: une Ile à sauver. *Biol. Conserv.*, **4**, 8–12.

Williamson, M. (1981) *Island Populations*. Oxford Univ. Press, Oxford.

CHAPTER 17

Marine Environment and Protection

GERARD M. WELLINGTON

University of Houston, Marine Science Program, Galveston, Texas, USA.

Contents

17.1.	Introduction	247
17.2.	Major Marine Habitats	248
	17.2.1. Rocky shores	248
	17.2.2. Vertical rock walls	249
	17.2.3. Sandy beaches	250
	17.2.4. Mangroves	250
	17.2.5. Coral reefs	250
17.3.	Inter-Island Regionalism	254
17.4.	Biogeographic Distributions and Affinities	255
17.5.	Plan for Protection	259
17.6.	Acknowledgements	261
	References	261

17.1. Introduction

'Hosts of Sally-lightfoots were the most brilliant spots of colour above the water in these islands, putting to shame the dull, drab hues of the terrestrial organisms and hinting at the glories of colourful animal life beneath the surface of the sea.'

William Beebe (1924, *Galápagos: World's End*, p. 92).

The Galápagos Islands have long held the interest and fascination of terrestrially-orientated biologists. Less well-known and explored, however, is the surrounding marine environment. This environment supports, either directly or indirectly, many of the vertebrate species that make Galápagos so unusual. For example marine iguanas, flightless cormorants, penguins, other seabirds and pinnipeds derive their livelihood directly from the productive nearshore waters. Within the marine environment proper there exists a diversity of habitats (e.g. rocky shore, sandy beaches, mangrove lagoons, coral reefs) which harbor an unusual mixture of temperate, subtropical and tropical marine organisms. This unlikely assemblage, at an equatorial location, is largely due to the unique hydrographic conditions surrounding the islands. The convergence of distinctly different water masses and the establishment of their representative biota at a distant island location is, to my

G – Q

knowledge, unparalleled elsewhere in the world. Isolation has led to the formation of marine communities which appear to be structured and organized quite differently than their mainland counterparts. What little is known about these communities suggests that important insights into how insular marine communities function and evolve may be gained from further study here.

In this chapter I will attempt to describe briefly the major marine biotopes and present some interesting aspects which contrast these communities with their mainland counterparts. A review of our current knowledge concerning the biogeographic affinities of several major taxonomic groups is presented. Lastly, I will outline steps presently being taken by the Ecuadorian Government to insure protection of these nearshore waters. This protection is not only imperative for esthetic, educational and scientific reasons, but also because the Galápagos phenomenon itself is ultimately dependent on a healthy marine environment.

17.2. Major Marine Habitats

17.2.1. Rocky shores

Given the volcanic origin of these youthful islands it is not surprising that much of the shoreline in Galápagos is composed of hard rocky substrates which are best described by Herman Melville (1856, from *Las Encantadas*): 'In many places the coast is rock-bound, or more properly, clinker-bound tumbled masses of blackish or greenish stuff like the dross of an iron furnace, forming dark clefts and caves here and there.'

In spite of its barren appearance the rocky intertidal areas are actually quite diverse in marine life although most organisms are relegated to cryptic habitats (Hedgepeth, 1969; Houvenaghel and Houvenaghel, 1974). Tidal fluctuations are substantial (>3 m) despite the equatorial position. The indicator species here are as follows: supralittoral zone; the littorinid gastropod, *Nodilittorina galapagiensis*; midlittoral zone, the barnacle, *Tetraclita squamosa milleporosa*; infralittoral zone, the barnacle, *Megabalanus galapaganus* and sea urchins such as *Eucidaris thouarsii* and *Echinometra vanbrunti*. The intertidal region supports an assemblage, or guild, of algal grazers represented by grapsoid crabs, particularly the abundant *Grapsus grapsus*, marine iguanas, chitons and neritid gastropods. Major invertebrate predators are various crabs and the gastropod, *Purpura columellaris*. Suspension feeders are mainly cryptic under rocks and in crevices with the notable exception of barnacles and some sea cucumbers. At the lowest tide level encrusting red algae form a distinct border. At some locations macrophytic algae such as *Blossevillea galapagensis* or *Sargassum* spp. are abundant.

The extent and degree of intertidal zonation varies throughout the islands and is largely a function of wave exposure. For example, along the rugged wave-exposed shores of southern Isabela and western Fernandina foliose algal cover is high throughout the intertidal zone while barnacle densities are high. In contrast, both algal biomass and barnacle numbers are extremely low or absent on rocky substrates in protected embayments.

As is the case along mainland shores the depauperate nature of open rock surfaces appears to be maintained by intense grazing and predation activities. The organization of intertidal communities in Galápagos differs from those along continental shores. For example, a larger and more diverse guild of herbivorous molluscs are present along the mainland and are largely responsible for reduced algal growth (Menge and Lubchenco, 1981). In Galápagos such grazers as *Siphonaria*, limpets and neritids are conspicuously absent or few in number. Rather, one finds high densities of grapsoid crabs, particularly the Sally-lightfoot, *Grapsus grapsus*, and the enigmatic marine iguana, *Amblyrhynchus cristatus*. These organisms seem to fill the role of mainland herbivores and thus maintain low algal biomass. Where temperatures are periodically cool due to intense upwelling, and wave action extreme, the activities of mobile herbivores appears to be reduced and algal communities flourish. The relationships between cause and effect of these physical and biological interactions have not been fully investigated. The diversity of rocky habitats in Galápagos makes this an ideal site to conduct such research.

Equally interesting is the conspicuous absence of the high intertidal barnacle, *Chthamalus*. Houvenaghel and Houvenaghel (1974) have argued that these barnacles have not successfully become established because the black lava substrate is subject to intense heating during low water exposures. Its apparent absence on other isolated eastern Pacific islands such as Cocos (Hertlein, 1963; Bakus, 1975) and Malpelo (Birkeland *et al.*, 1975) suggests that low dispersal ability rather than temperature may be the major factor in this case.

At the lower end of the intertidal and extending into subtidal areas are the sea anemone, *Anthopleura dovii*, and sea fans, *Pacifigorgia*. As in the intertidal zone, grazing is also intense at most subtidal locations. Urchins common at the infralittoral zone become even more abundant in shallow water. Grazing fishes such as *Prionurus laticlavius* (surgeonfish) and *Scarus ghobban* (parrotfish) are ubiquitous and occur in large schools. Except for a few algal species which apparently concentrate noxious toxins, most subtidal algal species persist as closely-cropped mats veneering the rock substrate. Besides grazing fishes, the green turtle, *Chelonia mydas agassizii*, and the marine iguana are important herbivores in this system.

In shallow water, damselfish foster algal gardens which provides a refuge for some algal species. These gardens are used as food, nesting and shelter sites by the damselfish. The species most abundant in Galápagos are *Eupomacentrus beebei*, *E. arcifrons* and *Nexilosus latifrons*.

By and large the most common invertebrate on subtidal rock substrates is the sessile gastropod, *Hipponix pilosus*. This species is inconspicuous and often concealed by an overlying algal mat. Shallow water rocky communities are also characterized by an abundance of planktivorous fishes, most notably *Paranthias colonus*, *Chromis atrilobata*, and the passer angelfish, *Holacanthus passer*. Many of these species, especially the first two, are an important source of food for boobies, particularly the nearshore-feeding blue-footed booby, *Sula dactylatra* (Harris, 1969). Also, numerous small benthic dwelling fishes provide food for the flightless cormorant, *Nannopterum harrisi* (Harris, 1979). The Galápagos penguin, *Spheniscus mendiculus* thrive on schools of fish fry.

The Galápagos shark (*Carcharhinus galapagensis*), white-tip (*C. albimarginatus*) and hammerhead (*Sphyrna lewini*) are common and often very abundant here. This abundance may be due to the high biomass of other fish present and also to the absence of an intense fishery effort in the Islands. Perhaps because prey is abundant the sharks in Galápagos are not aggressive towards man.

17.2.2. Vertical rock walls

Of the approximately 68 small islets and rocks scattered throughout the archipelago many are bordered by steep escarpments which drop vertically to a depth of 100 m or more. These walls are only interrupted occasionally by ledges previously eroded by wave action at a time when sea level was lower. These vertical walls are restricted to offshore islands and thus constitute a unique insular habitat. Encrusting the substrate are a myriad of brightly-colored colonial and solitary invertebrates not found in abundance elsewhere in the islands. Superior space competitors such as rapidly growing sponges (*Verongia*), tube worms (*Salmacina*), ascidians (*Alphidium*, *Halocynthia*, *Polyantrocarpa*) and bryozoans (*Borgiola*, *Heteropora*) predominate, but also hydroids and ahermatypic corals (*Tubastraea*) are commonly found on the undersides of ledges and in crevices.

Black corals are also found in this habitat. Two species are extant in Galápagos waters: *Antipathes panamensis* and *A. galapagensis*, the latter endemic to Galápagos. The horny skeleton of both species is black but the living polyps of *A. galapagensis* are bright yellow and those of *A. panamensis* golden brown. Both forms are erect and bushy in habit and can reach up to 2 m in height. Unfortunately, recent exploitation by local entrepreneurs has led to a marked decline in population abundance over the last few years, particularly for *A. panamensis*. Given the exceedingly slow growth rates and the longevity of harvested colonies, measures to control exploitation are clearly needed. Efforts are currently being made to estimate the impact of this harvesting (Robinson, personal communication).

17.2.3. Sandy beaches

In comparison to other eastern Pacific insular sites, sandy shore environments are well represented in Galápagos. This habitat is not only abundant but also quite varied. Sediment composition for beach sand ranges from predominantly carbonate (i.e., derived from physical breakdown and bioerosion of corals, calcareous algae, barnacle and shells, with examples on Floreana, Santa Cruz, and San Cristóbal) to tufa (e.g. Bartolomé, Santiago and Floreana) or basalt (e.g. Marchena, Pinta and Isabela); for further analysis see Chapter 2.8.4.

Intertidally, ghost crabs (*Ocypode gaudichaudii*) and hermit crabs (*Coenobita compressa*) are the conspicuous organisms present. Both are opportunistic scavengers which forage up and down with the tide. Mole crabs, *Hippa denticulata*, are found partially burrowed in the sand at the surf line where they filter-feed. Extending into the subtidal are sand dollars, *Encope* spp., and burrowing anemones, *Cerianthus* sp. Very little research has been done on this community in Galápagos, with the exception of the interstitial fauna (i.e. those animals which live between the sand grains) (Ax and Schmidt, 1973; Schmidt, 1974). These authors have found a high diversity of species with a high incidence of endemism. This high endemism is not surprising, however, since the interstitial fauna is not well-known anywhere, especially along mainland shores.

17.2.4. Mangroves

Four species of mangroves occur in Galápagos: the red mangrove, *Rhizophora mangle*; black mangrove, *Avicennia germinans*; white mangrove, *Laguncularia racemosa*; and, the button mangrove, *Conocarpus erecta*, all of which have extensive ranges in the islands (Wiggins and Porter, 1971). In terms of development, the red and black mangroves are most extensive. The best examples are found at Cartago and Elizabeth Bays bordering Isabela.

This habitat supports a characteristic assemblage of algae and invertebrates. Epiphytic on the stilt roots are several species of red algae, *Bostrychia calliptera*, *Caloglossa lepriuvii*, and *Catnella repens*. Gastropods such as *Ellobium stagnalis* and *Melampus carolinus* are obligate mangrove-dwellers and found on the soft muds trapped at the base of the stilt roots. The fiddler crab, *Uca helleri*, a Galápagos endemic, is also a resident of mangrove areas. Within embayments bordered by mangroves, green turtles, bat rays, snook (*Centropomus*) and an endemic fish, *Archosargus pourtalesii*, are common.

17.2.5. Coral reefs

Historically, the eastern Pacific has been considered depauperate in coral reef assemblages (Yonge, 1940; Rosenblatt, 1963). However, recent literature describes reef or coral communities as occurring in the Gulf of California (Squires, 1959; Dana and Wolfson, 1970; Barham *et al.*, 1970, Brusca and Thomson, 1977), along the Mexican coast (Greenfield *et al.*, 1970), Panama (Glynn *et al.*, 1972; Glynn, 1976; Rosenblatt *et al.*, 1972), Colombia (Prahl *et al.*, 1979) and from offshore islands (Clipperton Island, Sachet, 1962; Cocos Island, Bakus, 1975; Malpelo Island, Birkeland *et al.*, 1975). Most recently Glynn and Wellington (1983) have presented a detailed report on the distribution and abundance of coral and coral reefs in the Galápagos Island.

In Galápagos the major reef-building species are the branching coral, *Pocillopora robusta*, and three massive species: *Pavona clavus*, *Pavona gigantea*, and *Porites lobata*. The detailed survey presented by Glynn and Wellington (1983) indicates that incipient reef building is widespread throughout the archipelago, occurring along most shorelines except where upwelling is intense (i.e. western Isabela and Fernandina). Moderately well-developed fringing reefs occur near Floreana. At the small islet known as Onslow, *Pocillopora* forms a dense monotypic stand over an area of approximately one hectare (Fig. 17.1a). Just east and south of Onslow,

Figure 17.1. Coral reef formations, (a) *Pocillopora* reef at Isla Onslow, Floreana. Reef build-up here is ca. 1 m. (b) and (c) show *Pavona* reef at Isla Champion near Floreana. (b) shows plating form of *Pavona gigantea* at a depth of 20 m, (c) columnar colonies of *Pavona clavus* at about 10 m.

at Champion Island, a *Pavona* reef extends 0.5 km along the western side of the island and is estimated to have a maximum vertical growth of about 10 m (Fig. 17.1b,c). Other areas showing substantial coral development include the south side of Bartolomé and along the eastern side of Wolf and at the southern tip of Darwin.

Glynn and Wellington (1983) attempt to correlate the distribution and abundance of corals within the islands to broad hydrographic and climatic patterns such as water temperatures and cloud cover, and also volcanic and tectonic events. One of the general conclusions reached by this study is that physical conditions in Galápagos are generally conducive to active coral growth. Local oceanographic conditions can limit growth where upwelling leads to the persistence of cool water (<18°C). Even in these situations, however, refugia are often present. At Punta Espinosa (Fernandina), where temperatures occasionally fall well below 18°C, *Pocillopora* are found thriving in protected mangrove areas where shoal waters are heated to several degrees above ambient nearshore waters. At locations where volcanic activity is high and lava flows reach the shoreline from time to time, local extinction of coral fauna probably occurs. The potential importance of tectonic events is well demonstrated by the emergent coral communities found at Urvina Bay (Chapter 2.7.1). Recent uplift activity at Punta Espinosa has resulted in the death of a *Pocillopora* patch reef (Glynn and Wellington, 1983).

The most interesting aspects of coral development in Galápagos are the biological interactions which also control the extent of coral growth. Glynn *et al.* (1979) have shown that the urchin, *Eucidaris thouarsii*, can have a major impact on reef growth. These urchins feed directly on living coral by breaking and ingesting coral skeletal fragments along with surface tissues (Fig. 17.2). Where densities are high and live coral coverage low net coral growth is close to zero. Urchins at Onslow Island are estimated to reduce coral production by 30%.

Eucidaris also occurs along mainland shores but, in contrast to Galápagos *Eucidaris*, they are smaller and cryptic in habit and do not normally feed on coral. Experiments have shown that key urchin predators such as pufferfish and triggerfish are either absent or in much lower densities in Galápagos compared to Panama. Thus, unrestrained by predators, these urchins have expanded their niche to include a novel yet nutritious food source. Corals along mainland shores however are not exempt from predation. At certain locations the sea star, *Acanthaster*, accounts for 3–4% annual mortality of the standing coral crop (Glynn, 1973). Also, grazing by the mollusc, *Jenneria pustulata*, and pufferfish, *Arothron* spp., consume 30% of the annual biomass production of coral in Panama (Glynn *et al.*, 1972). Interestingly, both *Jenneria* and *Acanthaster* are absent from Galápagos.

Associated with shallow reef environments are small damselfish (ca. 7 cm length). These fish are sedentary and, as mentioned before, maintain algal gardens on nonliving coral substrates. These gardens are used for food, shelter and as nesting sites and are defended vigorously against intruding herbivorous fishes (e.g. parrotfish and surgeonfish) and potential egg predators (particularly *Arothron*). Observations by Glynn and Wellington (1983) indicate that damselfish will also eject urchins which wander into their territories. One possible explanation for this exclusion is that urchins are potential competitors for the occupation of shelter sites in the reef. These shelter sites are important to both urchins and damselfish for avoiding predatory fish. This ejection behavior has the indirect effect of reducing coral grazing immediate to damselfish territories and thereby may actually facilitate reef development.

A recent study by Wellington (1982) in Panama, where another species of damselfish occurs, has demonstrated that these fish can have a different yet major impact on coral communities. Here damselfish kill coral (mainly massive species) in order to expand the size of their algal gardens. It was found that massive corals suffered higher rates of mortality in shallow water areas than did branching corals (*Pocillopora*). This, in fact, leads to a predominance of branching corals in shallow water. However, because appropriate shelter for damselfish is less abundant in deeper water massive corals escape this mortality and consequently are more abundant there. Branching corals, on the other hand, suffer high mortality where damselfish are absent. This is due to the fact that damselfish defend their algal territories from egg predators such as pufferfish. These egg predators are also the major predator of juvenile *Pocillopora*. Thus, damselfish territories provide a refuge for the settlement of pocilloporid colonies. In Panama these interactions lead to a marked pattern of vertical zonation: *Pocillopora* in shallow water, *Pavona* in deep water.

In Galápagos, damselfish do not appear to kill reef building corals. The interactions between damselfish and potential coral predators, however, is similar. Therefore, damselfish probably enhance coral growth in Galápagos as well. Zonation of corals is also present probably because damselfish are excluded from deeper waters for much the same reason they are in Panama, i.e. no suitable shelter sites. Because damselfish do not kill coral here development of massive species is even more pronounced.

Figure 17.2. The urchin, *Eucidaris thouarsii* (arrows) feeding on *Pocillopora* colonies at Isla Onslow, Floreana.

In summary, the coral reef community is the best-studied marine habitat in Galápagos. The biological interactions responsible for shaping community structure in this insular environment contrast markedly with those occurring on mainland shores. Despite these differences the outcomes are surprisingly similar. Continued studies in this area will further our understanding of how isolation influences the organization of insular communities.

17.3. Inter-Island Regionalism

The Galápagos Archipelago extends over an area of 45,600 km² and is composed of 13 major islands as well as numerous lesser islands and rocks. Given this large geographic expanse and complex oceanographic setting, it is perhaps not surprising that nearshore environments are varied and composed of several distinct biotic assemblages. These marine communities are associated with water temperature regimes and reflect differences in nutrient and light levels (Chapter 3).

In an attempt to correlate productivity to the breeding cycles of marine birds, Harris (1969) proposed that the islands are comprised of several distinct regions based on hydrographic conditions: a northern, southern, western and two central areas (Fig. 17.3). The two most distinct zones are the northern and western sectors. The seasonally fluctuating North Equatorial Front, which separates tropical and subtropical water masses, lies just south of the northern islands of Darwin and Wolf for much of the year. Consequently these islands tend to be most tropical in their marine biota. The fish fauna in this region is dominated by many western Pacific and pelagic species, particularly the black surgeonfish, *Melichthys niger*, the Moorish idol, *Zanclus cornutus*, the wrasse *Thallasoma lutescens* and numerous moray eels. In addition, hermatypic corals proliferate, forming

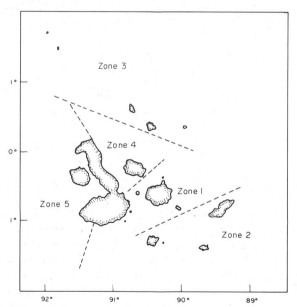

Figure 17.3. Sea surface temperature zones defined by Harris (1969). The western zone (5) and southern zone (2) are subject to cool water conditions; zone 3 is generally more tropical and thus warmer than the other zones. Zones 1 and 4 are characterized by moderate temperature variations. Compared to zone 1, zone 4 tends to be slightly cooler during the dry season (June to December).

extensive fringing reefs. Macrophytic algae are essentially absent here, probably due to lower nutrient availability and intense grazing by tropical fish algivores.

In the western sector, defined as western Isabela and Fernandina, upwelling of cool nutrient laden water via the Equatorial Undercurrent is often intense, particularly between the months of June and December. Temperatures as low as 14°C have been recorded (Wellington, personal observation). The dominant fish fauna in shallow water are species derived from South American warm temperate regions. These include the harlequin wrasse, *Bodianus eclancheri*, *Oplegnathus insignis*, and the damselfish, *Nexilosus latifrons*. These fish are extremely abundant in shallow water, but may occur elsewhere in the islands at low densities below the thermocline (ca 20–30 m). Earle (1980) has also noted this 'submergence phenomenon' for algal species. As she has pointed out, this situation provides an opportunity to explore the evolution of plant-herbivore interactions where temperate and tropical marine floras exist side-by-side.

With respect to invertebrates, the most striking example of regionalism is the shallow water urchin, *Caenocentrotus gibbosus*. This species is only abundant in the western sector; elsewhere it is replaced by the tropical species *Echinometra vanbrunti*. Hermatypic corals are scarce but the nonsymbiotic, ahermatypic fauna is rich. A recent survey at Caleta Tagus, Isabela revealed six common species, three of which are endemic to the islands (Wells, 1982, 1983).

Upwelling results in high nutrient levels and a diverse and abundant community of macrophytic algae. This algal biomass in turn supports dense populations of marine iguanas. The high productivity of this region is also reflected by the presence of flightless cormorants and penguins, species most uncommon at an equatorial location. Baleen whales such as the Sei, Fin and Humpback are regular visitors during the upwelling season.

Data presented by Pak and Zaneveld (1973) and Houvenaghel (1978) suggest that upwelling of the Equatorial Undercurrent may also influence the southern islands of Floreana and Española, especially along their western shores. This may account for the similarity of biotas between this region and the western sector. Also this southern region is farther from the Equatorial Front and thus is more under the influence of the cooler Peru Oceanic Current.

The central zones, comprising the east coast of Isabela, Santa Cruz, Santiago and perhaps Marchena and Pinta, undergo moderate seasonal temperature fluctuations (ca 10°C). This area contains a mixture of faunas, mainly dominated by eurythermic elements of the Mexican, Panamic and Peru-Chile Provinces as well as a distinct Galápagos endemic component.

17.4. Biogeographic Distributions and Affinities

Considering the oceanic origin of the islands there is little doubt that the present day littoral marine biota arrived via dispersal from nearby tropical and subtropical shores. The major avenues for immigration are the South Equatorial and Peru Oceanic Currents from the south and the Panama Current from the North.

While much of the marine biota has been poorly studied the better-known taxa indicate a strong similarity to the tropical Panamic Province (Table 17.1); a region extending from the Gulf of Tehuantepec (16°N) which contains the highest diversity of tropical elements found in the eastern pacific. This tropical fauna and flora, as a whole, bears little resemblance to the Western Pacific or Atlantic Provinces. To the west of Galápagos lies a large expanse of water separating the nearest Polynesian Islands from the American mainland. This barrier, termed the eastern Pacific Barrier (Ekman, 1953; Briggs, 1964), is believed to be highly effective in separating the biotas of the two regions. Only a small percentage of species in the eastern Pacific are regarded as transpacific. Briggs (1961, 1964) and Rosenblatt *et al.* (1972) list only 62 transpacific fish of which most, if not all, are derived from the western Pacific. Of these, 35 are apparently confined to offshore islands. If the two fish faunas from these regions are totalled this 62 species represents only 6%; in other words, the barrier has been 94% effective. Although distance is undoubtedly a major factor restricting the mixing of these two

Table 17.1. Summary of the biogeographic affinities and distributions of various marine taxa in the Galápagos Islands. Percentages of total species appear in parentheses.

Taxon	Number of Species	endemic	insular endemic	Biogeographic distribution Panamic	Temperate	Western Pacific/ Cosmopolitan	Atlantic	Source*
Algae	333	116 (35)	3 (<1)	133 (40)	13 (4)	33 (10)	46 (14)	1
Scleractinia (stony corals)								
–reef building	13	0	0	4 (31)	0	9 (69)	0	2
–nonreef building	31	10 (30)	0	6 (19)	?	11 (33)	4 (13)	2
Brachyura (true crabs)	117	25 (22)	4 (3)	82 (70)	11 (19)	9 (8)	8 (7)	3
Mollusca								
–gastropods	399	140 (35)	11 (2)	235 (59)	?	9 (2)	4 (1)	4
–chitons	11	7 (64)	0	2 (18)	1 (10)	—	—	5
Echinoderms								
–urchins	24	4 (17)	1 (4)	17 (71)	1 (4)	1 (4)	?	6
–sea stars	28	3 (11)	2 (7)	14 (58)	1 (3)	6 (21)	2 (7)	7
–sea cucumber	30	1 (3)	1 (3)	19 (63)	?	9 (30)	?	8
Fish	306	51 (17)	7 (2)	177 (58)	21 (7)	43 (14)	4 (1)	9

*1–Silva, 1966; Taylor, 1945; Wellington, 1975. 2–Wells, 1982, 1983. 3–Garth, 1946; Wellington, 1975. 4–Keen, 1971; Wellington, 1979. 5–Smith and Ferreira, 1977. 6–Clark, 1946. 7–M. Downey (pers. comm.). 8–Deichmann, 1941, 1958. 9–McCosker and Rosenblatt, Chapter 9.

faunas, the absence of a diverse coral reef habitat and potential interspecific competition may also be important considerations. Since the late Pliocene (Keigwin, 1978), the seaway which connected the Atlantic and Pacific oceans has been closed. The representative biotas have since diverged and probably less than 5% of the total biota are shared at the species level. Galápagos retains some species which are more closely related to Atlantic forms than those presently found elsewhere in the eastern Pacific. Examples are found in the fish fauna (see Chapter 9) and among the brachyuran crabs (Garth, 1946).

As previously mentioned, the majority of the Galápagos marine biota is derived from the Panamic Province. These species have most likely reached the islands directly from the continental shores of Ecuador and Colombia via the South Equatorial Current or indirectly via the North Equatorial Current. During periods of major current shifts when a prolonged and extensive warm water mass flows through the Galápagos from the north, organisms may come directly from Central America, However, this is less likely to occur since reproductive activity would probably be low along Central American shores at this time (Abbott, 1966). The more eurythermic elements of the Peruvian/Chilean Province have undoubtly been transported to Galápagos by the strong northward flowing Peru Current. There is little evidence to suggest that direct invasion from the west has taken place. Rather, these western Pacific organisms more likely reached Galápagos by way of Cocos and Clipperton Islands which are situated directly in the path of the North Equatorial Countercurrent flowing from west to east. One possible path of direct invasion is the subsurface Equatorial Undercurrent (Cromwell). This water mass is characterized by cool temperatures and thus would probably exclude transport of tropical larvae.

The phenomenon of 'insular confinement' involving the occurrence of a high proportion of west Pacific species on oceanic islands which are not present on eastern Pacific mainland shores has long been recognized. One of the best examples illustrating this pattern is found in the mollusca. Of the 52 species of west Pacific prosobranch gastropods and bivalves reported in the eastern Pacific, 38 (or 73%) are confined to offshore islands :Galápagos has 9 such species; Cocos, 4; Clipperton Atoll, 38; and the Revillagigedos, 6. Clipperton, the westernmost American outpost, is located directly in line with the North Equatorial Countercurrent. Of the 70 species of molluscs reported there 50% are west Pacific species (Emerson, 1967, 1968). This restricted distribution is probably a result of biological interactions (competition and predation) between mainland and invading species rather than a result of inability to reach distant shores.

The following synopses of selected taxa (Table 17.1) indicate a high percentage of endemism to the islands. The uniqueness of this biota was recognized by Ekman (1953); thus, many biogeographers conveniently recognize this area as the Galápagos Province (Briggs, 1974; Brusca and Wallerstein, 1979).

Algae

Since Silva's (1966) report on algal diversity and species distributions within the islands, more recent collecting efforts have added 22 more species (Wellington, 1975). These additions increase the known taxa to 333, of which 35% may be unique to the archipelago. This flora is represented by the following groups: Cyanophyaceae, 21 species with 4 endemic; Phaeophyceae, 43 spp. with 24 endemic; Xanthophyta, 1; Rhodophyceae, 223 with 82 endemic.

In view of the fact that the islands' marine flora has been little investigated it can be considered rich in comparison to other insular floras. For example, Mauritius has 360 spp. with 16% endemic. However, it far exceeds the flora of the lesser explored Juan Fernández which has but 100 spp. with 32% endemic (Silva, 1966). The high percentage of endemism in Galápagos must be considered tentative as further evaluation of taxonomic relationships will undoubtedly synonymize several species and more extensive collecting along the continent will reveal the presence of supposed Galápagos endemics.

Since our knowledge of South American algae is limited it is hard to make a meaningful evaluation of the floral affinities. However, it is possible to estimate from present knowledge that about 40% of the flora occurs on mainland shores from the Gulf of California to Chile. A small (4%) but significant number come from temperate South America and are represented mainly in the cooler southern and western portion of the archipelago. The western Pacific and Atlantic components of the flora can be considered as representative of a tropical flora. Surprisingly, many tropical genera are absent in Galápagos. These include members of the Chlorophyceae such as: *Avrainvillea*, *Boodlea*, *Chlorodesmis*, *Halimeda* and *Velonia*. One possible explanation may be the lack of suitable habitats for these genera. Most are associated with shallow, warm water with protected sandy-rock substrates. These habitats do exist in Galápagos but are not as extensive or well-developed as on mainland shores. Also conspicuously absent are marine phanerogams like *Halodule* and *Ruppia*. These species may have limited dispersal abilities and thus have not been able to reach Galápagos shores.

Scleractinia

Only a handful of scientific expeditions to Galápagos have been concerned with the collection and identification of the stony coral fauna. The first coral, *Placopsammia darwini*, was described by Duncan in 1876 from a single specimen collected by Darwin during his visit in 1835. The first coral report of any significance was made by Pourtales in 1875 from collections made by the *Hassler* Expedition in 1873. Further collections were made in subsequent years during the *Velero* Expeditions in the 1930's. Up until the early 1970's the known fauna stood at 32 spp.: 12 hermatypes (reef-building) and 20 ahermatypes (Durham, 1966).

The most recent and comprehensive study of Galápagos corals has now been completed by Wells (1982, 1983). Based on extensive collections by Glyn and Wellington (1983), Wells revised and updated the taxonomy of this group for much of the eastern Pacific. In this study 44 species are cited: 13 hermatypes and 31 ahermatypes. The hermatypic fauna is largely west Pacific in origin and, at the species level, bears little resemblance to the Caribbean fauna. Some authors have suggested that this fauna was derived from a post-Pliocene relict population previously extant in the Tethyan Sea (Heck and McCoy, 1978) while others favor the hypothesis that these corals recolonized this region through dispersal from the western Pacific since

Pleistocene times (Dana, 1975; see Glynn and Wellington, 1983 for elaboration of these conflicting hypotheses). There is no question that the Galápagos hermatypic coral fauna is more closely related to the western Pacific than to corals in the Caribbean.

Compared to other eastern Pacific sites, Galápagos corals are equally abundant and diverse. The ahermatypic fauna, in fact, is quite unique with 30% endemic. The richness of this fauna is directly related to high productivity in the western sector of the archipelago. At Caleta Tagus, for example, 6 species are very common and 3 of these are endemic.

Brachyura

The Galápagos brachyuran fauna is fairly well-known (Garth, 1946a,b; Wellington, 1975). Of the 117 species present, the majority (82 spp. or 70%) are probably derived from the Panamic Province. A smaller (25 or 22%) but significant number are endemic. This high affinity to the Panamic Province suggests invasion to the islands via the Peru Current. Although 11 species are reported in common with temperate American shores, only two, *Microphys aculeatus* and *Pinnaxodes chilensis*, can be considered true representatives of a cool water climate. This is somewhat surprising given that the Peru Current provides a direct avenue for transport of cool water species. Abbott (1966), however, has pointed out that when currents are strongest from this region's reproductive activities along Peru and Chile are expected to be lowest. The western Pacific is well represented with 10 species. All have been reported elsewhere in the eastern Pacific and most are obligate associates with the coral fauna.

It is notable that geocarcinids (land crabs) and sesarmids (aboreal crabs) are absent from Galápagos. Both groups are well represented along continental shores and even occur at a number of other eastern Pacific island locations, e.g. Clipperton, Cocos, Revillegigedos and Malpelo all support one or more species of land crabs. Suitable habitats appears to be available and these species apparently disperse well. Perhaps the arid shorelines in Galápagos are less suitable for colonization compared to other island situations in the eastern Pacific.

Mollusca

Numerous publications by a variety of authors (e.g. Emerson, 1967, 1968; Emerson and D'Attilio, 1970; Keen, 1971 and many others) have contributed significantly to our knowledge of the Galápagos molluscan fauna. Although the total fauna is far from completely known the number of species present is estimated to be approximately 600 (Emerson, 1967; Keen, 1971) or just about 20% of the molluscan species reported in the Panamic region. Of this, almost 400 are gastropods. As reflected in other taxa discussed here, nearly 60% of this fauna is common to the Panamic Province, with 35% endemic (Table 17.1).

Only nine (3%) of the species are in common with the western Pacific. Emerson (1967) concluded that the relative impoverishment of western Pacific species in the eastern Pacific is related to the paucity of diverse coral reefs. While the coral fauna is certainly poor in species numbers, moderately well developed reefs occur at a number of locations in the eastern Pacific, including the Galápagos. The validity of Emerson's argument is difficult to judge. For example, Clipperton Island has a gastropod fauna of 70 species of which nearly half are western Pacific. Only 50% of these forms have managed to reach mainland shores. Low dispersal is not a likely explanation given their mid-oceanic position. Neither does the diversity of coral there appear to differ substantially from that on the mainland.

The fossil record in Galápagos suggests a rapid turnover rate for some molluscan species. For example, the pelecypod *Pegophysema spherica* and the gastropod *Terebra albemarlensis* were predominant forms in late Pleistocene beach communities but apparently became extinct in recent times. Approximately 8% of the mollusc fauna found in Galápagos Pliocene fossil remains are now extinct in the islands although some still persist elsewhere in the eastern Pacific (Hertlein, 1972). This suggests that extinction and immigration rates may be rapid in this insular environment.

Echinodermata

The echinoderm fauna is moderately diverse. The echinoids (sea urchins) number 24 species, the asteroids (sea stars) 28 spp., and the holothurians (sea cucumbers) 30 spp. As is the case with most other taxa, the major contribution to our knowledge of this fauna has been made by the Allan Hancock Expeditions (1930–1938).

The echinoids have been thoroughly reviewed by H.L. Clark (1948) and a monographic treatment of the Panamic holothurians by Deichmann (1941, 1958) are still considered the major works for these taxa in this region. The asteroids have not been thoroughly examined. The diversity of asteroids presented here is largely the result of collections made by the author in collaboration with M. Downey.

The most common shallow water urchins in Galápagos are *Echinometra vanbrunti*, *Eucidaris thouarsii*, and *Diadema mexicanum*. All are widely distributed in the eastern tropical Pacific. One exception is *Lytechinus semituberculatus* which is considered to be a Galápagos endemic although there have been reports of this species from mainland Ecuador (Tortonese, 1953). Associated with sandy areas is a rich diversity of sand dollars (Clypeasteroids) in particular, *Clypeaster elongatus*, *C. europacificus* and *C. rotundas*, and heart urchins (Spatangoids) such as *Cassidulus pacificus* and *Agassizii scrobiculata*.

Most of the holothurians known from the islands are shallow water forms with the exception of 3 or 4 species. *Brandtothuria arenicola* is a circumtropical species and occurs commonly in the mid and lower intertidal zones. The upper levels of the tide are dominated by a Panamic species, *Selenkothuria theeli*. The most conspicuous sea cucumber in the subtidal region is *Isostichopus fuscus*. This is an extremely large animal reaching 25 cm or more in length and is easily recognized by its size and brown color and large yellowish tinged tubercules which cover the dorsal surface of the body. This species is restricted to the eastern Pacific and has a closely related counterpart in the Atlantic.

Sea stars are represented in the intertidal zone by the endemic sea stars, *Heliaster cumingii* and *H. multiradiata*. *Nidoriella armata*, *Pharia pyramidata* and *Phataria unifasicata* are ubiquitous in the lower intertidal and subtidal regions. Occurring in warmer water areas and associated with coral reefs are western Pacific species like *Mithrodia claverigera*, *Asteropsis carnifera* and *Leiaster callipelus*. Commonly associated with cooler sectors in the islands are *Luidia bellonae*, *Linckia columbiae*, *Astrometis sertulifera* and *Pauliella horrida galapagensis*. Also associated with this cool region is one of the largest sea stars known, *Luidia superba* (up to .5 m radius). This recently rediscovered species (Downey and Wellington, 1978) was first described by A.H. Clark from a single specimen collected off Colombia by the *Albatross* Expedition in 1880.

Comparisons of Galápagos echinoderms with conspecific counterparts along the mainland reveal marked differences in morphological and behavior characteristics. Biological and physical conditions differ between localities but it remains to be demonstrated whether these character differences are phenotypic responses to environmental variation or the result of natural selection on genetically isolated populations.

Fish

This group is covered extensively by McCosker and Rosenblatt in Chapter 9. A summary of the biogeographic distributions and affinities appears on Table 17.1.

In summary, the Galápagos marine environment possesses a rich and varied biota. For the most part this biota is derived from neighbouring shores; however, the apparent high endemic rate suggests that flow of propagules from the mainland is probably limited for many organisms. Biotic assemblages composed of elements from varying biogeographic lineages provides a unique opportunity to investigate ecological and evolutionary processes associated with insular environments. For example, the importance of dispersal, immigration and extinction of marine organisms to community structure on distant islands is not known. Certainly the best place to undertake such studies is in an area having little or no impact by man. Galápagos qualifies as such a place. In the next section I will briefly outline steps presently being taken to protect this environment.

17.5. Plan for Protection

(a) Justification for protection

With the development of the *Master Plan for the Protection and Use of the Galápagos National Park* in 1974 a recommendation was made to include the surrounding marine areas within the existing park boundaries. Soon after this recommendation a survey was undertaken to assess the diversity and uniqueness of this resource, to identify major habitats and significant features present, and to make recommendations for the protection and management of this resource (Wellington, 1975).

This survey concluded that the Galápagos marine communities, in relation to other insular areas, were represented by: a high diversity of species; a high degree of endemism; numerical abundance of many species, probably related to the absence of significant human disturbances; a strong phyto- and zoogeographic affinity to tropical and subtropical American shores but also represented by temperate American and western Pacific elements as well; and lastly, a diversity of habitats with distinct regionalism within the archipelago making Galápagos quite unlike other island systems.

While these factors alone justify protection of the marine environment it is also important to note that a fragile relationship exists between many of the semi-terrestrial organisms and their nearshore environments. As mentioned earlier, marine iguanas, sea birds and pinnipeds are directly linked to marine food webs. Unfortunately we know very little about these interrelationships. Moreover, we know almost nothing about the biological processes operating in marine insular systems, particularly those factors which control community structure and organization. All the evidence demonstrates that the Galápagos marine environment offers equally fascinating opportunities for basic biological studies as does the terrestrial environment. Further, this marine environment has been little modified by man's activities in comparison to most other locations and thus offers ideal conditions for monitoring global pollution. The educational and touristic merits of the marine environment are obvious. The underwater life has attracted the interests of many as evidenced by the increasing numbers of divers and snorkelers visiting the islands each year.

Because of these scientific, esthetic and educational values a plan has been developed with the aim of protecting the resource yet integrating man's present commercial activities in the islands. This plan calls for (1) extension of the National Park boundary to a distance of 5 km from the shore; this generally encompasses the 200 m depth contour which includes over 90% of the biota characteristic to the islands, (2) regulation and limitation of commercial and noncommercial interests through the establishment of a delimitation and zonation scheme and (3) protection of marine communities, particularly significant and fragile features, within the Park framework.

(b) Delimitation and Zonation.

Within the establishment of a marine zone extending 5 km from the shore nearly all littoral and sublittoral species and habitats to a 200 m depth contour will fall under Park protection and management. This distance will also provide protection for certain pelagic species, such as cetaceans which frequent inshore areas. This distance can also be realistically patrolled by Park Service personnel. The proposed areas to be included in this zone are shown on Fig. 17.4 and will encompass nearly 500,000 ha.

While the details of this plan have yet to be fully worked out a zonation scheme has been proposed based, with modifications, upon the terrestrial zoning scheme mentioned on pages 272–273.

(c) Legal Considerations

Ideally, National Parks authorities should have exclusive control over all human use of parklands and waters, exclusive responsibilities for all aspects of management, administration and development of the Park, and concurrent jurisdiction with local authorities in law enforcement and judgement within the Park. However, since the proposal for an extension of present Park boundaries into adjacent waters the necessary legislation has moved slowly. In part, this has been due to uncertainty regarding the jurisdictional powers of various sectors of government. A recent high level commission report issued in 1981, however, provides optimism that these problems may soon be resolved. The Commission has recommended that jurisdiction be vested and shared among the Ministries of Agriculture (within which the Park Service resides), Defense, and National Resources and Energy. The first of these has responsibility over administration and control of visitor-related activities within marine areas, including sport fisheries. The Ministry of Defense would have authority on issues involving sovereignty and marine laws; and the Ministry of National Resources and

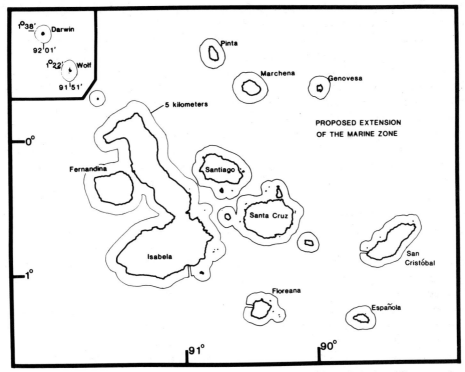

Figure 17.4. Shows the proposed 5 km extension of the National Park boundaries into adjacent marine areas.

Energy would control and establish regulations governing commercial fishing activities throughout the islands.

The establishment and management of the terrestrial portions of the Galápagos National Park have proven to be quite successful (see Chapter 18). This has largely resulted from outstanding cooperation between scientific and conservation interests, both in and out of Government. With this historical precedence I am certain that the marine areas will be incorporated into the Park in the very near future.

17.6 Acknowledgements

I thank Craig MacFarland, former Director of the Charles Darwin Research Station (CDRS) for his encouragement and support during my tenure at the CDRS (1973–1975). His efforts were instrumental in the formulation of the marine protection plan. Also I especially thank Pat Wellington for her most able assistance in the field. This work was financially supported by the US Peace Corps Program, the National Parks and Wildlife Service of Ecuador, and the Charles Darwin Foundation.

References

Abbott, D.P. (1966) Factors influencing the zoogeographic affinities of Galápagos inshore marine fauna. In *The Galápagos*. Edited by R.I. Bowman. Pages 108–122. U.C. Press Berkeley.

Ax, P. and Schmidt, P. (1973). Interstitielle fauna von Galápagos I. Einfuhrung. *Microfauna Mieresdonden*, **20**, 1–38.

Bakus, G.J. (1975) Marine zonation and ecology of Cocos Island, off Central America. *Atoll Res. Bull.*, **179**, 1–9.

Barham, E.G., Gowdy, R.W. and Wolfson, F.H. (1973) *Acanthaster* (Echinodermata, Asteroidea) in the Gulf of California. *Fish. Bull.*, **71**, 927–942.

Beebe, W. (1924) *Galápagos World's End*. G.P. Putnam's Sons, New York.

Birkeland, C., Meyer, D.L. Stames, J.P. and Buford, C.L. (1975) Subtidal communities of Malpelo Island. In *The Biological Investigations of Malpelo*. Edited by J.B. Graham. *Smithson. Contrib. Zoology.*, **176**, 55–68.

Briggs, J.C. (1961) The East Pacific barrier and the distribution of marine shore fishes. *Evolution*, **15**, 545–554.

Briggs, J.C. (1964) Additional transpacific shore-fishes. *Copeia 1964*, 706–708.

Briggs, J.C. (1974) *Marine Zoogeography*. McGraw-Hill Book Company, New York.

Brusca, R.C. and Thomson, D.A. (1977) Pulmo reef: the only coral reef in the Gulf of California. *Ciencias Marinas*, **1**, 37–53.

Brusca, R.C. and Wallerstein, B.R. (1979) Zoogeographic patterns of idoteid isopods in the Northeast Pacific, with a review of shallow water zoogeography of the area. *Bull. Biol. Soc., Wash.*, **3**, 67–105.

Clark, H.L. (1948) A report on the Echini of the warmer eastern Pacific based on the collection of the *Velero III*. *Allan Hancock Pacific Exped.*, **8**, 225–352.

Dana, T.F. (1975) Development of contemporary eastern Pacific coral reefs. *Mar. Biol.*, **33**, 355–374.

Dana, T.F. and Wolfson, A. (1970) Eastern Pacific crown-of-thorns starfish populations in the Gulf of California. *Trans. San Diego Soc. Nat. Hist.*, **16**, 83–90.

Deichmann, E. (1941) The Holothurioidea collected by the *Velero III* during the years 1932 to 1938. Part I. Dendrochirota. *Allan Hancock Pacific Exped.*, **8**, 61–195.

Deichmann, E. (1958) The Holothurioidea collected by the *Velero III* and *Velero IV* during the years 1932–1954. Part II. Aspidochirota. *Allan Hancock Pacific Exped.*, **11**, 253–349.

Downey, M. and Wellington, G.M. (1978) Rediscovery of the giant seastar, *Luidia superba*, A.H. Clark in the Galápagos Islands. *Bull. Mar. Sci.*, **28**, 375–376.

Durham, J.W. (1966) Coelenterates, especially stony corals, from the Galápagos and Cocos Islands. In *The Galápagos*. Edited by R.I. Bowman. Pages 123–135. U.C. Press, Berkeley.

Earle, S. (1980) Marine plant and animal distributions in relation to the Galápagos nearshore thermocline. *Not. de Galápagos*, **32**, 16–18.

Ekman, S. (1953) *Zoogeography of the Sea*. Sidgwick and Jackson, London.

Emerson, W.K. (1967) Indo-Pacific faunal elements in the tropical eastern Pacific with special reference to the mollusks. *Venus*, **25**, 85–93.

Emerson, W.K. (1968) New species of gastropoda from the east Pacific Ocean. *J. Conchol.*, **907**, 53–55.

Emerson, W.K. and D'Attilio, A. (1970) Three new species of muricacean gastropods from the eastern Pacific. *Veliger*, **12**, 270–274.

Garth, J. (1946a) Littoral brachyura fauna of the Galápagos Archipelago. *Allan Hancock Pacific Exped.*, **5**, 341–601.

Garth, J. (1946b) Distribution studies of Galápagos brachyura. *Allan Hancock Pacific Exped.*, **5**, 603–638.

Glynn, P.W. (1973) *Acanthaster*: effect on coral reef growth in Panama. *Science*, **180**, 504–506.

Glynn, P.W. (1976) Some physical and biological determinants of coral community structure in the eastern Pacific. *Ecol. Monogr.*, **46**, 431–456.

Glynn, P.W. and Wellington, G.M. (1983) *Corals and coral reefs of the Galápagos Islands*. U.C. Press, Berkeley

Glynn, P.W., Wellington, G.M. and Birkeland, C. (1979) Coral reef growth in the Galápagos: Limitation by sea urchins. *Science*, **203**, 47–49.

Glynn, P.W., Stewart, R.H. and McCosker, J.E. (1972) Pacific coral reefs of Panama: Structure, distribution and predators. *Geol. Rundschau.*, **61**, 483–519.

Harris, M.P. (1969) Breeding seasons of sea-birds in the Galápagos Islands. *J. Zool. Lond.*, **159**, 145–165.

Harris, M.P. (1979) Population dynamics of the Flightless Cormorant, *Nannopterum harrisi*. *The Ibis*, **121**, 135–146.

Heck, K.L. Jr. and McCoy, E.D. (1978) Long-distance dispersal of the reef-building corals of the eastern Pacific. *Mar. Biol.*, **48**, 349–356.

Hedgepeth, J.W. (1969) An intertidal reconnaissance of rock shores of Galápagos. *Wasmann J. Biol.*, **27**, 1–24.

Hertlein, L.G. (1963) Contributions to the biogeography of Cocos Islands, including a bibliography. *Proc. Cal. Acad. Sci.*, **32**, 219–289.

Hertlein, L.G. (1972) Pliocene fossils from Baltra (South Seymour) Island, Galápagos Islands. *Proc. Cal. Acad. Sci.*, **39**, 25–46.

Houvenaghel, G.T. (1978) Oceanographic conditions in the Galápagos Archipelago and this relationship with life on the islands. In *Upwelling Ecosystems*. Edited by R. Boje and M. Tomczak. Pages 181–200. Springer-Verlag, New York.

Houvenaghel, G.T. and Houvenaghel, N. (1974) Aspects écologiques de la zonation intertidale sur les côtes rocheuses des Iles Galápagos. *Mar. Biol.*, **26**, 135–152.

Keen, M. (1971) *Sea Shells of tropical West America, marine mollusks from Baja California to Peru*. Stanford Univ. Press, Stanford.

Keigwin, L.D. Jr., (1978) Pliocene closing at the Isthmus of Panama based on biostratigraphic evidence from nearby Pacific Ocean and Caribbean Sea cores. *Geology* **6**, 630–654.

Melville, H. (1856) *The Encantadas*. In *Four Short Novels*. Bantam paperbacks, New York (1959).

Menge, B.A. and Lubchenco, J. (1981) Community organization in temperate and tropical intertidal habitats: prey refuges in relation to consumer pressure gradients. *Ecol. Monogr.*, **51**, 429–450.

Pak, H. and Zanefeld, J.R.V. (1973) The Cromwell Current on the east side of the Galápagos Islands. *J. Geophys. Res.*, **78**, 7845–7859

Prahl, H. von, Guhl, F. and Grogl, M. (1979) *Gorgona*. Futura Grupo Editorial Ltda., Bogotá.

Rosenblatt, R.H. (1963) Some aspects of speciation in marine shore-fishes. In *Speciation in the Sea*. Edited by J.R. Harding and N. Tebble. Pages 171–180. The Systematics Assoc., London.

Rosenblatt, R.H., McCosker, J.E. and Rubinoff, I. (1972) Indo-West Pacific fishes from the Gulf of Chiriqui, Panama. *Los Angeles Nat. Hist. Mus. Contri. Sci*, **234**, 1–18.

Sachet, M.H. (1962) Geography and land ecology of Clipperton Island. *Atoll Res. Bull.*, **86**, 1–115.

Schmidt, P. (1974) Interstitielle fauna Galápagos. IV. Gastrotricha. *Mikrofauna Mieresboden*, **26**, 499–570.

Silva, P.L. (1966) Status of our knowledge of the Galápagos benthic marine algal flora prior to the Galápagos International Scientific Project. In *The Galápagos*. Edited by R.I. Bowman. Pages 149–156. U.C. Press, Berkeley.

Smith, A.G. and Ferreira, A.J. (1977) Chiton fauna of the Galápagos islands. *Veliger*, **20**, 82–96.

Squires, D.F. (1959) Results of the Puritan-America Museum of Natural History Expedition to western Mexico. 7. Corals and Coral Reefs in the Gulf of California. *Bull. Amer. Mus. Nat. Hist.*, **118**, 367–432.

Tortonese, E. (1953) On *Lytechinus* (Echinoidea) from the west coast of South America. *Annals and Magazine of Natural History*, **118**, 479–480.

Wellington, G.M. (1975) *The Galápagos Coastal Marine Environments: A resource report to the Department of National Parks and Wildlife.* Quito, Ecuador.

Wellington, G.M. (1982) Depth zonation of corals in the Gulf of Panama; control and facilitation by resident reef fishes. *Ecol. Monogr.*, **2**, 223–241.

Wells, J.W. (1982) New coral species from the Galápagos Islands. *Pac. Sci.*, **36**, in press.

Wells, J.W. (1983) Annotated list of the scleractinian corals of the Galápagos Islands. In P.W. Glynn and G.M. Wellington, *Corals and Coral Reefs of the Galápagos Islands.* U.C. Press, Berkeley.

Wiggins I. and Porter D. (1971) *Flora of the Galápagos.* Stanford Univ. Press, Stanford.

Yonge, C.M. (1940) The biology of reef-building corals. *Brit. Mus. (Nat. Hist.), Great Barrier Reef Exped., 1928–1929 Sci. Repts*, **1**, 353–391.

CHAPTER 18

The Path of Conservation
Part 1. The National Park and its Development

JUAN BLACK M.

Secretary-General, Charles Darwin Foundation

Contents

18.1.   The National Park and its Development   265
        18.1.1. The Changing Years   265
        18.1.2. Conservation Legislation   266
        18.1.3. Establishment of the Charles Darwin Research
                 Station   266
        18.1.4. Development of the Charles Darwin Research
                 Station (CDRS) and its Role in Conservation 267
        18.1.5. The Galapágos National Park Service (GNPS) 268

18.1. The National Park and its Development

18.1.1. The Changing Years

Ever since the discovery of the Galápagos by Fray Tomás de Berlanga, descriptions of the islands have exalted their geological wonders, their extraordinary fauna and flora, and their exceptional marine life. But it was the astute observations of Charles Darwin that revealed to the world the scientific importance of the islands. This resulted in numerous expeditions, with that of the California Academy of Sciences (1905–1906) being outstanding for its collections and volume of subsequent scientific publications.

Notwithstanding the unusual and bizarre history of the islands, each successive wave of visitors—pirates, the crews of warships, whalers, seal skin traders, colonists and scientists—has utilized the wildlife in one way or another. For some, it has been for subsistence; for others, it has been for commercial reasons; and for a growing number it has been for genuine scientific motives. But, ultimately, throughout these years of varying endeavour, thousands of tortoises, fur seals and birds have been killed or removed from the islands.

Despite the varied human activities, and despite the most recent and indirect pressures of colonization, the natural wonders of the Galápagos have survived to become of paramount importance among the key environments of the world.

18.1.2. Conservation Legislation

The first steps taken officially by the Government of Ecuador to safeguard native species of the Galápagos date from 1934. During the administration of Dr. Abelardo Montalvo, protection was given to certain animals of the islands and legal provision was made for the declaration of reserves and national parks. At the same time it was prohibited for anyone to take land in the archipelago without the prior permission of administrative authorities at Puerto Baquerizo Moreno. Authorized scientific expeditions were also to be limited (to collecting 3 specimens of any species of native animals), and the way was left open for the setting up of a scientific institution on the islands.

This legislation found its antecedents in the growing preoccupation in Ecuador and elsewhere in the world for the plight of the islands' fauna. The giant tortoises had been the subject of particular concern, with a request already having been made in 1930 for advice on measures that could be adopted by the government for their preservation on the islands (Townsend, in Bowman 1960).

In 1936, during the administration of Federico Páez, a decree was issued setting aside fourteen of the islands as reserves. Again, attention was given to the possibility of setting up a scientific station and to measures needed to prevent visitors to the islands from adding to the dangers already facing wildlife.

Growing interest in conservation in the islands, both in the United States and Europe, resulted in various communications between the Ecuadorian minister plenipotentiary in Washington, Colón Eloy Alfaro, and his government. These reaffirmed the need for adequate protection, for reserves and for a biological station to be set up in the Galápagos. Besides examining the ways and means by which these could be achieved, attention was given to the possible combined promotion of tourism with protection and research (Larrea, 1960).

That same year, the government organized its first National Scientific Commission. One of the participants in this was Misael Acosta-Solís, a botanist, who subsequently became involved over many years in steps for conserving the islands and their wildlife (Acosta-Solís, 1937). A further report (Samandaroff and Chalons, 1937), covering aspects of farming in the Galápagos, emphasized the touristic attractions of the islands. However, nothing had really been done to implement the various decrees and recommendations when the World War began in 1939.

Until 1957, interest in conserving the Galápagos was still mainly being expressed by individuals in Ecuador and scientific institutions overseas. But a considerable weight of opinion was growing for effective measures to be taken. The diplomat, the late Cristóbal Bonifaz Jijón, then persuaded the government in Quito to make a request to the United Nations Educational, Scientific and Cultural Organization (UNESCO) and the International Union for Conservation of Nature and Nature Resources (ICUN) for a special scientific mission to advise on conditions in the islands. The group that undertook this in 1957 was composed of Drs. Irenäus Eibl-Eibesfeldt (who had previously visited the islands and reported to UNESCO and IUCN) and Robert I. Bowman. Their task was to review the current status of wildlife, to recommend a site for the long-awaited research station and to advise on the setting up of effective reserves.

18.1.3. Establishment of the Charles Darwin Research Station

The reports of Eibl-Eibesfeldt and Bowman, the continuing efforts of other scientists and the formation of a Galápagos Committee at the International Congress of Zoology at London in 1958 all led to the creation of a special body, the Charles Darwin Foundation for the Galápagos Isles. Among its founding members and principal architects were Professor Victor van Straelen of Belgium and Sir Julian Huxley, first director-general of UNESCO. Legislation, concurrently drafted in Quito under the guidance of Cristóbal Bonifaz, underlined three crucial points:

—that the Galápagos Islands have strictly limited potential for agricultural development;

—that the islands possess a unique fauna and flora of outstanding importance to science;

—that the region has an incalculable potential for tourism.

In effect, the proposed decree repeated sentiment and ideas already expressed in the unimplemented legislation of 1934. But there were modifications: the entire archipelago would be converted into a national park, with the important exception that only those lands already legally assigned would be retained by colonists; that there would be created an Ecuadorian Institute for Scientific Research; and that the enforcement of laws would become the responsibility of administrative officials in the islands, known as *tenientes políticos*. This passed into law as an Emergency Decree on 4 July 1959. Later that month, in Brussels and under Belgian law, the Charles Darwin Foundation came into being.

18.1.4. Development of the Charles Darwin Research Station (CDRS) and its role in conservation

Between 1960 and 1964, the work of the new foundation was dedicated to the setting up of a research station at Bahía Academia on Santa Cruz. This was undertaken with the direct support of UNESCO, IUCN and the Government of Ecuador (Dorst and Laruelle, 1967). The station was officially inaugurated on 21 January 1964, at a ceremony attended by the highest representatives of the Government of Ecuador, by the ambassadors of countries supporting the Charles Darwin Foundation and by scientists from many countries. Immediately afterwards, an agreement was signed in Quito between the government and the foundation setting out the duties and functions of the research station.

Until that time no practical procedure had been laid down for the administration of the national park. Consequently, the government in its new agreement granted the CDRS authority to determine the reserve zones that were needed (an arrangement that, in the event, was complicated by the undetermined boundaries of farming areas) and to specify native plants and animals that required priority in conservation. Authorization was similarly given for the control or extermination of feral animals that were damaging the environment, and for measures to be taken to prevent the transfer of living organisms from the mainland and between the individual islands of the Galápagos. To carry out these duties the CDRS appointed the islands' first conservation officer in 1964.

Among the early duties of this official was the introduction of a bounty scheme for the control of feral pigs on Santa Cruz. Linked with this was the delimitation of a reserve area for the protection of the one sizeable population of giant tortoises remaining on the island.

As a next step, the CDRS communicated a document to the Government of Ecuador in 1967, signed by the foundation's honorary president, Sir Julian Huxley, advising on the inviolate reserve status of all unpopulated islands and on the setting up of protected zones on those islands with farming communities. This in effect gave the assurance needed by *bona fide* colonists that they would be free to engage in 'the development of legitimate farming pursuits.' In the short term, it signalled the more urgent need for the delimitation of national park and colonized areas—a difficult task that was only finally resolved after the creation of a Galápagos National Park Service. Ultimately, nearly nine-tenths of the land area of the archipelago became assigned as territory of the national park.

The difficulties that arose centred on incursions into areas that were technically (according to the 1959 decree) already part of the national park. Inevitably, uncertainties arose and some land speculation ensued, resulting, in extreme cases, even to the burning of native woodland in order to compromise a terrain's scientific value.

18.1.5. The Galápagos National Park Service (GNPS)

The two officials who arrived in 1968 to oversee the task of delimitation belonged to the Forestry Service of Ecuador and became, in effect, the nucleus of the embryonic National Park Service of Ecuador. It soon became apparent that their duties in the Galápagos were to be varied and manifold, though as yet they had little financial backing. Attempts were made not only to establish the reserves on inhabited islands, but to restrict feral animals and those human activities that were adversely affecting the environment. As tourism became a reality, they had the further tasks of controlling the activities of visitors.

During its first 18 months, the GNPS functioned closely with, and utilized the facilities of, the CDRS. There grew in fact a close working relationship, a symbiosis that became a key feature in the development of the subsequent scientific and conservation philosophy for the islands (page 272). Ultimately, this had wider repercussions, resulting in a greater awareness of the need for conservation legislation and practices on the mainland.

As a concluding step to the legal processes, the President of Ecuador, Dr. José María Velasco Ibarra, assigned to the Forestry Service responsibility for the setting up, and administration of, reserves and national parks in the country. At the same time, there were established rules for the use of these areas by tourist companies. One of the special requirements in the case of the Galápagos is the necessity for qualified guides to accompany each tour group—an obligation required of all companies arranging tours to the islands.

The organization of the Galápagos National Park Service was placed under a superintendent, with subsidiary officials responsible for administration, conservation and education. By June 1972, with the problems of delimitation finally resolved, activities extended to programmes for the protection of the tortoises (a project, involving interim captive breeding measures, which had been commenced by the CDRS) and the control of introduced animals. Eventually, goats were eliminated on the islands of Rábida, Santa Fé, Española and Marchena, and their numbers greatly reduced elsewhere (Chapter 8.3.1).

Between 1973 and 1978, with tourism bringing a steady 8,000 to 10,000 people annually to the islands, the National Park Service grew rapidly. There was an increase in the number of personnel, and a technical assistance programme of the Food and Agricultural Organization of the United Nations (FAO) was set up to guide future development in the islands. In September 1973, a Master Plan was formulated, drawing together a long-term conservation policy for the Galápagos and plans for possible development within the wider sphere of the province. The objectives emerging from this and explained further on page 273 were:
—the total protection of the landscapes and ecosystems of the islands;
—the suppression of harmful feral species and incompatible human activities;
—the development of facilities and explanatory information for visitors.

The following year, the National Planning Commission of Ecuador reduced into practical terms these objectives set out in the Master Plan. This resulted most importantly in a financial basis for the park. The significance of the islands to international science was reiterated, and there was established a specific working body for the conservation and development of the province. A further favourable development was the drafting of a broad conservation strategy for wildlife areas of outstanding beauty and interest on the mainland of Ecuador (Putney, 1976).

All these developments accentuated the growth of the Galápagos National Park Service. By 1978, besides a superintendent and supervisory staff of 10, the service employed 45 wardens and subsidiary personnel. With the ever-close collaboration of the Charles Darwin Research Station, there began new projects to safeguard populations of land and marine iguanas that were being threatened by feral dogs.

This work continues today. It is not always without difficulty, for the task of financing and maintaining active supervision in these remote islands poses many administrative challenges. But there is no faltering in the broad objective, to safeguard the Galápagos for science, for education and for their inestimable importance to Ecuador.

Part 2. The Alliance between National Government and International Science

G.T. CORLEY SMITH

Secretary-General, Charles Darwin Foundation 1972–82

Contents

18.2. The Alliance between National Government and
International Science   269
    18.2.1. The Origins   269
    18.2.2. The Charles Darwin Foundation   270
    18.2.3. The National Park Service   272
    18.2.4. Education   273
    18.2.5. A Unique Experiment   274
    References   275

18.2. The Alliance between National Government and International Science

18.2.1. The Origins

It took a quarter of a century to organize a system for conservation in the Galápagos. The movement began as the centenary of Charles Darwin's epoch-making visit in 1835 drew near. Before that, the few interested scientists had despaired of saving the unique wildlife and had actually made things worse by trying to collect as much as possible for preservation in museums. Occasional voices had also been raised in Ecuador about the lamentable condition of this remote and little known island possession, but until the 1930s no effective action had been proposed.

The Spaniards, who had claimed sovereignty for 300 years, never tried to colonize this cluster of volcanoes, apparently considering them better suited to tortoises than to human beings. When the newly independent Republic of Ecuador annexed the islands in 1832, immediate attempts were made to exploit them. Ecuador, then even more than now a 'developing' country, employed the only methods its limited resources permitted. Development in that age meant subduing the wilderness and introducing agriculture and animal husbandry.

269

There were no native inhabitants and, as there were few volunteers, the first settlements were largely peopled by political and other prisoners. The government was inadequately represented and was quite unable to control the foreign vessels that plundered the islands' only valuable natural resources—the rich stocks of whales, tortoises and fur seals. As there were no regular means of communication, mainland Ecuador knew little of the tryanny, suffering and bloodshed which characterized all attempts at development. A century after the annexation and the visit of Charles Darwin, the population of the entire archipelago was scarcely that of a modest village and poverty was general. The colonists did not thrive but, when they died or left, the domestic animals and plants they had introduced ran wild, multiplied and became a greater threat to the fragile ecosystems than man himself.

This was the background for the centenary of Darwin's visit. Small groups of scientists in California, London and New York urged the establishment of a research station in the islands but there seems to have been insufficient coordination either between them or with the small band of Ecuadorian activists who were aware of the threats to the Galápagos environment. When war broke out in 1939 the international scientists had achieved nothing beyond proclaiming the need for action and, although Ecuador had declared large parts of the archipelago to be nature reserves, the authorities never took steps to implement the decree. There was simply no agency in the islands to enforce it.

In the 1930s, nature conservation was a concept that had made little impact on the public mind but there had been an important change of atmosphere by the time of the next appropriate centenary, that of the publication of *The Origin of Species* in 1859. There had also been changes in the Galápagos that had altered the conservation problem both for better and for worse. During the war, Ecuador had authorized the United States to establish a temporary airforce base on the little island of Baltra; though little used after 1946, there was still a huge runway, capable of revolutionizing communications with the distant mainland. Meanwhile the human population of the archipelago had increased from a few hundreds to a few thousands, thus creating much larger vested interests than previously.

18.2.2. The Charles Darwin Foundation

In 1959 the conservationists' objectives were basically the same as in 1935: a national park with an international scientific station. But now, urged on by the International Zoological Congress and under the auspices of the United Nations Educational Scientific and Cultural Organization and the newly formed International Union for Conservation of Nature, a strong organizing committee was set up with representatives of Ecuador and several North Atlantic countries. At the same time the Government of Ecuador formally declared all unsettled areas of the archipelago to be a National Park.

The Charles Darwin Foundation for the Galápagos Isles (CDF) was singularly fortunate in the members of its first Executive Council, most of whom subsequently rose to international prominence in the world of science and conservation. Its council consisted largely of scientists and conservationists, a pattern which has been maintained. Steps were taken immediately to set up a research station on Santa Cruz Island. The task was made difficult not only by the lack of funds but even more by the lack of materials and means of transport and communication.

Nevertheless a field station, provided with water, electricity, laboratory, workshop and accommodation for staff and visiting scientists was set up amid the cactus and thorn scrub and was formally inaugurated in January 1964. An agreement was signed a few days later in Quito between the Government and the Foundation, empowering the latter to maintain and manage the research station for 25 years and to advise the national authorities on all matters affecting conservation and science in the archipelago. This was the beginning of a curious partnership which, in spite of all difficulties, has transformed the outlook for the Galápagos both from the point of view of science and conservation and from that of its human inhabitants.

Successive governments showed both courage and imagination in supporting the Charles Darwin

Foundation. In 1959 'conservation' and 'national park' were strange words and even stranger concepts to most people in Ecuador—and indeed in many other places. It must again be emphasized that Ecuador is a 'developing' country and that conservation all too often appears to be the antithesis of development. There was a persistent belief, fostered by their popular name of 'The Enchanted Isles' that, in spite of a century of failure, the Galápagos must have rich economic resources which only needed development. It was as natural as it was legitimate to ask: 'What was Ecuador to get out of this peculiar, generous and unprecedented deal with international science?' The eventual answer was: 'a tourist industry'. But this was anything but evident at the time. The islands were remote, communications and accommodations scant and primitive. Between the wars, millionaires had paid occasional visits in their yachts but few foreigners and few Ecuadorians ever went there. Nevertheless, it was argued that, if the government would support conservation, there was a strong probability that foreign tourists would want to see what was being conserved. Conservation would put the islands on the map. It was speculative, but tourism was definitely an official objective. This is clear from the report of a small expert team sent by the United Kingdom Government in 1965 at the request of the Government of Ecuador to make proposals for the future of the National Park. Their report was entitled: 'Recommendations on the Administration of the Proposed Galápagos National Park and the Development of its Tourist Potential' (Grimwood and Snow, 1966).

Therefore, from the beginning, there was an overt relationship between conservation and tourism. Obviously, as wildlife was the great attraction, the long-term possibilities of a tourist industry depended on its protection, including its protection against the future tourists themselves. The report proposed that tourism should be based principally on cruises, following, but more modestly, the pattern set by the millionaire yachtsmen, which would not only benefit visitors by enabling them to land on a number of the scattered islands, each of them so very different, but it would eliminate the need for hotels or other facilities within the boundaries of the National Park, as the tourists would sleep in the ships. When they went on shore they would be accompanied by authorized guides, who would protect both them and the wildlife.

This was the way in which tourism subsequently developed but these prophetic proposals raised doubts at the time and nobody could have foreseen to what extent and with what speed they would be realized. Rapid success led to fears that the great influx of tourists would endanger the environment and particularly the extraordinarily tame animals. This became a major preoccupation of the Charles Darwin Research Station but years of study of 'tourist impact' have revealed no serious or irreversible damage, and the creation of a Galápagos National Park Service combined with the training of official guides should give adequate protection for a considerable, though not unlimited, volume of tourist traffic. The inflow of foreign exchange has been a welcome supplement to the Ecuadorian economy and the new industry has led to marked improvements in the conditions of life in the islands. Directly and indirectly, tourism has also induced support for the Darwin Foundation and for conservation policy in general. Moreover, one cannot entirely ignore the satisfaction such visits have given to thousands. There are scientists who, because of the unique importance of the ecosystems to science, would like to see tourism banned and the settlers bought out and removed so that the whole archipelago could be devoted to research; and there are no doubt promoters who would like to see luxury hotels and other 'civilized' facilities, but the developments during the first 20 years of this experiment have on the whole been as satisfactory a compromise as could be hoped and more than could be expected (Anonymous, 1980). Certainly those founder members of the CDF who have lived to see the changes that have taken place can look back with pride on the work accomplished.

Another basic recommendation in the report was the organization of a National Park Service. This was eventually implemented (page 268) as confidence in the experiment grew, but during the early years the Charles Darwin Research Station was left in sole charge of conservation. It was no doubt undesirable that an international scientific body should be entrusted with such authority but there was no other agency to undertake the responsibility. Meanwhile the nature and extent of the national park had to be defined and the CDF submitted its proposals to the government. The 1959 decree had declared all unsettled areas of the archipelago to be national park and in due course this brought protected status to all the uninhabited islands, and large parts of the four others. The small island of Baltra, with its landing field and air force was entirely excluded. The remaining property rights within the boundaries of the park were extinguished and there are now no residents or developments other than a few simple jetties built from the local lava and discreetly marked trails for the visitors to follow. Even the research station and the headquarters of the park service are situated outside the park. Scientists and GNPS personnel working in the park sleep in tents or on board boats.

From the beginning the CDF had a triple mission: scientific investigation, conservation and education. Until the 1970s, the only resident scientists were the successive UNESCO-supported station directors, whose multiple administrative duties absorbed an ever-increasing share of their time, so that most research was (and still is) conducted by visiting scientists. The visitors, within broad limits set by the needs of conservation, devise their own projects and are funded by their universities or learned societies. Their numbers have steadily increased and must by now be approaching the one thousand mark. Some stay for weeks, others for years. Many of them have made substantial contributions to conservation and local education as well as to basic science but this has never been a condition of the acceptance of their projects. Only in more recent years has the Darwin Station had a strong scientific staff of its own.

From the beginning conservation was the dominant concern of the Charles Darwin Foundation within the limits imposed by the availability of men and money. Because of these limitations, the problems were more obvious than the solutions. After a century of degradation there was so much to be done and so few resources. Of the human threats, poaching proved one of the easiest to check but squatters still tried to settle in the park and farmers allowed their livestock to cross the boundaries, destroying the native vegetation and introducing seeds of alien plants. But the most immediate threats came from the introduced animals—goats, rats, cats, dogs, pigs and donkeys (Chapter 16). After 20 years of attempts at eradication, this still remains a most serious problem but encouragement may be derived from looking back on the gradual elimination of goats from islands where control was once considered impossible. Meanwhile, where endemic tortoises and land iguanas were in danger of extinction by the feral animals, highly-successful captive breeding programmes provided at any rate a temporary solution, while stands of endemic flora were protected by goat-proof fences (Chapter 16, Fig. 16.2).

18.2.3. The National Park Service

By 1968 the foundation had demonstrated the feasibility of conservation and organized touring had actually begun. It was clearly desirable that the sovereign power should assume direct control, so the Galápagos National Park Service (GNPS) was set up under the aegis of the Ministry of Agriculture. As the GNPS was built up gradually—the first park superintendent was not appointed until 1972—and in its early years used the Darwin Station's facilities, a close association grew up. In any case it is difficult to disentangle research and advice on conservation policy from its implementation. Similarly, on such matters as the control of tourists and the granting of permission to visiting scientists, day-by-day cooperation was fortunately inevitable. The first telephone link in the Galápagos was between the GNPS and the CDRS. There have been exchanges of leading personnel between the two organizations, both of which have grown to meet increasing demands on their services. The direct involvement of the State put new authority behind all conservation measures.

Once the National Park Service was firmly established, its role and that of the Darwin Station could be worked out in detail and a general management policy agreed. In 1973 a small team of national and international advisers, representing the Department of National Parks, the National Planning Board, FAO, UNESCO and CDF, drafted a Master Plan for the administration of the park. This was accepted by the Ministry as the basis for future policy.

The Master Plan (1974) confirmed, developed and defined previous pragmatic arrangements and made important new recommendations. Among these was the zoning of the park for specific purposes. As each island has different fauna, flora and other characteristics, it was impractical to allocate this one to science, that one to tourism. Instead, to simplify management, the entire park was divided into five types of zones:

Primitive-scientific Zones are areas that have remained essentially free from introduced species. They require the strictest protection to ensure their ecological integrity. Access permits will normally be granted by the park authorities only for scientific research under strict supervision.

Primitive Zones comprise much the largest area of the park. Although somewhat altered ecologically by introduced species, the maintenance of their primitive character is necessary to guarantee the preservation of the Galápagos ecosystems. One of their essential functions will be to serve as buffers between the Primitive-scientific Zones and the more frequented areas.

Extensive Use Zones are areas containing features of high interest to visitors but which cannot support heavy visitor loads for physical, biological or aesthetic reasons. No interference with nature will be allowed here apart from unobtrusive trails, small camps and a minimum of conservation and research facilities which do not intrude unduly on the wilderness.

Intensive Use Zones are a considerable number of carefully selected areas, small in extent, but of prime interest to visitors. They are deemed capable of withstanding relatively constant visitor use and the necessary minimum of visitor and administrative facilities will be permitted. Usually, scientific research will not be allowed here except for the regular monitoring of tourist impact on the flora and fauna. If the pressure of visitors exceeds the carrying capacity of the environment and deterioration is detected, access will be limited or suspended until the resources have regenerated.

Special Use Zones are lands bordering on the settled areas outside the park, which have suffered substantial alteration. They have traditionally been used by settlers for the supply of water, firewood, sand, salt, etc., and, for the present, these usages will continue on a permit basis. These zones have not the same high quality as the rest of the park but they nevertheless need careful management.

18.2.4. Education

The educational activities of the Charles Darwin Research Station have taken different forms to meet developments over the years. From the first, it was obviously desirable to reconcile the local population to the revolutionary idea of conservation. Natural history lessons were given in the little schools and courses were organized at the station for teachers and officials. After the creation of the National Park Service and the beginning of organized tourism, annual training courses for wardens were held and then rigorous courses followed by examinations for naturalist guides and auxiliary guides, whom the tourist companies were legally obliged to employ on all cruises. Together, wardens and guides have succeeded in regulating visits to the benefit of both the tourists and the environment.

Another development was to offer scholarships to Ecuadorian undergraduate and postgraduate students, enabling them to work at the station. Often they were attached to a visiting scientist as assistants and thus acquired practical experience of research in the field, for which there was formerly little provision in Ecuador. This stimulated the interest of the universities, and led in due course to calls for more and fuller opportunities. An essential provision of Ecuador's national plan was the training of scientists and technologists and it was felt that greater use should be made of the station's potential. As the CDF lacked the funds to engage numbers of highly-qualified scientists the authorities offered to meet the extra cost. Consequently since 1980 a number of specialist scientists have been added to the resident staff. These include an education coordinator, ornithologist, botanist, herpetologist, entomologist and marine biologist, each working with a small group of students. This not only gives expert training in field work but frequently provides the basis for degree theses. At the same time these scientist-student teams make it possible to pay greater attention to research specifically devoted to conservation.

Figure 18.1. As a part of its early policy, lessons in nature conservation have been arranged by the Charles Darwin Research Station for schoolchildren of the islands. Miguel Castro L. (at left) was the first Ecuadorian conservation official of the station, a role later embodied in the Galápagos National Park Service. (Photograph by Sven Gillsäter).

18.2.5. A Unique Experiment

According to Dr. Peter Kramer, who has had 20 years' experience of the islands as research scientist, station director and President of the Charles Darwin Foundation, 'the fact that there is no other archipelago at the same time as extensive, as isolated and as undisturbed by man makes the Galápagos of universal significance for evolutionary research' (Kramer, 1980). Much remains to be done but these extraordinary biological riches now seem to have been made safe for posterity. No known species has become extinct since the foundation was established and the tide of degradation has been halted and turned back. The spirit of Darwin reigns and hundreds of scientists, following in his wake, have worked at the Darwin Station since 1960, their papers and books enlarging and deepening knowledge. The pursuit of knowledge has been accompanied by improvements in the conditions of life of the local population, benefits to the Ecuadorian economy, stimulation to scientific education, pleasure and enlightenment for thousands of visitors and millions of television viewers.

None of this would have come about without the peculiar alliance between government and science. Neither could have done the job without the other. The Darwin Foundation, broadly international, non-governmental and non-bureaucratic, brought to the Galápagos a range of scientific talent that could not have been found in Ecuador, nor indeed in any single country. Successive governments showed commendable patience and tolerance and gave increasing moral and material support to this strange venture. The formation of such a symbiotic relationship was no doubt aided by special factors such as the Darwin legend, Ecuador's immense pride in its island possession and the international prestige arising from the success of the national park. Nevertheless it seems legitimate to ask whether the same basic formula, adapted to suit different local circumstances, might not serve the cause of conservation and science in other key environments. Relations between a sovereign power and a voluntary international body, particularly one bent on conservation in a developing country, are bound to be difficult; but the experiment has achieved success in Ecuador. Need the experiment remain unique? The Galápagos, once the despair of conservationists, was one of the first four natural areas to be declared a World Heritage by UNESCO.

References

Acosta-Solís, M. (1937) *Galápagos observado fitológicamente*. Universidad Central, Quito.

Anonymous (1974) Plan Maestro para la Protección y Uso del *Parque nacional Galápagos*. MAB-UNESCO-FAO, Santiago

Anonymous (1980) *Twenty Years of Conservation in the Galápagos*. Charles Darwin Foundation, Quito.

Bowman, R.I. (1960) *A Biological Reconnaissance of the Galápagos Islands during 1957*. UNESCO, Paris.

Dorst, J. and Laruelle, J. (1967) *The First Seven Years of the Charles Darwin Foundation for the Galápagos Isles 1959–1966*. Charles Darwin Foundation, Brussels.

Eibl-Eibesfeldt, I. (1959) Survey on the Galápagos Islands. *UNESCO Mission Reports*, **8**, 1–31.

Grimwood, I.R. and Snow, D.W. (1966). *Recomendaciones sobre la administración del propuesto Parque Nacional del Archipiélago de Galápagos y el desarrollo de su potencial turística*. Ministry of Overseas Development, London.

Kramer, P. (1980) Why We Need Galápagos. *Noticias de Galápagos*, **31**, 9–11.

Larrea, C.M. (1960) *El Archipiélago de Colón (Galápagos)*. Editorial de la Casa de la Cultura, Quito.

Putney, A.D. (1976) *Informe Final sobre Estrategia Preliminar para la Conservación de Areas Silvestres Sobresalientes del Ecuador*. Ministerio de Agricultura y Ganadería, Quito.

Samandaroff ,Y. and Chalons, M. (1937) *El Porvenir Agro-Pecuario del Archipiélago de Colón (Galápagos)*. Departamento de Agricultura, Quito.

CHAPTER 19

Contributions to Science from the Galápagos

ROBERT I. BOWMAN

San Francisco State University, San Francisco, California, USA

Contents

19.1.	Introduction	278
19.2.	Origin of the *'Origin of Species'*	279
19.3.	Origin of Life	280
19.4.	*El Niño* Phenomenon	283
19.5.	Satellite Reconnaissance of Galápagos Waters	285
19.6.	Geological Studies	287
	19.6.1. Darwin's contribution	287
	19.6.2. Caldera formation	287
	19.6.3. Planetary analogues of Galápagos calderas	290
19.7.	Disharmonic Biological Mixes	290
	19.7.1. Predator-prey relationships	291
	19.7.1.1. Sea-urchins and coral reefs	291
	19.7.1.2. Four-eyed blennies and flycatching	291
	19.7.1.3. Diurnal 'flighting' in storm petrels	291
	19.7.1.4. Tameness of animals	292
	19.7.1.5. Flightessness—an insular mockery of the evolutionary process!	294
	19.7.2. Adaptive radiation	294
	19.7.2.1. Plants	294
	19.7.2.2. Darwin's finches	295
19.8.	Adaptive Association between Galápagos Organisms	297
	19.8.1. Tomatoes, tortoises, and mockingbirds	297
	19.8.2. Cleaning symbiosis	297
	19.8.3. Finches and boobies	297
19.9.	Cryptic Faunas	298
19.10.	Genetics of Galápagos Organisms	299

Contents (*continued*)

19.1.1.   Breeding Behavior of Galápagos Organisms   301
    19.1.1.1.   Autogamy in Galápagos tomatoes   301
    19.1.1.2.   Development of ray flowers in *Scalesia*   302
    19.1.1.3.   Polyandry in Galápagos hawks   302
    19.1.1.4.   Adaptations for rapid breeding in Darwin's
                  finches   302
    19.1.1.5.   Reproductive 'strategies' of Galápagos
                  boobies   303
19.1.2.   Short-term Human Colonization of Galápagos   303
    19.1.2.1.   Prehistoric fishing settlements   303
    19.1.2.2.   A Utopian colonization scheme   304
19.1.3.   Conclusions   305
19.1.4.   Acknowledgments   307
          References   307

19.1. Introduction

No area on Earth of comparable size has inspired more fundamental changes in Man's perspective of himself and his environment than the Galápagos Islands. The unconventional flow of Nature on the land and in the sea has spawned revolutionary views on the origin, not only of new species, but also of life itself. The structural diversity of living forms, and the geological genesis of rock forms and edifices in the Galápagos, are inexorably linked to the evolutionary views of Charles Darwin.

Scientific exploration and study in the Galápagos spans the important period in which 19th-century science (natural history, descriptive and speculative) was transformed into its 20th-century mold (experimental, analytically rigorous, and integrative). But only since the establishment of the Charles Darwin Research Station at Academy Bay and the advent of tourism with accompanying modern transportation facilities has the Galápagos experienced a flush of multidisciplinary scientific activity.

In 1964 the two principal purposes of the Galápagos International Scientific Project (GISP) of the University of California and the United States National Science Foundation were to assess the status of our scientific knowledge of Galápagos, and to alert scientists throughout the world 'to the multifarious problems awaiting their study, particularly in the fields of geology, oceanography, meteorology, and evolutionary biology.' Both purposes have been fulfilled, the former through the publication of the GISP symposium proceedings (Bowman, 1966), and the latter through a virtual torrent of exciting new research. But so diverse in subject matter, and so far-flung in the world's scientific literature are the investigative results of the past 20 years, that it underscores the urgent need to reactivate, keep current, and make broadly available the computerized 'Galápagos Bibliography' initiated in 1972 by Drs. Tom Simkin and the late Robert Silberglied of the Smithsonian Institution.

It is quite apparent that scientific research in the Galápagos, although impressive by its sheer volume, has not progressed evenly over a broad front. Biological disciplines such as ichthyology, invertebrate zoology (especially marine), botany (exclusive of flowering plants), microbiology, paleontology and parasitology, are still very much in their infancy. The same is true of the physical sciences of pedology, hydrology, and climatology. Oceanographers and meteorologists, by virtue of the large-scale nature of the phenomena they study, must view the Galápagos as but a small piece of a much larger realm requiring the application of instrumentation of great sophistication, including deep-sea submersibles and remote sensing Earth-orbiting satellites.

In this overview of scientific contributions from the Galápagos, it has not been feasible to cite all of the many hundreds of scholarly publications well known to specialists, or to call attention to all active research areas, or to take note of the recent flourish of beautifully illustrated natural history books, which have helped in no small way to create world-wide popular appreciation of Galápagos Nature. What follows is an eclectic review, organized around principles, of curious, yet scientifically significant, discoveries made in the Galápagos Islands and the ocean around them.

From this general summary and the disciplinary reviews of my colleagues, writings, it is hoped that the reader will gain (a) a sense of the excitement that Galápagos science has brought its practitioners, (b) an appreciation of the depth, breadth, and world-wide significance of the research results, and (c) possibly an understanding of the manner in which honest differences of opinion among scientists have contributed to the discovery of truths about the organization of living things and their physical environment.

19.2. Origin of the *'Origin of Species'*

Of all Charles Darwin's observations during the voyage of H.M.S. *Beagle* it can be fairly said that island phenomena struck him as the most curious, and that the Galápagos conditions made some of the most profound impressions upon him. In his 'Ornithological Notebook' we find the key to his mesmeric fascination with the Galápagos. He observed that the mockingbirds were closely allied in appearance to those of Chile, but with a different song. Moreover, of the birds collected from four of the larger islands (page 177 and Fig. 19.1), he was 'astonished' to discover that adjacent islands, separated by narrow channels of the sea, were inhabited by slightly different varieties (see Bowman and Carter, 1971, and Abbott and Abbott, 1978). Although informed by a local official that the intra-archipelagic source of a given Galápagos tortoise could be ascertained from the characteristic shape of its carapace, only later, when considering the asserted difference between the wolf-like fox of East and West Falkland (Broad, 1982), did Darwin come to realize that all 'such facts [would] undermine the stability of Species' (Barlow, 1946). These words, written after his five-week stay in the Galápagos, are probably Darwin's first pronouncement of his suspicion that species were not

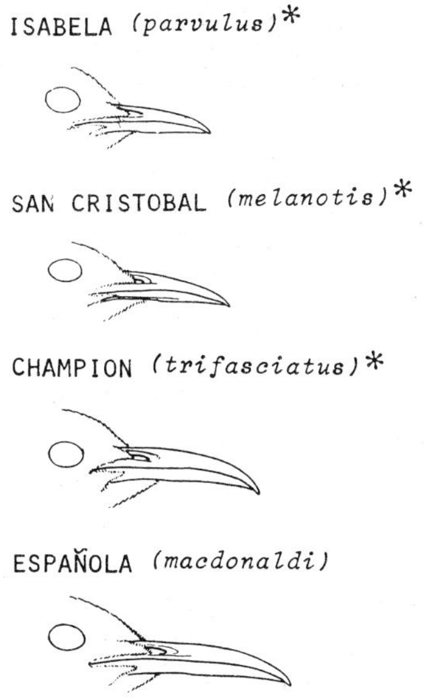

ISABELA *(parvulus)* *

SAN CRISTOBAL *(melanotis)* *

CHAMPION *(trifasciatus)* *

ESPAÑOLA *(macdonaldi)*

Figure 19.1. Variation in the size and shape of the bills of Galápagos mockingbirds (*Mimus* [*Nesomimus*] spp.). Species collected by Charles Darwin in 1835 are flagged by an asterisk. Drawings after Swarth, 1931.

immutable (Sulloway, 1982). By 1837, while working with the ornithologist John Gould, and musing about the different beak shapes of Galápagos finches, seeds of disbelief in the eternal constancy of species had germinated, and Charles Darwin became an evolutionist (Mayr, 1972). The facts of evolution triumphed over doubts about dogma or divine creation!

Although islands have had a small part to play in the grand sweep of evolution, they have, nevertheless, played a large part in the progress of our understanding of it. Clearly, insular phenomena played a crucial role in the *Origin of Species*, and from what we know of Darwin's interest in the Galápagos, it is not difficult to see the 'island model' in many of his arguments. It seems as if the Galápagos was used as an 'elastic template,' stretched to fit insular phenomena all over the world, delineating barriers, isolation, dispersion, and descent (Black, 1972).

Darwin's appreciation of the *space dimension* (= isolation) and the facts of species variability, so crucial to his theory of the transmutation of organisms by means of natural selection, had their origins in the peculiar conditions of the Galápagos setting. He acquired his first-hand understanding of the *time dimension* (= geology) from his earlier observations on fossiliferous deposits in the Patagonian plains and the Chilean Andes.

Over the past century, 'frontal attacks' by some religious fundamentalists and anti-intellectuals have been largely ineffectual, except among their clans, in promoting the belief that organic evolution is a mystery about which little is, or can be, known. Scientific studies on the genetics, ecology, and behavior of insular forms in the Galápagos, New Guinea, Hawaii, and elsewhere, have helped to dispel such a fallacy. As observed by Stanley (1981), Darwin's theory of evolution by means of natural selection is not just getting older, it is also getting better! Like any scientific concept that has long withstood the test of time, this one has suffered setbacks, but, time and again, has rebounded to become richer and stronger.

19.3. Origin of Life

The discovery of sea-floor spreading ENE of the Galápagos Islands (Heron and Heirtzler, 1967; see Chapter 2, Fig. 2.1), was followed, in 1977, by direct observation of hydrothermal vents from the manned submersible, *Alvin*, and the discovery of extraordinary and unique biological communities on the ocean floor at a depth of more than one and a half miles (Corliss, *et al.*, 1979). That these animal associations, including giant clams, yellow mussels, white crabs, and four-and-a-half-foot long pogonophoran worms, were primarily sustained by chemosynthetic bacteria was first proposed by John Baross and later demonstrated by Karl, *et al.* (1980). Many deep-sea bacteria are known to be pressure-tolerant and may represent recent arrivals from shallow surface waters. But certain forms are characteristically pressure-loving in their growth characteristics, and possibly have originated at great ocean depths (Jannasch, *et al.*, 1982).

It was probably inevitable that these discoveries would lead to speculation on the possibility that abiotic synthesis on Earth began in Archaean submarine hydrothermal systems (Corliss, Baross and Hoffman, 1981). Furthermore, it became apparent that submarine hydrothermal environments could have been the sites for protected evolutionary experimentation throughout the Precambrian, leading eventually to the Cambrian 'faunal explosion' (Baross, *et al*, 1980).

Not long after Pasteur (1862) demonstrated that contemporary organisms, even the most simple forms, do not arise spontaneously from non-living precursors, Huxley (1870) speculated that, in a remote period of Earth's history, living protoplasm evolved from 'not-living matter.' A competing model was suggested by Arrhenius (1908) that terrestrial life originated from simple extraterrestrial forms drifting through interstellar space (Shklovskii and Sagan, 1966). This hypothesis is still championed today by Crick and Orgel (1973), among others.

In the 1920's, A.I. Oparin (1924) and J.B.S. Haldane (1929) speculated on an abiological origin of life on Earth through the interaction of 'primary energy sources' with some set of 'primeval molecules.' Both reasoned that the common ancestor of all subsequent life on Earth was an anaerobic heterotroph which developed in a surface aqueous environment rich in biological and prebiological molecules—the 'organic soup.'

Acceptance of the organic soup model by most scientific investigators led to experiments in abiotic synthesis of organic molecules. In 1953, Miller succeeded in synthesizing for the first time amino acids from non-biogenic precursors using an electric discharge apparatus intended to simulate conditions in the atmosphere of the early Earth. Since those pioneering experiments, hundreds of organic molecules have been spontaneously generated using a variety of techniques, with electric discharge experiments being the most popular and productive methods. Part of the reason for the experimental longevity of electrical discharge experiments is that, prior to 1977, no plausible primeval environment for abiotic synthesis other than the 'organic soup' was thought to have existed. The *Alvin* submersible dives to the Galápagos hydrothermal vents not only discovered a previously unknown contemporary biological environment, but also opened a window on the past through which scientists could view ancient environments from a new perspective.

In 1980, Corliss, Baross and Hoffman (1981) developed a model which unified data from three different areas of scientific research—Archaean geology and paleontology, experimental biochemistry, and modern oceanography—to present a coherent and plausible scenario for the origin of life. They suggested that submarine hydrothermal systems such as are now known to exist along the Galápagos Rift, the East Pacific Rise, and other sea-floor rift zones, constitute ideal abiotic synthesis reactors. A critical corollary of this model is that Archaean 'greenstone belts' (i.e. zones of ancient weathered seafloor basalts) do, in fact, represent the oldest known oceanic crust and contain abundant evidence of Archaean hydrothermal activity (Hoffman, 1982).

When, at temperatures approaching 1100°C, newly-emplaced oceanic crusts interact with ambient bottom water (present day temperatures approximately 2°C; Archaean temperatures probably approximately 80°C), there is a continuing cycle of cooling, fracturing, crack propagation, further water penetration, cooling, fracturing, etc. As the water rises back up through the rock, a pressure head is established and cool ambient water is pulled in, which results in a self-propagating convection system (Fig. 19.2). Not only does the water cool the rock, but there is also a complex series of chemical exchange reactions leading to irreversible geochemical and mineralogical changes characteristic of hydrothermal systems (Maris and Bender, 1982). These characteristic geochemistries and mineralogies are ubiquitous in Archaean and Proterozoic greenstone belts (Hoffman, 1982).

As a result of the thermal and chemical interaction of seawater with hot, young oceanic crust, hydrothermal systems are characterized by high heat fluxes, chemically reducing conditions, abundant catalytic surfaces, and significant concentrations of important 'primeval' molecules and ions (CH_4, NH_3, H_2S, H_2, HCN, CO, CO_2, transition metals, etc. (see Fig. 19.2b). The self-propagating convective flow ensures a mixing gradient of temperature and composition which removes products from the site of the reaction. The existence of such a gradient makes it quite likely that the entire sequence of reactions, from the synthesis of simple prebiotic compounds to the synthesis of organic molecules (amino acid polymers and proteins) to protobionts (metabolizing organized structures) to self-replicating living organisms, could occur within and/or adjacent to these systems and their vents.

In contrast to other models, which require early micro-organisms to be anaerobic heterotrophs or phototrophs, the hydrothermal model strongly supports the contention that the first protocells were anaerobic chemo-autotrophs, capable of utilizing energy in the form of reduced sulfur compounds emitted from hydro-thermal vents. Such an organism would have more in common with Archaebacteria, a contention which is supported by microbiological work on vent organisms (Baross, *et al.*, 1980; Corliss, *et al.*, 1981; Karl, *et al.*, 1980). Furthermore, there are striking morphological similarities between micro-organisms which have been observed in scanning electron microscope photographs taken of chunks of rock and of hydrothermal sulfide chimneys from the Galápagos and East Pacific rises (Baross, *et al.*, 1980), and of Archaean fossil organisms described in the literature (Knoll and Barghoorn, 1977).

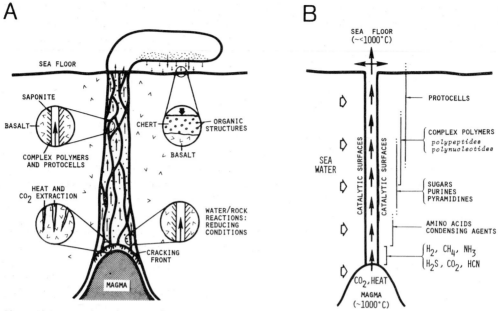

Figure 19.2. Hypothetical model (after Corliss, *et al.*, 1981), depicting a submarine hydrothermal system. This reactor features a continuous flow mixing gradient for the abiotic synthesis of living organisms or their immediate precursors. A. Supersaturated components of the low viscosity fluids rising through the confluent fracture system, precipitate out as they reach the sea-floor and mix rapidly with bottom water, forming chemical sediments around the vents. B. Proposed sequence of chemical biochemical events leading to the formation and development of 'protocells.'

The hydrothermal model for abiotic synthesis also provides a very convincing explanation for the rapid and early appearance of the Earth's biosphere. Evidence from the 3.5 billion year old Barberton Mountain Land of South Africa indicates that the rate of Archaean microbiological primary production was apparently of the order of magnitude as that in comparable present day sedimentary basins (Reimer, *et al.*, 1979). This cannot be explained by the organic soup model which is generally believed to require a vast length of time for the synthesis of the first living organism. Furthermore, there is no geological evidence that an organic soup ever existed. If, however, the floor of the Archaean ocean was riddled with rift zones, all of which necessarily resulted in the hydrothermal cooling of the newly-emplaced crust, then the sites for Archaean abiotic synthesis were abundant and essentially ubiquitous, and the process of abiotic synthesis was probably geologically instantaneous. Modern oceanic rift zones may provide homes for some of the oldest life associations on Earth.

The discovery of thermal hot spring communities on the sea-floor spreading zones of the Galápagos and East Pacific (lat. 15°N) rises—perhaps one of the greatest biological discoveries of the 20th century—raises the question of whether or not biogenesis is still possible, despite the presence of competing and predatory organisms that have originated over the past billion or more years.

Charles Darwin also wondered about the feasibility of modern day biogenesis on Earth, as evidenced by a thought expressed in a letter he wrote in 1871 (Morgulis, *in* Oparin, 1953):

'It is often said that all of the conditions for the first production of a living organism are now present, which could ever have been present. But if (and oh! what a big if) we could conceive in some warm little pond, with all sorts of ammonia and phosphoric salts, light, heat, electricity, etc. present, then a protein compound was chemically formed ready to undergo still more complex changes, at the present day, such matter would be instantly devoured or absorbed, which would not have been the case before living creatures were formed.'

Surely Darwin would have been amazed and delighted with the discovery of the bizarre ocean-bottom biological communities of the Galápagos, which flourish in a unique, totally dark world of high pressures, toxic metal compounds, extremes of volcanic heat and abyssal cold, and nurtured by microscopic sulfur-oxidizing heterotrophic bacteria. Such an ecosystem is almost the inverse ecological counterpart of the equally bizarre terrestrial and shallow water ecosystems of the Galápagos Islands, which are totally dependent on solar heat and photosynthetic fixation of carbon dioxide for their sustenance.

19.4. *El Niño* Phenomenon

The Galápagos Islands lie at the crossroads of oceanic currents (Fig. 19.3 and page 44), which largely control the distribution of maritime organisms and regulate the general character of the climate of the eastern tropical Pacific (Wyrtki, 1979; Palmer and Pyle, 1966). As a result of the anomolous variability of the ocean water at the Galápagos, there is an intermingling of faunas almost without parallel (e.g. fur seals, penguins, flying fish, corals, and tropic-birds). Large scale studies of the ocean-atmospheric processes affecting the seasonal 'battle of the currents,' have resulted from a need to understand better the impact of this fluctuating system on the anchovy fishery off Peru. In the 1960's, this fishery developed from almost nothing to the world's largest fishery based on a single species. The near total collapse of the anchovy catches following the *El Niño* event of 1973 (Idyll, 1973), accompanied by massive die-offs of seabirds because of starvation, prompted a concerted effort to advance our knowledge of the dynamics of ocean circulation in the eastern tropical Pacific, with a view towards predicting the reoccurrence of the event (Wyrtki, 1979). The Galápagos Islands occupy a strategic location for monitoring oceanic processes, and data from sea-level gauges on Baltra have helped oceanographers to understand certain aspects of the dynamic large scale fluctuations leading to an *El Niño* phenomenon.

As the term is used today by scientists, *El Niño* refers to a *large catastrophic* event in the fluctuating ocean-atmosphere system, which brings anomalously warm water to a broad area of the eastern Pacific, accompanied by torrential rains over the arid coastal regions of Ecuador and north Peru, westward to the Galápagos Islands (see Chapter 4.2). With respect to the Peruvian coastal waters, the event is characterized by its sporadic occurrence, its long persistence of more than a year, and its catastrophic biological consequences. As such, it has no equivalent anywhere in the oceans of the world (Wyrtki, 1979). In the Galápagos the

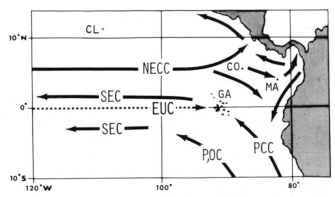

Figure 19.3. Generalized picture of the principal surface and sub-surface currents around the major oceanic islands of the eastern tropical Pacific Ocean. Islands shown are Clipperton (CL), Cocos (CO), Galápagos (GA), and Malpelo (MA). Surface currents indicated are North Equatorial Counter-current (NECC), Perú Coastal Current (PCC), Perú Oceanic Current (POC), and South Equatorial Current (SEC). Sub-surface current, indicated by the broken line, is the Equatorial Undercurrent (EUC). Based on Wyrtki (1965, 1966) and Knauss (1961).

massive displacement of normally cool, food-laden waters with abnormally warm food-barren waters, causes an 'ocean desert' to develop for sea-birds, which affects their reproductive success (Murphy, 1925; Harris, 1973, 1979; Boersma, 1978). Whereas *El Niño* causes a reduction in the local productivity of the ocean, the accompanying heavy rainfall brings widespread 'greening' of the land, with an extended growing season for vegetation and a prolonged breeding season for terrestrial based animals, and notably the finches (Grant and Boag, 1980).

A network of tide gauge stations was established in the equatorial Pacific Ocean from Guam and Rabaul in the western Pacific, to Manzanillo, Mexico, Easter Island, and the all-important station at Baltra in the Galápagos. By correlating data on sea-level changes, sea-surface topography across the equator, and the seasonal fluctuations in intensity of the southeast trade winds (Wyrtki, 1973, 1974, 1975 and 1977), a new theory for the occurrence of the *El Niño* event was proposed by Wyrtki (1975), namely, a response of the equatorial Pacific Ocean to atmospheric forcing. This theory, outlined by G. Houvenaghel in Chapter 3, has much in its support, but some unresolved problems remain. Since characteristics of each *El Niño* appear to be different, this supports the view that different 'El Niños' may have different causes (Cane, 1982).

Recent studies (Barnett, 1981), here summarized from the discussion of Kerr (1982), suggest that warm water in the equatorial Pacific can signal the onset of severe winters in north temperate latitudes around the globe. Atmospheric teleconnections are implicated. The first link is the conversion of potential energy to kinetic in the atmosphere over the *El Niño* anomaly in the tropics, where the winds are relatively light and the Coriolis effect weak. Consequently, a strong vertical atmospheric circulation can develop as heat released by the condensation of water vapor accelerates the ascent of air already warmed by the anomaly. As the thermodynamic circulation intensifies and reaches 10–25 km above the earth's surface, it makes itself felt thousands of kilometres to the north via a 'Rossby wave' (Horel and Wallace, 1981). Once these waves reach middle north latitudes, they may distort the wave pattern of the high-altitude westerly winds, so that extreme (cold) weather may be directed into North America.

If meteorologists could anticipate the sending of teleconnection signals from the equatorial region, they might be able to improve long-range weather predictions. For this to occur researchers must find a relation

Figure 19.4. Irregularities in the ocean surface between Española and Santa Fé, Galápagos on March 12, 1968. Rippled surface indicates areas of cool current amidst areas of smooth-surfaced warmer water.

between weather there and the weather elsewhere during the previous autumn or summer. Bjerknes (1966, 1969) suggested that *El Niño* in the eastern tropical Pacific, characterized by warming of surface waters off Ecuador and Peru westward to the Galápagos Islands and beyond, could affect weather in the middle latitudes, and Barnett (1981) discovered that sea surface temperatures of the *El Niño* region were the most useful of various Pacific regions studied to predict air temperatures in the United States a season ahead.

As noted by Kerr (1982), although the equatorial teleconnection is a reality, it has been quite elusive. Only one in five *El Niño* events of the past 30 years seems to have produced a dramatic effect on US weather, with the 1976–77 episode bringing record cold to the United States during the winter of 1977. Because of the intermittent nature of the equatorial teleconnections, many meteorologists are uncertain about their usefulness in long-range weather forecasting.

It is concluded that the events off the coast of Peru, Ecuador, and about the Galápagos Islands are not locally generated, but result from a large oscillation in the atmospheric-ocean system whose effects may be global (Covey, 1978; Horel and Wallace, 1981; Rasmusson and Carpenter, 1982; Wyrtki, 1979). A better understanding of the dynamics of the phenomenon in the eastern tropical Pacific Ocean is very important, since any major changes in summer precipitation over land or in oceanic circulation may have dramatic consequences for the economic well-being of the region through disruption of agriculture and fisheries.

19.5. Satellite Reconnaissance of Galápagos Waters

Within the equatorial latitudes of about 5°N and 5°S, and longitudes 85° and 100°W (Fig. 19.3), the North Equatorial Countercurrent from the west, which is characterized by clear pelagic water of a temperature ranging between 25° and 28°C, mingles with warm but less clear and saline water from the northward, and with cool Coastal Peru (Humboldt) Current water from the southeastward (Murphy, 1936). The picture sometimes results in alternating bands of surface water which differ in temperature by 5 or 10 degrees C or more, and with irregularities in sea-surface patterns (Wyrtki, 1979; see Fig. 19.4). Large scale patterns have been studied by McClain and Strong (1969) using photographs obtained by means of Applications Technology Satellite (ATS), which provides earth-synchronous coverage from an altitude of 38,800 km over the Equator in the eastern Pacific at 15 to 20 minute intervals during daylight hours.

As the sun moves from east to west, dark patches of water change to briefly reflectant 'sun-glint' areas. For example, such areas were repeatedly photographed during February and March, 1968 to the northwest and northeast of the Galápagos Islands (McClain and Strong, 1969). This is a region of very high marine productivity due to the pronounced upwelling (Wooster and Hedgpeth, 1966). To the west of the islands the Equatorial (Cromwell) Undercurrent is travelling eastward at about 3 knots, with upwelling and mixing taking place above it toward the surface, also producing areas of high marine productivity. This would allow the rather shallow thermocline in this region to break virtually through the surface (Houvenaghel, 1974; McClain and Strong, 1969).

On March 19, 1968, an ATS photograph revealed an enormous sun-glint area extending from Fernandina for over 400 km northwest of the archipelago. The timing and location of this phenomenon is important because of its possible relationship to a collapse of the caldera floor of Fernandina in June 1968 and for which evacuation of a subsurface magma chamber was needed (Simkin and Howard, 1970). Studies of caldera collapse elsewhere have indicated that there is often a balance between the volume of the collapse and the volume of the extruded products. But such appeared not to be the case at Fernandina, for which the collapse volume was far in excess of that accounted for by known subaerial products. Simkin and Howard (1970) suggested that additional flank flows may have gone unseen, and that the most likely place to look for the 'missing magma' would be on the submarine flanks of the volcano. The withdrawal of magma from below the caldera floor could have occurred at a time considerably in advance of actual floor collapse, with a high pressure concentration of gas in the evacuated space replacing the pre-existing structural support. McBirney and Williams (1969) have suggested that an outbreak of lava may have occurred at the base of the escarpment of the Galápagos platform just west of Fernandina. If this actually occurred there is the question of whether such a submarine eruption could have caused the extensive sun-glint area of March 19, 1968 (Fig. 19.5). It is likely that the calmer sea-state revealed as sun-glint was due to the wave dampening effect of upwelling, the

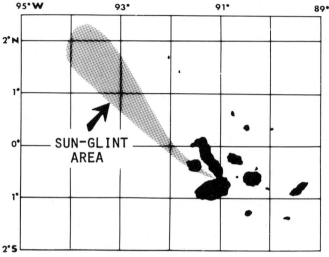

Figure 19.5. Location of 400 km long sun-glint area northwest of the Galápagos Islands, based on 'stationary' satellite photographs taken on 19 March 1968. Modified after Figs 4A, B and 7 in McLain and Strong (1969).

Figure 19.6. ATS III image dissector camera photograph taken on February 23, 1968, 1651:58 GMT, showing several regions of upwelling (dark areas indicated by pointers) between Galápagos Islands eastward to the Ecuadorian mainland. Photo supplied by A. E. Strong, U.S. National Environmental Satellite Center.

latter being generated by massive heat flow from a submarine lava vent on the western flank of Fernandina, and also possibly on the southeastern flank. The Peru Coastal Current, streaming through the archipelago, could have caused the upwelling water to drift in a northwesterly direction from the eruption site (Fig. 19.5).

Late in 1968 there was an onset of a modest *El Niño* that engulfed the eastern tropical Pacific from Galápagos to the South American continent (Quinn and Burt, 1970; Quinn, 1974). ATS photographs indicated numerous and variable sun-glint patches (upwellings) northeast and east of the Galápagos during February and March, 1968 (Fig. 19.6). Could these have been harbingers of the eastward surge of warm water (Equatorial Countercurrent, Fig. 3) from the western tropical Pacific that was to over-ride the cool waters of the Coastal Peru Current, resulting in the 1968–69 *El Niño* event.?

Future satellite monitoring will provide important links in the data-nexus used by oceanographers, meteorologists, and geologists to predict the onset of catastrophic physical events in the Galápagos area and beyond.

19.6. Geological Studies

19.6.1. Darwin's contribution

Previous to 1964, the geology of the Galápagos Islands was one of the least well-known of almost any region of the world, including the most remote oceanic archipelago (Hawaii) and the most inhospitable continent (Antarctica), and this despite the intriguing geological observations of Charles Darwin that were published 120 years earlier! For the most part, Darwin's biological observations and his speculations about them overshadowed his geological observations, although, as noted by the geologists McBirney and Williams (1969), they are no less incisive and significant. These same authors point out that on the basis of his 1835 field studies in the Galápagos, Darwin (1896) was probably the first to suggest the role of sea-water in the formation of palagonite tuffs, a porous stratified rock composed of compacted volcanic ash (Fig. 19.7); he was among the first to recognize crystal concentration—in a Buccaneer Bay lava flow—as resulting from sinking of relatively heavy crystals while the flow was still liquid (and that differentiation by gravity might explain differences between lavas, even from the same vent); he correctly discerned that settling and flotation are the major factors in the differentiation of crystal layers in lavas; and Darwin correctly concluded that in the absence of evidence of widespread geological uplift or subsidence, the present-day Galápagos Islands have always been isolated from each other and never connected with the mainland (see Cox, 1983 and Simpson, 1974).

One original theory erroneously attributed to Charles Darwin by Waldrop (1982) and others is that the Pacific Ocean basin gave rise to the Moon! Probably because of Darwin's extensive geological studies in the Pacific region, this confusion arose with the theory that was actually proposed by George Howard Darwin, an eminent scientist in his own right, and fifth child of Emma Wedgewood and Charles Robert Darwin (Brunn, 1982).

19.6.2. Caldera formation

With the beginning of systematic aerial photography in the early 1940's and of extensive ground-based surveys in the 1960's, it became clear that the principal volcanoes of the Galápagos Islands are enormous basaltic 'shields' (so-called because of their resemblance to the concave shields of early north European warriors) with large summit depressions termed calderas (Williams, 1966). See Fig. 19.8.

According to Williams (1941), calderas are formed by subsidence of surface material into some central space which becomes available at depth, and the Galápagos Islands are geologically well-known for their calderas and for their associated circumferential feeding vents (see Chapter 2.63). The actual collapse of caldera floors, however, is not common in historical time, and the Galápagos Islands are noteworthy for having provided the only large collapse known in the last 70 years. This was on Fernandina in 1968, and—because of modern remote sensing capabilities and prompt follow-up studies—it is the only historic caldera collapse with a detailed record (Simkin and Howard, 1970; Filson *et al.*, 1973).

Figure 19.7. Strata of volcanic tuff (palagonite), south shore of James Bay, Santiago. Below: Internal molds (1, 2, and 3) of fossil gastropods (*Strombus*) located at sea-level, Cerro Colorado, Santa Cruz. Age of fossil-bearing deposit is probably late Pliocene to early Pleistocene (*fide* M. J. James, Department of Paleontology, University of California, Berkeley; see Durham, 1965).

Figure 19.8. Above: East side of Volcán Darwin, Isabela, as viewed by a distinguished volcanologist, the late Howel Williams, in January, 1964. The upper regions of the highest peaks are clear of stratus clouds during the local 'summer' season. Below: Aerial view of Volcán Wolf (foreground) and Volcán Darwin (background), showing the inverted soup bowl-like form of Galápagos volcanic edifices on Isabela. During the local 'winter' season there is a pronounced air inversion layer above which the climate is arid. Photo taken from US Air Force Galápagos mission airplane on 4 July 1968.

19.6.3. Planetary analogues of Galápagos calderas

The last 15 years have seen an unprecedented expansion in the exploration of the Moon and planets by means of space probes, coupled with an unparalleled expansion of geophysical and geological exploration of Earth. Without 'ground-truth' information the large circular depressions on the planetary surfaces presented a problem of identification as to their origin (Malin, 1977). Were they impact craters or were they of volcanic origin, i.e. the result of a collapse phenomenon? Through application of the 'uniformatarianism principle' championed by Lyell (1830), the results of volcanism research on the Moon, Mars, Saturn, and other planets have been interpreted in conjunction with complementary field studies on Earth. Volcanoes and lava flows, such as those so splendidly displayed in the Galápagos, Hawaii, and Iceland, had suddenly taken on great significance.

Since the summits of the larger Galápagos calderas stand well above the moister regions at the inversion level, the dry conditions retard their erosion by water (Fig. 19.8). Thus they exhibit today geological details that give the impression of having formed in comparatively recent times, and, indeed, Fernandina has been dated at under one million years of age (Cox, 1983). This makes Galápagos volcanoes ideal for comparison with extra-mundane volcanic analogues. On the Moon, where the present rate of erosion (largely due to meteoric impact) is very slow, volcanic edifices one thousand million years old may still retain the essentials of their shape (Fielder and Wilson, 1975).

All shield volcanoes on Earth are dwarfed when compared with the giant shield volcano 'Olympus Mons' on Mars, which is probably the largest known volcano in the Solar System, i.e. with a basal diameter of 2000 km and standing some 20 km above sea-level (Fielder and Wilson, 1975). By contast, the impressive single Fernandina shield volcano in the Galápagos measures only 25–30 km across at sea-level and stands about 1.5 km above the sea-surface.

On the basis of aerial and ground reconnaissances of shield volcanoes in the Galápagos and elsewhere, it was concluded in advance of verification by actual planetary land probes that many of the lunar sinks were analogous, at least in broad outline, to large calderas and volcanic ring structures found on Earth. Features of Galápagos shield volcanoes such as step faulting, producing benches and multiple caldera walls, large central plateau (caldera floor), and multiple concentric circumferential fissures, are associated with caldera subsidence (Williams, 1966). The features of many large lunar sinks are also probably allied to volcano-tectonic subsidence of this sort. But no other volcano on Earth shows so well circumferential fissures traversing a wide flattish bench around the caldera summit as Fernandina in the Galápagos (Williams and McBirney, 1968).

19.7. Disharmonic Biological Mixes

Remote oceanic islands have been colonized by organisms with good to excellent dispersabilities (Carlquist, 1974; Porter, 1982; Vagvolgyi, 1975). For example, mainland terrestrial plants and animals that are poorly endowed with preadaptations for overseas transport (i.e. small dissemule size, resistance to desiccation, cold, salt water, etc.), or lacking in broad ecological tolerance (i.e. 'weediness'), generally make poor island colonists. The inability of many organisms to overcome such handicaps has resulted in 'disharmonic' floras and faunas on oceanic islands, characterized by the absence or poor representation of certain groups, e.g. hoofed and carnivorous mammals, amphibians, primary-division freshwater fishes, conifers, and large-seeded forest trees. Thus, out of an eclectic and impoverished mix of disparate mainland waif-weed species, which do not match the niches available to them on the islands, natural selection has shaped an array of ecological 'gap-filling,' compromising 'bedfellows,' which have established among themselves a new and unique, ecologically based 'harmonic' relationship. The extent of such realignments is often indicated by the degree of endemism shown by the various groups.

The Galápagos biota is replete with examples of 'make-shifts' in structure, behavior, and ecology, studies of which have furthered our understanding of ecosystem functioning on oceanic islands.

19.7.1. Predator-prey relationships

It is often remarked that oceanic islands like the Galápagos have diminished predatory pressures on their inhabitants (Lack, 1945; see Bowman, 1961). Such may have been the situation in the early stages of establishment, but subsequent evolution has brought about new and different predator-prey relationships between species.

19.7.1.1. Sea-urchins and coral reefs

Grazing by the sea-urchin, *Eucidaris thouarsii*, has been described in Chapter 17.2.5. In the insular setting, corals have acquired a new and unsuspected diurnal predator against which they have little protection, and the urchin has been 'freed,' presumably, of some of its mainland predators, thereby allowing divestiture of continental constraints on its feeding habits.

19.7.1.2. Four-eyed blennies and flycatching

The endemic Galápagos four-eyed blenny (*Dialommus fuscus*, see Chapter 9.51) is about as terrestrial in its foraging behavior as a marine fish might dare to be. Presumably, the absence or reduced numbers of predatory mammals, reptiles, birds, and amphibians along the intertidal splash zone has provided not only an escape route from efficient predatory fishes in the sea, but also a plentiful supply of foods such as small crustaceans and flies.

19.7.1.3. Diurnal 'flighting' in storm petrels

The large nesting colony of storm petrels, *Oceanodroma tethys* and *O. castro*, estimated at over 3000 birds on the southeast of Genovesa (Nelson, 1966), are conspicuous by their mass aerial mating manoeuvers ('flighting') during mid-day periods, under bright sunny skies. Their only predator at the nest site is the somewhat sluggish, partly diurnal, short-eared owl (*Asio galapagoensis*), which is not sufficiently numerous to take a significant toll (Nelson, 1979). Elsewhere, on continental islands (e.g. Farallones, 27 miles W of San Francisco, California), storm petrels and predatory diurnal gulls nest side by side, the petrels in burrows, the gulls on the surface. Since petrels are no match for gulls, and often have to pass within inches of a sitting gull in order to reach their nest burrows, storm petrels have adopted a nocturnal 'flighting' behavior, completely disappearing from view during the daylight hours in the vicinity of their colonial nesting island—the reverse behavior of the Galápagos storm petrels! The only populous gull in the Galápagos is the nocturnal-foraging fork-tailed gull (*Creagrus furcatus*)—a species, ironically, which is diurnally inactive during the early nesting season, presumably, in order to escape marauding frigate-birds that attack them when foraging and transporting food to their young (Hailman, 1964; Snow and Snow, 1968).

19.7.1.4. Tameness of animals

Darwin (1845) concluded his description of the natural history of the Galápagos Islands by describing the extreme tameness of birds—finches, mockingbirds, flycatchers, doves, and hawks. But tameness is not restricted to the birds, because *Grapsus* crabs, lava lizards, land and marine iguanas, fur seals, and sea-lions also permit very close approach of humans before exhibiting alarm. It should be noted, however, that

Figure 19.9. Land iguana (*Conolophus subcristatus*) on Fernandina keeps a watchful eye on a Galápagos hawk as it hovers overhead.

Galápagos Islands are not 'isles without fear', as some writers have characterized them. Darwin (1845) was careful to point out that the wildness of insular birds *with regard to man*, is a particular instinct directed against him, and not dependent on any general degree of caution arising from other sources of danger (Fig. 19.9). In the Galápagos, birds, lizards, and tortoises have been pursued and injured by man for over a century, but they have not yet learned a salutary dread of him (Moore, 1982). Jungius and Hirsch (1979) found that 'tame' Galápagos sea-birds on the nest site may be under severe physiological stress when approached to within 18 m, although no outward manifestations of the measured doubling or quadrupling of normal heart rate was detected by observers. In field experiments using dummy animals, Curio (1964, 1969) found that Darwin's finches feared carnivorous mammals substantially less than snakes or avian predators, which release a specific response. Specific recognition by the finches of resident avian predators, namely, the *Buteo* hawk and the *Asio* owl, is presumed to have evolved under geographically variable selection pressures for each, with the greatest fear reaction being expressed on islands where both predators occur, and least where neither occurs. Bowman

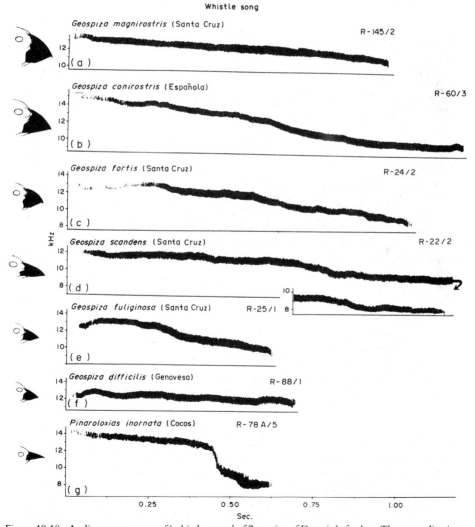

Figure 19.10. Audiospectrograms of 'whistle songs' of 7 species of Darwin's finches. These vocalizations are associated with pair-bonding and nest invitation behaviour. The tonal purity and imperceptable 'fade-in' and 'fade-out' of a sustained frequency sound provide no clues for its binaural spatial orientation. From Bowman, 1982.

(1983) has suggested that the high-pitched 'whistle songs' of Darwin's finches (frequency range of 9–15 kHz on average; see Fig. 19.10), which function in pair-bonding, are a form of 'acoustical camouflage' because they seem to defy binaural localization of their source by such ubiquitous nest predators as mockingbirds and short-eared owls.

19.7.1.5. Flightlessness—an insular mockery of the evolutionary process!

Oceanic islands are notorious for their great numbers of insects and birds that are flightless or with diminished powers of flight. In the Galápagos the most famous flightless birds are the penguin and the cormorant: the former is a diminutive, slightly altered equatorial derivative of a Subantarctic-Antarctic group, whereas the latter is a generically novel descendent of a northern hemisphere ancestor (Murphy, 1936).

The flightless cormorant (*Nannopterum harrisi*) is one of the most striking examples of genetic loss of wing function made possible by the safety of isolation. Whereas the absence of large terrestrial predatory reptiles and mammals has placed no check on the evolutionary loss of wing function, the presence of an abundant supply of sizeable eels, smaller fishes, and octopi, for which there are few avian competitors (Gifford, 1919; Harris, 1979; Snow, 1966), has placed a selective advantage on large body size. Because food resources are located immediately adjacent to the exposed lava flows, where the cormorants nest and rest with virtual impunity (Boersma, 1977; Harris, 1979), the flight adaptation is no longer needed for searching out foraging sites or for escape from land predators, despite occasional ineffectual advances by the smaller-sized *Buteo* hawk (Moore, 1982). Elsewhere in the world, cormorants use their wings for flying and for underwater swimming, which results in a functional compromise between minimal wing size necessary for aerial flight, and an optimal body size for underwater capture of foods, using wings and feet for propulsion and steering. The precarious balance struck by these evolutionary 'trade-offs' is apparent in the manoeuvrings for aerial take-off, which require a long 'runway' on the surface of the water. By juxtapositioning relaxed selection pressures for flight and increased selection pressures for large body size, natural selection, in the peculiar Galápagos setting, has produced one of the world's largest (heaviest) cormorants, with 'wings' more degenerate than those of the extinct great auk of eastern North America (Beebe, 1924).

19.7.2. Adaptive radiation

With respect to islands, this concept connotes 'entry' by an ancestral group of organisms into a variety of new and vacant niches, through cumulative successive ecological shifts (Carlquist, 1974). The implied condition predisposing a group to adaptive radiation is the absence or inefficient occupancy of available niches, the latter a consequence of an ecological 'disharmony' among the original island colonists (see preceding section). The Galápagos Islands exhibit a goodly number of instructive examples of adaptive radiation.

19.7.2.1. Plants

The most thoroughly studied examples of adaptive radiation occur in the genus *Scalesia* (Family Compositae), which includes a very diverse array of species (Eliasson, 1974 and Chapter 7.51), and in the genus *Opuntia* (Chapter 6.51).

In 1966, E. Yale Dawson suggested that the tree-like habit of many *Opuntia* species was a response to browsing by tortoises. On islands harboring tortoises, natural selection favored the arboreal form, with their pads out of bite-reach, and disfavored the prostrate and suberect forms, upon which the tortoise could readily feed. The tallest opuntias occur on tortoise-inhabited islands, and the shrubby forms occur on islands where tortoises are absent. Other details of structure and patterns of growth have been woven into the fabric of his

Figure 19.11. Adaptive radiation in the cactus genus *Opuntia*. Left: arborescent *O. echios barringtonensis*, up to 6 m tall and with trunk up to 1 m in diameter at the base, Isla Santa Fé. Right: shrubby *O. megasperma megasperma*, 3 m high, with rounded crown and freely proliferating branches (not visible in photo), Isla Champion (near Floreana).

hypothesis. As attractive as this idea at first appears, it does seem less plausible in the light of arguments set forth by Arp (1971), namely, that the imposing tree-like stature is the result of long-term interaction with other woody vegetation, because on most islands the cacti reach about the same average height as their associated vegetation.

As appears to be typical of many plant groups in the Galápagos, including *Scalesia*, *Opuntia*, *Acalypha*, *Alternanthera*, *Croton*, and others, variations in growth-form are often associated with environmental gradients in light, moisture, soil, and community structure (Arp, 1971; Eliasson, 1974; Hamann, 1979, 1981; Parkhurst and Loucks, 1972; and Reeder and Riechert, 1975; Wiggins and Porter, 1971).

19.7.2.2. Darwin's finches

Perhaps no other avian group has played a more central role in the development of ecological and evolutionary theory, or contributed more significantly to the scientific literature, than Darwin's finches. In the second revised edition of the *Voyage of the Beagle*, Darwin (1845) remarked 'Seeing this gradation and diversity of structure in one small, intimately related group of birds one might really fancy that from an original paucity of birds in this archipelago, one species had been taken and modified for different ends'—a first formulation of the principle of adaptive radiation (Fig. 19.1.2). Although this classical example of divergent evolution is often cited in textbooks—ironically, Darwin (1859) does not even mention the finches in his *Origin of Species*—the traditional pedagogical explanation of the variation in patterns of structure and behavior of the finches 'belies the complexity of the evolutionary processes they illustrate, the ambiguities of the evidence, and the differences of opinion amongst biologists about just how these birds evolved' (Grant, 1981). And despite decades of intensive field, laboratory, and museum studies on the finches, factual information about their biology has not kept pace with the evolutionary speculations about them (Abbott, 1980; Abbott, *et al.*, 1977; Bowman, 1961, 1963, 1983; Christian, 1970; Connor and Simberloff, 1978; Grant, 1981; Grant and Abbott, 1980; Grant and Grant, 1969; Hutchinson, 1959; Lack, 1945, 1947, 1969; Otte, 1974; Roth, 1981; Simberloff and Boecklen, 1981; Smith, *et al.*, 1978; Sulloway, 1982; Steadman, 1982; and Udvardy, 1970). Nonetheless such an outpouring of ideas from disciplined minds bodes well for continued progress in our understanding of the evolutionary processes of Nature.

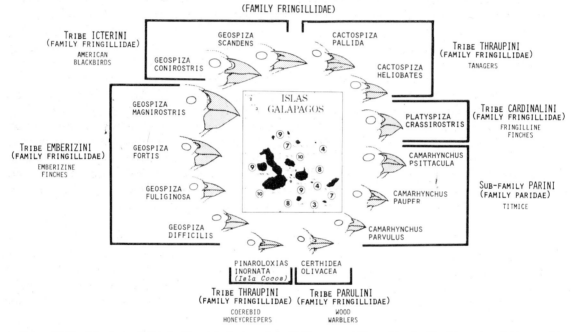

Figure 19.12. Adaptive radiation in Darwin's finches of the Galápagos and Cocos islands. The 14 species of the geospizine tribe (Family Fringillidae) show structural, ecological, and behavioral convergences with continental species distributed among 6 tribes of song-birds (nomenclature of Sibley and Ahlquist, pers. comm.). The number of geospizine species normally breeding on each of the major islands of the Galápagos is shown on the distribution map. Head profiles after Swarth (1931).

Unfortunately, and all too often, interpretations of data are narrowly tailored to a few currently fashionable disciplinary hypotheses. Biologists need to be reminded from time to time that in the analysis of community ecology, statistics must not be applied discriminately, without regard to the *total* ecology of the species concerned, including the manifold aspects of their physiology, behavior, and functional anatomy.

A note of irony regarding interspecific competition in Galápagos land birds has been pointed out by Abbott and Abbott (1978) in their important multivariate study of morphological variation in Galápagos and Ecuadorian mainland mockingbirds. These authors have correctly observed, although Darwin (1845) overlooked it—for which he may be reasonably excused—that the widely distributed Galápagos mockingbirds show just as much morphometric variation among islands as do Darwin's finches, yet they have no congeneric competitors anywhere in the archipelago to which this striking differentiation can or need be attributed (see Fig. 19.1). If inter-island differences in food resources are sufficient to explain the morphological variation in mockingbirds (see Bowman and Carter, 1971), then one wonders why population ecologists are so strongly compelled to invoke competition to explain similar morphological variation among the finches, which live on the same islands as the mockingbirds.

19.8. Adaptive Associations between Galápagos Organisms

19.8.1. Tomatoes, tortoises and mockingbirds

In arid regions of the world it is not uncommon to find seeds with hard to thick coats. These provide limited protection of the embryo from desiccation and from insect predation during the dry season. However, during the often short wet season, insufficient moisture, among other things, may inhibit the seed from breaking open its protective covering.

The seeds of all native Galápagos tomatoes (*Lycopersicon esculentum*) are subject to extreme dormancy, and without special treatment, less than 1% of them will germinate (Rick and Bowman, 1961). By careful excising or chemical softening of the seed coat, dormancy can be broken to a significant degree.

In a series of feeding experiments using a Galápagos tortoise and mockingbirds (*Mimus* [*Nesomimus*] *parvulus*), a startling improvement in percentage germination was achieved (Rick and Bowman, 1961; Rick, 1966). Passage through the guts of the tortoise (1–3 weeks' duration) and the mockingbird (less than 2 hours' duration), probably removed or diminished the mechanical obstruction of emergence by the seed coat.

These results suggest that tortoises and mockingbirds might be important natural agents not only in breaking seed dormancy, but also in widely dispersing the seeds. Such a mutualistic relationship provides nutrients to the predator species and enhances dispersal commensurate with the wanderings of the animals; however, the fate of the tomato rests almost entirely with the vagaries of the animals.

A somewhat similar behavioral interaction in thought to have occurred between the now extinct flightless dodo-bird (*Raphus cucullatus*) and the almost extinct forest tree (*Calvaria major*) on the island of Mauritius in the Indian Ocean. Presumably, the specially thickened endocarp of *Calvaria* seeds required abrasion of their 15 mm thick endocarp before germination could take place. The extinction of the dodo about 3 centuries ago correlates with the present-day rarity of *Calvaria* trees, most of which are extremely old. Feeding experiments revealed that after passage through the gut of turkeys—a kind of surrogate dodo!—the seed coats of *Calvaria* were sufficiently scarified to permit germination (Temple, 1977).

The evolutionary fates of co-evolving species on oceanic islands are precariously interwoven. Loss of one species in this ecological linkage threatens the evolutionary survival of the other.

19.8.2. Cleaning symbiosis

Reference has been made in previous chapters to Darwin's finches (*Geospiza* spp.) and Galápagos mockingbirds entering into a symbiotic cleaning relationship with tortoises and marine iguanas and removing ectoparasites from their skin. According to Hobson (1969), when marine iguanas are submerged, their molting skin is frequently picked off by the damselfish (*Abudefduf troschelii*). In Africa, the red-billed ox-pecker (*Buphaga erythrorhyncha*) grooms the hides of wild hoofed mammals. These mutualistic behaviors are especially significant because they often involve rather similar responses from distantly-related and widely-separated species, i.e. they demonstrate ethological convergence.

19.8.3. Finches and boobies

The blood-eating habit of *Geospiza difficilis* (Chapter 12.5.1) appears to have arisen as a mutualistic relationship, in which the booby was groomed of its parasitic flies, and the finch received a protein-rich meal. When the finch learned to draw blood directly, by puncturing the skin of the booby and drinking blood as it coursed down the quills, the relationship changed to one of partial parasitism. Blood constitutes a small but significant part of the diet of the sharp-beaked ground-finch, and is available only at those times of the year (usually the end of the 'dry season') when the boobies are 'tied' to land for nesting.

19.9 Cryptic Faunas

On oceanic islands, lava tubes are, geologically, among the youngest of all caves (Fig. 19.13; for their formation, see page 21). Comparatively few scientists have studied these volcanic formations in the Galápagos (Balasz, 1972; Stoops, 1967; Montoriol-Pous and de Mier, 1977) or the rich assortment of recent and fossiliferous vertebrate remains trapped within their confines (Broom, 1929; Niethammer, 1964; Steadman, 1981).

Figure 19.13. Cueva de Kübler, a lava tube north of Academy Bay, Santa Cruz, from which fossil remains of reptiles, birds, and mammals have been recovered, including extinct finch and rodent species (Steadman, 1981). Lava tubes are natural 'traps' for tortoises, lizards, and small mammals which accidentally fall through gaps in the tunnel roof (right).

Animals restricted to caves and other reclusive sites have long fascinated evolutionary biologists because of the partial or complete degeneration of their eyes and body pigments, and the considerable speciation that they exhibit. Surprisingly, it was not until 1964–65 that the scientific community was aware of the existence of a remarkably diverse cryptic fauna occupying coastal caves and crevasses, forest mulch, and dead trunks of trees—secluded niches that represent unique 'islands within islands.' Leleup (1967) and his party discovered many new species of arthropods, partially or completely depigmented or lacking in functional eyes, including crayfish, isopods, carabid beetles, earwigs, araneid spiders, pseudo-scorpions, among other species. With the help of the local De Roy family (De Roy, 1974), a blind or partially blind ophidiid fish (Cohen and Nielsen, 1978) was discovered in dark brackish pools, deep within crevasses close to shore. Pools bearing this new species (*Ogilbia galapagoensis*; see Poll and Leleup, 1965 and Cohen and Nielsen, 1978) showed some slight tidal fluctuations, thus indicating their indirect connection with the sea. Not altogether surprising was the subsequent discovery of yet another closely related ophidiid, *Ogilbia* [*Caecogilbia*] *deroyi* (Poll and van Mol, 1966), living in tidepools less than 1 km distant, which resembled the cave-dwelling species, but differed from it through the possession of functional eyes, skin pigment, etc. (van Mol, 1967).

Clearly, the search for trogloditic animals in the Galápagos has just begun, and, to judge from recent findings in Hawaiian lava tubes (Howarth, 1972, 1973, and 1981), many new and bizarre cryptic species await discovery.

The importance of studying cave creatures stems from the fact that once an organism invades the stable cave environment, selection probably no longer acts to maintain its ability to adjust ecologically and physiologically to variable conditions. The loss of adjustment on these levels may be associated with a decrease in genetic variability (Poulson and White, 1969; Wilkens, 1971; Laing, *et al.*, 1976). Trends toward lengthening of life and the lowering of population size and reproductive and metabolic rates, do not lead to success in variable and 'unpredictable' environments, so typical of the 'outside' world of Galápagos, where opportunism and adaptability are necessary strategies for survival.

19.10. Genetics of Galápagos Organisms

In recent years electrophoretic surveys of natural populations have led to examinations of the degree of genetic differentiation among local populations, species, and higher taxa. Such studies are of general interest to comparative biologists because they offer insights into the extent of genetic events occurring during the speciation process. Using electrophoretic data it is possible to measure genic variations in natural populations, including patterns of geographic variation, and determine the degree of relatedness among congeneric and distantly-related species. Such data can also clarify our understanding of morphological evolution in groups, evidence of hybridization, and the sequence and relative time of divergence of related taxa in relation to morphological evolution. The degree to which data sets based on allozyme and morphology are congruent, offers new opportunities for analyzing the phylogenetic history of adaptive radiation (Wake, 1981).

Terrestrial habitats of remote oceanic islands have been populated in large measure by means of long-distance dispersal. From a few founding individuals which chanced to reach the Galápagos, a variety of novel species has evolved. This has led to the inference that the founding events, involving a 'constricted gene pool,' does not permanently restrict the evolutionary potential of a species (Carson, 1981).

Species populations on oceanic islands, including both introduced and endemic, may ultimately become as genetically variable (i.e. polymorphic) as those of widespread continental species. For example, the levels of genetic heterozygosity in Darwin's finches (Yang and Patton, 1981) are similar to those found in other vertebrates, including continental song birds. This suggests that at the time of colonization there was no severe 'genetic bottleneck' impeding subsequent adaptive radiation and a large population build-up. Hybridization studies (i.e. DNA/DNA) on Darwin's finches (C. G. Sibley, in progress) are expected to identify nearest living relatives (i.e. 'sister groups') in the Americas, and resolve current differences of opinion based on gross structural, behavioral, and distributional information (see Bowman, 1961, 1983, and Steadman, 1982).

Phylogenetic relationships (i.e. genetic distances) between species of Darwin's finches, as deduced from allozymic data alone, are in overall agreement with the genetic grouping advocated by Swarth (1931), Lack (1945, but not 1947), and Bowman (1961), on the basis of bill shape and plumage, and by Bowman (1983) on the basis of song, among other things (Fig. 19.12). As shown by Jo (1983), the karyotype (i.e. chromosome number and configuration) of 12 species of Darwin's finches is so uniform that it contributes virtually nothing to our understanding of the group's radiative history. A somewhat parallel situation exists in the endemic plant genus *Scalesia* in which the chromosome number of all species examined is the same (i.e. 2n = 68), although structural variation in leaf, flower, and growth-form within the group is anything but uniform (Eliasson, 1974).

Genetic (allozymic) similarities between recently evolved Galápagos populations suggest that species can be formed with only minor alteration of the proteins encoded in structural genes. As pointed out by Wilson, *et al.*, (1974a, 1974b) and Carson (1981), this implies that regulatory genes are important in initial species differentiation. For example, using electrophoresis of blood plasma from seven races of Galápagos tortoise to identify 20 enzymes and other protein gene loci, Marlow and Patton (1981) have shown that there is little correspondence between inter-racial relationships based on biochemical data and those based on morphometric data (Fritts, 1983). The exaggerated 'saddle-back' races from Española, Pinzón, and Pinta do not form a genetically homogeneous group relative to the 'domed' races (i.e. from Santa Cruz), or 'intermediate' races from Isabela, Santiago, and San Cristóbal. They conclude that the saddle-back shaped carapace with associated structural conditions of smaller size, longer legs, longer necks, etc. was independently derived on several occasions (i.e. via convergent evolution) at the sites of their present-day occurrence. Similarly, Yang and Patton (1981) have concluded that allozymic differentiation has not been a component of the adaptive radiative process in Darwin's finches in the Galápagos.

The range of observed heterozygosity in island populations of Galápagos tortoises may be linked with severe reductions in population size that several races have experienced in recent history. For example, intrapopulational variability is greatest in the easternmost island of San Cristóbal, and becomes successively less variable towards the western islands, i.e. Santa Cruz, then Isabela. Tortoise populations showing virtually no genic variability, namely, those of Española, Santa Cruz, and Pinta, have suffered the heaviest depredations by humans for the past century or more, suggesting that a major 'genome constriction' has resulted from such severe population reductions (Marlow and Patton, 1981).

A recent study of introduced rat populations (*Rattus rattus*) in the Galápagos (Patton, *et al.*, 1975) demonstrates how genetic and anatomical characteristics can serve as 'tracers' of the origin and diversification of a species (see also Carson, 1970 for Hawaiian *Drosophila*).

On the basis of their chromosomal constitution, all Galápagos populations of the black rat belong to the karyotypic morph, 2n = 38, known from India, western Asia, Europe, Africa, North and South America, and Australia. It differs from the karyotypic morph, 2n = 42, known from eastern and southeastern Asia and the Indian subcontinent (Patton and Myers, 1974).

The level of concordance between allozyme frequencies and mensural characters of the skeleton, among other things, indicates that three population groups of introduced rats are recognizable according to the islands upon which they occur, as follows: Group 1, including Santiago and Bartolomé; Group 2, including Floreana, Isabela, Pinzón and San Cristóbal; and Group 3, including Santa Cruz and Baltra (Patton, *et al.*, 1975). According to these authors, an hypothesis of multiple origins of the black rat in the Galápagos seems to explain best the similarity relationships between islands of each group, and each represents a period of human activity in the archipelago.

Results of comparative immunological studies of serum proteins by Higgins and Rand (1974, 1975) indicate that the Galápagos marine iguana is immunologically, and therefore, genetically, more closely related to the Galápagos land iguana (*Conolophus pallidus* and *C. subcristatus*) than to the South American mainland *Iguana iguana*.

Among Galápagos plants, genetic variation has been intensively studied by Charles M. Rick and his associates in the endemic tomato, *Lycopersicon cheesmanii* (see references in Rick, 1983). They have demonstrated the presence of unique hereditary traits whose economic importance is just being realized. For example, irrigation has permitted farming in climates that would otherwise be too dry to support agriculture, but such practices often lead to the accumulation of high concentrations of salt in the soil. The interrelated stresses of salinity and drought make the cultivation of many plant foods impossible. Some plants, for example, populations of the Galápagos tomato, are tolerant of salty conditions often prevailing when they grow close to shore, but their fruits are very small, orange-colored, and largely inedible. Hybrid progeny of crosses with the common California (Walters) tomato produces a red, edible fruit the size of a 'cherry' tomato. Two-thirds of the hybrid plants survive in 70% seawater, and 15% of these yield tomato fruits (Marx, 1979). The goal of such studies of plant stress is to develop crops that can be irrigated with seawater in areas such as the Middle East and the coastal deserts of Africa, South America, and ironically, the Galápagos, where seawater is plentiful but freshwater scarce or inaccessible.

Insular floras are 'weedy' in character and often produce local races for dealing with environmental variation, which allows us to study the evolutionary 'strategies' that make them successful, i.e. tolerate a wide range of environmental conditions (Baker, 1971). The task of preserving genetic resources of such plants should be one of the major concerns of scientists. The American poet and philosopher, Ralph W. Emerson, defined a 'weed' as 'a plant whose virtues have not yet been discovered' (see Baker, 1974). Clearly, 'insular weeds' have tremendous potential for yielding new plants of agricultural and horticultural value, and serve as a reserve of primitive germplasms of crop plants and of chemical products, some with a value we have not yet begun to understand.

19.11. Breeding Behavior of Galápagos Organisms

For terrestrial organisms, long-distance dispersal to an island is a drastic event in the life history of a species, because genetic contact with the parental population is irretrievably broken or disrupted for long periods of time. The subsequent evolution of such a stock may be regarded as involving compensation for this broken contact (Carlquist, 1974).

19.11.1. Autogamy in Galápagos tomatoes

Rick (1983) has suggested that the ancestral tomato species from the western South American continent probably rafted to the Galápagos Islands where the occurrence of one species of bee (*Xylocopa darwini*)—a 'generalist' pollinator—severely limited the amount of possible insect cross-pollination. Extreme selection in the ancestral entomophilous plant probably took place for self-pollination (autogamy) and for generic tolerance of inbreeding. The result was the fixation of genotypes and the accumulation of mutant genes, which led to rapid differentiation.

Strict autogamy in Galápagos tomatoes was indicated from field and greenhouse studies which showed that whole populations of plants were morphologically uniform; unique deviant traits such as jointless pedicel, total anthocyan deficiency, were found in each case to be caused by a single recessive gene which was fixed throughout the wild populations; and the structure of floral parts favored automatic self-pollination. The absence of cross-pollination in insular plants is thought by some (Carlquist, 1974; Thomson and Barrett, 1981; Bawa, 1982; Willson, 1982) to restrict greatly the genetic vigor of such species and limit their adaptability and durability in the absence of occasional outcrossing. Neither of these evolutionary fates seems to have befallen Galápagos tomatoes, not yet, at least, and the same conclusion applies to other Galápagos self-pollinating angiosperms tested (Rick, 1966).

According to Bawa (1982), the claim that self-compatible hermaphrodites have more often established small populations on true islands, followed by selection for outcrossing and the evolution of dioecism (Baker, 1967; Gilmartin, 1968) has not been soundly substantiated by quantitative comparisons of insular and mainland flora or through abundant evidence of inbreeding suppression.

19.11.2. Development of ray flowers in *Scalesia*.

In the endemic composite genus, *Scalesia*, self-compatability and spontaneous self-pollination are known. It has been suggested by Carlquist (1961) that 'primitive' species of Compositae lack ray flowers, and Eliasson (1974) has demonstrated that ray flowers of *Scalesia* have developed from disc flowers. The same author has concluded that the occasional development of showy ray flowers is an adaptation for attracting the sole known pollinator, the *Xylocopa* carpenter bee. If insect pollinators were extremely rare, ray flowers might serve to increase the competitive ability of the floral head to attract the few available pollinators. On Isla Pinzón, where the carpenter bee does not occur, or does so only rarely, the *Scalesia* ray corollas are also extremely rare or absent from floral heads.

19.11.3. Polyandry in Galápagos hawks

In the Galápagos hawk, *Buteo galapagoensis*, the occurrence of a 'cooperative polyandrous' mating system has been demonstrated in which up to four males copulate with a single female throughout the breeding season (de Vries, 1975; Faaborg *et al.*, 1980; Chapter 12.41). The occurrence and frequency of polyandry varies considerably from island to island. Data are unavailable at present to determine whether group males survive to breed for longer periods than the average monogamous male, or to know genetic relatedness of the various males in a cooperative group, or the paternity within clutches. The latter feature could be revealed through electrophoretic studies (Sherman, 1981). Although Faaborg, *et al.*, (1980) are not yet able to explain, satisfactorily, why the Galápagos hawk has a polyandrous mating system rather than some other cooperative system, they suggest that among the ultimate causes might be the lack of suitable territories. Variation in resources and hawk survivorship from island to island may serve as proximate factors, which cause the variation in the frequency of polyandrous groups on these islands.

19.11.4. Adaptations for rapid breeding in Darwin's finches

Recent studies have suggested that physiological demands of reproduction may affect, in varying degrees, the body size of animals, including sexual dimorphism. Many species accumulate resources for laying eggs shortly before breeding occurs. If body size is small, the females of such species could accumulate resources relatively more quickly, and might be expected to have shorter breeding seasons than larger females. Accordingly, in regions such as the Galápagos, where environmental conditions fluctuate broadly and irregularly, there should be a selective advantage to being capable of breeding quickly, and small sized females would be at a selective advantage. Downhower (1976) found that on Isla Española, the small ground-finch, *Geospiza fuliginosa*, weighing 14 g on average, bred earlier than the larger 'cactus ground-finch,' *Geospiza conirostris*, weighing 30 g on average. By contrast, Grant and Grant (1980) did not find a parallel among the various-sized species of finch breeding on Genovesa, and they have suggested that other factors, including dietary differences and energetics, among other things, may be involved. The fact that Darwin's finches, especially the larger species, lay relatively small clutches of eggs, that are small in proportion to adult body weight, and have relatively short incubation periods, may also be considered to be adaptations that enhance repeated and rapid breeding at irregular intervals as dictated by vagaries of weather (Grant and Grant, 1982). Both Grant and Grant (1980a,b) and Downhower (1978) discuss patterns of mortality, infertility, nest predation, growth-rates, and feeding rates as they affect reproductive success.

19.11.5. Reproductive 'strategies' of Galápagos boobies

Perhaps no other group of sea-birds has been so thoroughly and masterfully monographed than the sulids (boobies and gannets) of the world, in large measure through the pen of Nelson (1968, 1978). This author explains in great detail and in readable style how the many aspects of the breeding biology of sea-birds, including the social structure of breeding groups, the timing of breeding, predation, feeding methods, and rate of recruitment are intimately linked, and how all are shaped by natural selection, not in isolation but rather as parts of the overall 'adaptedness' of the individual or pair or group (Nelson, 1970). By careful comparison of species in an evolutionary framework, Nelson has shown, in true Darwinian fashion, 'How far more interesting all the study of natural history becomes' (Darwin, 1859).

19.12. Short-term Human Colonization of Galápagos

19.121. Prehistoric fishing settlements

There was a general and widespread misconception, until the experimental voyage of the raft *Kon Tiki* in 1947, that the balsa rafts of Ecuador and Peru were incapable of navigation on the high seas (Heyerdahl, 1952). Once this myth was dispelled, it was reasonable to assume that the Galápagos Islands were readily within the reach of similar rafts piloted by native Americans from the coast of Ecuador and northern Peru. However, up to 1953, the many scientists who had visited the archipelago never made specific searches for archaeological remains, and no signs of early occupation had been reported, although man-made caves and broken Spanish jars and porcelain had been found and properly ascribed to the late 17th-century buccaneers and the 18th-century whalers (Heyerdahl and Skjölsvold, 1956).

Around the middle of this century two bits of information, one scientific, the other a fabrication, seemed to provide evidence of prehistoric visits to the Galápagos. Scientific studies of Hutchinson, *et al.*, (1947) on the genetics and evolution of cultivated cottons, suggested that the wild Galápagos variety, *Gossypium barbadense darwinii*, was closely related to the cotton cultivar (an allopolyploid) of the original civilizations on the north coast of Peru, and could, therefore, have been spread to the Galápagos since the establishment of aboriginal high cultures on the mainland coast. The problem of the 'transplanted Galápagos cotton' was considered to be an ethnobotanical one by Sauer (1950) and this encouraged Thor Heyerdahl to organize an archaeological expedition to the Galápagos in 1953. However, before setting out for the islands, Heyerdahl was shown a picture of a carved stone figure (Fig. 19.14), presumably taken in the Galápagos, which bore some resemblance to the stone statues on Tahiti, Fatu Hiva, and Easter Island in the south Pacific. Subsequently, Heyerdahl was to inspect the stone carving on Floreana and meet its creator, Heinz Wittmer (Fig. 19.14), a long-time German colonist, who sculptured the face in volcanic rock for the amusement of his children!

Results of later experiments on saltwater tolerance of cotton seeds (Stephens, 1967), coupled with the knowledge of the rate of drift westward by the Peru Coastal Current (Fig. 19.3), strongly suggested that the 500–600 mile saltwater barrier separating the South American mainland and the Galápagos Islands could have been breached by means of natural flotation of the ancestral Galápagos cotton seed.

From an analysis of artifacts recovered from sites in the Galápagos (see page 8), Heyerdahl and Skjölsvold (1956) were left with the 'impression that the pre-Spanish occupation did not have the characteristics of permanent or long-lasting habitat, but rather of temporary or possibly seasonal visits. The occupation sites ... did not contain material suggestive of organized settlements or communities,' and, indeed, the geographical conditions of these islands were far from favorable for permanent settlement because of the lack of freshwater along the coasts. No burials were uncovered nor were the funeral wares commonly associated

Figure 19.14. Left: giant human face carved into consolidated ash layer, Wittmer farm, highlands of Floreana. Right: the late Heinz Wittmer, German colonist who settled on Floreana in 1932 and carved the figure.

with the dead on the north coast of Peru. The exceptionally rich fishing grounds around the Galápagos Islands probably attracted fishermen from the mainland coast, from the earliest days of deep-sea navigation off Ecuador and northern Peru. So it would appear that these fishermen made casual or seasonal visits to the Galápagos, perhaps for centuries before the arrival of the first European visitors.

19.12.2. A Utopian colonization scheme

Few, if any, are the utopian movements which have been observed and studied by scholars from beginning to end. Luckily, one such has been documented by Faris, *et al.*, (1964) and involves a group of Americans led by a 'casual adventurer and scientific fiction reader,' who after reading an article on the Galápagos Islands, conceived an outrageous plan of founding a colony on San Cristóbal for the purpose of exploiting the island's resources.

The original venture conceived in 1959 developed into an 'ill-fated pursuit of a contemporary utopia.' Members of the colonizing group attempted to establish a new social pattern based on a vision of an ideal society whose members are withdrawn from the community at large, to embody the vision in experimental form. At least in a general way, such were the aspirations of the people who joined their leader, whose main purpose seems to have been economic profit. The following summary has been extracted from Faris, *et al.*, (1964).

The leader's ideal of society was one based on 'clear thinking and scientific principles.' On one of the Island Development Company's brochures it was stated that the main purpose of the Galápagos expedition was 'to show that a pioneer colonizing group, dedicated to furthering scientific research, can succeed, with this motivation replacing the religious or political motivations of many such new colonies in the past.'

The Galápagos Islands were perceived by the leader to be rich in marketable resources, and at various times he made mention of the possibilities of profit from coffee-growing, cattle-raising, lobster-fishing, seaweed-gathering, tourist-entertaining, and scientific research, especially biological studies. The plan of organization known as 'Filiate Science Antrorse' (meaning 'together with science we move forward') did not take into serious consideration the Ecuadorian residents of the islands. The final document of organization of F.S.A., despite internal inconsistencies and unworkability, satisfied the more than 100 persons, representing 36 family units, each of whom turned over $2,500 of their savings, and committed their future lives to this 'romantic' scheme.

Most of the recruits were drawn from applicants living in the State of Washington, USA. They were chiefly young persons with moderate incomes, including aircraft workers, farmers, truck drivers, firemen, salesmen, a janitor, a plumber, and some school teachers. One feature they all seemed to have in common was a dissatisfaction with their present condition of life, a mixture of idealism, and a yearning for a new and more exciting direction in a so-far adventureless career.

A series of disappointments, including lack of sea-worthiness of their ship, the *Alert*, lack of fishing skills among its members, depletion of the local lobster resource, irreparability of the refrigeration plant at Puerto Baquerizo Moreno, unavailability of their hoped-for coffee plantation in the highlands of San Cristóbal, political troubles in Ecuador resulting from this 'Yankee Invasion,' and debilitating diseases such as dysentery and hepatitis, resulted in a total collapse of the venture. By January, 1961, almost 14 months after the first group of colonists had reached San Cristóbal, all but one of the original colonizers had left the Galápagos. Thus, in little more than a year, 106 persons had come and gone from their utopian island, spent an estimated $165,000, experienced personal bankruptcy, and became generally disillusioned.

As Faris, *et al.* (1964) have stated, factors accounting for the failure of the expedition are abundant; there is hardly anything which could indicate a chance for success! The goal was impractical, marketing costs were out of reach of resources, social and religious traditions of the colonists contrasted with those of the Ecuadorian residents; leadership was deficient, everyone was unfamiliar with the Galápagos environment, and preparation and knowledge of requisite occupational skills were inadequate.

Thanks to the present overall national park status of the Galápagos Islands, other futile utopian experiments are unlikely to transpire in the archipelago; but the utopian idea still survives in the mind of Man.

19.13. Conclusions

The Galápagos Archipelago is indelibly enshrined in the history of science because it is the birthplace of theories on the origin, organization, and distribution of species, and factors shaping the Earth's physical environments. Because of their relatively pristine character, now effectively overseen by Ecuadorian conservators, the islands will continue to provide the factual basis for insights into an ever-widening range of scientific problems, so clearly illuminated under conditions of ecosystem simplicity.

The Galápagos have long held great interest and fascination for naturalists of all persuasions, often serving as a proving ground, or, more appropriately, a 'disproving ground' (Connor and Simberloff, 1978) for their heretical hypotheses. Were Charles Darwin's theory of evolution by means of natural selection to have stood un-challenged or unchanged until 1982—one hundred years after the man's death—one of the rarest achievements in science would have occurred, namely, a new vision of how the world works, understood and described perfectly the moment it is announced (Rensberger, 1982). Today, the truly challenging objections come not from the 'creationists,' who reject evolutionary theory in its totality, but instead from some of the leading authorities on the theory of natural selection itself. Unlike the creationists, these experts do not doubt that evolution took place or continues to unfold, but rather they question the traditional ideas of its *modus operandi*.

Science is usually understood to depict a universe of strict order and lawfulness, of rigorous economy. In the Galápagos there is an extravagant splendor of living Nature—proliferating luxuriantly at the expense of the sun's energy in the photic zone, and at the expense of magmatic and chemical energies in the dark abyssal depths. The lessons of a balanced view of Nature, learned by most scientists who have been privileged to visit the 'Enchanted Isles,' is that beauty connotes more than sheer orderliness. It postulates order compatible with uniqueness. As Weiss (1960) so aptly remarked, 'If there is any lesson in the study of organic Nature, it is that there is order in the gross with freedom of expression in the small.'

Although the stony bust of Charles Darwin stands silently on the sunlit shore of Puerto Baquerizo Moreno (Fig. 19.15), I sometimes think, as I gaze upon finches perched atop his bald pate, that the spirit of this great naturalist is very much alive and smiling with approval upon what he surveys around him, over a century and a half since the memorable *Beagle* visit to the Galápagos.

Hundreds of studies, with the illustrious beginning of those of Darwin in 1835, have brought widespread recognition to the Galápagos as one of the world's truly extraordinary areas for scientific investigations. We may confidently hope that the example of unspoiled Nature in the Galápagos, so esthetically pleasing to our sensibilities, will make the gift of life more valuable, and Man more worthy of the gift (Van Straelen, 1963).

Figure 19.15. Charles Darwin monument, Puerto Baquerizo Moreno, San Cristóbal, erected on the occasion of the 100th anniversary of the 1835 visit of the world-renowned naturalist and H.M.S. *Beagle* to the Galápagos.

19.14. Acknowledgments

I wish to express my sincere thanks to the following scientists for information and advice: Peter Glynn, Ole Hamann, Sarah Hoffman, John McCosker, Roger Perry, Gunter Seckel, Tom Simkin, Alan Strong, William Weber, Ira Wiggins, and Klaus Wyrtki. None of these helpful colleagues, however, are held accountable for the correctness of statements and interpretations appearing in this article; such is the sole responsibility of the author.

References

Abbott, I. (1980) Theories dealing with the ecology of landbirds on islands. *In* A. Macfadyen (ed.), *Advances in ecological research*, pp. 329–371. Academic Press.

Abbott, I. and L.K. Abbott (1978) Multivariate study of morphological variation in Galápagos and Ecuadorian mockingbirds. *Condor*, **80**, 302–308.

Abbott, I., L.K. Abbott, and P.R. Grant (1977) Comparative ecology of Galápagos ground-finches (*Geospiza* Gould): evaluation of the importance of floristic diversity and interspecific competition. *Ecol. Monogr.*, **47**, 151–184.

Arrhenius, S.A. (1908) *Worlds in the making: the evolution of the universe.* Harper and Bros., New York and London.

Arp, G.K. (1971) The Galápagos opuntias: another interpretation. *Noticias de Galápagos*, **21**, 33–37.

Baker, H.G. (1967) Support for Baker's Law—as a rule. *Evolution*, **32**, 853–856.

Baker, H.G. (1971) Human influences on plant evolution. *BioSci.*, **21**, 108.

Baker, H.G. (1974) The evolution of weeds. *Ann. Rev. Ecol. Syst.*, **5**, 1–24.

Balasz, D. (1972) Mapping of lava tunnels on Santa Cruz Island. *Noticias de Galápagos*, **19–20**, 10–11.

Barnett, T.P. (1981) Statistical prediction of North American air temperatures from Pacific predictors. *Monthly Weather Rev.*, **109**, 1021–1041.

Barlow, N. (1946) *Charles Darwin and the Voyage of H.M.S. "Beagle."* Philosophical Library, New York.

Baross, J.A., S.E. Hoffman, J.B. Corliss, L.I. Gordon, and M.D. Lilley (1980) Procaryotic 'coelocanths'; tube-forming microorganisms from submarine hydrothermal environments. *Oregon State Univ., School of Oceanography, Spec. Publ.*, Ref. 80–8.

Bawa, K.S. (1982) Outcrossing and the incidence of dioecism in island floras. *Amer. Nat.*, **119**, 866–871.

Beebe, W. (1924) *Galápagos: World's End.* G.P. Putnam's Sons, New York.

Bjerknes, J. (1966) A possible response of the atmospheric Hadley circulation to equatorial anomolies of ocean temperature. *Tellus*, **18**, 820–829.

Black, S. (1972) The role of insular phenomena in the "Origin of Species." Unpubl. Ms, Biol. 823, San Francisco State Univ., San Francisco.

Boersma, P.D. (1977) An ecological and behavioral study of the Galápagos penguin. *Living Bird*, **15**, 43–93.

Boersma, P.D. (1978) Breeding patterns of Galápagos penguins as an indicator of oceanographic conditions. *Science*, **200**, 1481–1483.

Bowman, R.I. (1961) Morphological differentiation and adaptation in the Galápagos finches. *Univ. Calif. Publ. Zool.*, **58**, 1–326.

Bowman, R.I. (1963) Evolutionary patterns in Darwin's finches. *Occas. Papers Calif. Acad. Sci.*, **44**, 107–140.

Bowman, R.I. (1983) The evolution of song in Darwin's finches. *In* R.I. Bowman, M. Berson, and A.E. Leviton (eds.), *Patterns of evolution in Galápagos Organisms*, pages 237–537. American Association for the Advancement of Science, Pacific Division, San Francisco, California.

Bowman, R.I. and A. Carter (1971) Egg-pecking behavior in Galápagos mockingbirds. *Living Bird*, **10**, 243–270.

Broad, W.J. (1982) Survival of the fittest in the Falklands. *Science*, **216**, 1389–1390, 1392.

Broom, R. (1929) On the extinct Galápagos tortoise that inhabited Charles Island. *Zoologica*, **9**, 313–320.

Brunn, J. (1982) George, not Charles. *Science*, **216**, 1274.

Cane, M. (1982) Summary of *El Niño* discussion at the equatorial theory panel meeting. *Trop. Ocean-Atmosphere Newsl.*, **10**, 2–3.

Carlquist, S. (1961) *Comparative plant anatomy.* Holt, Rinehart & Winston, New York.

Carlquist, S. (1974) *Island biology.* Columbia Univ. Press, New York.

Carson, H.L. (1970) Chromosome tracers of the origin of species. *Science*, **168**, 1414–1418.

Carson, H.L. (1981) Microevolution in insular ecosystems. *In* D. Mueller-Dombois, K.W. Bridges, and H.L. Carson (eds.), *Island Ecosystems: Biological Organization in Selected Hawaiian Communities*, pages 471–482. Hutchinson Ross Publishing Co., Stroudsburg, Pennsylvania.

Christian, J.J. (1970) Social subordination, population density, and mammalian evolution. *Science*, **168**, 84–90.

Cohen, D.M. and J.G. Nielsen (1978) Guide to the identification of genera of the fish order Ophidiiformes with a tentative classification of the order. *U.S. Dept. Commerce, NOAA Tech. Rep. NMFS Circ.*, **417**, 72pp.

Connor, E.F. and D. Simberloff (1978) Species number and compositional similarity of the Galápagos flora and avifauna. *Ecol. Monogr.*, **48**, 219–248.

Corliss, J.B., J. Dymond, L.I. Gordon, J.M. Edmond, R.P. von Herzen, R.D. Ballard, K. Green, D. Williams, A. Bainbridge, K. Craine, and T.H. van Andel (1979) Submarine thermal springs on the Galápagos Rift. *Science*, **203**, 1073–1083.

Corliss, J.B., J.A. Baross and S.E. Hoffman (1981) An hypothesis concerning the relationship between submarine hot springs and the origin of life on Earth. *Oceanologica Acta*, **1981**, 59–69.

Covey, D.L. (1978) The Pacific El Niño phenomenon and the Atlantic circulation. *Monthly Weather Rev.*, **106**, 1280–1287.

Cox, A. (1983) Ages of the Galápagos Islands. *In* R.I. Bowman, M. Berson, and A.E. Leviton (eds.), *Patterns of Evolution in Galápagos Organisms*, pages 11–23. American Association for the advancement of Science, Pacific Division, San Francisco, California.

Crick, F.H.C. and L.E. Orgel (1973) Directed panspermia. *Icarus*, **19**, 341–346.

Curio, E. (1964) Zur geographischen Variation des Feinderkennes einiger Darwinfinken (Geospizidae). *Verhandl. Deutch. Zoolog. Gesellschaft*, Kiel.

Curio, E. (1969) Funktionsweise und Stammensgeschichte der Flugfeinderkennens einiger Darwinfinken (Geospizinae). *Z. Tierpsychol.*, **26**, 394–487.

Darwin, C. (1845) *Journal of researches into the natural history and geology of the countries visited during the voyage of H.M.S. Beagle round the world, under the command of Capt. Fitz Roy, R.N.* 2d rev. ed. John Murray, London.

Darwin, C. (1859) *On the origin of species by means of natural selection, or the preservation of favored races in the struggle for life.* John Murray, London.

Darwin, C. (1896) *Geological observations on the volcanic islands and parts of South America visited during the voyage of H.M.S. 'Beagle.'* B. Appleton & Co., New York.

Dawson, E.Y. (1966) Cacti of the Galápagos Islands, with special reference to their relations with tortoises. *In* R.I. Bowman (ed.), *The Galápagos*, pp. 209–214. Univ. Calif. Press, Berkeley & Los Angeles.

De Roy, T.A. (1974) Discovering a new species. *Pacific Discov.*, **27**, 12–14.

De Vries, Tj. (1975) The breeding biology of the Galápagos hawk, *Buteo galapagoensis*. *Gerfaut*, **65**, 29–54.

Downhower, J.F. (1976) Darwin's finches and the evolution of sexual dimorphism in body size. *Nature*, **263**, 558–563.

Downhower, J.F. (1978) Observations on the nesting of the small ground finch *Geospiza fuliginosa* and the large cactus ground finch *G. conirostris* on Española, Galápagos. *Ibis*, **120**, 340–346.

Durham, J.W (1965) Geology of the Galápagos. *Pac. Discovery*, **18**, 3–6.

Eliasson, U. (1974) Studies in Galápagos plants. XIV. The genus *Scalesia* Arn. *Opera Botanica*, **36**, 1–117.

Faaborg, J., Tj. de Vries, C.B. Patterson, and C.R. Griffin (1980) Preliminary observations on the occurrence and evolution of polyandry in the Galápagos hawk (*Buteo galapagoensis*). *Auk*, **97**, 581–590.

Faris, R.E.L., W.R. Catton, Jr., and O.N. Larson (1964) The Galápagos expedition: failure in the pursuit of a contemporary secular utopia. *Pacific Sociol. Rev.*, **7**, 48–54.

Fielder, G. and L. Wilson (1975) *Volcanoes of the Earth, Moon and Mars.* St. Martin's Press, New York.

Filson, J., T. Simkin, and L-K. Leu (1973) Seismicity of a caldera collapse: Galápagos Islands 1968. *J. Geophys. Res.*, **78**, 8591.

Fritts, T.H. (1983) Morphometrics of Galápagos tortoises: evolutionary implications. *In* R.I. Bowman, M. Berson, and A.E. Leviton (eds.), *Patterns of Evolution in Galápagos Organisms*, pages 107–122. American Association for the Advancement of Science, Pacific Division, San Francisco, California.

Gifford, E.W. (1919) Field notes on the land birds of the Galápagos Islands and Cocos Island, Costa Rica. *Proc. Calif. Acad. Sci.*, **42**, 84–90.

Gilmartin, A.J. (1968) Baker's law and dioecism in the Hawaiian flora: an apparent contradiction. *Pac. Sci.*, **22**, 285–292.

Grant, B.R. and P.R Grant (1969) Darwin's finches: population variation and sympatric speciation. *Proc. Natl. Acad. Sci.*, **76**, 2359–2363.

Grant, P.R. (1981) Speciation and the adaptive radiation of Darwin's finches. *Amer. Sci.*, **69**, 653–663.

Grant, P.R. and I. Abbott (1980) Interspecific competition, null hypotheses and island biogeography. *Evolution*, **34**, 332–341.

Grant, P.R. and P.T. Boag (1980) Rainfall on the Galápagos and the demography of Darwin's finches. *Auk*, **97**, 227–244.

Grant, P.R. and B.R. Grant (1980a) The breeding and feeding characteristics of Darwin's finches on Isla Genovesa, Galápagos. *Ecol. Monogr.*, **50**, 381–410.

Grant P.R. and B.R. Grant (1980b) Annual variation in finch numbers, foraging and food supply on Isla Daphne Major, Galápagos. *Oecologia*, **46**, 55–62.

Hailman, J.P. (1964) The Galápagos swallow-tailed gull is nocturnal. *Wilson. Bull.*, **76**, 347–354.

Haldane, J.B.S. (1929) The origin of life. *Rationalist Annual*, **148**, 3.

Hamann, O. (1979) On climatic conditions, vegetation types, and leaf size in the Galápagos Islands. *Biotropica*, **11**, 101–122.

Hamann, O. (1981) Plant communities of the Galápagos Islands. *Dansk Botanisk Arkiv*, **34**, 1–163.

Harris, M.P. (1973) The biology of the waved albatross *Diomedia irrorata* of Hood Island, Galápagos. *Ibis*, **115**, 483–510.

Harris, M.P. (1979) Population dynamics of the fightless cormorant *Nannopterum harrisi*. *Ibis*, **121**, 120–146.

Herron, E.M. and J.R. Heirtzler (1967) Sea-floor spreading near the Galapagos. *Science*, **158**, 775–780.

Heyerdahl, T. (1952) *American Indians in the Pacific: the theory behind the Kon-Tiki expedition.* George Allen and Unwin, London.

Heyerdahl, T. and A. Skjölsvold (1956) Archaeological evidence of pre-Spanish visits to the Galápagos Islands. *Amer. Antiquity*, **22**, 1–71.

Higgins, P.J. and C.S. Rand (1974) A comparative immunological study of the serum proteins of several Galápagos iguanids. *Comp. Biochem. Physiol.*, **49A**, 347–355.

Higgins, P.J. and C.S. Rand (1975) Comparative immunology of Galápagos iguana hemoglobins. *J. Exp. Zool.*, **193**, 391–397.

Hobson, E.S. (1969) Remarks on aquatic habits of the Galápagos marine iguana, including submergence times, cleaning symbiosis, and the shark threat. *Copeia*, **1969**, 402–403.

Hoffman, S.E. (1982) Archaean hydrothermal systems. Unpubl. manuscr. School of Oceanography, Oregon State Univ., Corvallis.

Horel, J.D. and J.M. Wallace (1981) Planetary-scale atmospheric phenomena associated with the southern oscillation. *Monthly Weather Rev.*, **109**, 813–829.

Houvenaghel, G.T. (1974) Equatorial undercurrent and climate in the Galápagos Islands. *Nature*, **250**, 565–566.

Howarth, F.G. (1972) Cavernicoles in lava tubes on the island of Hawaii. *Science*, **175**, 325–326.

Howarth, F.G. (1973) The cavernicolous fauna of Hawaii lava tubes. 1. Introduction. *Pacif. Insects*, **15**, 139–151.

Howarth, F.G. (1981) Community structure and niche differentiation in Hawaiian lava tubes. *In* D. Mueller-Dombois, K.W. Bridges, and H.L. Carson (eds.), *Island ecosystems* (pages 318–336). Hutchinson Ross Publ. Co., Stroudsburg, Penn.

Hutchinson, G.E. (1959) Homage to Santa Rosalia, or why are there so many kinds of animals? *Amer. Nat.*, **93**, 145–159.

Hutchinson, J.B., R.A. Silow and S.G. Stephens (1947) *The evolution of Gossypium and the differentiation of the cultivated cottons.* Oxford Univ. Press.

Huxley, T.H. (1870) Biogenesis and abiogenesis. *In* T.H. Huxley, *Discourses: biological & geological.* Essays by Thomas H. Huxley, vol. 8, pages 229–271. MacMillan & Co., London, 1894.

Idyll, C.P. (1973) The anchovy crisis. *Sci. Amer.*, **228**, 22–29.

Jannasch, H.W., C.O. Wirsen, and C.D. Taylor (1982) Deep-sea bacteria: isolation in the absence of decompression. *Science*, **216**, 1315–1317.

Jo, N. (1983) Karyotypic analysis of Darwin's finches. *In* R.I. Bowman, M. Berson, and A. Leviton (eds.), *Patterns of Evolution in Galápagos Organisms*, pages 201–217. American Association for the Advancement of Science, Pacific Division, San Francisco, California.

Junguis, H. and U. Hirsch (1979) Herzfrequenzänderungen bei Brutvögeln in Galapagos als Folge von Störungen durch Besucher. *J. Orn.*, **120**, 229–310.

Karl, D.M., C.O. Wirsen, and H.W. Jannasch (1980) Deep-sea primary production at the Galapagos hydrothermal vents. *Science*, **207**, 2345–2347.

Kerr, R.A. (1982) U.S. weather and the equatorial connection. *Science*, **216**, 608–610.

Knauss, J.A. (1961) The Cromwell Current. *Sci. Amer.*, **204**, 105–116.

Knoll, A.H. and E.S. Barghoorn (1977) Archaean microfossils showing cell division from the Swaziland system of South Africa. *Science*, **198**, 396–398.

Lack, D. (1945) The Galápagos finches (Geospizinae): a study in variation. *Occas. Papers Calif. Acad. Sci.*, 21.

Lack, D. (1947) *Darwin's finches.* Cambridge Univ. Press.

Lack, D. (1969) Subspecies and sympatry in Darwin's finches. *Evolution*, **23**, 252–263.

Laing, C.D., G.R. Carmody, and S.B. Peck (1976) How common are sibling species in cave-inhabiting invertebrates? *Amer. Nat.*, **110**, 184–189.

Leleup, N. (1967) Existence d'une faune cryptique relictuelle aux îles Galapagos. *Noticias de Galápagos* 5/6 (1965), 4–16.

Lyell, C. (1830) *Principles of geology.* Vol. 1 John Murray, London.

Malin, M.C. (1977) Comparison of volcanic features of Elysium (Mars) and Tibesti (Earth). *Bull. Geol. Soc. Amer.*, **88**, 908–919.

Maris, C.R.P. and M.L. Bender (1982) Upwelling of hydrothermal solutions through ridge flank sediments shown by pore water profiles. *Science*, **216**, 623–626.

Marlow, R.W. and J.L. Patton (1981) Biochemical relationships of the Galápagos giant tortoises (*Geochelone elephantopus*). *J. Zool. (Lond.)*, **195**, 421–422.

Marx, J.K. (1979), Plants: can they live in salt water and like it? *Science*, **206**, 1168–1169.

Mayr, E. (1977) Darwin and natural selection. *Amer. Sci.*, **65**, 321–327.

McBirney, A.R. and H. Williams (1969) Geology and petrology of the Galápagos Islands. *Geol. Soc. Amer Memoir*, 118.

McClain, E.P. and A.E. Strong (1969) On anomalous dark patches in satellite-viewed sunglint areas. *Monthly Weather Rev. December.*, U.S. Dept. Comm., Washington. D.C.

Miller, S.L. (1953) A production of amino acids under possible primitive Earth conditions. *Science*, **117**, 528–529.

Montoriol-Pous, J. and J. de Mier (1977) Contribución al conocimiento vulcano-espeleológico de la isla de Santa Cruz (Galápagos, Ecuador). *Speleon*, **23**, 75–91.

Moore, T. de R. (1982) To eat and be eaten. *Pacific. Discovery*, **35**, 11–20.

Morgulis, S. (1953) Introduction to the second edition. *In* A.I. Oparin, *The origin of life*, pages v–xxii. 2nd ed. Dover Publ., New York.

Murphy, R.C. (1925) *Bird islands of Peru.* G.P. Putnam's Sons, New York.

Murphy, R.C. (1936) *Oceanic birds of South America.* Vol. 1. Amer. Mus. Nat. Hist., New York.

Nelson, J.B. (1966) Flighting behavior of Galápagos storm petrels. *Ibis*, **108**, 430–432.

Nelson, J.B. (1968) *Galapagos: islands of birds.* William Morrow & Co., New York.

Nelson, J.B. (1970) The relationship between behaviour and ecology in the Sulidae with reference to other sea birds. *Oceanogr. Mar. Biol. Ann. Rev.*, **8**, 501–574.

Nelson, J.B. (1978) *The Sulidae: gannets and boobies.* Oxford Univ. Press.

Nelson, J.B. (1979) *Seabirds: their biology and ecology.* A&W Publ., New York.

Niethammer, J. (1964) Contribution à la connaissance des mammifere terrestres de l'île Indefatigable (Santa Cruz), Galápagos. *Mammalia*, **28**, 593–606.

Oparin, A.I. (1924) *Proischogdenie Zhizni.* Moscovsky Robotchii, Moscow.

Otte, D. (1974) Effects and functions in the evolution of signaling systems. *Ann. Rev. Ecol. System.*, **5**, 385–417.

Palmer, C.E. and R.L. Pyle (1966) The climatological setting of the Galápagos. *In* R. I. Bowman (ed.), *The Galápagos*, pages 93–99. Univ. Calif. Press, Berkeley and Los Angeles.

Parkhurst, D.F. and O. L. Loucks (1972) Optimal leaf size in relation to environment. *J. Ecol.*, **60**, 505–537.

Pasteur, L. (1862) Mémoire sur les corpuscules organisés existent dans l'atmosphère. *Annales de Chimie et de Physique*, 64.

Patton, J.L. and P. Myers (1974) Chromosomal identity of black rats (*Rattus rattus*) from the Galápagos Islands, Ecuador. *Experientia*, **30**, 1140–1141.

Patton, J.L., S.Y. Yang, and P. Myers (1975) Genetic and morphologic divergence among introduced rat populations (*Rattus rattus*) of the Galápagos Archipelago, Ecuador. *Syst. Zool.* **24**, 296–310.

Poll, M. and N. Leleup (1965) Un poisson aveugle nouveau de la famille des *Brotulidae* provenant des îles Galapagos. *Bull. l'Acad. Royale Belgique cl. Sci. Ser.* 5, **51**, 464–474.

Poll, M. and J.J. van Mol (1966) Au subjet d'une espèce inconnue de Brotulidae littoral des îles Galapagos, apparentée a l'espèce aveugle *Caecogilbia galapagoensis* Poll et Leleup. *Bull. l'Acad. Royale Belgique cl. Sci. Ser. 5,* **52**, 1444–1461.

Porter, D. (1982) Vascular plants of the Galápagos: origins and dispersal. *In* R.I. Bowman, M. Berson, and A. Leviton (eds.), *Patterns of Evolution in Galápagos Organisms* pages 33–96. American Association for the Advancement of Science, Pacific Division, San Francisco, California.

Poulson, T.L. and W.B. White (1969) The cave environment. *Science,* **165**, 971–981.

Quinn, W.H. (1974) Monotoring and predicting El Niño invasions. *J. Appl. Meteorol.,* **13**, 825–830.

Quinn, W.H. and W.V. Burt (1970) Prediction of abnormally heavy precipitation over the Equatorial Pacific Dry Zone. *J. Appl. Meteorol.,* **9**, 20–28.

Rasmusson, E.M. and T.H. Carpenter (1982) Variations in tropical sea surface temperature and surface wind fields associated with the southern oscillation/El Niño. *Monthly Weather Rev.* **110**, 354–384.

Reeder, W.G. and S.E. Riechert (1975) Vegetation change along an altitudinal gradient, Santa Cruz Island, Galápagos. *Biotropica,* **7**, 162–175.

Reimer, T.O., E.S. Barghoorn, and L. Margulis (1979) Primary productivity in an early archaean microbial system. *Precambrian Res.,* **9**, 93–104.

Rensberger, B. (1982) Evolution since Darwin. *Science 82,* **3**, 40–45.

Rick, C.M. (1966) Some plant-animal relations on the Galápagos Islands. *In* R.I. Bowman (ed), *The Galápagos,* pages 215–244. Univ. Calif. Press, Berkeley and Los Angeles.

Rick, C.M. (1983) Genetic variation and evolution of Galápagos tomatoes. *In* R.I. Bowman, M. Berson, and A. Leviton (eds.), *Patterns of Evolution in Galápagos Organisms* pages 97–106. American Association for the Advancement of Science, Pacific Division, San Francisco, California.

Rick, C.M. and R.I. Bowman (1961) Galápagos tomatoes and tortoises. *Evolution* **15**, 407–417.

Roth, V.L. (1981) Constancy in the size ratios of sympatric species. *Amer. Nat.* **118**, 394–404.

Sauer, C.O. (1950) Cultivated plants of South and Central America. *In* J.H. Steward (ed.), *Handbook of South American Indians,* pages 487–543. *Bull. Bur. Amer. Ethnol.,* 143.

Seyfert, C.K. and L.A. Sirkin (1979). Earth history and plate tectonics. 2nd ed. Harper and Row, New York.

Sherman, P.W. (1981) Electrophoresis and avain genealogical analyses. *Auk,* **98**, 419–422.

Shklovskii, I.S. and C. Sagan 1966. *Intelligent life in the universe.* Holden-Day, San Francisco.

Simberloff, D. and W. Boecklen (1981) Santa Rosalia reconsidered: size ratios and competition. *Evolution,* **35**, 1206–1228.

Simkin, T. and K.A. Howard (1970) Caldera collapse in the Galápagos Islands, 1968. *Science,* **169**, 429–437.

Simpson, B.B. (1974) Glacial migrations of plants: island biogeographical evidence. *Science,* **185**, 698–700.

Smith, J.N.M., P.R. Grant, B.R. Grant, I.J. Abbott, and L.K. Abbott (1978) Seasonal variation in feeding habits of Darwin's ground finches. *Ecology,* **59**, 1137–1150.

Snow, B.K. (1966) Observations on the behaviour and ecology of the Flightless Cormorant *Nannopterum harrisi.* Ibis, **108**, 265–280.

Snow, B.K. and D.W. Snow (1968) Behavior of the swallow-tailed gull of the Galápagos. *Condor,* **70**, 252–264.

Stanley, S.M. (1981) *The new evolutionary timetable: fossils, genes, and the origin of species.* Basic Books, Inc., New York.

Steadman, D.W. (1981) Vertebrate fossils in lava tubes in the Galápagos Islands. *Proc. 8th Internatl. Congr. Speleology,* pages 549–550.

Steadman, D.W. (1982) The origin of Darwin's finches. *Trans. San Diego Soc. Nat. Hist.* **19**, 279–296.

Stephens, S.C. (1967) Evolution under domestication of the New World cottons (*Gossypium spp.*). *Ciência e Cultura,* **19**, 118–134.

Stoops, G. (1967) On the presence of lava tunnels on Isla Santa Cruz. *Noticias de Galápagos,* **5–6**, 17–18.

Sulloway, F.J. (1982) Darwin and his finches: the evolution of a legend. *J. Hist. Biol.,* **15**, 1–53.

Swarth, H.S. (1931) The avifauna of the Galápagos Islands. *Occas. Papers. Calif. Acad. Sci,* 18.

Temple, S.A. (1977) Plant-animal mutualism: coevolution with dodo leads to near extinction of plant. *Science,* **197**, 885–886.

Thomson, J.D. and S.C. Barrett (1981). Selection for outcrossing, sexual selection, and the evolution of dioecy in plants. *Amer. Nat.,* **118**, 443–449.

Udvardy, M.D.F. (1970) Mammalian evolution: is it due to social subordination? *Science,* **170**, 344–345.

Vagvolgyi, J. (1975) Body size, aerial dispersal, and origin of the Pacific land snail fauna. *Syst. Zool.,* **24**, 465–488.

Van Mol, J.J. (1967) Écologie comparée de deux espèces de Brotulidae (Pisces) des îles Galápagos: *Caecogilbia deroyi* Poll et Van Mol 1967 et *C. galapagoensis* Poll et Leleup 1965. *Bull. l'Acad. Royale cl. Sci., Ser. 5,* **53**, 232–248.

Van Straelen, V. (1963) Introduction. Galápagos Islands: a unique area for scientific investigations. *Ocas. Papers Calif. Acad. Sci.,* **44**, 5–9.

Wake, D.B. (1981) The application of allozyme evidence to problems in the evolution of morphology. *In* G.G.E. Scudder and J.L. Reveal (eds.), *Evolution today,* pages 257–270. Proc. 2nd Internatl. Congr. Syst. Evol. Biol.

Waldrop, M.M. (1982) The origin of the moon. *Science,* **216**, 606.

Weiss, P. (1960) *Organic form: scientific and esthetic aspects.* Daedalus (winter), 1960.

Wiggins, I.L. and D. Porter (1971) *Flora of the Galápagos Islands.* Stanford Univ. Press, Stanford, California.

Wilkens, H. (1971) Genetic interpretation of regressive evolutionary processes: study of hybrid eyes of two astyanax cave populations (Characidae, Pisces). *Evolution,* **25**, 530–544.

Williams, H. (1941) Calderas and their origin. *Univ. Calif. Publ. Bull. Geol. Sci.,* **25**, 239–346.

Williams, H. (1966) Geology of the Galápagos Islands. *In* R. I. Bowman (ed.), *The Galápagos,* pages 65–70. Univ. Calif. Press, Berkeley and Los Angeles.

Willson, N.F. (1982) Sexual selection and dicliny in angiosperms. *Amer. Nat.,* **119**, 579–583.

Wilson, A.C., L.R. Maxson, and V.M. Sarich (1974a) Two types of molecular evolution: evidence from studies of interspecific hybridization. *Proc. Natl. Acad. Sci.,* **71**, 2843–2847.

Wilson, A.C., V. M. Sarich, and L.R. Maxson (1974b) The importance of gene arrangement in evolution: evidence from studies on rates of chromosomal, protein, and anatomical evolution. *Proc. Natl. Acad. Sci.*, **71**, 3028–3030.

Wooster, W.S. and J.W. Hedgepeth (1966) The oceanographic setting of the Galápagos. *In* R. I. Bowman (ed.), *The Galápagos*, pages 100–107, Univ. Calif. Press, Berkeley and Los Angeles.

Wyrtki, K. (1965) Surface currents of the eastern tropical Pacific Ocean. *Bull. Inter-Amer. Trop. Tuna Comm.*, **9**, 271–304.

Wyrtki, K. (1966) Oceanography of the eastern equatorial Pacific Ocean. *Oceanogr. Mar. Biol. Ann. Rev.*, **4**, 33–68.

Wyrtki, K. (1973) Teleconnections in the equatorial Pacific Ocean. *Science*, **180**, 66–68.

Wyrtki, K. (1974) Equatorial currents in the Pacific 1950 to 1970 and their relations to the trade winds. *J. Phys. Oceanogr.*, **4**, 372–380.

Wyrtki, K. (1975) *El Niño*—the dynamic response of the equatorial Pacific Ocean to atmospheric forcing. *J. Phys. Oceanogr.*, **5**, 572–584.

Wyrtki, K. (1976) The response of sea surface topography to the 1976 El Niño. *J. Phys. Oceanogr.*, **9**, 1223–1231.

Wyrtki, K. (1977) Sea level during the 1972 El Niño. *J. Phys. Oceanogr.*, **7**, 779–787.

Wyrtki, K. (1979) El Niño. *La Recherche*, **10**, 1212–1220.

Yang, S.Y. and J.L. Patton (1981) Genic variability and differentiation in the Galápagos finches. *Auk*, **98**, 230–242.

Index

Academy (schooner) 13
Adaptive radiation 13, 294
  in Darwin's finches 176, 177–8, 187, 295–7
  in giant tortoises 146 (Table), 154–5
  in iguanas 159, 165
  in mockingbirds 176–7, 296–7
  in native rats 226–9
  in vascular plants 94–6, 97, 294–5
Age of islands 17–18
Agricultural land
  effects of clearance for 11, 127, 129, 204
  products of 10, 11
Albatross expeditions 135, 259
Algae
  affinities of marine 256
  as food for marine iguana 161, 248
  intertidal 248, 250
  richness of marine 257
Allan Hancock (*Velero*) expeditions 13, 135, 257, 258
Altitudinal zonation 4, 102–3, 116
Amphibia, absence from Galápagos 7
Andean area, floral affinities with Galápagos 82, 98
Angiosperm families 88, 89
Antarctic Intermediate Water 47
Arid (coastal) Zone 73–74, 77, 97, 102, 120, 122, 129
  plants as pioneer species 129
Ascension Island 199
Auckland Island 236

Balsa Pacífica 8
Barnacles 249
Bats 226
Beagle, H.M.S. 12, 133
Bees 104, 301, 302
Birds (*see also* Darwin's finches)
  adaptive radiation in 176–8
  as dispersal agents for plants 5, 73, 99
  breeding seasons 180–1, 199–204
  colonization of new islands 187
  cooperative breeding 180, 302
  distribution of breeding populations 178, 179 (*Table*), 194
  evolution in 186–8, 302
  extinctions in 178, 188
  feeding diversity 185–6, 195–6
  flightlessness in 294

  introduced to Galápagos 242
  migratory in Galápagos 193
  population size and fluctuations 179, 182, 184
  predation upon 204–5, 291
  recent arrivals on Galápagos 5, 178
  seasonal variation in food 62, 181, 186, 196–9
  species (*listed*) 176, 194
Bogs 63, 128
British Isles, flora as compared with Galápagos 92
Brown Zone 77, 102, 129
Bryophytes
  dispersal capacity 81
  distribution 76–80
  ecological restrictions 80–1
  endemism in 81–2
  relationships of Galápagos 82–3
Buccaneers 8, 18, 303
Butterflies, migrant 5

Cacti
  adaptive radiation in 94
  growth form of Galápagos 294–5
Calderas 28–32, 287–8, 290
California Academy of Sciences expedition 13, 178, 237, 265
Canary Islands 92, 93
Cape Verde Islands 92, 93
Caribbean Area, floral affinities with Galápagos 82, 98
Carnegie Ridge 16, 136
Cats (feral) 241
Cattle (feral) 128, 234–6
Caves 298
  fauna of 298–9
  formation of lava 21
  fossil evidence from 227
Central America, floral affinities with Galápagos 5, 82, 98
Cephalopoda 195, 209, 218
Cerralvo Island 157
Charles Darwin Foundation 13, 266–7, 270–2
Charles Darwin Research Station 13, 36, 49, 148, 266–8, 270–2, 273–4
Christmas Island (Pacific) 199
Cinder cones 24
Climatic conditions 57ff
Clipperton Island 256, 257, 258
Cocos Island 82, 138, 186, 187, 249, 256, 257, 258, 296

Cocos Ridge   16
Colonization of islands by new species   187, 256–7
Compositae   87, 111
Conservation (see also National Park)
  education   273–4
  legislation   13, 243, 266ff
  management programmes   117, 128, 238, 267
  priorities   66, 130, 204–5, 231, 243, 249
  under National Park Service   268, 271, 272
  zones   267, 272–3
Continental islands   92
Coral reefs   61, 137, 250–2, 254–5
Corals
  affinities of Galápagos   256
  black   249
  endemism in   258
  interactions with associated species   252–3, 291
  stony   250–2, 254–5, 257–8
Coriolis Force   45, 56, 284
Cottons   94, 303
Crabs   165, 250, 256, 258
Craters, pit   30
Cryptic faunas   298–9
Currents of the ocean   283 (Figure)
  California   44
  Cromwell (or Equatorial Under-)   44, 45–6, 51–2, 62, 192, 255
  El Niño   60
  Equatorial Counter-   44–5
  Humboldt (or Peru)   7, 44, 56, 60, 61, 192, 193, 256, 258
  North Equatorial   44, 256
  Panama   255
  Peru Subsuperficial   45
  South Equatorial   45, 53, 255, 256
  surface waters   46–7

Damselfish   249, 252–3
Darwin, Charles
  observations on Galápagos   12–13, 21, 116, 134, 152, 175, 237, 279, 287, 295
Darwin's finches (Geospizidae)   175–88
  distribution   178, 179 (Table)
  extinctions in   178, 188
  evolution in   186–8, 302
  feeding diversity in   185–6
  genetic variation in   187–8, 299–300
  haemophagous habit   186, 298
  levels of differentiation in   177–8
  variation in songs   187, 293–4
Decres (corvette)   117
Dispersal agencies/mechanisms   5, 73, 91, 98–9
  in Galápagos cottons   303
  in Galápagos tomatoes   297
  in native rodents   225
  in Scalesia   104–6
  in shorefish   138
  in tortoises   6, 146
Distribution changes, in Darwin's finches   178–9
Dogs (feral)   239–41
  as predators   147, 204–5, 217
Doldrums   55–6
Donkeys (feral)   116, 147, 238

Earthquakes   29, 36
Earthworms   117
Easter Island   137
Eastern Pacific Barrier   255
Echinoderms   256, 258–9
Ekman layer   45
El Junco (lake)   63–8
El Niño phenomenon   47–8, 60, 180–1, 198, 283–5, 287
Endemic species as dominant components of vegetation   129
Endemism in Galápagos   96, 129–30
  bryophytes   81–2
  corals   255, 258
  ferns and fern allies   91
  interstitial fauna   250
  lichens   81–2
  marine algae   257
  marine mollusca   258
  rats   226–9
  shorefishes   138
  vascular plants   90–3
Epiphytes   77, 107, 110, 250
Eruptions, volcanic (see under, Volcanic activity)
Essex (frigate)   237
Establishment of plants on Galápagos   76, 91, 303
Evolution   13, 76, 93ff, 176, 186–8, 279–80, 295–7
Extinctions in Galápagos,   13–14
  birds   178, 188
  giant tortoises   147
  land iguanas   165, 172
  native rats   228–9
  vascular plants   129

Fault systems   27–34
Fauna
  cryptic   298–9
  introduced (listed)   235
Faunal affinities   5, 137–8, 256, (Table)
Fenced quadrats as living seed banks   120, 238
Ferns   24, 91, 94
Fern-sedge Zone   74, 77, 79, 102, 127–8
Fish   133–44
  grazing   249
  numbers of species   137
  relationship of larval forms to endemism   138
  sequential protogynous hermaphroditism in   141
Fish fauna
  compared to other island groups   137
  endemism in   138
  relationships of   137–8, 255, 256
Fishing industry   143–4, 218
Flora
  disharmonic   101, 290
  of islands   92–3
Floral affinities of Galápagos   82, 98, 256
Floristic composition
  as determinant for secondary succession   121
  of Scalesia forest   107–9
Forests
  deciduous   113, 120
  defined as   103
  depletion on Galápagos   111, 267
  evergreen   112–13
  Scalesia   104–12, 124, 129

steppe 113, 120
Fossil pollen analysis 97
Fossil remains 18, 136, 258, 288, 298
Fumaroles 24
Fur seal, Galápagos 215–23
    adaptations to local conditions 215–16, 218–19
    distribution 217
    food and habitat 218
    population size 217
    reproduction 219–23
    taxonomy 216–17

Galápagos International Scientific Project 13, 72, 136, 278
Galápagos Islands
    age 17–18, 136
    area 3
    climate 3, 57ff
    dating of lake sediments in 65
    discovery 1
    early scientific visitors 13, 72, 134–5
    English names 9
    geology 16ff
    lakes 31, 63–8
    map 2
    Master Plan for, 259, 268, 272
    nomenclature 10
    oceanographic setting 43–53, 283
    origin 16
    origin of life on 4–7
    physical features (of islands)
        Baltra 34, 35, 272
        Bartolomé 20, 38
        Champion 23
        Daphne Major 183
        Fernandina 20, 28, 29, 31, 57, 98, 290
        Floreana 10–11, 32
        Genovesa 28, 59, 64
        Isabela 3, 22, 28–9, 30, 34, 59, 63, 250, 289
        Marchena 23, 28, 32, 38
        Pinta 27
        Plaza 34, 168
        Rábida 32
        San Cristóbal 59, 64
        Santa Cruz 32, 34
        Santiago 20, 23, 59
        Santa Fé 34
        Tortuga 38
    population 11
    rainfall 4, 37, 58ff, 152, 180
    settlement 10–11, 270, 303–5
    under Ecuadorian sovereignty 10, 269
Galápagos Spreading Center 16–17, 25, 27, 34, 36
Germination of seeds 104, 297
Goats (feral) 111, 237–8
    as food competitors 147, 230
    on Española 147, 237
    on Pinta 117, 123–4, 237
    on Santa Fé 120–1, 122, 237, 244
    on Santiago 116, 120, 237
Growth strategy in *Scalesia* 104, 109, 124

Hassler (American Galápagos Expedition, 1873) 135, 257

Hawaiian Islands 16, 18, 92
Hepaticae 76–83
Hydrothermal vent communities 16, 280–3

Ice-age events affecting Galápagos 66
Iguanas
    immunological studies in 300
    Land (*Conolophus*) 165–72
        captive breeding programme 172, 240
        reproduction 171
        subspeciation 165
        territoriality 168–70
    Marine (*Amblyrhynchus*) 157–65
        marine adaptations 160–1
        predation upon 165, 240
        reproduction 162–4
        subspeciation 159 (*Table*)
Indo-Pacific Area, affinities with Galápagos shorefish 138
Insects
    introduced to Galápagos 239, 242–3
    migratory 5
    pollination 104, 301, 302
Insular confinement 256
Interisland variation (*see also*, Adaptive radiation) 13
International Union for Nature Conservation 266, 267
Intertropical Convergence Zone 44, 52–3, 55–60, 67–8
Introduced fauna
    distribution on Galápagos 236 (*Table*)
    effects of 111, 116–18, 165, 204–5, 217, 229, 234ff
    eradication of 117, 238, 242
    facilitating invasion by new species 117
    vulnerability of native biota to 225
Isla de la Plata 192

Juan Fernández Islands 92–3, 257
Julia E. Whalen (Stanford Galápagos Expedition, 1898–1899) 13, 135

Klipfishes 138, 139–40, 291

Lakes 31, 63–7
Lava
    dating of 17–18
    flows and tubes 19–20
    types of 20–1
    weathering of 37
La Venus (French Galápagos Expedition, 1838) 135
Leaf structure, variation in *Scalesia* 95
Lichen flora 72–6
    affinities of 75
    dispersal 5, 73
    evolution of 76
Limestone 34
Littoral Zone 73, 97
Liverworts 76–83
Lizards, marine adaptations in 157–8, 160–1

Magma 19, 21ff
Malpelo Island 136, 138, 157, 192, 249, 258

Mammals
  introduced to Galápagos 234–42
  native land 225–31
  paucity on oceanic islands 225, 290
  pinnipeds 207–223
Mangroves 250
Marine erosion 38
Marine environment
  biogeographic distributions and affinities 255–9
  habitats
    coral reefs 250–4
    mangroves 250
    rocky shores 248–9
    sandy beaches 250
    vertical rock walls 249
  inter-island regionalism 254–5
  intertidal communities in Galápagos 248
  plan for protection of 259–61
Mauritius 239, 257, 297
Mexican Province
  faunal affinities with Galápagos 255
  floral affinities with Galápagos 98
Miconia Zone 78, 102, 127, 129
Migration
  altitudinal, in tortoises 149
  marine bird 193
Mockingbirds 165, 171, 176–7, 180, 187, 279, 296–7
Mollusca 248, 249, 256–7, 258
Mosses 24, 76–83

National Park 240
  administration 260, 267–8, 271–2
  establishment of 266, 267
  Master Plan for protection and use of 259, 272
  spread of alien plants into 118, 128
Nematodes 29
Neotropical Region, floral affinities with Galápagos 82
New Caldeonia 92
Niche expansion in Galápagos garden eels 142
North Equatorial Front 254
Nossi Bé Island 158
Nouvelle Amsterdam Island 236
Nutrient levels in sea 50, 61, 255, 285

Ocean current systems, see Currents
Oceanic islands 92, 233–4, 256, 290, 294
Orchids 91, 107
Orchil (dye) 11, 72
Origin of Species 13, 133, 279–80

Palagonite 37, 287, 288
Panamic Province/Area
  faunal affinities with Galápagos 137, 255, 256, 258
  floral affinities with Galápagos 82, 98, 256
Parasites
  symbiotic removal of 153–4, 165, 171–2, 186, 298
Parrotfishes
  distribution in relation to sea temperature 137
  occurrence 249
Pelagic crustacea 195
Pigs (feral) 111, 147, 204, 239, 267

Pit craters 30, 32
Plankton biomass 51
Plant distribution
  agents of 73, 98–9, 105–6
Plants
  endemism in Galápagos 81–2, 85, 86–7, 90ff, 129–30
  evolutionary patterns in Galápagos 93ff, 294–5
  extinct on Galápagos 129
  introduced by man 80, 86, 88, 99, 117, 119 (Table)
  native Galápagos 85, 88
  numbers of species of Galápagos 85–6, 87
Plate tectonics 16
Pollen-dating studies 97
Pollinators 91, 104, 301
Polyandry in Galápagos hawks 180, 302
Pre-Columbian visits to Galápagos
  possible evidence for 7–8, 227, 303–4
Predator-prey relationships 291

Rainfall 4, 37, 58ff, 152, 180
Rats
  introduced (feral) 241–2
    as predators 147, 149, 165, 204–5, 229
    chromosome studies in 300
  native (oryzomine) 226–31
    arrival on Galápagos 225
    distribution 226–9
    ecology of 230
    extinction in 228 (Table), 229
    origin and taxonomy 226–7, 229
Reefs, ecology of Galápagos 250–4
Regeneration of vegetation 121, 123, 125–7
Relict species 90, 92, 96, 257
Revillagigedos Island 258
Rift systems 16, 27, 281
Rodents
  cricetine 227, 229
  introduced species 241–2, 300
  native 226–31
Rock (see also Lava)
  composition 24–5
  weathering and decomposition 37

Salinity of sea 50
Santa Catalina Island 237
Scalesia Zone 74, 78, 102, 104ff, 129
Sea anemones 249
Sea fans 249
Sea level changes 67
Sea lion, Galápagos 207–14
  care of young 211–13
  food and habitat 208–9
  population size 214
  reproduction 209–11
Sea surface temperature 48–9, 61, 137, 198, 254
Seal hunters 217
Seaweeds (see under Algae)
Sedimentation
  lake 63–7
  marine 38, 250
Seed germination 104, 297
Settlement of Galápagos 10–11, 303–5

Sharks 141, 214, 218, 220–1, 249
Shorefishes (*see also* Fish) 133–44
Snake (*Dromicus*) 165, 172
Solfataras 24
Soils, Galápagos 37
Spatter cones 24, 33
Speciation
    allopatric 176, 178
    number of species as function of island size 178
    sympatric 187
Spore dispersal 5, 73, 91
St. Helena 92, 237
Stratus cloud layer 57, 63, 67, 289
Submergence 36
Succession (secondary)
    on Pinta 123
    on Santa Fé 121–2
Sulphur deposits 11, 24
Symbiotic relationships
    finch and booby 186, 298
    iguana and finch 171–2
    in lichens 72, 76
    orchids and fungi 91
    tortoise and finch 153–4

Tameness of Galápagos animals 14, 216, 230, 292–3
Tephra 21
Terrestrial environment
    changes brought about by man 77, 116–17
    habitat diversity 96
Tethyan Sea 257
Thermoregulatory behaviour
    in fur seals 218–19
    in marine iguanas 161–2
Tomatoes, Galápagos
    autogamy in 301
    genetic variation in 300–1
    germination of 297
Tortoise, Giant (*Geochelone*) 13, 145–56
    arrival on Galápagos 6, 146
    breeding programme 148–9
    distribution and status 146, (*Table*)
    exploitation of 146–7
    food and food competitors 147, 152
    growth of lichens on 76
    natural regulation of populations 149
    predation upon 147, 149, 152, 242
    reproduction 149–50
    subspeciation in 146, 153, 154–5, 300
Tourism 12, 204, 266, 268, 271, 273
Transition Zone 74, 77–8, 102
Tristan da Cunha 236
Tuff 288
    cones 22–3, 37–8
    formation of 21, 287
Turtles, marine 239, 249

UNESCO 226, 267, 272
Uplift, geological 34–6, 252

Upwelling of ocean water 46, 51–2, 57, 61–2, 217, 252, 255, 285–7
Utopian colonization scheme in Galápagos 304–5

Vascular plants 85–9, 94
Vegetation
    altitudinal zonation 4, 102–3, 116
    climax forest (classified as) 103
    endangered types 129
    impact of colonization on 116–17, 124
    impact of introduced animals on 111, 113, 117, 119ff
    mesophytic 124–8
    monitoring changes in 30, 119ff
    regeneration following cessation of overgrazing 121, 123
    xerophytic (*see also* Arid Zone) 120–4
Vegetation changes on
    Española 237
    Floreana 111
    Isabela 129
    Pinta 113, 122–4, 125–7, 237
    San Cristóbal 124, 127, 129
    Santa Cruz 128
    Santa Fé 120–2
    Santiago 111, 120, 124, 237
Velero expeditions (*see under* Allan Hancock)
Vent systems
    circumferential 27–8, 32–3
    formation of 19
    radial 27, 32
Volcanic activity 3, 16
    base surge effects 21–2
    eruptions 18–19, 27
    explosive 21–4
    interpretation by satellite reconnaissance 285–7
Volcanoes
    calderas 28–32, 287–8
    development of Galápagos 26
    Hawaiian 16, 18, 32, 33
    submarine 24, 33

Weathering of rocks 37
Weedy species 96, 117, 118, 301
Whales 255
Whaling industry 8, 135, 147, 234
Wind
    as agent in spore dispersal 5, 91, 99
    effect on formation of volcanic cones 22
    prevailing trade- 3, 45, 46, 56, 57

Xenoliths 25

Zonation
    altitudinal 4, 102–3
    intertidal 248
    Intertropical Convergence 44, 52–3, 55–60, 67–8
    marine protection 260
    national park 272–3

Species Index

Abudefduf troschelii 297
Agassizii scrobiculata 259
Alternanthera halimifola 107, 110
Amblyrhynchus cristatus 157–65, 248, 249, 300
Anas bahamensis 29
Anoectangium aestivum 79
Anous stolidus 192, 194ff, 199, 202
Anthoceros sp. 79, 83
Anthopleura dovii 249
Anthracothecium ochraceoflavum 73
Antipathes spp. 249
Archosargus pourtalesii 137, 138, 250
Arctocephalus galapagoensis 209, 215–23
Ardea herodias 165
Arothron spp. 252
Arthothelium galapagoensis 73
Asio flammeus 152, 181, 201, 204, 230
Asplenium auritum 106, 107
Asteropsis carnifera 259
Astrometis sertulifera 259
Audubon's Shearwater 192, 194ff, 199, 200, 201
Azolla spp. 66, 91

Band-rumped Storm Petrel 192, 194, 199, 200, 291
Bazzania teretiuscula 80
Black Surgeonfish 254
Blossevillea galapagensis 248
Blue-footed Booby 184, 192, 193, 194ff, 199, 202, 249
Bodianus eclancheri 140–1, 255
Borreria ericaefolia 130
Brachycereus nesioticus 87, 93, 94, 96
Brachymenium fabronioides 83
Brandtothuria arenicola 259
Breutelia tomentosa 79, 80
Brown Noddy 192, 194ff, 199, 202
Brown Pelican 192, 194ff, 199, 202
Bryopteris liebmanniana 75
Bryum argenteum 83
Bubulcus ibis 7
Buellia galapagona 73
Bursera graveolens 60, 113, 122, 130
Bursera malacophylla 93
Buteo galapagoensis 152, 165, 172, 180, 188, 204, 230, 302
Butorides sundevalli 165, 182

Cactospiza heliobates 178, 186
Cactospiza pallida 181, 184, 185–6
Cactus Ground Finch 180, 181, 182, 184, 185
Caenocentrotus gibbosus 255
Calandrina galapagosa 129
Callechelys galapagensis 138
Caloplaca isidiosa 73
Camarhynchus psittacula 186
Campylopus galapagoensis 77, 79
Carcharhinus spp. 141, 249
Cassidulus pacificus 259
Castela galapageia 123, 130
Cattle Egret 7
Ceratodon spp. 79, 83
Certhidea olivacea 181
Charles Island Mockingbird 176, 177
Chelonia mydas 239, 249, 250
Chromis atrilobata 249
Cinchona succirubra 119, 128
Cirrhites rivulatus 165
Citrus spp. 80, 117, 118, 119
Cladia aggregata 74
Cladina spp. 74, 76
Cladonia spp. 74
Clerodendrum molle 130
Clypeaster spp. 259
Coccyzus melacorhyphus 179, 184
Coenobita compressa 250
Coffea arabica 80
Common Egret 182
Conolophus pallidus 165ff, 300
Conolophus subcristatus 154, 165–72, 292, 300
Cordia lutea 118, 120
Cranichis lichenophila 86
Creagrus furcatus 192, 193, 194ff, 199ff
Croton scouleri 111, 112, 113, 123
Cyathea weatherbiana 67, 80, 102, 128

Danaus spp. 5
Dark-billed Cuckoo 179, 184
Dark-rumped Petrel 194, 199, 200, 204–5
Darwiniothamnus spp. 86, 87, 94, 97
Darwin's Finches 154, 176ff, 293, 295–7, 298, 299–300, 302
Diadema mexicanum 259
Dialommus fuscus 139–40, 291
Digitaria decumbens 119

Diomedea irrorata   192, 193, 194ff, 199ff
Dromicus spp.   165, 172

Echinometra vanbrunti   248, 255, 259
Entosthodon bonplandii   79
Epidendrum spicatum   107
Erpodium domingense   77
Erythrina velutina   113, 120
Eucidaris thouarsii   248, 252–3, 259
Eugenia jambos   80, 119
Eumetopias jubata   221
Eupomacentrus spp.   249
Everniastrum spp.   74

Fire Ant   235, 242–3
Fissidens sp.   77
Flightless Cormorant   192, 193, 194, 198, 199ff, 294
Fossombronia pusilla   83
Fregata magnificens   192, 193, 194ff, 199, 200
Fregata minor   192, 194ff, 199, 200
Frullania spp.   77, 78
Funaria spp.   79, 83
Furcraea cubensis   119

Galápagos Batfish   141–2
Galápagos Bee   104, 301, 302
Galápagos Black Coral   249
Galápagos Cotton   94, 303
Galápagos Dove   178, 181, 184
Galápagos Fiddler Crab   250
Galápagos Four-eyed Blenny   139–40, 291
Galápagos Fur Seal   209, 215–23
Galápagos Giant Rat   227–9
Galápagos Giant Tortoise   6, 145–56
Galápagos Hawk   152, 165, 172, 180, 188, 204, 230, 302
Galápagos Mockingbirds (see under *Nesomimus*)
Galápagos Penguin   62, 192, 194ff, 199, 202, 204, 294
Galápagos Pintail   29
Galápagos Rail   178, 179, 180, 181
Galápagos Rats (see under *Megaoryzomys, Nesoryzomys, Oryzomys*)
Galápagos Red Bat   226
Galápagos Reef Shark   141, 249
Galápagos Sea Lion   141, 164, 207–14
Galápagos Snakes   165, 172
Galápagos Tomatoes   94, 297, 300–1
Garden Eel   142
Geochelone elephantopus   6, 145–56
Geochelone gigantea   146
Geochelone spp.   146
Geospiza conirostris   187, 302
Geospiza difficilis   178, 181, 186, 298
Geospiza fortis   154, 165, 179, 180, 182, 184, 186
Geospiza fuliginosa   154, 165, 178, 179, 186, 302
Geospiza magnirostris   178, 179, 181, 188
Geospiza scandens   180, 181, 182, 184, 185
Ghost Crab   250
Giant Tortoise   6, 145–56
Gossypium spp.   94, 303
Grapsus grapsus   165, 248
Great Blue Heron   165
Great Frigatebird   192, 194ff, 199, 200

Green Turtle   239, 249, 250
Groutiella mucronifolia   78

Hammerhead Shark   249
Harlequin Wrasse   140–1, 255
Hawkfish   165
Heliaster spp.   259
Herbertus pensilis   79, 80
Hermit Crab   250
Hippomane mancinella   113
Hipponix pilosus   249
Hoary Bat   226
Holacanthus passer   249
Hood Island Mockingbird   176, 177

Isopterygium sp.   79
Isostichopus fuscus   259

Jasminocereus thouarsii   87, 94, 120, 168
Jigger Flea   239

Kalanchoe pinnata   119

Labrisomus multiporosus   138
Land Iguana   154, 165–72, 292, 300
Lantana camara   119
Lantana peduncularis   113, 123
Large Cactus Ground Finch   187
Large Ground Finch   178, 179, 181, 188
Large Tree Finch   186
Larus fuliginosus   192, 194ff, 199, 202
Lasiurus spp.   226
Laterallus spilonotus   178, 179, 180, 181
Lava Gull   192, 194ff, 199, 202
Lava Heron   165, 182
Lecanora pseudopinguis   73
Lecocarpus spp.   86, 87, 90, 94
Leiaster callipelus   259
Leptogium spp.   74
Leptolejeunea elliptica   83
Linckia columbiae   259
Lippia spp.   111, 130
Lobipes lobatus   193
Lophocolea trapezoidea   80
Luidia spp.   259
Lycopersicon spp.   94, 297, 300–1
Lycopodium setaceum   86
Lytechinus semituberculatus   259

Macraea laricifolia   86, 87, 93, 94, 130
Magnificent Frigatebird   192, 193, 194ff, 199, 200
Mangrove Finch   178, 186
Marchantia sp.   79, 83
Marchesinia brachiata   74
Marine Iguana   157–65, 248, 249, 300
Masked Booby   192, 193, 194ff, 199, 200
Medium Ground Finch   179, 180, 182, 184, 186
Megabalanus galapaganus   248

Megaoryzomys curioi   227–9
Melichthys niger   254
Miconia robinsoniana   80, 102, 127
Microphys aculeatus   258
Mithrodia claverigera   259
Mollugo snodgrassii   97
Moorish Idol   254
Mureana argus   136

Nannopterum harrisi   192, 193, 194, 198, 199ff, 294
Neocrex erythrops   7, 176, 178
Nephrolepis cordifolia   106, 107
Nesomimus spp.   165, 171, 176, 180, 187, 279, 296–7
Nesoryzomys spp.   227–30
Nexilosus latifrons   249, 255
Nidoriella armata   259
Night Heron   182
Nodilittorina galapagiensis   248
Nyctanassa violacea   182

Oceanites gracilis   192, 194, 199
Oceanodroma castro   192, 194, 199, 200, 291
Oceanodroma tethys   192, 194, 199, 200, 291
Ocypode gaudichaudii   250
Ogcocephalus darwini   141–2
Ogilbia spp.   299
Onychoteuthis banksi   218
Oplegnathus insignis   255
Opuntia echios   118, 120, 121, 130, 244
Opuntia galapageia   122
Opuntia insularis   112
Opuntia spp.   94, 96, 237, 294–5
Oryzomys bauri   227–30
Oryzomys galapagoensis   226–7, 228

Paint-billed Crake   7, 176, 178
Paranthias colonus   249
Passiflora colinvauxii   107, 109
Pauliella horrida   259
Pavona spp.   250–2
Pegophysema spherica   258
Pelecanus occidentalis   192, 194ff, 199, 202
Pennisetum purpureum   119
Persea americana   118, 119
Phaethon aethereus   192, 193, 194ff, 199, 200ff
Pharia pyramidata   259
Phataria unifasicata   259
Phoradendron henslovii   107
Pinnaxodes chilensis   258
Piscidia carthagenensis   113, 130
Pisonia floribunda   112, 113, 124, 130
Placopsammia darwini   257
Plagiochasma rupestris   81
Plagiochila scabrifolia   80
Platyspiza crassirostris   178, 181
Pocillopora robusta   137, 250–2
Polytrichum juniperinum   79
Porites lobata   137, 250
Prionurus laticlavius   249
Pseudocyphellaria spp.   74
Psidium galapageium   111, 112, 113, 120, 124, 129, 130

Psidium guajava   80, 111, 112, 119
Psychotria angustata   129
Psychotria rufipes   105, 111, 130
Pterodroma phaeopygia   194, 199, 200, 204–5
Pterodroma spp.   205
Pufferfish   252
Puffinus lherminieri   192, 194ff, 199, 200, 201
Purpura columellaris   248
Pyrenula cerina   73
Pyrocephalus rubinus   176, 187

Ramalina spp.   73, 74
Red-billed Tropicbird   192, 193, 194ff, 199, 200ff
Red-footed Booby   192, 193, 194ff, 199, 202
Red-necked Phalarope   193
Riccia sp.   79, 83
Roccella babingtonii   11, 72–4
Roccella galapagoensis   73

Sargassum spp.   248
Sauteria berteroana   80, 83
Scalesia baurii   123
Scalesia cordata   112, 129
Scalesia microcephala   86, 112, 129
Scalesia pedunculata   104–6, 109–12, 124, 129, 130, 237
Scalesia spp.   94, 95, 111, 117, 129, 300, 302
Scarus ghobban   249
Schistophoron tenue   75
Selenkothuria theeli   259
Semicossyphus darwini   134
Sesuvium edmonstonei   93
Sharp-beaked Ground Finch   178, 181, 186, 298
Short-eared Owl   152, 181, 201, 204, 230
Sicyocaulis pentagonus   87, 93, 94
Sisyrinchium galapagense   86
Small Ground Finch   178, 179, 186
Solanum erianthum   113, 127
Sooty Tern   192, 194, 199, 202
Sphagnum spp.   79, 128
Spheniscus mendiculus   62, 192, 194ff, 199, 202, 204, 294
Sphyrna lewini   249
Squamidium spp.   77, 78
Steller's Sea Lion   221
Stereocaulon spp.   74
Sterna fuscata   192, 194, 199, 202
Sticta spp.   74
Strombus sp.   288
Sula dactylatra   192, 193, 194ff, 199, 200, 249
Sula nebouxii   184, 192, 193, 194ff, 199, 202
Sula sula   192, 193, 194ff, 199, 202
Surgeonfish   249
Swallow-tailed Gull   192, 193, 194ff, 199ff

Taenioconger sp.   142
Targionia stellaris   80, 83
Teloschistes flavicans   73
Terebra albemarlensis   258
Tetraclita squamosa   248
Thallasoma lutescens   254
Thuidium recognitum   79
Tillandsia insularis   112

Tunca penetrans   239

Uca helleri   250

Vegetarian Finch   178, 181
Vermilion Flycatcher   176, 187

Warbler Finch   181
Wasmannia auropunctata   235, 242–3
Waved Albatross   192, 193, 194ff, 199ff
Wedge-rumped Storm Petrel   192, 194, 199, 200, 291

Weissia controversa   83
White-tip Shark   249
White-vented Storm Petrel   192, 194, 199
Woodpecker Finch   181, 184, 185–6

Xylocopa darwinii   104, 301, 302

Zalophus californianus wollebaeki   141, 164, 207–14
Zanclus cornutus   254
Zanthoxylum fagara   111, 112, 113, 125, 237
Zelometeorium patulum   78, 79
Zenaida galapagoensis   178, 181, 184

KEY ENVIRONMENTS

Other Titles in the Series

AMAZONIA *Edited by:* G. Prance and T. Lovejoy

ANTARCTICA *Edited by:* N. Bonner and D. Walton

GALAPAGOS *Edited by:* R. Perry

MADAGASCAR *Edited by:* A. Jolly, P. Oberlé and R. Albignac

MALAYSIA *Edited by:* The Earl of Cranbrook

RED SEA *Edited by:* A. Edwards and S. Head

SAHARA DESERT *Edited by:* J. L. Cloudsley-Thompson

WESTERN MEDITERRANEAN *Edited by:* R. Margalef